MARX
Selections

THE GREAT PHILOSOPHERS

Paul Edwards, General Editor

MARX
Selections

Edited,
with Introduction, Notes, and
Bibliography, by

ALLEN W. WOOD
Cornell University

A Scribner/Macmillan Book

Macmillan Publishing Company
NEW YORK

Collier Macmillan Publishers
LONDON

Macmillan Publishing Company
866 Third Avenue, New York, New York 10022

Collier Macmillan Canada, Inc.

Library of Congress Cataloging-in-Publication Data

Marx, Karl, 1818-1883.
    Marx selections.

    (The Great philosophers series)
    Bibliography: p.
    1. Philosophy.   I. Wood, Allen W.   II. Title.
III. Series.
B3305.M72E5 1988   335.4   87-32741
ISBN 0-02-429521-3

Printing: 3 4 5 6 7   Year: 8 9 0 1 2 3 4

ACKNOWLEDGMENTS

"Critique of Hegel's Philosophy of Right: Introduction," selections from "Excerpt Notebooks"
and selections from "Economic and Philosophic Manuscripts," translation copyright © 1967, are here
reprinted with the generous permission of the translators, Loyd D. Easton and Kurt H. Guddat.
    "Theses on Feuerbach," translation copyright © 1976, selections from *The German Ideology*, transla-
tion copyright © 1976 excerpt from Marx's letter to P. V. Annenkov, translation copyright © 1955,
excerpts from *The Poverty of Philosophy*, translation copyright © 1976, Preface to *Toward a Critique of
Political Economy*, translation copyright © 1970, *The Communist Manifesto*, English text of 1888, and
excerpt from *The Civil War in France*, English text of 1871, are here reprinted with the kind permission
of International Publishers, New York.
    Excerpts from *The Eighteenth Brumaire of Louis Bonaparte*, translation copyright © 1973 by Ben
Fowkes, from *Surveys from Exile: Political Writings*, Volume 2, edited by David Fernbach, "Critique
of the Gotha Program," translation copyright © 1974 by Joris de Bres, from *The First International and
After: Political Writings*, Volume 3, edited by David Fernbach, and selections from *Capital: A Critique
of Political Economy*, translation copyright © 1976 by Ben Fowkes, all reprinted by permission of
Random House, Inc., New York and Penguin Books, Ltd., London.
    In the editing of this volume I have had the helpful advice of Professors G. A. Cohen, Paul
Edwards, Loyd D. Easton, and Edward Lee, to all of whom I am grateful. I am also especially
grateful for both the helpful advice and the personal inspiration of Mr. Harold Goldstein.

ISBN 0-02-429521-3

To Stephen

Contents

MARX
Selections

Introduction

MARX AND PHILOSOPHY

Although his principal academic training was in philosophy, Karl Marx has not traditionally been considered a "philosopher" in the technical or academic sense of the term. Yet the scope of his thought and the depth with which it has gripped people certainly warrant applying the term to him in a more everyday sense. In fact, to find someone whose thought has had a greater general impact on the human world, one would have to seek among the founders of the great world religions. And when we consider Marx alongside the prophets and holy men whose influence has been comparable, he stands out at once as the sole *philosopher* in the entire company, the only one who rests his teachings not on mystical insight, supernatural inspiration, or personal holiness but simply on unaided, fallible human reason grappling with hard, dry empirical facts.

This anomaly of Marx the philosopher—the uniquely successful philosopher, the great "scientist-prophet"—makes Marx's teachings an object of continuing fascination even to those who have scant sympathy with his conclusions. For modern society usually thinks of itself as founded on secular reason, and Marx is the only secular thinker whose ideas have had an impact on modern culture comparable to that of a religion. Whatever the extent of our eventual agreement or disagreement with Marx's ideas, we surely learn something about ourselves by coming to understand them and their appeal to the modern world.

If Marx's thought is the only modern philosophy to have the impact of a religion, deplorably often it has been treated both by its enthusiasts and its enemies as if it were a religion in the sense that ordinary canons of reason are suspended with respect to it. Self-described Marxists have often regarded Marx's writings and doctrines as if they were a sort of infallible, sacred canon, any deviation from which places the heretic both outside the truth and in hostile opposition to those who are its chosen guardians. And non-Marxists (especially Americans) have usually behaved as if they thought it would be wicked to read Marx for any purpose other than that of proving to themselves and the world once and for all that the whole of Marx's dangerous teachings should be dismissed without qualification.

Everyone knows that the philosophy of Marx is "dialectical materialism". But this pretentious term conveys little except the mislead-

ing impression that Marx's thought is much more esoteric and more systematic than it actually is; and its use immediately interposes between
us and Marx's thought the quite irrelevant task of explaining what "dialec-
tics" is, and how it might be combined with "materialism". The term
"dialectical materialism" was never used by Marx or Engels themselves
(though it was coined on the basis of language Engels uses in some of his
popular polemical writings). But it has been popular, probably because it
simultaneously serves the needs of those who must reduce Marx's thought
to credal formulas for incantation and those whose sole interest in Marx
is to ridicule and reject what he has to say.

In recent years, however, Marx has at last become a "philosopher" in
a highly precise and technical sense—he has become an object of serious
study by academic philosophers. Of course he has already been this on
the continent of Europe for several generations. But it is only during the
last twenty years that Marx has gained a position of respectability in the
English-speaking philosophical world. (It is indicative that no volume of
Marx selections was included, for instance, in the ancestor of the present
series of books, the Scribner's "Modern Student's Library".) Yet as the
Bibliography of the present volume amply documents, English-speaking
philosophers in the past twenty years, and perhaps most notably those
trained in the so-called "analytic" tradition, have also begun to regard
Marx as an important contributor to the tradition of social thought in
which they see themselves.

The reasons why this is so are many and complex, but the fact itself
is firmly rooted in the spirit of our age. Late twentieth century philosophy
has repudiated the metatheoretic formalism characteristic both of early
twentieth century positivism and of such continental analogues as
phenomenology, whose common (and often anxious) concern was to establish "philosophy" as a distinct discipline, with a subject matter clearly
marked off from those of the empirical sciences. Late twentieth-century
philosophy, by contrast, unashamedly directs itself toward the historical,
the empirical, and the substantive, especially in the areas of ethics, social
theory, and philosophy of science; and this is matched by an equally
notable trend in the sciences themselves toward the philosophical, toward
asking big questions and attempting to answer them with grand theories.
Both trends duplicate tendencies which were at work in German intellectual life during the period when Marx wrote, and they make us more
receptive to Marx as a thinker who ambitiously combined empirical inquiry with theories of philosophical scope, and had scant respect for the
supposed boundary lines between different empirical disciplines or between philosophy and empirical research. The interest in Marx also provides a focus for the annoyingly persistent strength of leftist ideas in the
intellectual community during an era in which offical public ideology in

the dominant English-speaking nations was supposed to have moved decisively to the right along with official state policies.

Whatever its causes, one beneficial effect of the recent trend in Marx scholarship has been to raise the level at which Marx's philosophy can be discussed. In place of grotesque, jargon-addicted "-isms", with their claims and counter-claims to orthodoxy and heresy, it has initiated a tradition in which Marx may perhaps at last be treated as it makes sense to treat any important philosopher—to see him as a figure whose questions, doctrines, arguments, and vocabulary belong to the common store from which we draw in trying to define and solve our fundamental cultural problems, and as a great but fallible thinker from whom we can learn equally by attaining to his insights and by exposing his mistakes. If so-called "analytical Marxism" can succeed in getting people to expound Marx's ideas rigorously and criticize them on their merits, then it may have almost as much to offer the tradition of Marxist theory as Marxism has to offer English-speaking culture.

KARL MARX: BIOGRAPHICAL

Karl Heinrich Marx was born on May 5, 1818 in the city of Trier, in the Prussian Rhineland. He came from a Jewish family of rabbinical background, but in 1824 his father converted to Christianity, so that Karl Marx was not raised as a Jew. Heinrich Marx was a successful lawyer of conservative political sentiments. He expected his son to follow in the legal profession and sent him to the University of Bonn in 1835 with this in mind. A year later, however, Marx transferred to the University of Berlin and exchanged the study of law for philosophy, allying himself with the atheistic and politically radical Young Hegelian movement, apparently planning on an academic career in philosophy. To this end he completed a doctoral dissertation on the philosophies of Democritus and Epicurus at the University of Jena in 1841.

But in 1840 Friedrich Wilhelm IV succeeded to the Prussian throne. The new king was a romantic-reactionary suspicious of Hegelian rationalism and especially hostile to the Young Hegelian radicals. Under him, the Prussian Ministry of Culture dismissed some Young Hegelians from their academic chairs and barred the way to an academic career for their students. Marx therefore turned his talents to journalism, editing the *Rheinische Zeitung*, a radical newspaper in Cologne, until increasing censorship of the publication prompted his resignation in the spring of 1843. He then joined with the Young Hegelian Arnold Ruge in another publishing effort, the *Deutsch-Französische Jahrbücher* (German-French Annals). In June of the same year Marx married his childhood sweetheart, Jenny von Westphalen (1814–1881), after an engagement of six years. Despite the hardships of later years, their marriage seems to have been a happy one.

Marx's collaboration with Ruge brought him to Paris in November, 1843, where he met radicals from many countries, most notably his fellow Young Hegelian Friedrich Engels (1820–1895), with whom he not only formed a lifelong friendship, but also began a lifetime of literary and political collaboration. It was Engels who introduced Marx both to the study of political economy and to the British working class movement. Before 1844 was over, Marx and Engels had ventured on their first writing project together, a critique of Young Hegelian philosophy entitled *The Holy Family*.

In January, 1845, Prussian diplomacy succeeded in getting Marx banished from Paris, and he took up residence in Brussels. There in 1847 he and Engels joined the Communist League, whose famous *Manifesto* was published on the eve of the French revolution of February, 1848. The revolution brought Marx first back to Paris, and then to Cologne, where he edited the radical *Neue Rheinische Zeitung* until the revolution in Germany collapsed. After successfully defending himself and his associates in a Cologne court against charges of "inciting to revolt," Marx was expelled from Prussian territories in 1849 and soon took up residence in London, where he was to spend virtually the rest of his life.

During the first years in England, the Marx family endured a poverty as bitter and brutal as any Marx was ever to describe in his writings. Three of the six children died of want before 1856, and Marx was beset by illnesses from which he would never fully recover. Despite this, whenever not confined to his bed by sickness he regularly spent ten hours a day in the British Museum, studying and writing; after returning home, he often wrote far into the night. The chief object of his efforts was *Capital*, his critical analysis of capitalism and the political economy which studied it. The first volume of Marx's great work was published in 1867; the rest of the project was left unfinished at his death.

Marx was instrumental in founding the International Workingmen's Association in 1864, and he guided it through six congresses in the next nine years. The history of the First International was one of struggle not only against the oppressing classes, but also internally. Marx's chief opponents in the early years were the followers of Pierre Proudhon (1809–1865); later Marx combatted the clandestine intrigues of the anarchist Mikhail Bakunin (1814–1876), who was expelled from the International in 1872. After 1873, Marx's bad health was chronic, and he was less and less able to work. Jenny Marx, who always edited the manuscripts written in her husband's notoriously illegible hand, fell ill with cancer in 1878 and died in 1881. Marx himself died on March 14, 1883. Engels then took over the task of editing the unfinished volumes of *Capital*. He published Volume 2 in 1885 and Volume 3 in 1894, a year before his own death.

EARLY WRITINGS

Young Hegelianism

The origin of Marx's thought is to be found in his ambivalent relation to the so-called "Young Hegelian" movement in philosophy which arose in Germany during the 1830s and 1840s. The Young Hegelians were philosophers who began as followers of Georg Wilhelm Friedrich Hegel (1770–1831), but drew unorthodox and even revolutionary conclusions from their Hegelianism, first in theology and then later in morality and politics. The two seminal works of the Young Hegelian movement were *The Life of Jesus* (1835) by David Friedrich Strauss (1808–1874), and *The Essence of Christianity* (1841) by Ludwig Feuerbach (1804–1872). Other prominent Young Hegelian philosophers, besides Marx and Engels, were Arnold Ruge (1802–1880), Max Stirner (the literary pseudonym of Kaspar Schmidt) (1806–1856), Bruno Bauer (1809–1882), his brother Edgar Bauer (1820–1886), and Moses Hess (1812–1875).

Hegel's *Philosophy of Right* (1821) proclaimed that the rational is actual and the actual is rational. Just as Hegel's metaphysics attempted to portray the Christian religion as containing the truths of rational speculative philosophy in a figurative form, so Hegel's philosophy of the state presented a profound vision of the spiritual nature of modern humanity, and attempted to display the modern state as its actualization and fulfillment. Hegel conceived of modern human beings as destined to freedom, to the harmonious and unfettered development both of individuality and community according to reason; and Hegel's philosophy tried to understand the modern state as the objectification of this freedom.

To the Young Hegelians, Hegel's philosophy was at once a profound truth and a cruel deception. They shared Hegel's aspiration to the self-actualization of human freedom both in philosophy and in society, but they regarded both Christianity and the existing social order not as the objectification of freedom but as systems of servitude and self-alienation. Their task was to rethink critically the rational core of Hegelian philosophy, and to turn critical reason both against the outward, mystifying form of Hegel's system and against the forms of spiritual and social unreason with which Hegelian apologetics had made common cause. The task of philosophy is not to contemplate the actuality of the rational but to make reason actual in the world, by revolutionizing both philosophical thinking and social reality.

Alienation and Practice

What is distinctive from the very beginning about Marx's approach to this task is the fact that he conceives it as a practical and not a theoretical one. As Marx sees it, the error of the Young Hegelian philosophers (especially Bruno Bauer and Ludwig Feuerbach, the two Marx takes most seriously) is that they begin from the standpoint of critical thinking or contemplative knowledge. They conceive of both unfreedom and human emancipation, both self-alienation and self-actualization, fundamentally as states of mind or consciousness. For them, the criticism of religion is the starting point for all criticism because liberation is fundamentally an act of critical thinking, and religion is for them the fundamental form of mystification, of mental or spiritual unfreedom and self-alienation.

In the Preface to his 1859 *Toward a Critique of Political Economy* (below, p. 135), Marx reports that the starting point for his social thought was his criticism of Hegel's philosophy of right, whose first published form was his 1843 essay "Toward the Critique of Hegel's *Philosophy of Right*: Introduction" (pp. 23–35). In this essay, Marx accepts the idea that "the criticism of religion is the premise of all criticism," but he holds that the criticism of religious illusions leads inevitably to criticism of the real world that produces them. Thus Marx seeks the "basis" of religious criticism elsewhere, in criticism of the "the human world," "this state, this society" which gives rise both to religion and to the need for it (p. 23). Equally, Marx seeks elsewhere than in critical thinking or theory the power to actualize philosophy. He seeks it in *practice* (p. 29), and specifically, in the revolutionary practice of a "class with radical chains, a class in civil society that is not of civil society"—the proletariat (p. 34). Philosophy is the source of the proletariat's revolutionary consciousness, while the proletariat is the material agency which will actualize philosophy (p. 34).

In seeking a social basis for criticism and human emancipation, it was natural for Marx to look to what Hegel had seen as the distinctive mark of the modern world and called "civil society"—the social organization of labor through a market system distinct from the political state and based on private property. It was equally natural for Marx to turn his attention to political economy, the science of civil society. Marx's first critical reflections on political economy and the civil society it studies are found in his Paris notebooks and manuscripts of 1844. These manuscripts, not published until 1930, reveal his continuing preoccupation with human self-actualization, conceived in the form of "production" in a genuinely "human" form, consciously actualizing people's social nature by producing explicitly for social needs (pp. 36–39); and with the critical project of understanding the way in which human labor in present society takes an "alienated" form, in which human beings do not actualize their essence but frustrate it (pp. 44–49).

The theory of "alienation" present in the 1844 manuscripts provides us with the first version of three characteristic Marxian ideas which take a different form in Marx's mature thought. First, Marx regards the evils and irrationalities of modern society as constituting a single interconnected whole, which in the 1844 manuscripts he attempts to grasp through the concept of "alienation." Second, Marx insists that what is fundamental about this system is something about the kind of laboring activity which goes on within it. The 1844 manuscripts thus claim that the alienated relation of workers to their own labor is the fundamental form of alienation (p. 46). Third, Marx views this kind of labor as characteristic of a transitory phase of human history, a critical stage in the generally progressive movement of human self-development and self-actualization.

In his writings after 1844, Marx continues to employ the concept of alienation in a descriptive or diagnostic way; but it no longer plays the fundamental, explanatory role assigned to it in the 1844 manuscripts. The three ideas just mentioned are no longer expressed in the philosophical jargon of alienation. Instead, they take the form of a programmatic theory of history which attempts to identify the fundamental dynamic of what Hegel called "civil society" and then to understand all human history, the history of politics, law, philosophy, religion, in terms of the history of civil society. What Marx had earlier called "alienated labor" is henceforth understood in terms of the relations of production characteristic of a historically determinate and transitory mode of production.

THE MATERIALIST CONCEPTION OF HISTORY

The Primacy of Production

The "materialist conception of history" was first worked out by Marx and Engels in the years 1845–1846, in their long unpublished manuscript *The German Ideology* (see pp. 85–108). But perhaps its most definitive programmatic expression is found much later in the 1859 Preface (see pp. 134–137). According to the materialist conception of history, the foundation of any social form is the prevailing form of "civil society", what the *German Ideology* calls its "form of intercourse" but Marx's later writings usually describe as its *social relations of production*. Social relations of production consist in relationships between the occupants of determinate social roles, relating to their degree and manner of effective control over the means and processes of social production. Master/slave, lord/serf, landlord/tenant and capitalist/wage-laborer are a few examples of relations of production. Historical materialism sees human history as consisting of a series of identifiable stages, or *modes of production*, each fundamentally characterized by a determinate set of such social relations.

The historical sequence of modes of production, however, is determined by something even more fundamental, the *productive powers* or *productive forces* of society, that is, the means and techniques of production available to the society. In Marx's view, the productive powers of a society tend to be employed efficiently, and on the whole they tend to grow, though their growth under certain modes of production is much more rapid than their growth under others. The prevailing relations of production are those which facilitiate the employment of society's productive powers at a given stage of their growth, and which enable the productive powers to grow even further. At a certain stage in their development, however, society's productive powers will come into conflict with the prevailing relations of production. As Marx puts it, "from forms of development of the productive forces, these relations turn into their fetters" (p. 135). In order to make way for the further progressive development of the productive forces, the relations of production must be burst asunder and replaced by new relations. The process by which old relations of production are overthrown and replaced by new ones is a *social revolution*.

The Class Struggle

The mechanism through which a social revolution occurs is the class struggle. Relations of production define social groups with a common situation and common interests. If the members of these groups become conscious of these interests and form a social and political movement to further their interests, they constitute a *class*. Or as Marx occasionally puts it, the articulation of the group's common situation and collective interests in a distinctive intellectual and political form transforms the group from a class "potentially" or "in itself" into a class "actually" or "for itself" (p. 120). In the process of organizing themselves into a class, individuals acquire new goals and aspirations, largely coinciding with their shared individual interests but sometimes requiring the sacrifice of individual interests for the class's common purpose. These larger, collective goals are *class interests*.

According to historical materialism, the history of past societies has been fundamentally a history of the struggles of class interests. The basic class interests of any class, whether consciously recognized or not, consist in the establishment and defense of a certain set of relations of production, under which the members of that class exercise domination over social production. That class tends to be dominant at any stage whose class interests are bound up with the relations of production corresponding to the existing stage of the society's productive forces. When these relations of production come into conflict with the developing productive forces, there arises a revolutionary class, that class whose interests are bound up with the relations of production which suit the emerging state of the productive forces. The adjustment of production relations to productive forces is effected by a social revolution, carried out by the revolutionary class.

The class struggle, and its foundation in the conflict of productive forces and production relations, is in the view of Marx and Engels the secret of history, the key to its coherence (p. 112). It is a secret in the sense that up until now class struggles were often not carried on consciously *as* class struggles. That is, class movements usually did not understand their own class basis, but took the illusory form of religion or philosophy, and they attributed their social power to truths of divine revelation or moral reason rather than to the material conditions of life to which they gave expression. The ruling ideas of an epoch are typically the ideas of its ruling class, or at any rate the ideas whose currency helps to perpetuate and stabilize its rule. Revolutionary ideas are the ideas of a revolutionary class, ideas which consciously move individuals to further its class interests.

Ideology

The standard Marxian term for a system of thoughts which thus serves a class function in ignorance of their true social character, is *ideology*. Historical materialism proposes to understand potent religious, philosophical, moral, aesthetic, and political ideas as ideological in this sense. And in *The German Ideology*, Marx and Engels accuse the Young Hegelians of being "ideologues" in their attempt to liberate the human race simply through the device of "critical" thinking, through philosophy. Just as they see alienation as fundamentally a mental or spiritual phenomenon, so they see its cure as an intellectual act of liberation. For Marx, however, alienation is a real state of human beings, owing its causes to real, social obstacles to human self-actualization. What is needed is not a new understanding of reality, but a new reality, a new society: "The philosophers have only *interpreted* the world in various ways; the point is to *change* it" (p. 82). There is a role for "philosophy" in human emancipation, but only if it finally recognizes its rootedness in the historical process and makes its task that of lending to the revolutionary class—to the proletariat—the self-transparency to accomplish its historical mission with full consciousness. The reason for this is that, in contrast to earlier revolutionary classes, the proletariat will do its work not mystified by ideology but with a sober, scientific appreciation of the historical meaning of what it does. The proletariat's mission of universal human emancipation is bound up with the historical self-transparency of proletarian practice.

Marx's theory of history has often been represented as "economic determinism"—another term never used by Marx. The label would be harmless enough if it did no more than emphasize the fundamental role which productive powers and economic relations play in history according to Marx. But it becomes mischievous when it is used to depict Marx's theory as one hostile to human freedom and personality, in which human individuals become mere ciphers in an impersonal process and their actions are determined robot-like by cold economic facts. Though Marx's theory in no way denies the uniqueness of human individuals or the reality of their choices, it discloses to us the social struggles in which our actions are inevitably caught up, and it forces us to see these actions in light of an objective historical meaning, of which we are often unaware, and which we would often prefer them not to have. It therefore may have a disorienting and unsettling effect on us comparable to that of the deterministic doctrines with which it is frequently confused.

Like Freud, but in a very different way, Marx has taught us that we are often the victims of systematic illusions about ourselves and the meaning of our actions. Unlike Freudian psychoanalysis, Marxian historical materialism does not claim that people's motives and intentions are different from what the actors think they are. But it does tell us that the objective historical significance of our actions is not to be sought in their conformity to some moral or religious code of conduct but in their impact on a struggle of social classes, a struggle of which we may not be aware, and from which we would often prefer to distance ourselves. Further, it exhibits our most cherished philosophical and religious ideas themselves in an embarrassing light—as class ideologies—and suggests that so long as we choose to see these ideas in some more exalted aspect we are the victims of illusions which enable us to be manipulated by historical forces and movements to which we may never have freely given our allegiance. As with Freud, the intended function of traumatic self-knowledge is to liberate—for we can become free historical agents when we understand fully the historical significance of our options and choose our course in light of that.

COMMUNISM AND THE WORKING CLASS MOVEMENT

Revolutionary Practice and "Ideals"

It is typical, and it may even seem inevitable, for a social reformer or revolutionary to begin with a conception of how the world ought to be, with an ideal goal to be attained, with a notion of the society to be brought about, or else with a principle or set of principles of social justice, and then look for a way of achieving that goal, realizing the ideal, or making the world conform to the principles. When people approach Marx's writings with this preconception, the first thing they look for is Marx's "ideal" of communism, or the principles of distributive justice he wants to impose on society. Often this preconception is so strong that even Marx's most explicit and emphatic statements are powerless to persuade those in its grip that what they are looking for simply isn't there. Marx's whole approach is one to which practice based on ideal goals and moral principles is fundamentally alien.

Marx believes that through an understanding of the historical process, we can discern a movement of human self-actualization and emancipation in history and identify the mechanisms through which it operates. The task of revolutionary practice is to identify ourselves with this movement and aid it in its accomplishment of its historic mission. The goals of the movement, its programs, its class consciousness (including its "principles" and "ideals") may change as the movement develops; the actual movement is the foundation of its conscious aims, while they are only the changing conscious forms of its developing activity. For Marx, the fundamental thing is the actual movement; conscious goals are secondary, and a given set of such goals represents at most a transitory stage in a developing history.

Historical materialism identifies the class struggle as the foundation of this process, and progressive human agency as the pursuit by a revolutionary class of its class interest in transforming the economic structure of society. Even when they represent a revolutionary class, reformers who begin with ideal goals or principles are *ideologues*, victims of historical self-ignorance and illusion, because their starting point is a class-ideology and not an understanding of the historical process. Self-transparent revolutionary practice is the conscious practice of a revolutionary class, unmasked and undistorted by ideology.

Marx's view depends on a judgment that human history presents us with a generally developmental or progressive process, whose foundation is the expansion of human productive powers. But this judgment is not based on any values or principles beyond history itself. For Marx, to understand the movement of history is to identify the forms of human agency which develop and emancipate human beings. But there is no goal of the historical process to be legislated to that process from outside it. We measure human freedom and self-actualization in history by standards that are themselves products of history and which change along with changes in human beings and in their conception of themselves. The practice of human emancipation consists in discerning which class is the revolutionary class, identifying oneself with that class, and developing oneself (together with one's "goals" and "principles") along with its development.

Communism

Marx holds that in the mid-nineteenth century, revolutionary practice is the practice of the revolutionary proletariat, struggling to overthrow the capitalist mode of production and the class rule of the bourgeoisie. The identification of the proletariat as the revolutionary class, along with the materialist interpretation of modern capitalist society, depends on a concrete understanding of the historical process through which capitalist society was generated and through which it is passing away. Marx and Engels summarize their understanding of this process in Part I of *The Communist*

Manifesto. In Part II they identify "communism" as the social movement which represents the class interests of the proletariat.

For Marx and Engels, therefore, "communism" does not refer to a conception of how society should be, an ideal social order or program to be imposed on society by a revolutionary elite. Rather, "communism" denotes a class movement, whose ultimate goals for the most part remain still to be defined. As they had already put it in *The German Ideology*: "*Communism* is for us not a *state of affairs* which is to be established, an *ideal* to which reality [will] have to adjust itself. We call communism the *real* movement which abolishes the present state of things" (p. 98). If Marx believes the communist revolution will abolish private property in the means of production, that is only because he believes private property in the means of production is the fundamental feature of capitalist society, the basis of bourgeois class rule. To say that bourgeois private property will be abolished is to say no more than that that it is the mission of the revolutionary proletariat to overthrow the bourgeoisie and to abolish capitalism. Beyond this, Marx has little or no conception of what "communist" society will be like.

The ten "communist" measures listed in the *Manifesto* (p. 158) are not blueprints for a new society. (Just notice how many of them have already been implemented, at least partially, within capitalist societies.) They are instead the first cautious steps toward a new society, the steps still close enough to us that we can pretend to foresee them. Of greater interest to Marx is the foretaste of what the proletariat will actually do when it comes to power, which—he thinks—we can see in the Paris Commune of 1871 (see pp. 170–181).

The Critique of Justice

We look in vain in Marx's writings for an "ideal" of communist society. Equally absent from Marx's thinking is any principle of right or justice on which such a society might be founded. Those who coax such ideals or principles from the Marxian texts succeed only in obscuring precisely what is most original and challenging in Marx's conception of revolutionary practice; and they usually replace some of Marx's most original thoughts with just that familiar and banal moralism whose ideological mystifications Marx set out to expose.

Marx's *Critique of the Gotha Program* (pp. 184–199) does make conjectures about the mode of distribution in communist society. But Marx's discussion of communist distribution is put forward there with the sole aim of showing that no distributive proposals of any kind belong in any working class program. His whole idea is that the entire standpoint of distributive "right" is ideological, bourgeois rather than proletarian in origin and import. The fact that the distributive system in the first phase of communist society will be based on some principle of right is a simple consequence of the fact that communist society at its inception will be limited by the conditions of its origin, "still stamped with the birth-marks of the old society from which it emerges" (pp. 188–89). Marx discusses distributive proposals based on "equal right" precisely to show that they are all inherently *defective*. He attacks the program's demands for "a just distribution" and "equal right" as "ideological humbug" and "obsolete verbal rubbish," subversive of the "realistic outlook" won by the workers' part "at the cost of immense effort" (p. 190).

Far from criticizing capitalism on the basis of rights or principles of justice, Marx does not even believe that capitalism is an unjust system. Marx answers the Gotha Program's demand for a "just distribution" by asking rhetorically "Does not the bourgeoisie claim that the present system of distribution is 'just'? And is it not, in fact, the only 'just' system of distribution on the basis of the present mode of production? Are economic relations regulated by legal concepts of right or is the opposite not the case, that legal relations spring from economic ones?" According to Marx, capitalism alienates and exploits, but it violates no one's rights and does no one an injustice.

For Marx, relations of right are part of the moral and legal superstructure of society, whose basis is its social relations of production. Consequently, the justice of a transaction consists simply in its correspondence to the prevailing mode of production (see pp. 276–277). That capitalism should turn out to be just for Marx should therefore not surprise us, and the fact that it is just should not incline us in any way to think better of capitalist exploitation. But it should convince working class parties not to fill their programs with ideological trash about right and justice.

CAPITAL

In Marx's own view, his main contribution to science and his chief life work was *Capital*, a critical analysis of political economy and of its subject matter, the capitalist mode of production. The economic method of *Capital* is not made entirely explicit by Marx in its pages, and its conception of the aims and methods of economic science differs not only from that of the classical political economists (the tradition of Adam Smith and David Ricardo) but even more from the neoclassical or marginalist tradition on which present day economic theory is based. Marx's strategy is to begin with the most basic and abstract category of capitalist production, the commodity, and work toward a more concrete understanding of the actual capitalist world by successively developing out of this category the other categories which manifest themselves in capitalist society. His method is motivated by the (distinctly antipositivist) conviction that the aim of science is not merely to systematize observations, but to discern the underlying structure of reality. In the case of social science, this task takes a special form because Marx believes that social reality in capitalist hides or disguises itself, that capitalism is a system which embodies systematic illusions about itself, both in theory and in practice. *Capital* is subtitled "A Critique of Political Economy" because Marx believes the science of political economy itself has been a victim of these illusions.

Commodities, Value and Capital

Capital begins in effect with an extremely simple model of commodity production, based on private property, assuming perfect competition and perfect sensitivity of the market to production costs, but deliberately ignoring the effect of all production costs except labor and treating all commodities as freely reproducible. Within this model it will be true that the relative price of a commodity is proportional to what Marx calls "value": the amount of labor time socially necessary to produce it (p. 212). The relevance of this model to the actual world depends on our seeing it, as Marx did, as exhibiting (through "the force of abstraction") the essential features of commodity production, which still are present in the surface phenomena of actual capitalism, though in a much modified form. The object of Marx's theory is to use this model to generate successively the different factors which effect this modification, enabling us to understand the real significance of these factors. From the "value form" of commodities, Marx first generates the "money form", and then the capital form.

Capital is money used to purchase means of production and labor-power; Marx calls the former "constant capital" and the latter "variable capital". Through the capitalist production process, capital somehow produces commodities of greater value than that of the original capital. Marx finds the secret of this increment or "surplus value" to lie in the fact that labor-power is a commodity which has the unique property that through its use, it not only replaces its own value but adds a surplus to that value. In other words, it is possible for money to function as capital because the value of a day's labor-power (that is, the amount of labor time socially necessary to induce the worker to work for a day) is less than the value the worker produces during a day (that is, the amount of time the worker labors that day). In effect, the working day is divided into two parts: the "necessary labor" the worker does to replace the value paid in a day's wages and the "surplus labor" the worker does gratis for the capitalist. The secret of surplus value is that one component of capital is used to purchase a commodity (labor-power) whose use yields greater value than that of the commodity itself—that is why Marx calls it "variable" capital. Or in other words, surplus value results from the fact that labor is *exploited*.

Exploitation

Marx states his theory of exploitation in terms of his labor theory of value. But the basic idea behind his view that workers are exploited by capital does not depend on this theory. Capitalists own the means of production, or the purchasing power required to buy them, and they also command the purchasing power the worker needs in order to live in a commodity-producing society. Workers own little but their capacity to labor, and have no acceptable alternative to making their living by employing the means of production with which capitalists provide them. Ownership of the means of production gives the capitalist class a decisive bargaining advantage over the working class, with the result that the worker must in effect offer something to the capitalist to induce the capitalist to devote purchasing power to the worker's means of production and wages rather than putting it to some other use. The extraction of this inducement is what Marx means by capital's exploitation of labor.

Marx's theory of value enables him to represent the inducement in an especially graphic way, as a portion of each working day during which the worker is forced to work for the capitalist. But the power-relations between capitalist and worker, based on the fact that the former has effective control over the means of production and the latter needs to employ those means in order to live, do not depend on any theoretical representation of them. Of course they can be obfuscated, as when the capitalist's constant threat of withdrawing purchasing power from the production process is represented as a socially beneficial act of "abstinence". The capitalist could employ all the purchasing power he has to satisfy his own present wants, but instead he devotes some of it to workers' wages and means of production; and for this, the apologists say, he is entitled to a "reward". Of course it is true that production won't be carried on if the social resources necessary for it are otherwise consumed, and in that sense everyone (the worker as well as the capitalist) must "abstain" from using up these resources. Because capitalists own the resources, they are in a position, as the workers are not, to demand a "reward" in return for this abstinence. But the demand does not rest on any special burden of deprivation which capitalists bear for the sake of the productive process; on the contrary, the bargaining advantage they hold in virtue of their ownership of the means of production enables capitalists not only to exploit others but also to impose such burdens mainly on others.

The Tendencies of Capitalist Accumulation

The commodities produced in the capitalist process are produced for sale; when they are sold, their surplus value is realized and then employed as capital to purchase more labor-power and means of production. Volume

2 of *Capital* deals with the circulation process of capital. Volume 3 treats the division of surplus value into profit, interest and rent, and propounds a theory of prices intended to modify and concretize the theory of value used provisionally in Volume 1.

According to Marx, the capitalist process is not simply homeostatic or self-reproducing, but embodies certain directional tendencies. Capital has an inherent tendency to self-expansion or accumulation. It tends to raise the ratio of surplus labor to necessary labor by every means at its disposal, by prolonging the working day and reducing the value of labor-power. Marx holds that along with these tendencies, and involved in them, there is also a tendency for the constant component of capital (capital invested in means of production) to rise faster than the variable component (capital spent on labor-power) (p. 263).

Marx thinks there are inherent dysfunctions or "contradictions" lurking in these tendencies, and he sees them as indications that capitalist relations of production are becoming incompatible with the tremendous productive forces capitalism has generated. He believes the long-term effects of the tendency to accumulation, and to the increased ratio of constant capital to variable capital, are disruptive to the capitalist economy in a number of ways. They deprive the workers of the purchasing power needed to buy commodities, realize capital and thereby sustain the cycle of accumulation; and the tendency of the constant component of capital to grow larger and larger also involves a long-term tendency of the rate of profit to fall, interfering with the process of accumulation by which capital lives and grows. Capitalism involves itself in periodic crises of general overproduction, which threaten the social stability of the capitalist system by further increasing the poverty and discontent of the masses exploited by it. Capital tends more and more to be concentrated in the hands of a few, while the size of the working class, and its misery, grow larger and larger, so that its capacity and motivation to overthrow the rule of capital tends to grow stronger and stronger. Marx is confident that the mass of the people will inevitably do what it has powerful, urgent, and continuing reasons to do: expropriate the expropriators and overthrow the capitalist mode of production (p. 274).

MARX TODAY

The goals Marx set for himself were anything but modest. In the realm of theory, he aspired to nothing less than a scientific comprehension of history, which would enable him to anticipate the large scale social changes taking place in modern society. Practically, he attempted to identify and intellectually to equip a social movement which would lead the way to nothing less than universal human emancipation. With such goals as these, it is hardly surprising that Marx's record is one of failure as well as success. A century's hindsight makes it all too easy to identify some of the failures.

Capitalism has proven much more resilient and resourceful than Marx thought it would be. Organized labor in prosperous nations has extracted significant concessions from capital, and Keynesian techniques of state intervention (chiefly the accumulation of massive state debt) have controlled capitalism's periodic crises. Capitalism does not seem likely to be overthrown by a working class revolution in the foreseeable future. Workers in many capitalist societies have organized, as Marx urged them to, but they have not formed a movement of international scope, as he hoped they would. Workers' organizations have also largely lost their radical or revolutionary character; they see themselves merely as advancing the special interests of one group among others within the capitalist system. The phenomenon of multinational corporations, with their awesome political influence and their capacity to defeat working class organization by utilizing the labor market on a worldwide scale, might make it truer to say, with bitter irony, that it is the bourgeoisie and not the proletariat which has seized power by organizing internationally.

Historic revolutions have been made in Marx's name. But they have not occurred in the prosperous nations of Western Europe where Marx most expected them. Instead, they have happened in poorer countries which lacked the traditions of European bourgeois democracy which Marx took for granted as part of the revolutionary proletariat's cultural heritage. Systems founded in Marx's name have set certain limits to the empire of international capitalism, and they have consistently done better than comparably poor capitalist countries in providing for a minimally tolerable standard of living for all. Yet is far from clear that the Russian and Chinese revolutions represent deeds of the organized proletariat as Marx conceived of it, and doubtful that they have initiated anything like what Marx hoped the revolutionary proletariat would accomplish. Nominally Marxist political regimes often differ from the fascist dictatorships in comparable capitalist countries only by being more successfully repressive, and so more stable politically. But stability is a dubious virtue in political systems with many vices. It looks as if we must conclude that the revolution Marx worked for either has turned out rather badly thus far, or else has not occurred yet at all.

Marx showed bold imagination in portraying the immediate future of modern society as a historic war to the death between two great social classes, with the fate of the human race hanging in the balance and his own theory serving the revolutionary class as an intellectual weapon. But even he was unequal to the hideous nightmare-vision of a world at the mercy of two monstrous, hostile empires, each using Marx's teachings (one side the professed devotion to them, the other side fear and hatred of them) as a pretext for whatever atrocities it enters their heads to commit, both empires starving the world's poor and stunting human civilization in order to squander the resources of modern society arming themselves many times over with weapons which have long since had the capacity at a moment's notice to extinguish all life on earth.

Marxian historical materialism has importantly influenced several generations of historians, but it has often not been well understood either by those who attempted to practice it or by those who attempted to refute it, and its vision has been neither confirmed nor disconfirmed. Even after a full century, Marxian economic theory still presents a challenge to orthodox economics: but largely because the capitalist system still remains an enigma to everyone, and not because the isolated and embattled scientific subculture of Marxian economics has been able to boast any special successes. The scientific promise of Marxian social theory, if it is anywhere near as great as Marx thought it was, is still very far from being realized.

Yet the historic role of ideas is seldom what their creators think it will be. Marx emphasized this truth, but inevitably fancied his own ideas exempt from it. The power of Marx's thought is best appreciated not by measuring it against its own ambitious self-conception, but by looking at its actual effects.

In the century since Marx wrote, capitalism has changed, as he predicted it would, and for many of the reasons he predicted it would. Halfway through that century, it nearly destroyed itself through one of the general crises of underconsumption which Marx was the first to study. If Marx's predictions have proven false, his theories have provided some of the best keys to understanding what has happened instead. More importantly, however, Marx has changed the way modern society looks at itself. Capitalism no longer dares pretend that it is inevitable, "natural" or inherently stable. Seeing itself, however reluctantly, through post-Marxian eyes, it now recognizes itself as a system torn by tensions and conflicts, a whole in process of constant change, an enigma and sometimes a threat to itself, and above all as a way of life to which alternatives exist, and to which further alternatives can be invented. It is to Marx that we owe the fact that despite attempts to deny it, capitalism for us is a problem rather than a solution. It is this above all which makes Marx's name so powerful a symbol of fear to some and of hope to others.

But along with this, Marx is also virtually the creator of modern radicalism, not only of its science and its theory, but also of its style and rhetoric: he is its poet as well as its methodologist, the original voice of revolutionary emotions and instincts as much as the author of radical theory's concepts and principles. Not only movements of class emancipation, but also those of racial, national, and sexual liberation, have derived their radical spirit, their conception of their emancipation—and that means their conception of themselves—from Marx. Marx is not only the great preacher of modern society's self-doubt and self-hatred, but also the great prophet of its will to revolutionize, transform, and transfigure.

The principal historic significance of Marx's thought lies not so much in the specific programs and parties which have adopted his name as in the way in which his theories have provided the modern revolutionary impulse with its self-understanding. As soon as we appreciate this fact, we can see right away what is fundamentally wrong with the common practice of applying to Marx a scorecard of theoretical and practical successes and failures, correct and incorrect predictions, good and evil results. For then we can see immediately that the history of Marx's thought is still our own history, its fate is bound up with a reality whose possibilities are still radically open, within our grasp yet beyond our ken, exceeding the best and the worst we can pretend to imagine and even casting doubt on our capacity to apply terms like "good," "evil," "best," and "worst" to such an open future.

Whenever we pronounce condescendingly on what history has shown us about the fate of Marx's thought, we speak as if we ourselves, our own collective life and history, were something already settled, as if we had long since come to terms with all humanity's possible futures. Our condescension to Marx is only the complacent mask worn by our comfortable, falsifying flight from ourselves—not only from our unresolved social questions and self-dissatisfactions, but even more from our own historical openness and self-opacity, and above all from the specter of radical social revolution which has haunted modern society for the past two centuries, and which continues to challenge, allure, and terrify us. The history of Marx's thought will remain unfinished as long as revolutionary possibilities still live for us and Marx's thought is still their principal source.

I
Early Philosophical Writings
(1843–1845)

Toward a Critique of Hegel's *Philosophy of Right*: Introduction (1843) (*Complete*)

During the years 1842–1843, Marx wrote a critical discussion of Hegel's philosophy of the state as presented in *The Philosophy of Right*, with the apparent intention of eventually publishing a thorough critique of Hegel's political philosophy from a Young Hegelian point of view. The brief essay below, written for the *German-French Annals* in 1843, was apparently intended as an introduction to that more extensive critique, which never appeared.

But the 1843 essay shows also Marx's reservations about the Young Hegelian standpoint. Where the Young Hegelians emphasize the criticism of religion, Marx sees religious consciousness as nothing but a symptom of social conditions which are in need not of intellectual critique but of practical revolution. The essay also exhibits Marx's nascent acquaintance with the working class movement, which was soon drastically to change the direction of his study, thought, and action. This essay is the birth-place, in fact, of the Marxian concept of the proletariat as the revolutionary class whose mission is universal human emancipation. Translated from the German by Loyd D. Easton and Kurt H. Guddat.

For Germany the *criticism of religion* has been essentially completed, and criticism of religion is the premise of all criticism.

The *profane* existence of error is compromised when its *heavenly oratio pro aris et focis* [defense of altar and hearth] has been refuted. Man, who has found only the *reflection* of himself in the fantastic reality of heaven where he sought a supernatural being, will no longer be inclined to find the *semblance* of himself, only the non-human being, where he seeks and must seek his true reality.

The basis of irreligious criticism is: *Man makes religion*, religion does not make man. And indeed religion is the self-consciousness and self-regard of man who has either not yet found or has already lost himself. But *man* is not an abstract being squatting outside the world. Man is the *world of men*, the state, society. This state and this society produce religion, which is an *inverted consciousness of the world* because they are an *inverted world*. Religion is the generalized theory of this world, its encyclopaedic compendium, its logic in popular form, its spiritualistic point d'honneur, its enthusiasm, its moral sanction, its solemn complement, its general ground of consolation and justification. It is the *fantastic realization* of the human essence inasmuch as the *human essence* possesses no true reality. The struggle against religion is therefore indirectly the struggle against *that world* whose spiritual *aroma* is religion.

Religious suffering is the *expression* of real suffering and at the same time the *protest* against real suffering. Religion is the sigh of the oppressed creature, the heart of a heartless world, as it is the spirit of spiritless conditions. It is the *opium* of the people.

The abolition of religion as people's illusory happiness is the demand for their *real* happiness. The demand to abandon illusions about their condition is a *demand to abandon a condition which requires illusions*. The criticism of religion is thus in *embryo* a *criticism of the vale of tears* whose *halo* is religion.

Criticism has plucked imaginary flowers from the chain, not so that man will wear the chain that is without fantasy or consolation but so that he will throw it off and pluck the living flower. The criticism of religion disillusions man so that he thinks, acts, and shapes his reality like a disillusioned man who has come to his senses, so that he revolves around himself and thus around his true sun. Religion is only the illusory sun that revolves around man so long as he does not revolve about himself.

Thus it is the *task of history*, once the *otherworldly truth* has disappeared, to establish the *truth of this world*. The immediate *task of philosophy* which is in the service of history is to unmask human self-alienation in its *unholy forms* now that it has been unmasked in in its *holy form*. Thus the criticism of heavy turns into the criticism of the earth, the *criticism of religion*, into the criticism of law, and the *criticism of theology* into the *criticism of politics*.

The following exposition—a contribution to this undertaking [developed from the unpublished "Critique of Hegel's Philosophy of the State" written in Kreuznach]—does not directly pertain to the original but to a copy, the German *philosophy* of the state and law, for the simple reason that it deals with *Germany*.

If one were to proceed from the *status quo* itself in Germany, even in the only appropriate way, *that is*, negatively, the result would still be an *anachronism*. Even the negation of our political present is already a dusty fact in the historical lumber room of modern nations. If I negate powdered wigs, I am still left with unpowdered wigs. If I negate German conditions of 1843, I am hardly, according to French chronology, in the year 1789 and still less in the focus of the present.

Indeed, German history plumes itself on a development no nation in the historical firmament previously exhibited or will ever copy. We have in point of fact shared in the restorations of the modern nations without sharing in their revolutions. We have been restored, first because other nations dared to make revolutions, and secondly because other nations suffered counter-revolutions—on the one hand because our masters were afraid, and on the other because they were not afraid. Led by our shepherds, we found ourselves in the company of freedom only once, on the *day of its burial.*

A school of thought that legitimizes today's infamy by yesterday's, a school of thought that explains every cry of the serf against the knout as rebellion once the knout is time-honored, ancestral, and historical, a school to which history shows only its *a posteriori*, as the God of Israel did to his servant Moses—the Historical School of Law[1]—might have invented German history if it were not an invention of German history. A Shylock, but a servile Shylock, that school swears on its bond, on its historical bond, its Christian-Germanic bond, for every pound of flesh cut from the heart of the people.

Good-natured enthusiasts, German chauvinists by extraction and liberals by reflection, on the other hand, seek our history of freedom beyond our history in the primeval Teutonic forests. But how does the history of our freedom differ from the history of the wild boar's freedom if it is only to be found in the forests? As the proverb says, what is shouted into the forest, the forest echoes back. So peace to the primeval Teutonic forests!

War on German conditions! By all means! They are *below the level of history, beneath all criticism,* but they are still an object of criticism just as the criminal below the level of humanity is still an object of the *executioner.* In its struggle against these conditions criticism is not a passion of the head but the head of passion. It is not a lancet, it is a weapon. Its object is an *enemy* it wants not to refute but to *destroy.* For the spirit of these conditions has already been refuted. In and for themselves they are objects not *worthy of thought* but *existences* as despicable as they are despised. Criticism itself does not even need to be concerned with this matter, for it is already clear about it. Criticism is no longer an *end in itself* but simply a *means.* Its essential pathos is *indignation*, its essential task, *denunciation.*

It is a matter of describing the pervasive, suffocating pressure of all social spheres on one another, the general but passive dejection, the narrowness that recognizes but misunderstands itself—this framed in a system of government that lives on the conservation of all meanness and is nothing but *meanness in government.*

What a sight! Society is forever splitting into the most varied races opposing one another with petty antipathies, bad consciences, and brutal mediocrity, and precisely because of their mutually ambiguous and distrustful situation they are all treated by their *rulers* as merely *tolerated existences*, without exception, though with varying formalities. And they are forced to recognize and acknowledge their being *dominated, ruled,* and *possessed* as a *concession from heaven*! On the other side are the rulers themselves whose greatness is inversely proportional to their number!

The criticism dealing with this matter is criticism in *hand-to-hand* combat, and in such a combat the point is not whether the opponent is noble, equal, or *interesting*, the point is to *strike* him. The point is to permit the Germans not even a moment of self-deception and resignation. We must make the actual pressure more pressing by adding to it the consciousness of pressure and make the shame more shameful by publicizing it. Every sphere of German society must be shown as the *partie honteuse* of German society, and we have to make these petrified social relations dance by singing their own tune! The people must be taught to be *terrified* of themselves to give them *courage*. This will fulfill an imperative need of the German nation, and the needs of nations are themselves the ultimate grounds of their satisfaction.

And even for *modern* nations this struggle against the restricted content of the German *status quo* cannot be without interest, for the German *status quo* is the *open fulfillment of the Ancien Régime,* and the *Ancien Régime* is the *hidden deficiency of the modern state.* The struggle against the German political present is the struggle against the past of modern nations, and they are still burdened with reminders of that past. It is instructive for them to see the *Ancien Régime,* which lived through its *tragedy* with them, play its *comedy* as a German ghost. The history of the *Ancien Régime* was *tragic* so long as it was the established power in the world, while freedom on the other hand was a personal notion—in short, as long as it believed and had to believe in its own validity. As long as the *Ancien Régime* as an existing world order struggled against a world that was just coming into being, there was on its side a historical but not a personal error. Its downfall was therefore tragic.

On the other hand, the present German regime—an anachronism, a flagrant contradiction of generally accepted axioms, the nullity of the *Ancien Régime* exhibited to the whole world—only imagines that it believes in itself and demands that the world imagine the same thing. If it is believed in its own *nature*, would it try to hide that nature under the *semblance* of an alien nature and seek its salvation in hypocrisy and sophism? The modern *Ancien Régime* is merely the *comedian* in a world whose *real heroes* are dead. History is thorough and goes through many phases as it conducts an old form to the grave. The final phase of a world-historical form is *comedy.* The Greek gods, already tragically and mortally wounded in Aeschylus' *Prometheus Bound*, had to die again comically in Lucian's dialogues.[2] Why this course of history? So that mankind may part from its past *happily.* This *happy* historical destiny we vindicate for the political authorities of Germany.

But once *modern* political and social reality itself is subjected to criticism, once criticism arrives at truly human problems, it either finds itself outside the German *status quo* or it would deal with its object at *a level below* its objects. For example! The relation of industry and the world of wealth in general to the political world is a major problem of modern times. In what form is this problem beginning to preoccupy the Germans? In the form of *protective tariffs*, the *system of prohibition*, and *political economy*. German chauvinism has gone from man to matter and thus one fine day our barons of cotton and heroes of iron saw themselves transformed into patriots. Thus in Germany we are beginning to recognize the sovereignty of monopoly at home by investing it with *sovereignty abroad*. We are about to begin in Germany where France and England are about to end. The old rotten condition against which these countries are revolting in theory and which they bear as chains is greeted in Germany as the dawn of a glorious future which as yet hardly dares to pass from *crafty* [*listigen*:-Friedrich List][3] theory to the most ruthless practice. Whereas the problem in France and England reads: *political economy* or the *rule of society over wealth*, in Germany it reads: *political economy* or the *rule of private property over nationality*. Thus in France and England it is a question of abolishing monopoly that has developed to its final consequences; in Germany it is a question of proceeding to the final consequences of monopoly. There it is a question of solution; here, still a question of collision. This is an adequate example of the *German* form of modern problems, an example of how our history, like a raw recruit, still has had to do extra drill on matters threshed over in history.

If the *total* German development were not in advance of its *political* development, a German could at the most have a share in the problems of the present like that of a *Russian*. But if the single individual is not bound by the limitations of his nation, still less is the nation as a whole liberated by the liberation of one individual. The Scythians made no progress toward Greek culture even though Greece had a Scythian among her philosophers.[4]

Fortunately we Germans are not Scythians.

As the ancient countries lived their pre-history in imagination, in *mythology*, so we Germans have lived our post-history in thought, in *philosophy*. We are *philosophical* contemporaries of the present without being its *historical* contemporaries. German philosophy is the *ideal extension* of German history. If, therefore, we criticize the *oeuvres posthumes* of our ideal history—*philosophy*—instead of the *oeuvres incomplètes* of our real history, our criticism is in the center of questions of which the present says: *That is the question*. That which in progressive nations is a *practical* break with modern political conditions is in Germany, where these conditions do not yet exist, just a *critical* break with the philosophical reflection of those conditions.

The *German philosophy of law and of the state* is the only *German history* which stands *al pari* with the *official* modern present. The German nation must therefore join its dream-history to its present conditions and criticize not only these present conditions but also their abstract continuation. Its future can be *limited* neither to the direct negation of its real political and legal conditions nor to their direct fulfillment, for it has the direct negation of its real conditions in its ideal conditions and has almost *outlived* the direct fulfillment of its ideal conditions in the view of neighboring countries. Hence, the *practical* political party in Germany rightly demands the *negation of philosophy.* It is wrong not in its demand but in stopping at the demand it neither seriously fulfills nor can fulfill. It supposes that it accomplishes that negation by turning its back on philosophy, looking aside, and muttering a few petulant and trite phrases about it. Because its outlook is so limited it does not even count philosophy as part of *German* actuality or even imagines it is *beneath* German practice and its theories. You demand starting from *actual germs of life* but forget that the actual life-germ of the German nation has so far sprouted only inside its *cranium.* In short: *you cannot transcend [aufheben] philosophy without actualizing it.*

The same error, but with the factors *reversed*, was committed by the *theoretical* party which originated in philosophy.

In the present struggle the theoretical party saw *only* the *critical struggle of philosophy against the German world.* It did not consider that *previous philosophy* itself belongs to this world and is its *complement*, although an ideal one. Critical toward its counterpart, it was not critical of itself. Starting from the *presuppositions* of philosophy, it either stopped at philosophy's given results or passed off demands and results from somewhere else as direct demands and results from philosophy. But these latter—their legitimacy assumed—can only be obtained by the *negation of previous philosophy*, by the negation of philosophy as philosophy. We shall later give a closer account of this party. Its main defect may be summarized as follows: *It believed that it could actualize philosophy without transcending it.*

The criticism of the *German philosophy of the state and law*, which attained its most consistent, profound, and final formulation with *Hegel*, is at once a critical analysis of the modern state and the actuality connected with it and also the decisive negation of all previous *forms of German political and legal consciousness whose* most prominent and general expression at the level of *science is* precisely the *speculative philosophy of law.* If the speculative philosophy of law—that abstract and extravagant *thinking* about the modern state whose reality remains in the beyond, if only beyond the Rhine— was possible only in Germany, conversely the *German* conception of the modern state in abstraction from *actual man* was possible only because and insofar as the modern state abstracts itself from *actual man* or satisfies the *whole* man only in an illusory way. In politics the Germans have *thought* what other nations have *done*.[5] Germany has been their *theoretical conscience*. The abstraction and presumption of its thought always kept pace with the one-sided and stunted character of their actuality. If the *status quo* of the *German political system [Staatswesen]* expresses *the completion of the Ancien Régime*, the thorn in the flesh of the modern state, the *status quo* of *German political science [Staatswissen]* expresses the *incompletion of the modern state*, the damage to the flesh itself.

As the resolute opponent of the previous mode of *German* political consciousness, the criticism of speculative philosophy of law does not proceed in its own sphere but proceeds to *tasks* that can be solved by only one means—practice [*Praxis*].

The question arises: Can Germany reach a practice *à la hauteur des principes, that is, a revolution*, which will raise it not only to the *official level* of modern nations but to the *human level* which will be their immediate future?

The weapon of criticism obviously cannot replace the criticism of weapons. Material force must be overthrown by material force. But theory also becomes a material force once it has gripped the masses. Theory is capable of gripping the masses when it demonstrates *ad hominem*, and it demonstrates *ad hominem* when it becomes radical. To be radical is to grasp things by the root. But for man the root is man himself. The clear proof of the radicalism of German theory and hence of its political energy is that it proceeds from the decisive *positive* transcendence of religion. The criticism of religion ends with the doctrine that *man is the highest being for man*, hence with the *categorical imperative to overthrow all conditions* in which man is a degraded, enslaved, neglected, contemptible being—conditions that cannot better be described than by the exclamation of a Frenchman on the occasion of a proposed dog tax: Poor dogs! They want to treat you like human beings!

Even historically, theoretical emancipation has a specific practical significance for Germany. For Germany's *revolutionary* past is theoretical—it is the *Reformation*. As the revolution then began in the brain of the *monk*, now it begins in the brain of the *philosopher*.

Luther, to be sure, overcame bondage based on *devotion* by replacing it with bondage based on *conviction*. He shattered faith in authority by restoring the authority of faith. He turned priests into laymen by turning laymen into priests. He freed man from outward religiosity by making religiosity the inwardness of man. He emancipated the body from its chains by putting chains on the heart.

But if Protestantism was not the true solution, it was the true formulation of the problem. The question was no longer the struggle of the layman against the *priest external to him* but of his struggle against *his own inner priest*, his *priestly nature*. And if the Protestant transformation of German laymen into priests emancipated the lay popes—the *princes* with their clerical set, the privileged, and the Philistines—the philosophical transformation of priestly Germans into men will emancipate the *people*. But little as emancipation stops with princes, just as little will *secularization* of property stop with the *confiscation of church property* set in motion chiefly by hypocritical Prussia. At that time the Peasants' War, the most radical fact of German history, came to grief because of theology. Today, when theology itself has come to grief, the most unfree fact of German history— our *status quo*—will be shattered by philosophy. On the eve of the Reformation official Germany was the most abject vassal of Rome. On the eve of its revolution Germany is the abject vassal of something less than Rome—of Prussia and Austria, of ignorant country squires and Philistines.

But a major difficulty seems to stand in the way of a *radical* German revolution.

Revolutions require a *passive* element, a *material* basis. Theory is actualized in a people only insofar as it actualizes their needs. But will the enormous discrepancy between the demands of German thought and the answers of German actuality correspond to a similar discrepancy between civil society and the state, and within civil society itself? Will theoretical needs be immediate practical needs? It is not enough that thought should seek its actualization; actuality must itself strive toward thought.

But Germany has not risen to the intermediate stages of political emancipation at the same time as the modern nations. It has not yet reached in practice even the stages it has surpassed in theory. How can it clear with a *salto mortale* not only its own limitations but also those of modern nations—limitations which in actuality it must experience and strive for as an emancipation from its actual limitations? A radical revolution can only be a revolution of radical needs whose preconditions and birthplaces appear to be lacking.

But if Germany has attended the development of modern nations only through the abstract activity of thought without taking an active part in the real struggles of this development, it has also shared the *sufferings* of this development without sharing its enjoyments or partial satisfaction. Abstract activity on one side corresponds to abstract suffering on the other. One fine day Germany will find itself at the level of European decadence before ever having reached the level of European emancipation. It will be comparable to a *fetishist* wasting away from the diseases of Christianity.

Considering *German governments*, we find that owing to the circumstances of the time, the situation of Germany, the outlook of German culture, and finally their own fortunate instinct they are driven to combine the *civilized deficiencies* of the *modern political order* (whose advantages we do not enjoy) with the *barbarous deficiencies* of the *Ancien Régime* (which we enjoy in full). Hence Germany must participate more and more if not in the sense [*Verstand*] at least in the nonsense [*Unverstand*] of those political forms transcending its *status quo*. Is there, for example, another country in the whole world which as naïvely as so-called constitutional Germany shares all the illusions of constitutional statehood without sharing its realities? And was it not, necessarily, a German government's bright idea to combine the tortures of censorship with the tortures of the French September laws [of 1835][6] presupposing freedom of the press? As the *gods* of all nations were found in the Roman Pantheon, the *sins* of all forms of the state will be found in the Holy German Empire. That this eclecticism will reach an unprecedented height is particularly guaranteed by the *politico-aesthetic gourmanderie* of a German king [Friedrich Wilhelm IV][7] who plans to play all the roles of monarchy—feudal or bureaucratic, absolute or constitutional, autocratic or democratic—if not in the person of the people at least in his *own*, and if not for the people at least for *himself*. *As the deficiency of the political present erected into a system, Germany* will not be able to shed the specifically German limitations without shedding the general limitations of the political present.

   Radical revolution, *universal human* emancipation, is not a utopian dream for Germany. What is utopian is the partial, the *merely* political revolution, the revolution which would leave the pillars of the house standing. What is the basis of a partial and merely political revolution? It is *part of civil society* emancipating itself and attaining *universal* supremacy, a particular class by virtue of its *special situation* undertaking the general emancipation of society. This class emancipates the whole of society but only on the condition that the whole of society is in the same position as this class, *for example*, that it has or can easily acquire money and education.

   No class in civil society can take this role without arousing an impulse of enthusiasm in itself and in the masses, an impulse in which it fraternizes and merges with society at large, identifies itself with it, and is experienced and recognized as its *general representative*—an impulse in which its claims and rights are truly the rights and claims of society itself and in which it is actually the social head and the social heart. Only in the name of the general rights of society can a particular class claim general supremacy. Revolutionary energy and intellectual self-confidence are not by themselves sufficient to seize this emancipatory position and hence the political control of all spheres of society in the interest of its own. If a *popular revolution is to coincide with the emancipation of a particular class* of civil society, if *one* class is to stand for the whole society, all the defects of society must conversely be concentrated in another class. A particular class must be the class of general offense and the incorporation of general limitation. A particular social sphere must stand for the *notorious crime* of society as a whole so that emancipation from this sphere appears as general self-emancipation. For *one* class to be the class of emancipation *par excellence*, conversely another must be the obvious class of oppression. The negative, general significance of the French nobility and clergy determined the positive, general significance of the *bourgeoisie* standing next to and opposing them.

But in Germany every class lacks not only the consistency, penetration, courage, and ruthlessness which could stamp it as the negative representative of society. There is equally lacking in every class that breadth of soul which identifies itself, if only momentarily, with the soul of the people—that genius for inspiring material force toward political power, that revolutionary boldness which flings at its adversary the defiant words, *I am nothing and I should be everything*. The main feature of German morality and honor in classes as well as individuals is rather a *modest egoism* displaying its narrowness and allowing it to be displayed against itself. The relationship of the different spheres of German society is therefore not dramatic but epic. Each of them begins to be aware of itself and place itself beside the others, not as soon as it is oppressed but as soon as circumstances, without its initiative, create a social layer on which it can exert pressure in turn. Even the *moral self-esteem of the German middle class* rests only on its awareness of being the general representative of the philistine mediocrity of all the other classes. Hence, not only do German kings ascend their thrones *mal à propos*, but every section of civil society goes through a defeat before it celebrates victory, develops its own obstacles before it overcomes those facing it, asserts its narrow-minded nature before it can assert its generosity so that even the opportunity of playing a great role has always passed before it actually existed and each class is involved in a struggle against the class beneath as soon as it begins to struggle with the class above it. Hence princes struggle against kings, the bureaucrat against the nobility, and the bourgeoisie against them all, while the proletariat is already beginning to struggle against the bourgeoisie. The middle class hardly dares to conceive the idea of emancipation from its own perspective. The development of social conditions and the progress of political theory show that perspective to be already antiquated or at least problematic.

In France it is enough to be something for one to want to be everything. In Germany no one can be anything unless he is prepared to renounce everything. In France partial emancipation is the basis of universal emancipation. In Germany universal emancipation is the *conditio sine qua non* of any partial emancipation. In France it is the actuality, in Germany the impossibility, of gradual emancipation which must give birth to complete freedom. In France every class of the nation is *politically idealistic* and experiences itself first of all not as a particular class but as representing the general needs of society. The role of *emancipator* thus passes successively and dramatically to different classes of people until it finally reaches the class which actualizes social freedom, no longer assuming certain conditions external to man and yet created by human society but rather organizing all the conditions of human existence on the basis of social freedom. In Germany, by contrast, where practical life is as mindless as mental life is impractical, no class in civil society has any need or capacity for general emancipation until it is forced to it by its *immediate* condition, by *material* necessity, by its *very chains.*

Where, then, is the *positive* possibility of German emancipation?

Answer: In the formation of a class with *radical chains,* a class in civil society that is not of civil society, a class that is the dissolution of all classes, a sphere of society having a universal character because of its universal suffering and claiming no *particular* right because no *particular wrong* but *unqualified wrong* is perpetrated on it; a sphere that can invoke no *traditional* title but only a *human* title, which does not partially oppose the consequences but totally opposes the premises of the German political system; a sphere, finally, that cannot emancipate itself without emancipating itself from all the other spheres of society, thereby emancipating them; a sphere, in short, that is the *complete loss* of humanity and can only redeem itself through the *total redemption of humanity.* This dissolution of society as a particular class is the *proletariat.*

The proletariat is only beginning to appear in Germany as a result of the rising *industrial* movement. For it is not poverty from *natural circumstances* but *artificially produced* poverty, not the human masses mechanically oppressed by the weight of society but the masses resulting from the *acute disintegration* of society, and particularly of the middle class, which gives rise to the proletariat—though also, needless to say, poverty from natural circumstances and Christian-Germanic serfdom gradually join the proletariat.

Heralding the *dissolution of the existing order of things,* the proletariat merely announces the *secret of its own existence* because it is the *real* dissolution of this order. Demanding the *negation of private property,* the proletariat merely raises to the *principle of society* what society has raised to the principle *of the proletariat,* what the proletariat already embodies as the negative result of society without its action. The proletarian thus has the same right in the emerging order of things as the *German king* has in the existing order when he calls the people *his* people or a horse *his* horse. Declaring the people to be his private property, the king merely proclaims that the private owner is king.

As philosophy finds its *material* weapons in the proletariat, the proletariat finds its *intellectual* weapons in philosophy. And once the lighting of thought has deeply struck this unsophisticated soil of the people, the *Germans* will emancipate themselves to become *men*.

Let us summarize the result:

The only emancipation of Germany possible *in practice* is emancipation based on *the* theory proclaiming that man is the highest essence of man. In Germany emancipation from the *Middle Ages* is possible only as emancipation at the same time from *partial* victories over the Middle Ages. In Germany *no* brand of bondage can be broken without *every* brand of bondage being broken. Always seeking *fundamentals*, Germany can only make a *fundamental* revolution. The *emancipation of the German* is the *emancipation of mankind*. The *head* of this emancipation is *philosophy*, its *heart* is the *proletariat*. Philosophy cannot be actualized without the transcendence [*Aufhebung*] of the proletariat, the proletariat cannot be transcended without the actualization of philosophy.

When all the inner conditions are fulfilled, the *day of German resurrection* will be announced by the *crowing of the French rooster.*

NOTES TO "TOWARD A CRITIQUE OF HEGEL'S *PHILOSOPHY OF RIGHT*: INTRODUCTION"

1. The Historical School of Law was a movement in early nineteenth-century German jurisprudence. Two of its chief exponents were Friedrich Karl von Savigny (1779–1861) (professor of law in Berlin), author of *On the Calling of Our Age for Legislation and Jurisprudence* (1814) and Gustav Ritter von Hugo (1764–1844) (professor of law in Göttingen), author of *Textbook of Roman Law* (1790). The spirit of the historical school was empirical but romantic, reacting against the legal rationalism of the eighteenth century. It emphasized the historical origins of law, celebrating native German culture and opposing attempts to "adulterate" it with alien (chiefly French) influences, such as proposals to codify law after the model of the Napoleonic Code. Explicit criticisms of Hugo and implicit criticisms of Savigny are to be found in Hegel's *Philosophy of Right*. Marx had attended Savigny's lectures in Berlin, but preferred the lectures of Hegel's protégé, Eduard Gans (1798–1839).

2. Aeschylus' (525–456 B.C.) tragedy *Prometheus Bound* tells the story of the titan who stole fire from the gods and gave it to man; Lucian (120–180 A.D.), a Greek satirist of skeptical temper; his *Dialogues on the Gods* were witty commentaries on pagan religion.

3. The German political economist Friedrich List (1789–1846) was author of *The National System of Political Economy* (1840). He advocated industrial capitalism, along with nationalist and protectionist trade policies.

4. The Scythians were an ancient people from southern Russia, regarded by the Greeks as the least civilized of all the barbarians. Yet according to Diogenes Laertius, *Lives of the Philosophers* I Prologue 13, Anacharsis the Scythian was numbered by some among the Greek sages. cf. Aristotle, *Nicomachean Ethics* 1176b34.

5. This is an allusion to Hegel, who says, comparing Kant's moral philosophy to the French revolution, "Among the Germans this view assumed no other form than that of tranquil theory; but the French wished to give it practical effect" (*The Philosophy of History*, tr. J. Sibree. New York: Dover, 1956, p. 443).
6. The laws of September, 1835 increased financial guarantees required of newspapers and imposed fines on publications deemed subversive.
7. The romantic-reactionary Friedrich Wilhelm IV acceded to the Prussian throne in 1840.

Excerpt Notebooks (1844)
(*Excerpt*)

Marx began his study of political economy in 1844, reading and commenting on a French translation of *The Elements of Political Economy* by James Mill (1773–1836), father of John Stuart Mill. In the following excerpt from his notes on Mill's *Elements*, Marx criticizes the political economists for seeing the process of production in terms conditioned by the institution of private property, instead of recognizing the true nature of production as the exercise of the social essence of humanity. Translated from the German by Loyd D. Easton and Kurt H. Guddat.

. . . It is the basic presupposition of private property that man *produces* only in order to *own*. The purpose of production is to *own*. It not only has such a *useful* purpose; it also has a *selfish* purpose. Man only produces in order to *own* something for himself. The object of his production is the objectification of his *immediate*, selfish *need*. Man—in his wild, barbaric condition—determines his production by the *extent* of his immediate need whose content is the *immediately* produced object itself.

In that condition man produces *no more* than he immediately needs. The *limit of his need* is the *limit of his production*. Demand and supply coincide. Production is *determined* by need. Either no exchange takes place or the exchange is reduced to the exchange of man's labor for the product of his labor, and this exchange is the latent form (the germ) of real exchange.

As soon as exchange occurs, there is an overproduction beyond the immediate boundary of ownership. But this overproduction does not exceed selfish need. Rather it is only an *indirect* way of satisfying a need which finds its objectification in the production of another person. Production has become a *source of income*, labor for profit. While formerly need determined the extent of production, now production, or rather the *owning of the product*, determines how far needs can be satisfied.

I have produced for myself and not for you, just as you have produced for yourself and not for me. The result of my production as such has as little direct connection with you as the result of your production has with me, that is, our production is not production of man for man as man, not *socialized* production. No one is gratified by the product of another. Our mutual production means nothing for us as human beings. Our exchange, therefore, cannot be the mediating movement in which it would be acknowledged that my product means anything for you because it is an *objectification* of your being, your need. *Human nature* is not the bond of our production for each other. Exchange can only set in *motion* and confirm the *relationship* which each of us has to his own product and to the production of the other person. Each of us sees in his product only his *own* objectified self-interest and in the product of another person, *another* self-interest which is independent, alien, and objectified.

As a human being, however, you do have a human relation to my product; you *want* my product. It is the object of your desire and your will. But your want, desire, and will for my product are impotent. In other words, your *human* nature, necessarily and intimately related to my human production, is not your *power*, not your sharing in this production, because the *power* of human nature is not acknowledged in my production. Rather it is the *bond* which makes you dependent upon me because it makes you dependent on my product. It is far from being the *means* of giving you *power* over my production; rather it is the *means* of giving me power over you.

When I produce *more* than I can consume, I subtly *reckon* with your need. I produce only the *semblance* of a surplus of the object. In truth I produce a *different* object, the object of your production which I plan to exchange for this surplus, an exchange already accomplished in thought. My *social* relationship with you and my labor for your want is just plain *deception* and our mutual reintegration is *deception* just as well. Mutual pillaging is its base. Its background is the intent to pillage, to defraud. Since our exchange is selfish on your side as well as mine and since every self-interest attempts to surpass that of another person, we necessarily attempt to defraud each other. The power I give my object over yours, however, requires your *acknowledgment* to become real. Our mutual acknowledgment of the mutual power of our objects is a battle and the one with more insight, energy, power, and cleverness is the winner. If my physical strength suffices, I pillage you directly. If there is no physical power, we mutually dissemble and the more adroit comes out on top. It makes no difference for the *entire* relationship who the winner is, for the *ideal* and *intended* victory takes place on both sides; in his own judgment each of the two has overcome the other.

On both sides exchange necessarily requires the *object* of mutual production and mutual ownership. The ideal relationship to the mutual objects of our production is our mutual need. But the *real* and *truly effective* relationship is only the mutually *exclusive ownership* of mutual production. It is your *object*, the *equivalent* of my object, that gives your want for my object *value*, *dignity*, and *efficacy* for me. Our mutual product, therefore, is the *means*, the *intermediary*, the *instrument*, the *acknowledged power* of our mutual needs. Your *demand* and the *equivalent of your property* are terms which for me are *synonymous* and equally valid, and your demand is effective only when it has an effect on me. Without this effect your demand is merely an unsatisfied effort on your part and without consequence for me. You have no relationship to my object as a human being because I *myself* have no human relation to it. But the *means* is the *real power* over an object, and we mutually regard our product as the *power* each one has over the other and over himself. In other words, our own product is turned against us. It appeared to be our property, but actually we are its property. We ourselves are excluded from *true* property because our *property* excludes the other human being.

Our objects in their relation to one another constitute the only intelligible language we use with one another. We would not understand a human language, and it would remain without effect. On the one hand, it would be felt and spoken as a plea, as begging, and as *humiliation* and hence uttered with shame and with a feeling of supplication; on the other hand, it would be heard and rejected as *effrontery* or *madness*. We are so much mutually alienated from human nature that the direct language of this nature is an *injury to human dignity* for us, while the alienated language of objective values appears as justified, self-confident, and self-accepted human dignity.

To be sure, from your point of view your product is an *instrument*, a *means* for the appropriation of my product and for the satisfaction of your need. But from my point of view it is the *goal* of our exchange. I regard you as a means and instrument for the production of this object, that is, my goal, and much more so than I regard you as related to my object. But (1) each of us actually *does* what the other thinks he is doing. You actually made yourself the means, the instrument, and the producer of *your* own object in order to appropriate mine; (2) for you, your own object is only the *sensuous shell* and *concealed form* of my object; its production *means* and *expressly* is the *acquisition* of my object. You indeed become the *means* and instrument of your object; your greed is the *slave* of this object, and you performed slavish services so that the object is never again a remission of your greed. This mutual servitude to the object is actually manifested to us at the beginning of its development as the relationship of *lordship* and *slavery*, and is only the *crude* and *frank* expression of our *essential* relationship.

Our *mutual* value is the *value* of our mutual objects for us. Man himself, therefore, is mutually *valueless* for us.

Suppose we had produced things as human beings: in his production each of us would have *twice affirmed* himself and the other. (1) In my *production* I would have objectified my *individuality* and its *particularity*, and in the course of the activity I would have enjoyed an individual *life*; in viewing the object I would have experienced the individual joy of knowing my personality as an *objective, sensuously perceptible*, and *indubitable* power. (2) In your satisfaction and your use of my product I would have had the *direct* and conscious satisfaction that my work satisfied a *human* need, that it objectified *human* nature, and that it created an object appropriate to the need of another *human* being. (3) I would have been the *mediator* between you and the species and you would have experienced me as a redintegration of your own nature and a necessary part of your self; I would have been affirmed in your thought as well as your love. (4) In my individual life I would have directly created your life; in my individual activity I would have immediately *confirmed* and *realized* my true *human* and *social* nature.

Our productions would be so many mirrors reflecting our nature.

What happens so far as I am concerned would also apply to you.

Let us summarize the various factors in the supposition above:

My labor would be a *free manifestation of life* and an *enjoyment of life*. Under the presupposition of private property it is an *externalization of life* because I work *in order to live* and provide for myself the *means* of living. Working is *not* living.

Furthermore, in my labor the *particularity* of my individuality would be affirmed because my *individual* life is affirmed. Labor then would be *true, active property*. Under the presupposition of private property my individuality is externalized to the point where I *hate* this *activity* and where it is a *torment* for me. Rather it is then only the *semblance* of an activity, only a *forced* activity, imposed upon me only by *external* and accidental necessity and *not* by an *internal* and *determined* necessity. . . .

Economic and Philosophic Manuscripts (1844) (*Selections*)

Marx's study of political economy in 1844 led him to the project of a systematic critique both of this science and of the society it studies. The result was a series of manuscripts, first summarizing the results of political economy and then criticizing them from the perspective of Young Hegelian philosophy—especially from the perspective of Feuerbach. The project was never completed, but the manuscripts, first published in 1932, have been highly influential on Marxian philosophy in the twentieth century. The selections printed here include the Preface to the projected series of essays, and the best known manuscripts: "Alienated Labor," "Private Property and Communism" and "Critique of the Hegelian Dialectic and Philosophy in General". Translated from the German by Loyd D. Easton and Kurt H. Guddat.

PREFACE

In the *Deutsch-Französische Jahrbücher* I announced a critique of jurisprudence and political science in the form of a critique of the *Hegelian* philosophy of law. Preparing this for publication, I found that the combination of criticism directed solely against speculation with criticism of various subjects would be quite unsuitable; it would impede the development of the argument and render comprehension difficult. Moreover, the wealth and diversity of the subjects to be dealt with could have been accommodated in a *single* work only in a very aphoristic style, and such aphoristic presentation would have given the *impression* of arbitrary systematization. Therefore, I shall issue the critique of law, morals, politics, etc., in separate, independent brochures, and finally attempt to give in a separate work the unity of the whole, the relation of the separate parts, and eventually a critique of the speculative treatment of the material. Hence in the present work the relationships of political economy with the state, law, morals, civil life, etc., are touched upon only insofar as political economy itself, ex professo, deals with these subjects.

It is hardly necessary to assure the reader familiar with political economy that my conclusions have been obtained through an entirely empirical analysis, based on a thorough, critical study of political economy.

The uninformed reviewer, however, who tries to hide his complete ignorance and poverty of thought by hurling *"utopian phrase"* at the positive critic's head or such phrases as "the entirely pure, entirely decisive, entirely critical criticism," the "not merely legal but social, entirely social society," the "compact, massy mass," the "outspoken spokesman of the massy mass"—this reviewer [Bruno Bauer][1] has yet to furnish the first proof that outside his theological family affairs he has anything to contribute to *worldly* matters.))*

It is a matter of course that in addition to the French and English socialists I have also used German socialist works. The significant and *original* German contributions on this subject—apart from Weitling's[2] writings—amount to no more than the essays by Hess in *Twenty-one Sheets[3]* [*From Switzerland*] and Engels' "Outlines of a Critique of Political Economy" in the *Deutsch-Französische Jahrbücher* where I indicated the basic elements of the present work in a very general way.

((Besides the criticism concerned with political economy, positive criticism in general, and thus also German positive criticism of political economy, is really founded on the discoveries of *Feuerbach* against whose *Philosophy of the Future* and "Theses on the Reform of Philosophy" in the *Anekdota* the petty envy of some and the loud rage of others seem to have instigated an organized conspiracy of *silence*, despite the tacit use that is made of Feuerbach's works.))[4]

Positive humanistic and naturalistic criticism begins with *Feuerbach*. The less vociferous *Feuerbach's* writings are, the more certain, profound, extensive, and lasting is their influence—the only writings since Hegel's *Phenomenology of Spirit* and *Logic* containing a real theoretical revolution.

In contrast to the *critical theologians* of our time[5] [Bruno Bauer and followers] I have regarded the concluding chapter of the present work—the discussion of the *Hegelian dialectic* and philosophy in general—to be absolutely necessary because such a task has not yet been accomplished. This lack of *thoroughness* is inevitable because even the *critical* theologian remains a *theologian*. Either he must proceed from certain presuppositions of philosophy, accepting them as authoritative, or else, if in the course of criticism and as a result of other persons' discoveries doubts arise in his mind about the philosophical presuppositions, he abandons them in a cowardly, indefensible manner, *abstracts* from them, and manifests his servitude to these very presuppositions and his vexation over this servitude in a negative, unconscious, and sophistical way.

((manifests this only negatively and unconsciously, on the one hand,

[*Material within double parentheses, from here on, vertically crossed out by Marx.]

in constantly repeating the assurance of the *purity* of his own criticism, and on the other hand, in trying to present the appearance that criticism only has to do with a limited form of the criticism outside—say that of the eighteenth century—and with the obtuseness of the *mass,* in order to divert the observer's eyes as well as his own from the *necessary* clash between *criticism* and its birthplace—Hegelian *dialectic* and German philosophy in general—and from the necessary advancement of modern criticism beyond its own narrowness and natural origin. Finally, however, when discoveries such as *Feuerbach's* are made about the nature of his own philosophical presuppositions, the critical theologian may claim to have made the discovery *himself* and pretend this by hurling *catch phrases,* the results of the discovery which he was not able to develop, at writers who are still caught in philosophy. He may even manage to secure the sense of his superiority to that discovery, not by attempting, even if he could, to bring into their proper relations the elements of Hegelian *dialectic* which he still finds missing in the criticism of Hegelian dialectic not yet served up to him, but rather by employing those elements in veiled, mischievous, and sceptical ways, in a secretive manner, against the criticism of Hegelian dialectic—such as the category of mediating proof against the category of positive, self-originating truth, the [. . .], etc.—in the form *peculiar* to Hegelian dialectic. The theological critic finds it quite natural that everything is to be *done* by philosophy so that he can *chatter* about purity, resoluteness, about the very critical criticism. He fancies himself the true *conqueror of philosophy* whenever he happens to *feel* that some moment in Hegel is lacking in relation to Feuerbach—for however much the theological critic practices the spiritualistic idolatry of "*Self-Consciousness*" and "Spirit," he can not go beyond feeling and achieve consciousness.))

Considered closely, *theological criticism*—while in the beginning of the movement an actual factor of progress—in the final analysis is nothing but the culmination and consequence of the old *philosophical* transcendence, particularly *Hegelian transcendence,* distorted into a *theological caricature.* On another occasion [subsequently in *The Holy Family*] I shall describe in detail this interesting historical justice, this historical nemesis, which is inducing theology, ever the sore point of philosophy, to exhibit in itself the negative dissolution of philosophy—that is, its decomposition process.

((To what extent *Feuerbach's* discoveries about the nature of philosophy still require—at least for their *proof*—a critical analysis of philosophical dialectic will be learned from my exposition itself.))

ALIENATED LABOR

We have proceeded from the presuppositions of political economy. We have accepted its language and its laws. We presupposed private property, the separation of labor, capital and land, hence of wages, profit of capital and rent, likewise the division of labor, competition, the concept of exchange value, etc. From political economy itself, in its own words, we have shown that the worker sinks to the level of a commodity, the most miserable commodity; that the misery of the worker is inversely proportional to the power and volume of his production; that the necessary result of competition is the accumulation of capital in a few hands and thus the revival of monopoly in a more frightful form; and finally that the distinction between capitalist and landowner, between agricultural laborer and industrial worker, disappears and the whole society must divide into the two classes of *proprietors* and propertyless *workers*.

Political economy proceeds from the fact of private property. It does not explain private property. It grasps the actual, *material* process of private property in abstract and general formulae which it then takes as *laws*. It does not *comprehend* these laws, that is, does not prove them as proceeding from the nature of private property. Political economy does not disclose the reason for the division between capital and labor, between capital and land. When, for example, the relation of wages to profits is determined, the ultimate basis is taken to be the interest of the capitalists; that is, political economy assumes what it should develop. Similarly, competition is referred to at every point and explained from external circumstances. Political economy teaches us nothing about the extent to which these external, apparently accidental circumstances are simply the expression of a necessary development. We have seen how political economy regards exchange itself as an accidental fact. The only wheels which political economy puts in motion are *greed* and the *war among the greedy, competition*.

Just because political economy does not grasp the interconnections within the movement, the doctrine of competition could stand opposed to the doctrine of monopoly, the doctrine of freedom of craft to that of the guild, the doctrine of the division of landed property to that of the great estate. Competition, freedom of craft, and division of landed property were developed and conceived only as accidental, deliberate, forced consequences of monopoly, the guild, and feudal property, rather than necessary, inevitable, natural consequences.

We now have to grasp the essential connection among private property, greed, division of labor, capital and landownership, and the connection of exchange with competition, of value with the devaluation of men, of monopoly with competition, etc., and of this whole alienation with the *money*-system.

Let us not put ourselves in a fictitious primordial state like a political economist trying to clarify things. Such a primordial state clarifies nothing. It merely pushes the issue into a gray, misty distance. It acknowledges as a fact or event what it should deduce, namely, the necessary relation between two things for example, between division of labor and exchange.

In such a manner theology explains the origin of evil by the fall of man. That is, it asserts as a fact in the form of history what it should explain.

We proceed from a *present* fact of political economy.

The worker becomes poorer the more wealth he produces, the more his production increases in power and extent. The worker becomes a cheaper commodity the more commodities he produces. The *increase in value* of the world of things is directly proportional to the *decrease in value* of the human world. Labor not only produces commodities. It also produces itself and the worker as a *commodity*, and indeed in the same proportion as it produces commodities in general.

This fact simply indicates that the object which labor produces, its product, stands opposed to it as an *alien thing*, as a *power independent* of the producer. The product of labor is labor embodied and made objective in a thing. It is the *objectification* of labor. The realization of labor is its objectification. In the viewpoint of political economy this realization of labor appears as the *diminution* of the worker, the objectification as the *loss of and subservience to the object*, and the appropriation as *alienation* [*Entfremdung*], as externalization [*Entäusserung*].

So much does the realization of labor appear as diminution that the worker is diminished to the point of starvation. So much does objectification appear as loss of the object that the worker is robbed of the most essential objects not only of life but also of work. Indeed, work itself becomes a thing of which he can take possession only with the greatest effort and with the most unpredictable interruptions. So much does the appropriation of the object appear as alienation that the more objects the worker produces, the fewer he can own and the more he falls under the domination of his product, of capital.

All these consequences follow from the fact that the worker is related to the *product of his labor* as to an *alien* object. For it is clear according to this premise: The more the worker exerts himself, the more powerful becomes the alien objective world which he fashions against himself, the poorer he and his inner world become, the less there is that belongs to him. It is the same in religion. The more man attributes to God, the less he retains in himself. The worker puts his life into the object; then it no longer belongs to him but to the object. The greater this activity, the poorer is the worker. What the product of his work is, he is not. The greater this product is, the smaller he is himself. The *externalization* of the worker in his product means not only that his work becomes an object, an *external* existence, but also that it exists *outside him* independently, alien, an autonomous power, opposed to him. The life he has given to the object confronts him as hostile and alien.

Let us now consider more closely the *objectification*, the worker's production and with it the *alienation* and *loss* of the object, his product.

The worker can make nothing without *nature*, without the *sensuous external world.* It is the material wherein his labor realizes itself, wherein it is active, out of which and by means of which it produces.

But as nature furnishes to labor the *means of life* in the sense that labor cannot *live* without objects upon which labor is exercised, nature also furnishes the *means of life* in the narrower sense, namely, the means of physical subsistence of the *worker* himself.

The more the worker *appropriates* the external world and sensuous nature through his labor, the more he deprives himself of the *means of life* in two respects: first, that the sensuous external world gradually ceases to be an object belonging to his labor, a *means of life* of his work; secondly, that it gradually ceases to be a *means of life* in the immediate sense, a means of physical subsistence of the worker.

In these two respects, therefore, the worker becomes a slave to his objects; first, in that he receives an *object of labor*, that is, he receives *labor*, and secondly that he receives the *means of subsistence*. The first enables him to exist as a *worker* and the second as a *physical subject*. The terminus of this slavery is that he can only maintain himself as a *physical subject* so far as he is a *worker*, and only as a *physical subject* is he a worker.

(The alienation of the worker in his object is expressed according to the laws of political economy as follows: the more the worker produces, the less he has to consume; the more values he creates the more worthless and unworthy he becomes; the better shaped his product, the more mis-shapen is he; the more civilized his product, the more barbaric is the worker; the more powerful the work, the more powerless becomes the worker; the more intelligence the work has, the more witless is the worker and the more he becomes a slave of nature.)

Political economy conceals the alienation in the nature of labor by ignoring the direct relationship between the worker (labor) *and production.* To be sure, labor produces marvels for the wealthy but it produces deprivation for the worker. It produces palaces, but hovels for the worker. It produces beauty, but mutilation for the worker. It displaces labor through machines, but it throws some workers back into barbarous labor and turns others into machines. It produces intelligence, but for the worker it produces imbecility and cretinism.

The direct relationship of labor to its products is the relationship of the worker to the objects of his production. The relationship of the rich to the objects of production and to production itself is only a *consequence* of this first relationship and confirms it. Later we shall observe the latter aspect.

Thus, when we ask, What is the essential relationship of labor? we ask about the relationship of the *worker* to production.

Up to now we have considered the alienation, the externalization of the worker only from one side: his *relationship to the products of his labor.* But alienation is shown not only in the result but also in the *process of production*, in the *producing activity* itself. How could the worker stand in an alien relationship to the product of his activity if he did not alienate himself from himself in the very act of production? After all, the product is only the résumé of activity, of production. If the product of work is externalization, production itself must be active externalization, externalization of activity, activity of externalization. Only alienation—and externalization in the activity of labor itself—is summarized in the alienation of the object of labor.

What constitutes the externalization of labor?

First is the fact that labor is *external* to the laborer—that is, it is not part of his nature—and that the worker does not affirm himself in his work but denies himself, feels miserable and unhappy, develops no free physical and mental energy but mortifies his flesh and ruins his mind. The worker, therefore feels at ease only outside work, and during work he is outside himself. He is at home when he is not working and when he is working he is not at home. His work, therefore, is not voluntary, but coerced, *forced labor.* It is not the satisfaction of a need but only a *means* to satisfy other needs. Its alien character is obvious from the fact that as soon as no physical or other pressure exists, labor is avoided like the plague. External labor, labor in which man is externalized, is labor of self-sacrifice, of penance. Finally, the external nature of work for the worker appears in the fact that it is not his own but another person's, that in work he does not belong to himself but to someone else. In religion the spontaneity of human imagination, the spontaneity of the human brain and heart, acts independently of the individual as an alien, divine or devilish activity. Similarly, the activity of the worker is not his own spontaneous activity. It belongs to another. It is the loss of his own self.

The result, therefore, is that man (the worker) feels that he is acting freely only in his animal functions—eating, drinking, and procreating, or at most in his shelter and finery—while in his human functions he feels only like an animal. The animalistic becomes the human and the human the animalistic.

To be sure, eating, drinking, and procreation are genuine human functions. In abstraction, however, and separated from the remaining sphere of human activities and turned into final and sole ends, they are animal functions.

We have considered labor, the act of alienation of practical human activity, in two aspects: (1) the relationship of the worker to the *product of labor* as an alien object dominating him. This relationship is at the same time the relationship to the sensuous external world, to natural objects as an alien world hostile to him; (2) the relationship of labor to the *act of production* in *labor.* This relationship is that of the worker to his own activity as alien and not belonging to him, activity as passivity, power as weakness, procreation as emasculation, the worker's *own* physical and spiritual energy, his personal life—for what else is life but activity—as an activity turned against him, independent of him, and not belonging to him. *Self-alienation*, as against the alienation of the *object*, stated above.

We have now to derive a third aspect of *alienated labor* from the two previous ones.

Man is a species-being [*Gattungswesen*] not only in that he practically and theoretically makes his own species as well as that of other things his object, but also—and this is only another expression for the same thing—in that as present and living species he considers himself to be a *universal* and consequently free being.

The life of the species in man as in animals is physical in that man, (like the animal) lives by inorganic nature. And as man is more universal than the animal, the realm of inorganic nature by which he lives is more universal. As plants, animals, minerals, air, light, etc., in theory form a part of human consciousness, partly as objects of natural science, partly as objects of art—his spiritual inorganic nature or spiritual means of life which he first must prepare for enjoyment and assimilation—so they also form in practice a part of human life and human activity. Man lives physically only by these products of nature; they may appear in the form of food, heat, clothing, housing, etc. The universality of man appears in practice in the universality which makes the whole of nature his *inorganic* body: (1) as a direct means of life, and (2) as the matter, object, and instrument of his life activity. Nature is the *inorganic body* of man, that is, nature insofar as it is not the human body. Man *lives* by nature. This means that nature is his *body* with which he must remain in perpetual process in order not to die. That the physical and spiritual life of man is tied up with nature is another way of saying that nature is linked to itself, for man is a part of nature.

In alienating (1) nature from man, and (2) man from himself, his own active function, his life activity, alienated labor also alienates the *species* from him; it makes *species-life* the means of individual life. In the first place it alienates species-life and the individual life, and secondly it turns the latter in its abstraction into the purpose of the former, also in its abstract and alienated form.

For labor, *life activity*, and *productive life* appear to man at first only as a *means* to satisfy a need, the need to maintain physical existence. Productive life, however, is species-life. It is life begetting life. In the mode of life activity lies the entire character of a species, its species-character; and free conscious activity is the species-character of man. Life itself appears only as a *means of life*.

The animal is immediately one with its life activity, not distinct from it. The animal *is its life activity*. Man makes his life activity itself into an object of will and consciousness. He has conscious life activity. It is not a determination with which he immediately identifies. Conscious life activity distinguishes man immediately from the life activity of the animal.

Only thereby is he a species-being. Or rather, he is only a conscious being—that is, his own life is an object for him—since he is a species-being. Only on that account is his activity free activity. Alienated labor reverses the relationship in that man; since he is a conscious being, makes his life activity, his *essence*, only a means for his *existence*.

The practical creation of an *objective world*, the *treatment* of inorganic nature, is proof that man is a conscious species-being, that is, a being which is related to its species as to its own essence or is related to itself as a species-being. To be sure animals also produce. They build themselves nests, dwelling places, like the bees, beavers, ants, etc. But the animal produces only what is immediately necessary for itself or its young. It produces in a one-sided way while man produces universally. The animal produces under the domination of immediate physical need while man produces free of physical need and only genuinely so in freedom from such need. The animal only produces itself while man reproduces the whole of nature. The animal's product belongs immediately to its physical body while man is free when he confronts his product. The animal builds only according to the standard and need of the species to which it belongs while man knows how to produce according to the standard of any species and at all times knows how to apply an intrinsic standard to the object. Thus man creates also according to the laws of beauty.

In the treatment of the objective world, therefore, man proves himself to be genuinely a *species-being*. This production is his active species-life. Through it nature appears as *his* work and his actuality. The object of labor is thus the *objectification of man's species-life*: he produces himself not only intellectually, as in consciousness, but also actively in a real sense and sees himself in a world he made. In taking from man the object of his production, alienated labor takes from his *species-life*, his actual and objective existence as a species. It changes his superiority to the animal to inferiority, since he is deprived of nature, his inorganic body.

By degrading free spontaneous activity to the level of a means, alienated labor makes the species-life of man a means of his physical existence.

The consciousness which man has from his species is altered through alienation, so that species-life becomes a means for him.

(3) Alienated labor hence turns the *species-existence of man*, and also nature as his mental species-capacity, into an existence *alien* to him, into the *means* of his *individual existence*. It alienates his spiritual nature, his *human essence*, from his own body and likewise from nature outside him.

(4) A direct consequence of man's alienation from the product of his work, from his life activity, and from his species-existence, is the *alienation of man* from *man*. When man confronts himself, he confronts *other* men. What holds true of man's relationship to his work, to the product of his work, and to himself, also holds true of man's relationship to other men, to their labor, and the object of their labor.

In general, the statement that man is alienated from his species-existence means that one man is alienated from another just as each man is alienated from human nature.

The alienation of man, the relation of man to himself, is realized and expressed in the relation between man and other men.

Thus in the relation of alienated labor every man sees the others according to the standard and the relation in which he finds himself as a worker.

We began with an economic fact, the alienation of the worker and his product. We have given expression to the concept of this fact: *alienated, externalized* labor. We have analyzed this concept and have thus analyzed merely a fact of political economy.

Let us now see further how the concept of alienated, externalized labor must express and represent itself in actuality.

If the product of labor is alien to me, confronts me as an alien power, to whom then does it belong?

If my own activity does not belong to me, if it is an alien and forced activity, to whom then does it belong?

To a being *other* than myself.

Who is this being?

Gods? To be sure, in early times the main production, for example, the building of temples in Egypt, India, and Mexico, appears to be in the service of the gods, just as the product belongs to the gods. But gods alone were never workmasters. The same is true of *nature*. And what a contradiction it would be if the more man subjugates nature through his work and the more the miracles of gods are rendered superfluous by the marvels of industry, man should renounce his joy in producing and the enjoyment of his product for love of these powers.

The *alien* being who owns labor and the product of labor, whom labor serves and whom the product of labor satisfies can only be *man* himself.

That the product of labor does not belong to the worker and an alien power confronts him is possible only because this product belongs to *a man other than the worker*. If his activity is torment for him, it must be the *pleasure* and the life-enjoyment for another. Not gods, not nature, but only man himself can be this alien power over man.

Let us consider the statement previously made, that the relationship of man to himself is *objective* and *actual* to him only through his relationship to other men. If man is related to the product of his labor, to his objectified labor, as to an *alien*, hostile, powerful object independent of him, he is so related that another alien, hostile, powerful man independent of him is the lord of this object. If he is unfree in relation to his own activity, he is related to it as bonded activity, activity under the domination, coercion, and yoke of another man.

Every self-alienation of man, from himself and from nature, appears in the relationship which he postulates between other men and himself and nature. Thus religious self-alienation appears necessarily in the relation of laity to priest, or also to a mediator, since we are here now concerned with the spiritual world. In the practical real world self-alienation can appear only in the practical real relationships to other men. The means whereby the alienation proceeds is a *practical* means. Through alienated labor man thus not only produces his relationship to the object and to the act of production as an alien man at enmity with him. He also creates the relation in which other men stand to his production and product, and the relation in which he stands to these other men. Just as he begets his own production as loss of his reality, as his punishment; just as he begets his own product, as a loss, a product not belonging to him, so he begets the domination of the nonproducer over production and over product. As he alienates his own activity from himself, he confers upon the stranger an activity which is not his own.

Up to this point, we have investigated the relationship only from the side of the worker and will later investigate it also from the side of the non-worker.

Thus through *alienated externalized* labor does the worker create the relation to this work of man alienated to labor and standing outside it. The relation of the worker to labor produces the relation of the capitalist to labor, or whatever one wishes to call the lord of labor. *Private property* is thus product, result, and necessary consequence of *externalized labor*, of the external relation of the worker to nature and to himself.

Private property thus is derived, through analysis, from the concept of *externalized labor*, that is, *externalized man*, alienated labor, alienated life, and *alienated* man.

We have obtained the concept of *externalized labor* (*externalized life*) from political economy as a result of the *movement of private property*. But the analysis of this idea shows that though private property appears to be the ground and cause of externalized labor, it is rather a consequence of externalized labor, just as gods are *originally* not the cause but the effect of an aberration of the human mind. Later this relationship reverses.

Only at the final culmination of the development of private property does this, its secret, reappear—namely, that on the one hand it is the *product* of externalized labor and that secondly it is the *means* through which labor externalizes itself, the *realization of this externalization*.

This development throws light on several conflicts hitherto unresolved.

(1) Political economy proceeds from labor as the very soul of production and yet gives labor nothing, private property everything. From this contradiction Proudhon decided in favor of labor and against private property. We perceive, however, that this apparent contradiction is the contradiction of *alienated labor* with itself and that political economy has only formulated the laws of alienated labor.

Therefore we also perceive that *wages* and *private property* are identical: for when the product, the object of labor, pays for the labor itself, wages are only a necessary consequence of the alienation of labor. In wages labor appears not as an end in itself but as the servant of wages. We shall develop this later and now only draw some conclusions.

An enforced *raising of wages* (disregarding all other difficulties, including that this anomaly could only be maintained forcibly) would therefore be nothing but a *better slave-salary* and would not achieve either for the worker or for labor human significance and dignity.

Even the *equality of wages*, as advanced by Proudhon, would only convert the relation of the contemporary worker to his work into the relation of all men to labor.[6] Society would then be conceived as an abstract capitalist.

Wages are a direct result of alienated labor, and alienated labor is the direct cause of private property. The downfall of one is necessarily the downfall of the other.

(2) From the relation of alienated labor to private property it follows further that the emancipation of society from private property, etc., from servitude, is expressed in its *political* form as the *emancipation of workers*, not as though it is only a question of their emancipation but because in their emancipation is contained universal human emancipation. It is contained in their emancipation because the whole of human servitude is involved in the relation of worker to production, and all relations of servitude are only modifications and consequences of the worker's relation to production.

As we have found the concept of *private property* through *analysis* from the concept of *alienated, externalized labor*, so we can develop all the *categories* of political economy with the aid of these two factors, and we shall again find in each category—for example, barter, competition, capital, money—only a *particular* and *developed expression* of these primary foundations.

Before considering this configuration, however, let us try to solve two problems.

(1) To determine the general *nature of private property* as a result of alienated labor in its relation to *truly human* and *social property*.

(2) We have taken the *alienation of labor* and its *externalization* as a fact and analyzed this fact. How, we ask now, does it happen that *man externalizes* his *labor*, alienates it? How is this alienation rooted in the nature of human development? We have already achieved much in resolving the problem by *transforming* the question concerning the *origin of private property* into the question concerning the relationship of *externalized labor* to evolution of humanity. In talking about *private property* one believes he is dealing with something external to man. Talking of labor, one is immediately dealing with man himself. This new formulation of the problem already contains its solution.

On (1) *The general nature of private property and its relation to truly human property.*

We have resolved alienated labor into two parts which mutually determine each other or rather are only different expressions of one and the same relationship. *Appropriation* appears as *alienation*, as *externalization; externalization* as *appropriation; alienation* as the true *naturalization*.

We considered the one side, *externalized* labor, in relation to the *worker* himself, that is, the *relation of externalized labor to itself*. We have found the *property relation of the non-worker* to the *worker* and *labor* to be the product, the necessary result, of this relationship. *Private property* as the material, summarized expression of externalized labor embraces both relationships—the *relationship of worker to labor, the product of his work, and the non-worker*; and the relationship of the *non-worker to the worker* and *the product of his labor*.

As we have seen that in relation to the worker who *appropriates* nature through his labor the appropriation appears as alienation—self-activity as activity for another and of another, living as the sacrifice of life, production of the object as loss of it to an alien power, an *alien* man—we now consider the relationship of this *alien* man to the worker, to labor and its object.

It should be noted first that everything which appears with the worker as an *activity of externalization* and an *activity of alienation* appears with the non-worker as a *condition of externalization*, a *condition of alienation*.

Secondly, that the *actual, practical attitude* of the worker in production and to his product (as a condition of mind) appears as a *theoretical* attitude in the non-worker confronting him.

Thirdly, the non-worker does everything against the worker which the worker does against himself, but he does not do against his own self what he does against the worker.[7]

Let us consider more closely these three relationships. [Here the manuscript breaks off, unfinished.]

PRIVATE PROPERTY AND COMMUNISM

The antithesis between *propertylessness* and *property*, however, still remains indifferent, not grasped in its *active connection* with its *internal* relationship as *contradiction*, so long as it is not understood as the antithesis of *labor* and *capital*. This antithesis can be expressed in the *first* form even without the advanced development of private property as in ancient Rome, in Turkey, etc. It does not yet *appear* as instituted by private property itself. But labor, the subjective essence of private property as exclusion of property, and capital, objective labor as the exclusion of labor, is *private property* as its developed relation of contradiction, hence a dynamic relation driving toward resolution.

The overcoming [*Aufhebung*] of self-alienation follows the same course as self-alienation. *Private property* is first considered only in its objective aspect—but still with labor as its essence. Its form of existence is therefore *capital which is to be overcome "as such" (Proudhon)*. *Or the particular form* of labor—leveled down, parceled, and thus unfree labor—is taken as the source of the *perniciousness* of private property and its humanly alienated existence. *Fourier* agreeing with the physiocrats, thus regards *agricultural labor* as being at least *exemplary*, while *Saint-Simon* on the other hand holds *industrial labor* as such to be the essence of labor and thus seeks the *exclusive* predominance of the industrialists and the improvement of the workers' condition.[8] *Communism* is ultimately the *positive* expression of private property as overcome [*aufgehoben*]. Immediately it is *universal* private property. In taking this relation in its *universality* communism is: (1) In its first form only a *universalization* and *completion* of this relationship. As such it appears in a double pattern: On the one hand the domination of *material* property bulks so large that it wants to destroy *everything* which cannot be possessed by everyone as *private property*. It wants to abstract from talent, etc., by *force*. Immediate, physical *possession* is for it the sole aim of life and existence. The condition of the *laborer* is not overcome but extended to all men. The relationship of private property remains the relationship of the community to the world of things. Ultimately this movement which contrasts universal private property to private property is expressed in the animalistic form that *marriage* (surely a *form* of *exclusive private property*) is counterposed to the *community of women* where they become *communal* and *common* property. We might say that this idea of the *community of women* is the *open secret* of this still very crude, unthinking communism. As women go from marriage into universal prostitution, so the whole world of wealth—that is, the objective essence of man—passes from the relationship of exclusive marriage with the private owner into the relationship of universal prostitution with the community. This communism—in that it negates man's *personality* everywhere—is only the logical expression of the private property which is this negation. Universal *envy* establishing itself as a power is only the disguised form in which *greed* reestablishes and satisfies itself in *another* way. The thought of every piece of private property as such is *at the very least* turned against *richer* private property as envy and the desire to level so that envy and the desire to level in fact constitute the essence of competition. Crude communism is only the fulfillment of this envy and leveling on the basis of a *preconceived* minimum. It has a *definite delimited* measure. How little this overcoming of private property is an actual appropriation is shown precisely by the abstract negation of the entire world of culture and civilization, the reversion to the *unnatural* simplicity of the *poor* and wantless man who has not gone beyond private property, has not yet even achieved it.

The community is only a community of *labor* and an equality of *wages* which the communal capital, the *community* as universal capitalist, pays out. Both sides of the relationship are raised to a *supposed* universality—

labor as the condition in which everyone is put, *capital* as the recognized universality and power of the community.

In the relationship with *woman*, as the spoil and handmaid of communal lust, is expressed the infinite degradation in which man exists for himself since the secret of this relationship has its *unambiguous*, decisive, *plain*, and revealed expression in the relationship of *man* to *woman* and in the way in which the *immediate*, *natural* species-relationship of human being to human being is the *relationship* of *man* to *woman*. In this *natural* species-relationship man's relationship to nature is immediately his relationship to man, as his relationship to man is immediately his relationship to nature, to his own *natural* condition. In this relationship the extent to which the human essence has become nature for man or nature has become the human essence of man is *sensuously manifested*, reduced to a perceptible *fact*. From this relationship one can thus judge the entire level of mankind's development. From the character of his relationship follows the extent to which *man* has become and comprehended himself as a *generic being*, as *man*; the relationship of man to women is the *most natural* relationship of human being to human being. It thus indicates the extent to which man's *natural* behavior has become *human* or the extent to which his *human* essence has become a *natural* essence for him, the extent to which his *human nature* has become *nature* to him. In this relationship is also apparent the extent to which man's *need* has become *human*, thus the extent to which the *other* human being, as human being, has become a need for him, the extent to which he in his most individual existence is at the same time a social being.

The first positive overcoming of private property—*crude* communism— is thus only an *apparent form* of the vileness of private property trying to set itself up as the *positive community*.

(2) Communism (a) still of political nature, democratic or despotic; (b) with the overcoming of the state, but still incomplete and influenced by private property, that is, by the alienation of man. In both forms communism already knows itself as the reintegration or return of man to himself, as the overcoming of human self-alienation, but since it has not yet understood the positive essence of private property and just as little the *human* nature of needs, it still remains captive to and infected by private property. It has, indeed, grasped its concept but still not its essence.

(3) *Communism* as *positive* overcoming of *private property* as *human self-alienation*, and thus as the actual *appropriation of the human* essence through and for man; therefore as the complete and conscious restoration of man to himself within the total wealth of previous development, the restoration of man as a *social*, that is, human being. This communism as completed naturalism is humanism, as completed humanism it is naturalism. It is the *genuine* resolution of the antagonism between man and nature and

between man and man; it is the true resolution of the conflict between existence and essence, objectification and self-affirmation, freedom and necessity, individual and species. It is the riddle of history solved and knows itself as this solution.

The entire movement of history is therefore both its *actual* genesis—the birth of its empirical existence—and also for its thinking awareness the *conceived* and *conscious* movement of its *becoming* whereas the other yet undeveloped communism seeks in certain historical forms opposed to private property a *historical* proof, a proof in what explicitly exists. It thereby tears particular moments out of the movement (Cabet, Villegardelle[9] etc., particularly ride this horse) and marks them as proofs of its historical pedigree. Thus it makes clear that the far greater part of this movement contradicts its claims and that if it once existed, its *past* existence refutes the pretension of its *essence*.

It is easy to see the necessity that the whole revolutionary movement finds both its empirical as well as theoretical basis in the development of *private property*—in the economy, to be exact.

This *material*, immediately *perceptible* private property is the material, sensuous expression of *alienated human* life. Its movement—production and consumption—is the *sensuous* manifestation of the movement of all previous production, that is, the realization or actuality of man. Religion, family, state, law, morality, science, art, etc., are only *particular* forms of production and fall under its general law. The positive overcoming of *private property* as the appropriation of *human* life is thus the positive overcoming of all alienation and the return of man from religion, family, state, etc., to his *human*, that is, *social* existence. Religious alienation as such occurs only in the sphere of the inner human *consciousness*, but economic alienation belongs to *actual life*—its overcoming thus includes both aspects. It is obvious that the movement has its *first* beginning among different peoples depending on whether their true *acknowledged* life proceeds more in consciousness or in the external world, is more ideal or real. Communism thus begins (*Owen*[10]) with atheism, but atheism is at the beginning still far from being *communism* since it is mostly an *abstraction*.[a]—The philanthropy of atheism is at first therefore only a *philosophical*, abstract philanthropy; that of communism is at once *real* and immediately bent toward *action*.

On the assumption that private property has been positively overcome we have seen how man produces man, himself, and other men; how the object, the immediate activity of his individuality, is at the same time his own existence for other men, their existence, and their existence for him.

---

[a] Prostitution is only a *particular* expression of the *general* prostitution of the *laborer*, and since prostitution is a relationship which includes not only the prostituted but also the prostitution—whose vileness is still greater—so also the capitalist, etc. falls in this category [Marx's footnote].

Similarly, however, both the material of labor and man as subject are equally the result and beginning of the movement (and the historical *necessity* of private property lies precisely in the fact that they must be this *beginning*). Thus is the *social* character the general character of the whole movement; as society itself produces *man* as *man*, so it is *produced* by him. Activity and satisfaction [*Genuss*], both in their content and *mode of existence*, are *social*, *social* activity and *social* satisfaction. The *human* essence of nature primarily exists only for *social* man, because only here is nature a *link* with *man*, as his existence for others and their existence for him, as the life-element of human actuality—only here is nature the *foundation* of man's own *human* existence. Only here has the *natural* existence of man become his *human* existence and nature become human. Thus *society* is the completed, essential unity of man with nature, the true resurrection of nature, the fulfilled naturalism of man and humanism of nature.

Social activity and satisfaction by no means exist *merely* in the form of an *immediate* communal activity and immediate *communal* satisfaction. Nevertheless such activity and satisfaction, expressed and confirmed immediately in *actual association* with other men, will occur wherever that *immediate* expression of sociality is essentially grounded in its content and adequate to its nature.

Even as I am *scientifically* active, etc.—an activity I can seldom pursue in direct community with others—I am *socially* active because I am active as a *man*. Not only is the material of my activity—such as the language in which the thinker is active—given to me as a social product, but my *own* existence *is* social activity; what I make from myself I make for society, conscious of my nature as social.

My *general* consciousness is only the *theoretical* form of that whose *living* form is the *real* community, the social essence, although at present *general* consciousness is an abstraction from actual life and antagonistically opposed to it. Consequently the *activity* of my general consciousness is thus, as activity, my *theoretical* existence as a social being.

To be avoided above all is establishing "society" once again as an abstraction over against the individual. The individual *is* the *social being*. The expression of his life—even if it does not appear immediately in the form of a *communal* expression carried out together with others—is therefore an expression and assertion of *social life*. The individual and generic life of man are not *distinct*, however much—and necessarily so—the mode of existence of individual life is either a more *particular* or more *general* mode of generic life, or generic life a more *particular* or *universal* mode of individual life.

As *generic consciousness* man asserts his real *social life* and merely repeats his actual existence in thought just as, conversely, generic existence asserts itself in generic consciousness and in its universality exists explicitly as a thinking being. Though man is therefore a *particular* individual—and precisely his particularity makes him an individual, an actual *individual* communal being—he is equally the *totality*, the ideal totality, the subjective existence of society explicitly thought and experienced. Likewise he also exists in actuality both as perception and actual satisfaction of social existence and as a totality of human expression of life.

Thinking and being, to be sure, are thus *distinct* but at the same time in *unity* with one another.

Death seems to be a harsh victory of the species over the particular individual and to contradict the species' unity, but the particular individual is only a *particular generic being* and as such mortal.

(((4) Just as *private property* is only the sensuous expression of the fact that man becomes *objective* for himself and at the same time becomes an alien and inhuman object for himself, that his expression of life is his externalization of life and his realization a loss of reality, an *alien* actuality, so the positive overcoming of private property—that is, the *sensuous* appropriation of the human essence—and life, of objective man and of human *works* by and for man—is not to be grasped only as *immediate*, exclusive *satisfaction* or as *possession*, as *having*. Man appropriates to himself his manifold essence in an all-sided way, thus as a whole man. Every one of his *human* relations to the world—seeing, hearing, smelling, tasting, feeling, thinking, perceiving, sensing, wishing, acting, loving—in short, all the organs of his individuality, which are immediately communal in form, are an appropriation of the object in their *objective* relation [*Verhalten*] or their *relation to it*. This appropriation of *human* actuality and its relation to the object is the *confirmation of human actuality*. It is therefore as varied as are the *determinations* of the human *essence* and *activities*. It is human *efficacy* and human *suffering*, for suffering, humanly conceived, is a satisfaction of the self in man.

Private property has made us so stupid and one-sided that an object is *ours* only if we have it, if it exists for us as a capital or is immediately possessed by us, eaten, drunk, worn, lived in, etc., in short, *used*; but private property grasps all these immediate forms of possession only as *means of living*, and the life they serve is the *life* of *private property*, labor, and capitalization.

Hence *all* the physical and spiritual senses have been replaced by the simple alienation of them *all*, the sense of *having*. Human nature had to be reduced to this absolute poverty so that it could give birth to its inner wealth. (On the category of *having*, see *Hess* in *Twenty-one Sheets*.)

The overcoming of private property means therefore the complete *emancipation* of all human senses and aptitudes [*Eigenschaften*], but it means this emancipation precisely because these senses and aptitudes have become *human* both subjectively and objectively. The eye has become a *human* eye, just as its *object* has become a social, *human* object derived from and for man. The *senses* have therefore become *theoreticians* immediately in their *praxis*. They try to relate themselves to their *subject matter [Sache]* for its own sake, but the subject matter itself is an *objective human* relation to itself and to man,[b] and vice versa. Need or satisfaction have thus lost their *egoistic* nature, and nature has lost its mere *utility* by use becoming *human* use.

Similarly the senses and satisfactions of other men have become my *own* appropriation. Besides these immediate organs, *social* organs are therefore developed in the *form* of society; for example, activity in direct association with others, etc., has become an organ of a *life-expression* and a way of appropriating *human* life.

It is obvious that the *human* eye appreciates differently from the crude, inhuman eye, the human *ear* differently from the crude ear, etc.

Only if man's object, we have seen, becomes for him a *human* object or objective man, is he not lost in it. This is possible only when the object becomes *social* and he himself becomes social just as society becomes essential for him in this object.

On the one hand, therefore, it is only when objective actuality generally becomes for man in society the actuality of essential human capacities, human actuality, and thus the actuality of his *own* capacities that all *objects* become for him the *objectification* of himself, become objects which confirm and realize his individuality as *his* objects, that is, *he himself* becomes the object. *How* they become his depends on the *nature* of the *object* and the nature of the *essential capacity* corresponding to *it*, for it is precisely the *determinateness* of this relationship which shapes the particular, *actual* mode of affirmation. For the *eye* an object is different than for the *ear*, and the object of the eye *is* another object than that of the *ear*. The peculiarity of each essential capacity is precisely its *characteristic essence* and thus also the characteristic mode of its objectification, of its *objectively actual*, living *being*. Thus man is affirmed in the objective world not only in thought but with *all* his senses.

On the other hand and from the subjective point of view, as music alone awakens man's musical sense and the most beautiful music has *no* meaning for the unmusical ear—is no object for it, because my object can only be the confirmation of one of my essential capacities and can therefore only be so for me insofar as my essential capacity exists explicitly as a subjective capacity, because the meaning of an object for me reaches only as far as *my* senses go (only makes sense for a corresponding sense)—for this reason the *senses* of social man *differ* from those of the unsocial. Only through the objectively unfolded wealth of human nature is the wealth of the subjective *human* sensibility either cultivated or created—a musical

---

[b] I can practically relate myself to the subject matter in a human way only if it is itself humanly related to man [Marx's footnote].

ear, an eye for the beauty of form, in short, *senses* capable of human satisfaction, confirming themselves as essential *human* capacities. For not only the five senses but also the so-called spiritual and moral senses (will, love, etc.), in a word, *human* sense and the humanity of the senses come into being only through the existence of *their* object, through nature *humanized*. The *development* of the five senses is a labor of the whole previous history of the world. *Sense* subordinated to crude, practical need has only a *narrow* meaning.)) For the starving man food does not exist in its human form but only in its abstract character as food. It could be available in its crudest form and one could not say wherein the starving man's eating differs from that of *animals*. The care-laden, needy man has no mind for the most beautiful play. The dealer in minerals sees only their market value but not their beauty and special nature; he has no mineralogical sensitivity. Hence the objectification of the human essence, both theoretically and practically, is necessary to *humanize* man's *senses* and also create a *human sense* corresponding to the entire wealth of humanity and nature.

((Just as the coming society finds at hand all the material for this *cultural development [Bildung]* through the movement of *private property*, its wealth as well as its poverty both material and spiritual, *so* the fully *constituted* society produces man in this entire wealth of his being, produces the *rich*, deep, and *entirely sensitive* man as its enduring actuality.))

It is apparent how subjectivism and objectivism, spiritualism and materialism, activity and passivity lose their opposition and thus their existence as antitheses only in the social situation; ((it is apparent how the resolution of *theoretical* antitheses is possible *only* in a *practical* way, only through man's practical energy, and hence their resolution is in no way merely a problem of knowledge but a *real* problem of life which *philosophy* could not solve because it grasped the problem as *only* theoretical.))

((It is apparent how the history of *industry*, industry as *objectively* existing, is the *open* book of *man's essential powers*, the observably present human *psychology*, which has not been thus far grasped in its connection with man's *essential* nature but only in an external utilitarian way because in the perspective of alienation only the general existence of man—religion or history in its abstract-general character as politics, art, literature, etc.—was grasped as the actuality of man's essential powers and his *human generic action*. We have before us the *objectified essential powers* of man in the form of *sensuous, alien, useful objects*—in the form of alienation—in *ordinary material industry* (which can be conceived as a part of that general movement just as that movement can be grasped as a *particular* part of industry since all human activity up to the present has been labor, industry, activity alienated from itself). A *psychology* for which this book, that is, the most observably present and accessible part of history, remains closed cannot become an actual, substantial, and *real* science.)) What indeed should one think of a science which *arbitrarily* abstracts from this large area of human labor and is unaware of its own incompleteness while such an extended wealth of human activity means no more to it than can be expressed in one word—*"need," "common need"*?

The *natural sciences* have become enormously active and have accumulated an ever growing subject-matter. But philosophy has remained as alien to them as they have to it. Their momentary unity was only a *fantastic illusion*. The will was there, but the means were missing. Historiography itself only occasionally takes account of natural science as a moment of enlightenment, utility, some particular great discoveries. But natural science has penetrated and transformed human life all the more *practically* through industry, preparing for human emancipation however much it immediately had to accentuate dehumanization. *Industry* is the *actual* historical relationship of nature, and thus of natural science, to man. If it is grasped as the *exoteric* manifestation of man's *essential powers*, the *human* essence of nature or the *natural* essence of man can also be understood. Hence, natural science will lose its abstract material—or rather idealistic—tendency and become the basis of *human* science as it has already become, though in an alienated form, the basis of actual human life. One basis for life and *another* for *science* is in itself a lie. ((Nature developing in human history—the creation of human society—is the *actual* nature of man; hence nature as it develops through industry, though in an *alienated* form, is true *anthropological* nature.))

Sense perception (see Feuerbach) must be the basis of all science. Science is only *actual* when it proceeds from sense perception in the twofold form of both *sensuous* awareness and *sensuous* need, that is, from nature. The whole of history is a preparation for *"man"* to become the object of *sensuous* awareness and for the needs of "man as man" to become sensuous needs. History itself is an *actual* part of *natural history*, of nature's development into man. Natural science will in time include the science of man as the science of man will include natural science: There will be *one* science.

Man is the immediate object of natural science because immediately *perceptible nature* is for man, immediately, human sense perception (an identical statement) as the *other* man immediately perceptible for him. His own sense perception only exists as human sense perception for himself through the *other* man. But *nature* is the direct object of the *science of man*. The first object for man—man himself—is nature, sense perception; and the particular, perceptible, and essential powers of man can attain self-knowledge only in natural science because they are objectively developed only in *natural* objects. The element of thought itself, the element of the life-expression of thought, *language*, is perceptible nature. The *social* actuality of nature and *human* natural science or the *natural science of man* are identical expressions.

((It is apparent how the *rich man* and wide *human* need appear in place of economic *wealth* and *poverty*. The rich man is simultaneously one who *needs* a totality of human manifestations of life and in whom his own realization exists as inner necessity, as *need*. Not only the *wealth* but also the *poverty* of man equally acquire—under the premise of socialism—a *human* and thus social meaning. It is the passive bond which lets man experience the greatest wealth, the *other* human being, as need. The domination of the objective essence within me, the sensuous eruption of my essential activity, is *emotion* which thereby becomes the *activity* of my nature.))

(5) A *being* only regards himself as independent when he stands on his own feet, and he stands on his own feet only when he owes his *existence* to himself. A man who lives by the favor of another considers himself dependent. But I live entirely by the favor of another if I owe him not only the maintenance of my life but also its *creation*, its *source*. My life necessarily has such an external ground if it is not my own creation. The notion of *creation* is thus very difficult to expel from popular consciousness. For such consciousness the self-subsistence of nature and man is *inconceivable* because it contradicts all the *palpable facts* of practical life.

The creation of the *earth* has been severely shaken by *geognosy* [rather: by *geogony*], the science which presents the formation and development of the earth as a self-generative process. Generatio aequivoca is the only practical refutation of the theory of creation.

It is easy indeed to tell a particular individual what Aristotle said: You were begotten by your father and mother, so in you the mating of two human beings, a generic act of mankind, produced another. You see therefore that man owes even his physical existence to another. Here you must not keep in view only *one* of the two aspects, the *infinite* progression, and ask further, Who begot my father? Who his grandfather? etc. You must also keep in mind the *circular movement* sensibly apparent in that process whereby man reproduces himself in procreation; thus *man* always remains the subject. But you will answer: I grant this circular movement but you must allow the progression which leads even further until I ask, Who created the first man and nature as a whole? I can only answer: Your question is itself a product of abstraction. Ask yourself how you arrive at that question, whether it does not arise from a standpoint to which I cannot reply because it is twisted. Ask yourself whether that progression exists as such for rational thought. If you ask about the creation of nature and man, you thus abstract from man and nature. You assert them as *non-existent* and yet want me to prove them to you as *existing*. I say to you: Give up your abstraction and you will also give up your question. Or if you want to maintain your abstraction, be consistent and if you think of man and nature as *non-existent*, think of yourself as non-existent as you too are nature and man. Do not think, do not question me, for as soon as you think and question, your *abstraction* from the existence of nature and man makes no sense. Or are you such an egoist that you assert everything as nothing and yet want yourself to exist?

You may reply to me: I do not want to assert the nothingness of nature, etc. I only ask about its *genesis* as I ask the anatomist about the formation of bones, etc.

Since for socialist man, however, the *entire so-called world history* is only the creation of man through human labor and the development of nature for man, he has evident and incontrovertible proof of his *self-creation*, his own *formation process*. Since the *essential dependence* of man in nature—man for man as the existence of nature and nature for man as the existence of man—has become practical, sensuous and perceptible, the question about an *alien* being beyond man and nature (a question which implies the unreality of nature and man) has become impossible in practice. *Atheism* as a denial of this unreality no longer makes sense because it is a *negation of God* and through this negation asserts the *existence of man*. But socialism as such no longer needs such mediation. It begins with the *sensuous perception, theoretically and practically,* of man and nature as *essential beings*. It is man's *positive self-consciousness*, no longer attained through the overcoming of religion, just as *actual life* is positive actuality no longer attained through the overcoming of private property, through *communism*. The position of communism is the negation of the negation and hence, for the next stage of historical development, the necessary *actual* phase of man's emancipation and rehabilitation. *Communism* is the necessary form and dynamic principle of the immediate future but not as such the goal of human development—the form of human society.

CRITIQUE OF HEGELIAN DIALECTIC
AND PHILOSOPHY IN GENERAL

This is perhaps the place at which to make some comments explaining and justifying what has been said about Hegel's dialectic in general, particularly its exposition in the *Phenomenology* [*of Spirit*] and *Logic*, and finally about its relation to the modern critical movement.

Modern German criticism has been so much preoccupied with the past, so much restricted by the development of its subject matter, that it has had a completely uncritical attitude toward methods of criticism and has been completely oblivious to the *seemingly formal* but actually *essential* question: How do we now stand in relation to the Hegelian *dialectic*? This lack of awareness concerning the relation of modern criticism to Hegel's philosophy in general and his dialectic in particular has been so great that critics like *Strauss* and *Bruno Bauer* have been completely entrapped in the Hegelian logic—the former completely and the latter at least implicitly in his [*Critique of the Gospel History of the*] *Synoptics*[11] (where he substitutes the "self-consciousness" of abstract man for the substance of "abstract nature," in opposition to Strauss) and even in his *Revealed Christianity*[12] where you find, for example: "As though self-consciousness in producing the world did not produce its difference and thereby produce itself in what it produced since it again transcends the distinction between what is produced and itself, since it exists only in this production and movement—as though it should not have its purpose in this movement," etc. Or again: "They (the French materialists) could not yet see that the movement of the universe has only become actual for itself and unified with itself as the movement of self-consciousness." Such expressions not only verbally agree with the Hegelian perspective but reproduce it literally.

How little awareness there was in relation to the Hegelian dialectic during the act of criticism (Bauer, *Synoptics*) and how little this awareness appeared even after the act of substantial criticism is shown by Bauer in his *Good Cause of Freedom*[13] [*and My Own Concern*] when he discusses Herr Gruppe's[14] impertinent question—"What about logic now?"—and refers it to future critics.

But now that *Feuerbach* in his "Theses" appearing in the *Anekdota* and more fully in his [*Principles of the*] *Philosophy of the Future* has destroyed the inner principle of the old dialectic and philosophy, the school of criticism which was unable to do this by itself but has seen it done has proclaimed itself pure, decisive, absolute, and entirely clear with itself. In its spiritual pride it has reduced the entire process of history to the relation between the rest of the world—which falls under the category of "the Mass"—and itself and has reduced dogmatic antitheses into the one between its own cleverness and the stupidity of the world, between the critical Christ and "Humanity" as the "*rabble.*" Daily and hourly it has demonstrated its own excellence against the stupidity of the masses and has finally announced the critical *last judgment* to the effect that the day is at hand when the whole of fallen humanity will assemble before it and be divided into groups with each particular mob receiving its testimonium paupertatis. Now that this school of criticism has publicized its superiority to human feelings as well as to the whole world, above which it sits enthroned in sublime solitude, from time to time letting fall from its sarcastic lips the laughter of the Olympian gods—even now after all these entertaining antics of idealism (of Young Hegelianism) expiring in the form of criticism—even now it has not once expressed the suspicion that there must be a reckoning with its own source, the Hegelian dialectic. It has not even indicated a critical relation to Feuerbach's dialectic. This is a procedure with a completely uncritical attitude toward itself.

Feuerbach is the only one who has a *serious, critical* relation to Hegel's dialectic, who has made genuine discoveries in this field, and who above all is the true conqueror of the old philosophy. The magnitude of Feuerbach's achievement and the unpretentious simplicity with which he presents it to the world stand in a strikingly opposite inverse ratio.

Feuerbach's great achievement is: (1) proof that philosophy is nothing more than religion brought to and developed in reflection, and thus is equally to be condemned as another form and mode of the alienation of man's nature;

(2) the establishment of *true materialism* and *real science* by making the social relationship of "man to man" the fundamental principle of his theory;

(3) opposing to the negation of the negation, which claims to be the absolute positive, the self-subsistent positive positively grounded on itself.

Feuerbach explains Hegel's dialectic (and thereby justifies starting out from the positive, from sense certainty) in the following way:

Hegel proceeds from the alienation of substance (logically, from the infinite, abstract universal), from absolute and fixed abstraction—that is, in popular language, he proceeds from religion and theology.

Secondly, he transcends [*hebt auf*] the infinite and posits the actual, the perceptible, the real, the finite, the particular (philosophy, the transcendence of religion and theology).

Thirdly, he then transcends the positive and re-establishes abstraction, the infinite. Re-establishment of religion and theology.

Feuerbach thus views the negation of the negation as *merely* a contradiction of philosophy with itself, as philosophy which affirms theology (the transcendent, etc.) after having denied it, thus affirming it in opposition to itself.

The positing or self-affirmation and self-confirmation in the negation of the negation is taken to be a positing which is still not sure of itself and hence is burdened with its opposite, is still doubtful of itself and hence is in need of proof, and is thus not demonstrated by its own existence and not grasped as a self-justifying position and hence directly and immediately confronts the self-grounded position of sense certainty.

Because Hegel conceived the negation of the negation from the aspect of the positive relation inherent in it as the only true positive, and from the aspect of the negative relation inherent in it as the only true and self-confirming act of all being, he found only the *abstract, logical, speculative* expression of the movement of history, not the *actual* history of man as a given subject but only man's *genesis*, the *history of his origin*. We shall explain both the abstract form of this movement and the difference between this movement as conceived by Hegel and, in contrast, by modern criticism in Feuerbach's *Essence of Christianity*[15] or rather the *critical* form of this movement which is still uncritical with Hegel.

Let us take a look at Hegel's system. We must begin with his *Phenomenology*, the true birthplace and secret of his philosophy.

PHENOMENOLOGY

A. Self-consciousness

  I. *Consciousness.*

   (α) Sense certainty or the "this" and *meaning.*

   (β) *Perception* or the thing with its properties and *illusion.*

   (γ) Force and understanding, phenomenon and supersensible world.

  II. *Self-consciousness.* The truth of self-certainty.

   (a) Independence and dependence of self-consciousness, lordship and bondage.

   (b) Freedom of self-consciousness. Stoicism, scepticism, the unhappy consciousness.

  III. *Reason.* Certainty and truth of reason.

   (a) Observational reason; observation of nature and self-consciousness.

   (b) The realization of rational self-consciousness through itself. Pleasure and necessity. The law of the heart and the frenzy of vanity. Virtue and the way of the world.

   (c) Individuality which is real in and for itself. The spiritual animal kingdom and deception or the real fact. Law-giving reason. Law-testing reason.

B. *Spirit [Geist]*

  I. *True spirit*, ethicality.

  II. Self-alienated spirit, culture.

  III. Spirit certain of itself, morality.

C. *Religion*

  Natural religion, *religion as art, revealed* religion.

D. *Absolute Knowledge*

Since Hegel's *Encyclopedia* begins with logic, with *pure speculative thought*, and ends with *absolute knowledge*— with self-consciousness, self-comprehending or absolute, that is, superhuman, abstract mind [*Geist*]—it is altogether nothing but the *expanded essence* of the philosophical mind, its self-objectification. And the philosophical mind is only the alienated world-mind thinking within its self-alienation, that is, comprehending itself abstractly. Logic—the *currency* of mind, the speculative *thought-value* of man and nature, their essence indifferent to any actual determinate character and hence unreal—is *thought externalized* and hence *thought* abstracting from nature and actual men. It is *abstract* thinking. The *externality of this abstract thinking . . . nature* as it exists for this abstract thought. Nature is external to it, its self-loss, and is also conceived as something external, as abstract thought but as externalized abstract thought. Finally, [there is] *mind*, thinking which returns to its own birthplace and which as anthropological, phenomenological, psychological, ethical, and artistic-religious is not valid for itself until ultimately it finds itself and relates itself to itself as *absolute* knowledge in the absolute (i.e. abstract) mind containing its conscious and corresponding local existence. For its actual existence is *abstraction*.

Hegel makes a double mistake.

The first appears most clearly in the *Phenomenology*, the birthplace of the Hegelian philosophy. Where Hegel, to be specific, conceives wealth, state power, etc. as entities alienated from *man's* nature, this only happens in their thought form . . . They are thought-entities and hence merely an alienation of *pure*, that is, abstract, philosophical thinking. The whole movement, accordingly, ends with absolute knowledge. It is precisely abstract thought from which these objects are alienated and which they confront with their presumption of actuality. The *philosopher*—himself an abstract form of alienated man—sets himself up as the *measuring rod* of the alienated world. The entire *history of externalization* and the *withdrawal* from externalization is therefore nothing but the *history of the production* of abstract, that is, of absolute, logical, speculative thought. The *alienation* thus forming the real interest and transcendence of this externalization is the opposition of *in itself* and *for itself*, of *consciousness* and *self-consciousness*, of *object and subject*—that is, the opposition within thought itself between abstract thinking and sensuous actuality or actual sensibility. All other contradictions and their movements are only the *appearance*, the *cloak*, the *exoteric* form of these uniquely interesting opposites which constitute the *meaning* of the other profane contradictions. It is not that the human being *objectifies* himself *inhumanly* in opposition to himself, but that he *objectifies* himself by *distinction* from and in *opposition* to abstract thought—this is the essence of alienation as given and as to be transcended. The appropriation of man's essential capacities which have become things, even alien things, is thus primarily only an *appropriation* taking place in *consciousness*, in *pure thought*, that is, in *abstraction*. It is the appropriation of these objects as *thoughts* and *thought processes*. Hence there is already implicit in the *Phenomenology* as a germ, potentiality, and secret—despite its thoroughly negative and critical appearance and despite the actual criticism it contains which often anticipates later developments—the uncritical positivism and equally uncritical idealism of Hegel's later works, the philosophical dissolution and restoration of the existing empirical world.

Secondly, the vindication of the objective world for man—for example, the recognition that *sense* perception is no *abstract* sense perception but *human* sense perception, that religion, wealth, etc., are only the alienated actuality of *human* objectification, of *man's* essential capacities put to work, and therefore are only the *path* to genuine *human* actuality—this appropriation or insight into this process appears in Hegel as the affirmation that *sensuousness, religion,* state power, etc., are *mental* entities since *spirit* alone is the *genuine* essence of man and the true form of spirit is the thinking spirit, the logical, speculative mind. The *human quality* of nature, of nature produced through history, and of man's products appears in their being *products* of abstract spirit and hence phases of *mind, thought-entities.* The *Phenomenology* is thus concealed and mystifying criticism, unclear to itself, but inasmuch as it firmly grasps the *alienation* of man—even though man appears only as mind—*all* the elements of criticism are implicit in it, already *prepared* and *elaborated* in a manner far surpassing the Hegelian standpoint. The sections on the "unhappy consciousness," the "honest consciousness," the struggle between the "noble and base consciousness," etc., etc., contain the *critical* elements—though still in an alienated form—of whole spheres such as religion, the state, civil life, etc. Just as the *entity* or *object* appears as a thought-entity, so is the *subject* always *consciousness* or *self-consciousness*; or rather the object appears only as *abstract* consciousness, man only as *self-consciousness*, and the diverse forms of alienation which make their appearance are therefore only different forms of consciousness and self-consciousness. Since abstract consciousness— the form in which the object is conceived—is *in itself* only a moment of distinction in self-consciousness, the result of the movement is the iden- tity of self-consciousness with consciousness (absolute knowledge) or the movement of abstract thought no longer directed outward but proceeding only within itself. That is to say, the dialectic of pure thought is the result.

The great thing in Hegel's *Phenomenology* and its final result—the dialec- tic of negativity as the moving and productive principle—is simply that Hegel grasps the self-development of man as a process, objectification as loss of the object, as alienation and transcendence of this alienation; that he thus grasps the nature of *work* and comprehends objective man, authen- tic because actual, as the result of his *own work.* The *actual,* active relation of man to himself as a species-being or the confirmation of his species- being as an actual, that is, human, being is only possible so far as he actually brings forth all his *species-powers*—which in turn is only possible through the collective effort of mankind, only as the result of history—and treats them as objects, something which immediately is again only possi- ble in the form of alienation.

We shall now indicate in detail Hegel's one-sidedness and limitations in the closing chapter of the *Phenomenology* on absolute knowledge—a chapter containing the pervasive spirit of the whole book, its relation to speculative dialectic, and Hegel's *consciousness* of both and their inter- relationship.

Provisionally, let us say this much in advance: Hegel's standpoint is that of modern political economy. He views *labor* as the *essence,* the self- confirming essence of man; he sees only the positive side of labor, not its negative side. Labor is *man's coming-to-be for himself* within *externalization* or as *externalized* man. The only labor Hegel knows and recognizes is *abstract, mental* labor. So that which above all constitutes the *essence* of philosophy—the *externalization of man knowing himself or externalized* knowledge *thinking itself*—Hegel grasps as its essence. Therefore, he is able to collect the separate elements of preceding philosophy and present his own as *the* philosophy. What other philosophers did—grasp separate phases of nature and human life as phases of self-consciousness, indeed, abstract self-consciousness—Hegel *knows* from *doing* philosophy. Hence his science is absolute.

Let us now proceed to our subject.

Absolute knowledge. The last chapter of the Phenomenology.

The main point is that the *object* of *consciousness* is nothing else but *self-consciousness*, or that the object is only *objectified self-consciousness*, self-consciousness as object. (Assume man = self-consciousness.)

It is a question, therefore, of surmounting the *object of consciousness*. *Objectivity* as such is regarded as an *alienated* human relationship which does not correspond to the *essence of man*, to self-consciousness. *Reappropriation* of the objective essence of man, developed as something alien and determined by alienation, means not only the overcoming of *alienation* but also of *objectivity*—that is, man is regarded as a *non-objective, spiritual* being.

The process of *surmounting the object of consciousness* is described by Hegel as follows:

The *object* does not reveal itself as *returning* into the *self* (for Hegel that is a *one-sided* view of the movement, grasping only one aspect). Man is assumed as equivalent to self. But the self is only man conceived *abstractly*, derived through abstraction. Man is a *self*. His eye, his ear, etc., belong to a *self*; every one of his essential capacities has the quality of *selfhood*. But on that account it is quite false to say that *self-consciousness* has eyes, ears, essential capacities. Self-consciousness is rather a quality of human nature, of the human eye, etc.; human nature is not a quality of *self-consciousness*.

The self, abstracted and fixed for itself, is man as *abstract egoist*, purely abstract *egoism* raised to the level of thought. (We shall return to this later.)

For Hegel *human nature, man*, is equivalent to *self-consciousness*. All alienation of human nature is thus *nothing* but the *alienation of self-consciousness*. The alienation of self-consciousness is not taken to be an expression of the *actual* alienation of human nature reflected in knowledge and thought. *Actual* alienation, that which appears real, is rather in its *innermost* and concealed character (which philosophy only brings to light) only the *appearance* of the alienation of actual human nature, of *self-consciousness*. The science which grasps this is therefore called *phenomenology*. All reappropriation of that alienated objective nature thus appears as an incorporation into self-consciousness. The man who takes possession of his nature is *only* self-consciousness taking possession of its objective nature. Hence the return of the object into the self is its reappropriation.

Expressed *comprehensively*, the *surmounting* of the *object of consciousness* amounts to this: (1) that the object as such presents itself to consciousness as something vanishing; (2) that it is the externalization of self-consciousness which establishes thinghood; (3) that this externalization has not only a *negative* but a *positive* significance as well; (4) that it has this significance not only *for us* or in itself but for *self-consciousness itself*; (5) *for self-consciousness* the negative of the object or its self-transcendence thereby has *positive* significance—*self-consciousness* thus *knows* this negativity of the object— since self-consciousness externalizes itself and in this externalization establishes *itself* as object or establishes the object as itself on behalf of the indivisible unity of *being-for-self*; (6) on the other hand, there is also present this other moment in the process, that self-consciousness has transcended and reabsorbed into itself this externalization, this objectivity, and is thus at one with itself in *its* other-being *as such*; (7) this is the movement of consciousness, and consciousness is therefore the totality of its phases; (8) consciousness must similarly have related itself to the object in all its aspects and have grasped the object in terms of each of them. This totality of its aspects gives the object *implicitly a spiritual nature*, and it truly becomes this nature for consciousness through the apprehension of every one of these aspects as belonging to the *self* or through what was earlier called the *spiritual* relation to them.

ad (1) that the object as such presents itself to consciousness as something vanishing—this is the *return of the object into the self* mentioned above.

ad (2) the *externalization of self-consciousness* establishes *thinghood*. Since man equals self-consciousness, his externalized objective nature or *thinghood* is equivalent to externalized *self-consciousness* and *thinghood* is established through this externalization. (Thinghood is that which is *an object for man* and an object is truly only for him if it is essential to him and thus his *objective* essence. Since it is not *actual man* and therefore also not *nature*—man being *nature as human*—who as such becomes a subject but only the abstraction of man, self-consciousness, thinghood can only be externalized self-consciousness.) It is entirely to be expected that a living, natural being endowed with objective (i.e. material) capacities should have *real natural objects* corresponding to its nature and also that its self-externalization should establish an *actual* objective world but a world in the form of *externality*, one which does not belong to such a being's nature, an overpowering world. There is nothing incomprehensible or mysterious in this. The contrary, rather, would be mysterious. But it is equally clear that a *self-consciousness*, that is, its externalization, can only establish *thinghood*, that is, only an abstract thing, a thing of abstraction and no *actual* thing. It is further clear that thinghood thus completely lacks *independence*, *essentiality*, over and against self-consciousness but is a mere artifice *established* by self-consciousness. And what is established, instead of confirming itself, is only a confirmation of the act of establishing which for a moment, but only a moment, fixes its energy as product and *apparently* gives it the role of an independent, actual nature.

When actual, corporeal *man* with his feet firmly planted on the solid ground, inhaling and exhaling all of nature's energies *establishes* his actual, objective *essential capacities* as alien objects through his externalization, the *establishing* is not the subject but the subjectivity of *objective* capacities whose action must therefore also be *objective*. An objective being acts objectively and would not act objectively if objectivity did not lie in its essential nature. It creates and establishes *only objects because* it is established through objects, because it is fundamentally part of *nature*. In the act of establishing, this objective being does not therefore descend from its "pure activity" to the *creation* of the *object*, but its *objective* product merely confirms its *objective activity*, its activity as that of an objective, natural being.

We see here how a consistent naturalism or humanism is distinguished from both idealism and materialism as well, and at the same time is the unifying truth of both. We also see how only naturalism is able to comprehend the act of world history.

((Immediately, *man is a natural being*. As a living natural being he is, in one aspect, endowed with the *natural capacities* and *vital powers* of an *active* natural being. These capacities exist in him as tendencies and capabilities, as *drives*. In another aspect as a natural, living, sentient and objective being man is a *suffering*, conditioned, and limited creature like an animal or plant. The *objects* of his drives, that is to say, exist outside him as independent, yet they are *objects* of his *need*, essential and indispensable to the exercise and confirmation of his *essential capacities*. The fact that man is a *corporeal*, actual, sentient, objective being with natural capacities means that he has *actual, sensuous objects* for his nature as objects of his life-expression, or that he can only *express* his life in actual sensuous objects. *To be* objective, natural, sentient and at the same time have an object, nature, and sense outside oneself or be oneself object, nature, and sense for a third person is one and the same thing.)) *Hunger* is a natural *need*; it thus requires *nature and an object* outside itself to be satisfied and quieted. Hunger is the objective need of a body for an *object* existing outside itself, indispensable to its integration and the expression of its nature. The sun is the *object* of the plant, indispensable to it and confirming its life, just as the plant is object for the sun *expressing* its life-awakening, its *objective* and essential power.

A being which does not have its nature outside itself is not a *natural* one and has no part in the system of nature. A being which has no object outside itself is not objective. A being which is not itself an object for a third being has no being for its *object*, that is, is not related objectively, its being is not objective.

An unobjective being is a *nonentity*.

Suppose there is a being which is not an object itself and does not have one. First of all, such a being would be the *only* being; no other being would exist outside of it; it would be solitary and alone. For as soon as there are objects outside of me, as soon as I am not *alone*, I am *another, another actuality* from the object outside me. For this third object I am thus an *other actuality* than it, that is, *its* object. To assume a being which is not the object of another is thus to suppose that *no* objective being exists. As soon as I have an object, it has me for its object. But a *non-objective* being is an unactual, non-sensuous, merely conceived being. It is merely imagined, an abstraction. To be *sensuous* or actual is to be an object of sense or *sensuous* object and thus to have sensuous objects outside oneself, objects of sensibility. To be sentient is to *suffer*.

As an objective sentient being man is therefore a *suffering* being, and since he feels his suffering, he is a *passionate* being. Passion is man's essential capacity energetically bent on its object.

((But man is not only a natural being; he is a *human* natural being. That is, he is a being for himself and hence a *species-being*; as such he must confirm and express himself as much in his being as in his knowing. Accordingly, *human* objects are not natural objects as they immediately present themselves nor is *human* sense immediately and objectively *human* sensibility, human objectivity. Neither objective nor subjective nature is immediately presented in a form adequate to the *human* being.)) And as everything natural must *have its genesis, man* too has his genetic act, *history*, which is for him, however, known and hence consciously self-transcending. History is the true natural history of mankind. (We shall return to this later.)

Thirdly, since this establishment of thinghood is itself only an appearance, an act contradicting the essence of pure activity, it must again be transcended and thinghood must be denied.

ad 3, 4, 5, 6. (3) This externalization of consciousness has not only a *negative* significance but a *positive* significance as well, and (4) it has this positive significance not only *for us* or in itself but for consciousness itself. (5) For *consciousness* the negative of the object or its transcendence of its own self thereby has the *positive* significance or thereby *knows* the nullity of the object by the fact that it externalizes its *own self*, because in this externalization it *knows* itself as object or the object as its own self, serving the indivisible unity of *being-for-self*. (6) On the other hand there is equally present here the other moment or aspect, that consciousness has also transcended and reabsorbed this externalization and objectivity and is thus *at one with itself in its other-being as such*.

As we have already seen, the appropriation of alienated, objective being or the transcendence of objectivity in the mode of *alienation*—which must proceed from indifferent otherness to actual, antagonistic alienation—for Hegel means also or primarily the transcendence of *objectivity* since the *objective* character of the object for self-consciousness, not its *determinateness*, is the scandal of alienation. Hence the object is something negative, a self-transcendence, a *nullity*. This nullity of the object has not merely a negative but also a *positive* meaning for consciousness because it is precisely the self-*confirmation* of non-objectivity, of the *abstraction* of itself. For *consciousness itself* this nullity therefore has a positive significance in that it *knows* this nullity, objective being, as its *self-externalization* and knows that it exists only as a result of its self-externalization. . . .

The way in which consciousness is and the way in which something is for it is *knowing*. Knowing is its only act. Hence something comes to exist for consciousness insofar as consciousness *knows* that *something*. Knowing is its sole objective relation. Consciousness knows, then, the nullity of the object (i.e., knows the non-existence of the distinction between object and itself, the non-existence of the object for it) because it knows the object is its *self-externalization*; that is, it knows itself—knowing as object— in that the object is only the *appearance* of an object, a deception, which essentially is nothing but knowing itself which has confronted itself with itself and hence with a *nullity*, with a something which has *no* objectivity outside the knowing. Or, knowing knows that in relating itself to an object it is merely *outside* itself externalized, that *it* only *appears to itself*, as object or that what appears to it as object is only itself.

On the other hand, says Hegel, there is equally present here the other moment or aspect, that consciousness has also transcended and reabsorbed this externalization and objectivity and thus is *at one with itself* in its *other-being as such*.

All the illusions of speculation are assembled in this discussion.

First, consciousness—self-consciousness—is *at one with itself* in *its other-being as such*. Hence if we here abstract from Hegel's abstraction and replace consciousness with the self-consciousness of man, it is *at one with itself* in its *other-being as such*. This means, for one thing, that consciousness—knowing as knowing, thinking as thinking—claims to be immediately the *other* of itself, sensibility, actuality, life—thought surpassing itself in thought. (Feuerbach.) This aspect is present inasmuch as consciousness as mere consciousness is offended at *objectivity as such*, not alienated objectivity.

Secondly, this implies that self-conscious man, insofar as he has recognized and transcended the spiritual world—or the general spiritual existence of his world—as self-externalization, then reaffirms it in this externalized form and presents it as his authentic existence, re-establishes it, and pretends to be *at one in his other-being as such*. Thus after transcending religion, for example, and recognizing it as a product of self-externalization, he yet finds confirmation of himself in *religion as religion*. Here *is* the root of Hegel's *false* positivism or of his merely *apparent* criticism which Feuerbach noted as the positing, negation, and reestablishment of religion or theology—but which has to be conceived in more general terms. Thus reason is at one with itself in unreason as unreason. Having recognized that man leads an externalized life in law, politics, etc., man leads in this externalized life as such his truly human life. Self-affirmation and self-confirmation in *contradiction* with itself and with the knowledge and essence of the object is thus authentic *knowledge* and authentic *life*.

There can thus no longer be any question about Hegel's accommodation in regard to religion, the state, etc., since this lie is the lie of his principle.

If I *know* that religion is the *externalized* self-consciousness of man, what I know in it as religion is not my self-consciousness but my externalized self-consciousness confirmed in it. Then I know my own self and its essential self-consciousness not as confirmed in *religion* but rather in the *suppression* and *transcendence* of religion.

Thus with Hegel the negation of the negation is not the confirmation of my authentic nature even through the negation of its appearance. It is the confirmation of the apparent or self-alienated nature in its denial—the denial of the apparent nature as objective, as existing outside and independent of man—and its transformation into a subject. *Transcendence*, therefore, has a special role in which *denial* and preservation, denial and affirmation, are bound together.

Thus in Hegel's philosophy of law, for example, *private right* transcended is *morality*, morality transcended is the *family*, the family transcended is *civil society*, civil society transcended is the *state*, the state transcended is *world history*. In *actuality* private right, morality, the family, civil society, the state, etc., remain in existence only as they have become *moments* or aspects, modes of the particular existence of man, which are meaningless in isolation but mutually dissolve and generate one another. They are *moments of process*.

In their actual existence their *process*-nature is hidden. It first appears and becomes manifest in thought, in philosophy. Hence my authentic religious existence is my existence in *philosophy of religion*, my authentic political existence is my existence in *philosophy of law*, my authentic natural existence is my existence in *philosophy of nature*, my authentic aesthetic existence is my existence in *philosophy of art*, and my authentic human existence is my existence in *philosophy*. Likewise the authentic existence of religion, the state, nature, and art is the *philosophy* of religion, of the state, of nature, and of art. But if the philosophy of religion, etc., is for me the only authentic existence of religion, I am only truly religious as a *philosopher of religion* and hence I deny *actual* religious feeling and the actually *religious* man. But at the same time I *assert* them, partly in my own particular existence or in the alien existence which I oppose to them—for this *is* only their *philosophical* expression—and partly in their particular original form, since for me they mean only the *apparent* other-being as allegories, forms of their own authentic existence concealed in sensuous coverings, that is, forms of my *philosophical* existence.

In the same way, *quality* transcended is *quantity*, quantity transcended is *magnitude*, magnitude transcended is *essence*, essence transcended is *phenomenon*, phenomenon transcended is *actuality*, actuality transcended is the *concept*, the concept transcended is *objectivity*, objectivity transcended is *absolute Idea*, the absolute Idea transcended is *nature*, nature transcended is *subjective* spirit, subjective spirit transcended is the *ethical* objective Spirit, the ethical objective Spirit transcended is *art*, art transcended is *religion*, and religion transcended is *absolute Knowledge*.

On the one hand this transcendence is transcendence of a thought-entity; thus private property as *thought* is transcended in the *thought* of morality. And because thought imagines itself to be immediately the other of itself or *sensuous actuality*—thus taking its own action for *actual, sensuous* action—this transcendence in thought which leaves its object intact in actuality believes it has actually overcome it. On the other hand, the object, having become a moment of thought for this transcendence, hence also becomes in its actuality a self-confirmation of the same transcendence, of self-consciousness, of abstraction.

From one aspect, the particular existence which Hegel *transcends* in philosophy is therefore not *actual* religion, not the *actual* state, and not *actual* nature but religion as already an object of knowledge, that is, *dogmatics*. (Similarly with *jurisprudence, political science*, and *natural science*.) In this respect he thus opposes both the *actual nature* of the object and the immediate unphilosophical *knowledge*—the unphilosophical concepts—of that nature. He therefore contradicts conventional *concepts*.

From the other aspect, the religious man, etc., can find his ultimate justification in Hegel.

Now the *positive* moments or aspects of the Hegelian dialectic—within the category of alienation—must be considered.

(a) *Transcendence* as an objective movement *reabsorbing* externalization into itself. —((This is the insight into the *appropriation* of objective being, expressed within alienation, through the transcendence of its alienation. It is the alienated insight into the *actual objectification* of man and into the actual appropriation of his objective nature by the destruction of the *alienated* character of the objective world, by the transcendence of the objective world in its alienated existence, just as atheism which transcends God is the emergence of theoretical humanism, and communism which transcends private property is the vindication of actual human life as man's property, the emergence of practical humanism. Or, atheism is humanism mediated through itself by the transcendence of religion, and communism is humanism mediated through itself by the transcendence of private property. Only through the transcendence of private property. Only through the transcendence of this mediation—which is, however, a necessary presupposition—emerges *positive* humanism, humanism emerging positively from itself.))

But atheism and communism are no flight from, no abstraction from, no loss of the objective world created by man as his essential capacities objectified. They are no impoverished return to unnatural, primitive simplicity. Rather they are primarily the actual emergence and the actual, developed realization of man's nature as something actual.

In grasping the *positive* significance of self-referring negation—even if again in an alienated way—Hegel thus grasps man's self-alienation, the externalization of his nature, his loss of objectivity and actualization as finding of self, expression of his nature, objectification, and realization. ((In short, he grasps labor, within the realm of abstraction, as man's *act of self-creation*, his relation to himself as something alien, and the manifestation of his developing *species-consciousness* and *species-life* as something alien.))

(b) But in Hegel—apart from or rather as a result of the inversion already described—this act of self-creation appears, first, as *merely formal* because it is abstract and because human nature itself is viewed only as *abstract*, as *thinking*, as self-consciousness.

Secondly, since the conception is *formal* and *abstract*, the transcendence of externalization affirms the externalization. Or, for Hegel the process of *self-creation* and *self-objectification* in the form of *self-externalization and self-alienation* is the *absolute* and hence final *expression of human life* which has itself as its goal, is at peace with itself, and is at one with its essence.

This movement in its abstract form as dialectic is therefore regarded as *authentic human life*, and since it is still an abstraction, an alienation of human life, it is regarded as a *divine process* and hence the divine process of mankind—a process carried out by man's abstract, pure, absolute nature as distinguished from himself.

Thirdly: This process must have a bearer, a subject. But the subject only emerges as a result—namely, the subject knowing itself as absolute self-consciousness which is therefore *God, Absolute Spirit, the self-knowing and self-manifesting Idea.* Actual man and actual nature become merely predicates or symbols of this concealed, unreal man and nature. Hence subject and predicate are absolutely inverted in relation to each other. There is a *mystical subject-object* or a *subjectivity passing beyond the object*, the *absolute subject* as a *process* of self-*externalization* and returning from this externalization into itself but at the same time reabsorbing it into itself. And there is the subject as this process—a pure, restless revolving within itself.

First, the *formal and abstract* conception of man's act of self-creation or self-objectification.

With Hegel's identification of man and self-consciousness, the alienated object or alienated essence of man is nothing but *consciousness*, merely the thought of alienation, its *abstract* and hence empty and unreal expression, *negation*. The transcendence of externalization is thus also nothing but an abstract, empty transcendence of that empty abstraction, the *negation of the negation*. The rich, living, sensuous, concrete activity of self-objectification therefore becomes its mere abstraction, *absolute negativity*, an abstraction fixed as such and regarded as independent activity, as activity itself. Since this so-called negativity is only the *abstract, empty* form of that real living act, its content can only be *formal*, derived by abstraction from all content. Hence there are general, abstract *forms of abstraction*—thought forms and logical categories detached from *actual* spirit and *actual* nature—pertaining to any content and indifferent to all and valid for every content. (We shall develop the *logical* content of absolute negativity later.)

Hegel's positive achievement here (in his speculative logic) is his view that *determinate concepts*, universal *fixed thought-forms* independent of nature and spirit, are a necessary result of the universal alienation of human nature and human thought. Hegel has collated and presented them as moments of the abstraction process. For example, Being transcended is Essence, Essence transcended is Concept, Concept transcended . . . Absolute Idea. But what, then, is the Absolute Idea? It must again transcend its own self unless it wants to go through once more from the beginning the whole movement of abstraction and remain content with being a collection of abstractions or a self-comprehending abstraction. But a self-comprehending abstraction knows itself to be nothing; it must abandon itself as abstraction to arrive at something which is its exact opposite, *nature*. Hence the entire Logic is proof that abstract thought is nothing for itself, that the Absolute Idea is nothing for itself; and only *nature* is something.

The Absolute Idea, the *Abstract Idea* which "considered in its unity with itself is *intuiting*" [*Anschauen*] (Hegel's *Encyclopedia*, 3rd ed., p. 222 [¶ 244]) and which "in its own absolute truth *decides* to let the moment of its particularity or of initial determination and other-being, the *immediate idea* as its reflection, freely *proceed from itself as nature*" *(ibid.)*—this entire Idea which behaves in such a peculiar and extravagant way and has given the Hegelians such terrible headaches is from beginning to end nothing but *abstraction*, that is, the abstract thinker. It is abstraction which, wise from experience and enlightened concerning its truth, decides under various conditions, themselves false and still abstract, to *release* itself and establish its other-being, the particular, and the determinate, in place of its oneness with itself, non-being, universality, and in-determinateness. It decides to let *nature*, which it hid within itself as a mere abstraction or thought entity, *proceed freely from itself*—that is, it decides to forsake abstraction and for once pay attention to nature *free* of abstraction. The abstract idea which becomes unmediated *intuiting* is through and through nothing but abstract thought abandoning itself and deciding on *intuition*. This entire transition from Logic to Philosophy of Nature is nothing but the transition from *abstracting to intuiting*, very difficult for the abstract thinker and hence so quixotically described by him. The *mystical* feeling which drives a philosopher from abstract thinking to intuiting is *boredom*, the longing for a content.

(Man alienated from himself is also the thinker alienated from his *nature*, that is, from his natural and human essence. Hence his thoughts are fixed, ghostly spirits outside nature and man. Hegel has imprisoned all these spirits together in his Logic, conceiving each of them first as negation, as *externalization of human* thought, and then as the negation of the negation, the transcendence of this externalization as *actual* externalization of human thought. But since this negation of the negation is still itself imprisoned in alienation, it partly re-establishes these fixed spirits in their alienation and partly halts at the last step of alienation, self-reference, as their authentic existence.[c] Insofar as this abstraction apprehends itself and experiences an infinite boredom with itself, Hegel abandons abstract thinking moving solely within thinking—without eyes, teeth, ears, everything—as he decides to recognize *nature* as essential being and devote himself to intuition.)

But *nature* too, taken abstractly, for itself, and fixedly isolated from man, is *nothing* for man. It is obvious that the abstract thinker who has committed himself to intuiting, intuits nature abstractly. As nature lay enclosed in the thinker as absolute Idea, as a *thought-entity* in a form hidden and mysterious to the thinker himself, what he has in truth let proceed from himself was only this *abstract nature*, only nature as a thought-entity, but now with the significance of the other-being of thought, actual and perceived nature distinguished from abstract thought. Or, to speak in human terms, the abstract thinker perceives in his intuition of nature that the entities he thought he was creating out of nothing from pure abstraction, in a divine dialectic as pure products of the labor of thought weaving within itself and never perceiving outward actuality—these entities he thought he was creating are merely *abstractions* from *nature's characteristics*. The whole of nature thus only repeats logical abstractions to him in a sensuous, external form.—He again *analyzes* nature and

---

[c] That is, Hegel puts in place of these fixed abstractions the act of abstraction revolving within itself. He has thereby performed the service, in the first place, of having indicated the source of all these inappropriate concepts originally belonging to different philosophies, of having brought them together, and of having created the entire range of abstraction rather than some specific abstraction as the object of criticism. (Later we shall see why Hegel separates thinking from *subject*. But now it is already clear that if man is not human, his characteristic externalization cannot exist and hence thinking itself could not be viewed as the characteristic externalization of man as a human and natural subject with eyes, ears, etc., living in society, the world, and nature.) [Marx's parenthetical remark within the paragraph of the manuscript.]

these abstractions. His intuition of nature is thus only the act of confirming his abstraction by the intuition of nature, his conscious re-enactment of the process of producing his abstraction. Thus, for example, Time is its own self-related Negativity (*loc. cit.*, p. 238). To Becoming transcended as particular Being there corresponds, in natural form, Movement transcended as Matter. In *natural* form Light is *Reflection-in-itself*. Body as *Moon* and *Comet* is the *natural* form of the *opposition* which the Logic on one side calls the *positive grounded on itself* and on the other, the *negative* grounded on itself. The Earth is the *natural* form of the logical *ground* as the negative unity of the opposition, etc.

Nature as nature, that is, so far as it is sensuously distinguished from that secret meaning hidden within it, nature separated and distinguished from these abstractions, is *nothing*, a *nothing proving* itself to be *nothing*. It is *meaningless* or only means an externality which has been transcended.

"In the finite-*teleological* point of view is to be found the correct premise that nature does not contain in itself the absolute end or purpose" (p. 225 [¶245]). Its purpose is the confirmation of abstraction. "Nature has revealed itself as the Idea in the *form of other-being*. Since the *Idea* in this form is the negative of itself or *outside itself*, nature is not just relatively outside this Idea [. . .] but *externality* determines how it exists as nature" (p. 227 [¶247]).

Externality is not to be understood here as *self-externalizing sensuousness* open to the light and to the *sensibility* of sensuous man. It is here to be taken as externalization, error, a defect which ought not be. For what is true is still the Idea. Nature is only the *form* of the *other-being* of the Idea. And since abstract thought is the *essence* of things, something external to it is in essence merely *external*. The abstract thinker also recognizes that *sensuousness, externality* as distinguished from thought weaving *within itself*, is the essence of nature. But at the same time he expresses this distinction in such a way as to make this *externality of nature*, its *contrast* to thought, its *defect*. And inasmuch as nature is distinct from abstraction it is something defective. Something which is defective not only for me, in my eyes, but also in itself has something outside itself which it lacks. That is to say, its essence is something other than itself. For the abstract thinker nature must consequently transcend itself since it is already promulgated by him as a potentially *transcended* existence.

"*For us, Spirit has nature* as its *presupposition* since it is nature's *truth* and hence its *absolute prius*. In this truth nature has *disappeared* and Spirit has yielded to the Idea as Being-for-itself whose *object* as well as *subject* is the *Concept*. This identity is *absolute negativity* because in nature the Concept has its complete external objectivity but here its externalization has been transcended and in this transcedence the Concept has become self-identical. It is this identity only in being a return from nature" (p. 392 [¶381]).

"*Revelation, as the abstract* idea, is unmediated transition, the *becoming* of nature; as revelation of Spirit which is free it *establishes* nature as *its own* world. This establishing as reflection is likewise the *presupposition* of the world as independently existing nature. Revelation conceptually is the creation of nature as Spirit's own being in which Spirit gives itself the *affirmation and truth* of its freedom." "The *Absolute is Spirit*; this is the highest definition of the Absolute" [¶384].

NOTES TO "ECONOMIC AND PHILOSOPHIC MANUSCRIPTS"

1. Bauer reviewed books, articles and pamphlets on the Jewish question in the *Allgemeine Literatur-Zeitung* 1 (December, 1843), 4 (March, 1844); he also wrote an article on the same subject in the *Allgemeine Literatur-Zeitung* 8 (July, 1844).
2. Wilhelm Weitling (1808–1871), a German communist writer, author of *Guarantees of Harmony and Freedom* (1842).
3. Moses Hess, *Twenty-One Sheets from Switzerland* (1844).
4. Ludwig Feuerbach, *Principles of the Philosophy of the Future* (1843); *Preliminary Theses on the Reformation of Philosophy*, published in *Anekdota zur Neuesten deutschen Philosophie und Publicistik* 2 (1843), edited by Arnold Ruge. Two articles by Marx appeared in the same publication.
5. Marx is referring to Bruno Bauer and other contributors to the *Allgemeine Literatur-Zeitung*.
6. Pierre-Joseph Proudhon (1809–1865), French socialist writer and precursor of anarchism, author of *What Is Property?* (1841).
7. This paragraph is an allusion to Hegel's famous discussion of the "master and servant" (or "lord and bondsman") in *The Phenomenology of Spirit*: "[The lord's] essential nature is to exist for himself; he is sheer negative power for whom the thing is nothing. Thus he is the pure, essential action in this relationship, while the bondsman is impure an unessential. For recognition proper the moment is lacking, that what the lord does to the other he also does to himself, and what the bondsman does to himself he should also do to the other" (Hegel, *The Phenomenology of Spirit*, translated by A. V. Miller. Oxford: Clarendon Press, 1977. ¶182).
8. Charles Fourier (1772–1837) and Henri Saint-Simon (1760–1825), French socialist writers. The Physiocrats were a school of eighteenth century political economists, whose foremost representative was Francois Quesnay (1694–1774).
9. Etienne Cabet (1788–1856), French communist, author of *Travels in Icaria* (1840); Francois Villegardelle (1810–1856), French communist writer and follower of Fourier.
10. Robert Owen (1771–1858), British communist and founder of utopian colonies.
11. Bruno Bauer, *Critique of the Gospel History of the Synoptics* (1841).
12. Bruno Bauer, *Revealed Christianity* (1843).
13. Bruno Bauer, *The Good Cause of Freedom and My Own Concern* (1842).
14. Otto Friedrich Gruppe (1804–1876), anti-Hegelian polemicist, regarded by some as a precursor of twentieth century linguistic philosophy.
15. Ludwig Feuerbach, *The Essence of Christianity* (1841).

Theses on Feuerbach (1845)
(*Complete*)

These notes were written by Marx in the spring of 1845 in Brussels. They were first published by Engels as an appendix to his 1888 pamphlet *Ludwig Feuerbach and the End of Classical German Philosophy.* The Theses signify Marx's decisive break with the philosophy of Feuerbach, shortly to be given fuller expression in *The German Ideology.* The translation printed here follows Marx's original manuscript rather than Engels' edited version.

1

The chief defect of all previous materialism (that of Feuerbach included) is that things [*Gegenstand*], reality, sensuousness are conceived only in the form of the *object, or of contemplation,* but not as *sensuous human activity, practice,* not subjectively. Hence, in contradistinction to materialism, the *active* side was set forth abstractly by idealism—which, of course, does not know real, sensuous activity as such. Feuerbach wants sensuous objects, really distinct from conceptual objects, but he does not conceive human activity itself as *objective* activity. In *The Essence of Christianity* he therefore regards the theoretical attitude as the only genuinely human attitude, while practice is conceived and defined only in its dirty-Jewish form of appearance.[1] Hence he does not grasp the significance of "revolutionary", of "practical-critical", activity.

2

The question whether objective truth can be attributed to human thinking is not a question of theory but is a *practical* question. Man must prove the truth, i.e., the reality and power, the this-worldliness of his thinking in practice. The dispute over the reality or non-reality of thinking which is isolated from practice is a purely *scholastic* question.

3

The materialist doctrine concerning the changing of circumstances and upbringing forgets that circumstances are changed by men and that the educator must himself be educated. This doctrine must, therefore, divide society into two parts, one of which is superior to society.

The coincidence of the changing of circumstances and of human activity or self-change can be conceived and rationally understood only as *revolutionary practice*.

4

Feuerbach starts out from the fact of religious self-estrangement, of the duplication of the world into a religious world and a secular one. His work consists in resolving the religious world into its secular basis. But that the secular basis lifts off from itself and establishes itself as an independent realm in the clouds can only be explained by the inner strife and intrinsic contradictoriness of this secular basis. The latter must, therefore, itself be both understood in its contradiction and revolutionised in practice. Thus, for instance, once the earthly family is discovered to be the secret of the holy family, the former must then itself be destroyed in theory and in practice.

5

Feuerbach, not satisfied with *abstract thinking*, wants [*sensuous*] *contemplation*; but he does not conceive sensuousness as *practical*, human-sensuous activity.

6

Feuerbach resolves the essence of religion into the essence of *man*. But the essence of man is no abstraction inherent in each single individual. In its reality it is the ensemble of the social relations.

Feuerbach, who does not enter upon a criticism of this real essence, is hence obliged:

1. To abstract from the historical process and to define the religious sentiment [*Gemüt*] by itself, and to presuppose an abstract—*isolated*—human individual.

2. Essence, therefore, can be regarded only as "species", as an inner, mute, general character which unites the many individuals *in a natural way*.

7

Feuerbach, consequently, does not see that the "religious sentiment" is itself a social product, and that the abstract individual which he analyses belongs to a particular form of society.

8

All social life is essentially *practical*. All mysteries which lead theory to mysticism find their rational solution in human practice and in the comprehension of this practice.

9

The highest point reached by contemplative materialism, that is, materialism which does not comprehend sensuousness as practical activity, is the contemplation of single individuals and of civil society.

10

The standpoint of the old materialism is civil society; the standpoint of the new is human society, or social humanity.

11

The philosophers have only *interpreted* the world in various ways; the point is to *change* it.

NOTE TO "THESES ON FEUERBACH"

1. Feuerbach's *Essence of Christianity* praises the Greeks' pure, disinterested, theoretical attitude toward nature, which he contrasts with the tainted, interested, practical attitude characteristic of religion, and specifically of the Hebrew religious tradition (including, of course, Christianity).

II
The Materialist Conception of History
(1845–1859)

Marx and Engels
The German Ideology (1845–1846)
(*Selections*)

Though much of the five hundred-page manuscript of *The German Ideology* consists of lengthy and unprofitable polemics against Feuerbach, Bauer, Stirner, and others, it would be difficult to overestimate the importance of this manuscript for the development of Marx's thought. It represents his final break with Young Hegelian philosophy and, even more importantly, it contains the first formulation of the materialist theory of history. Written jointly by Marx and Engels in Brussels in 1845–1846, it was first published in 1932. Selections from Part One translated from the German by W. Lough; selections from later parts ("[Personal Interests and Class Interests]" and "[Self-Enjoyment, Morality and Historical Materialism]") translated by Clemens Dutt.

[IDEOLOGY IN GENERAL
GERMAN IDEOLOGY IN PARTICULAR]

German criticism has, right up to its latest efforts, never left the realm of philosophy. It by no means examines its general philosophic premises, but in fact all its problems originate in a definite philosophical system, that of Hegel. Not only in its answers, even in its questions there was a mystification. This dependence on Hegel is the reason why not one of these modern critics has even attempted a comprehensive criticism of the Hegelian system, however much each professes to have advanced beyond Hegel. Their polemics against Hegel and against one another are confined to this—each takes one aspect of the Hegelian system and turns this against the whole system as well as against the aspects chosen by the others. To begin with they took pure, unfalsified Hegelian categories such as "substance" and "self-consciousness", later they secularised these categories by giving them more profane names such as "species", "the unique", "man", etc.[1]

The entire body of German philosophical criticism from Strauss to Stirner is confined to criticism of *religious* conceptions. The critics started from real religion and theology proper. What religious consciousness and religious conception are was subsequently defined in various ways. The advance consisted in including the allegedly dominant metaphysical, political, juridical, moral and other conceptions under the category of religious or theological conceptions; and similarly in declaring that political, juridical, moral consciousness was religious or theological consciousness, and that the political, juridical, moral man—"Man" in the last resort—was religious. The dominance of religion was presupposed. Gradually every dominant relationship was declared to be a religious relationship and transformed into a cult, a cult of law, a cult of the state, etc. It was throughout merely a question of dogmas and belief in dogmas. The world was sanctified to an ever-increasing extent till at last the venerable Saint Max[2] was able to canonise it *en bloc* and thus dispose of it once for all.

The Old Hegelians had *understood* everything as soon as it was reduced to a Hegelian logical category. The Young Hegelians *criticised* everything by ascribing religious conceptions to it or by declaring that it is a theological matter. The Young Hegelians are in agreement with the Old Hegelians in their belief in the rule of religion, of concepts, of a universal principle in the existing world. Except that the one party attacks this rule as usurpation, while the other extols it as legitimate.

Since the Young Hegelians consider conceptions, thoughts, ideas, in fact all the products of consciousness, to which they attribute an independent existence, as the real chains of men (just as the Old Hegelians declare them the true bonds of human society), it is evident that the Young Hegelians have to fight only against these illusions of consciousness. Since, according to their fantasy, the relations of men, all their doings, their fetters and their limitations are products of their consciousness, the Young Hegelians logically put to men the moral postulate of exchanging their present consciousness for human, critical or egoistic consciousness[3] and thus of removing their limitations. This demand to change consciousness amounts to a demand to interpret the existing world in a different way, i.e., to recognise it by means of a different interpretation. The Young Hegelian ideologists, in spite of their allegedly "world-shattering" phrases, are the staunchest conservatives. The most recent of them have found the correct expression for their activity when they declare they are only fighting against *"phrases"*. They forget, however, that they themselves are opposing nothing but phrases to these phrases, and that they are in no way combating the real existing world when they are combating solely the phrases of this world. The only results which this philosophic criticism was able to achieve were a few (and at that one-sided) elucidations of Christianity from the point of view of religious history; all the rest of their assertions are only further embellishments of their claim to have furnished, in these unimportant elucidations, discoveries of world-historic importance.

It has not occurred to any one of these philosophers to inquire into the connection of German philosophy with German reality, the connection of their criticism with their own material surroundings.

[PREMISES OF THE MATERIALIST CONCEPTION OF HISTORY]

The premises from which we begin are not arbitrary ones, not dogmas, but real premises from which abstraction can only be made in the imagination. They are the real individuals, their activity and the material conditions of their life, both those which they find already existing and those produced by their activity. These premises can thus be verified in a purely empirical way.

The first premise of all human history is, of course, the existence of living human individuals. Thus the first fact to be established is the physical organisation of these individuals and their consequent relation to the rest of nature. Of course, we cannot here go either into the actual physical nature of man, or into the natural conditions in which man finds himself—geological, oro-hydrographical, climatic and so on. All historical writing must set out from these natural bases and their modification in the course of history through the action of men.

Men can be distinguished from animals by consciousness, by religion or anything else you like. They themselves begin to distinguish themselves from animals as soon as they begin to *produce* their means of subsistence, a step which is conditioned by their physical organisation. By producing their means of subsistence men are indirectly producing their material life.

The way in which men produce their means of subsistence depends first of all on the nature of the means of subsistence they actually find in existence and have to reproduce.

This mode of production must not be considered simply as being the reproduction of the physical existence of the individuals. Rather it is a definite form of activity of these individuals, a definite form of expressing their life, a definite *mode of life* on their part. As individuals express their life, so they are. What they are, therefore, coincides with their production, both with *what* they produce and with *how* they produce. Hence what individuals are depends on the material conditions of their production.

This production only makes its appearance with the *increase of population*. In its turn this presupposes the *intercourse [Verkehr]* of individuals with one another. The form of this intercourse is again determined by production.

[PRODUCTION AND INTERCOURSE. DIVISION OF LABOUR AND FORMS OF PROPERTY—TRIBAL, ANCIENT, FEUDAL]

The relations of different nations among themselves depend upon the extent to which each has developed its productive forces, the division of labour and internal intercourse. This proposition is generally recognised. But not only the relation of one nation to others, but also the whole internal structure of the nation itself depends on the stage of development reached by its production and its internal and external intercourse. How far the productive forces of a nation are developed is shown most manifestly by the degree to which the division of labour has been carried. Each new productive force, insofar as it is not merely a quantitative extension of productive forces already known (for instance, the bringing into cultivation of fresh land), causes a further development of the division of labour.

The division of labour inside a nation leads at first to the separation of industrial and commercial from agricultural labour, and hence to the separation of *town* and *country* and to the conflict of their interests. Its further development leads to the separation of commercial from industrial labour. At the same time through the division of labour inside these various branches there develop various divisions among the individuals co-operating in definite kinds of labour. The relative position of these individual groups is determined by the way work is organised in agriculture, industry and commerce (patriarchalism, slavery, estates, classes). These same conditions are to be seen (given a more developed intercourse) in the relations of different nations to one another.

The various stages of development in the division of labour are just so many different forms of property, i.e., the existing stage in the division of labour determines also the relations of individuals to one another with reference to the material, instrument and product of labour.

The first form of property is tribal property [*Stammeigentum*]. It corresponds to the undeveloped stage of production, at which a people lives by hunting and fishing, by cattle-raising or, at most, by agriculture. In the latter case it presupposes a great mass of uncultivated stretches of land. The division of labour is at this stage still very elementary and is confined to a further extension of the natural division of labour existing in the family. The social structure is, therefore, limited to an extension of the family: patriarchal chieftains, below them the members of the tribe, finally slaves. The slavery latent in the family only develops gradually with the increase of population, the growth of wants, and with the extension of external intercourse, both of war and of barter.

The second form is the ancient communal and state property, which proceeds especially from the union of several tribes into a *city* by agreement or by conquest, and which is still accompanied by slavery. Beside communal property we already find movable, and later also immovable, private property developing, but as an abnormal form subordinate to communal property. The citizens hold power over their labouring slaves only in their community, and even on this account alone they are bound to the form of communal property. It constitutes the communal private property of the active citizens who, in relation to their slaves, are compelled to remain in this spontaneously derived form of association. For this reason the whole structure of society based on this communal property, and with it the power of the people, decays in the same measure in which immovable private property evolves. The division of labour is already more developed. We already find the opposition of town and country; later the opposition between those states which represent town interests and those which represent country interests, and inside the towns themselves the opposition between industry and maritime commerce. The class relations between citizens and slaves are now completely developed.

With the development of private property, we find here for the first time the same relations which we shall find again, only on a more extensive scale, with modern private property. On the one hand, the concentration of private property, which began very early in Rome (as the Licinian agrarian law[4] proves) and proceeded very rapidly from the time of the civil wars and especially under the emperors, on the other hand, coupled with this, the transformation of the plebeian small peasantry into a proletariat, which, however, owing to its intermediate position between propertied citizens and slaves, never achieved an independent development.

The third form is feudal or estate property. If antiquity started out from the *town* and its small territory, the Middle Ages started out from the *country*. This different starting-point was determined by the sparseness of the population at that time, which was scattered over a large area and which received no large increases from the conquerors. In contrast to Greece and Rome, feudal development, therefore, begins over a much wider territory, prepared by the Roman conquests and the spread of agriculture at first associated with them. The last centuries of the declining Roman Empire and its conquest by the barbarians destroyed a considerable part of the productive forces; agriculture had declined, industry had decayed for want of a market, trade had died out or been violently interrupted, the rural and urban population had decreased. These conditions and the mode of organisation of the conquest determined by them, together with the influence of the Germanic military constitution, led to the development of feudal property. Like tribal and communal property, it is also based on a community; but the directly producing class standing over against it is not, as in the case of the ancient community, the slaves, but the enserfed small peasantry. As soon as feudalism is fully developed, there also arises antagonism to the towns. The hierarchical structure of landownership, and the armed bodies of retainers associated with it, gave the nobility power over the serfs. This feudal organisation was, just as much as the ancient communal property, an association against a subjected producing class; but the form of association and the relation to the direct producers were different because of the different conditions of production.

This feudal structure of landownership had its counterpart in the *towns* in the shape of corporative property, the feudal organisation of trades. Here property consisted chiefly in the labour of each individual. The

necessity for associating against the association of the robber-nobility, the
need for communal covered markets in an age when the industrialist was
at the same time a merchant, the growing competition of the escaped
serfs swarming into the rising towns, the feudal structure of the whole
country: these combined to bring about the *guilds*. The gradually accumulated small capital of individual craftsmen and their stable numbers, as
against the growing population, evolved the relation of journeyman and
apprentice, which brought into being in the towns a hierarchy similar to
that in the country.

Thus property during the feudal epoch primarily consisted on the one
hand of landed property with serf labour chained to it, and on the other
of the personal labour of the individual who with his small capital com-
mands the labour of journeymen. The organisation of both was determined by the restricted conditions of production—the scanty and primitive cultivation of the land, and the craft type of industry. There was little
division of labour in the heyday of feudalism. Each country bore in itself
the antithesis of town and country; the division into estates was certainly
strongly marked; but apart from the differentiation of princes, nobility,
clergy and peasants in the country, and masters, journeymen, apprentices
and soon also the rabble of casual labourers in the towns, there was no
important division. In agriculture it was rendered difficult by the strip-sys-
tem, beside which the cottage industry of the peasants themselves
emerged. In industry there was no division of labour in the individual
trades and very little between them. The separation of industry and
commerce was found already in existence in older towns; in the newer it
only developed later, when the towns entered into mutual relations.

The grouping of larger territories into feudal kingdoms was a necessity
for the landed nobility as for the towns. The organisation of the ruling
class, the nobility, had, therefore, everywhere a monarch at its head.

[THE ESSENCE OF THE MATERIALIST CONCEPTION OF HISTORY SOCIAL BEING AND SOCIAL CONSCIOUSNESS]

The fact is, therefore, that definite individuals who are productively active
in a definite way enter into these definite social and political relations.
Empirical observation must in each separate instance bring out empirically,
and without any mystification and speculation, the connection of the social
and political structure with production. The social structure and the state
are continually evolving out of the life-process of definite individuals, however, of these individuals, not as they may appear in their own or other
people's imagination, but as they *actually* are, i.e., as they act, produce
materially, and hence as they work under definite material limits, presuppositions and conditions independent of their will.

The production of ideas, of conceptions, of consciousness, is at first directly interwoven with the material activity and the material intercourse of men—the language of real life. Conceiving, thinking, the mental intercourse of men at this stage still appear as the direct efflux of their material behaviour. The same applies to mental production as expressed in the language of the politics, laws, morality, religion, metaphysics, etc., of a people. Men are the producers of their conceptions, ideas, etc., that is, real, active men, as they are conditioned by a definite development of their productive forces and of the intercourse corresponding to these, up to its furthest forms. Consciousness [*das Bewusstsein*] can never be anything else than conscious being [*das bewusste Sein*], and the being of men is their actual life-process. If in all ideology men and their relations appear upside-down as in a *camera obscura*, this phenomenon arises just as much from their historical life-process as the inversion of objects on the retina does from their physical life-process.

In direct contrast to German philosophy which descends from heaven to earth, here it is a matter of ascending from earth to heaven. That is to say, not of setting out from what men say, imagine, conceive, nor from men as narrated, thought of, imagined, conceived, in order to arrive at men in the flesh; but setting out from real, active men, and on the basis of their real life-process demonstrating the development of the ideological reflexes and echoes of this life-process. The phantoms formed in the brains of men are also, necessarily, sublimates of their material life-process, which is empirically verifiable and bound to material premises. Morality, religion, metaphysics, and all the rest of ideology as well as the forms of consciousness corresponding to these, thus no longer retain the semblance of independence. They have no history, no development; but men, developing their material production and their material intercourse, alter, along with this their actual world, also their thinking and the products of their thinking. It is not consciousness that determines life, but life that determines consciousness. For the first manner of approach the starting-point is consciousness taken as the living individual; for the second manner of approach, which conforms to real life, it is the real living individuals themselves, and consciousness is considered solely as *their* consciousness.

This manner of approach is not devoid of premises. It starts out from the real premises and does not abandon them for a moment. Its premises are men, not in any fantastic isolation and fixity, but in their actual, empirically perceptible process of development under definite conditions. As soon as this active life-process is described, history ceases to be a collection of dead facts, as it is with the empiricists (themselves still abstract), or an imagined activity of imagined subjects, as with the idealists.

Where speculation ends, where real life starts, there consequently begins real, positive science, the expounding of the practical activity, of the practical process of development of men. Empty phrases about consciousness end, and real knowledge has to take their place. When the reality is described, a self-sufficient philosophy [*die selbständige Philosophie*] loses its medium of existence. At the best its place can only be taken by a summing-up of the most general results, abstractions which are derived from the observation of the historical development of men. These abstractions in themselves, divorced from real history, have no value whatsoever. They can only serve to facilitate the arrangement of historical material, to indicate the sequence of its separate strata. But they by no means afford a recipe or schema, as does philosophy, for neatly trimming the epochs of history. On the contrary, the difficulties begin only when one sets about the examination and arrangement of the material—whether of a past epoch or of the present—and its actual presentation. The removal of these difficulties is governed by premises which certainly cannot be stated here, but which only the study of the actual life-process and the activity of the individuals of each epoch will make evident. We shall select here some of these abstractions, which we use in contradistinction to ideology, and shall illustrate them by historical examples. . . .

[PRIMARY HISTORICAL RELATIONS, OR THE BASIC ASPECTS OF SOCIAL ACTIVITY: PRODUCTION OF THE MEANS OF SUBSISTENCE, PRODUCTION OF NEW NEEDS, REPRODUCTION OF MEN (THE FAMILY). SOCIAL INTERCOURSE, CONSCIOUSNESS]

Since we are dealing with the Germans, who are devoid of premises, we must begin by stating the first premise of all human existence and, therefore, of all history, the premise, namely, that men must be in a position to live in order to be able to "make history". But life involves before everything else eating and drinking, housing, clothing and various other things. The first historical act is thus the production of the means to satisfy these needs, the production of material life itself. And indeed this is an historical act, a fundamental condition of all history, which today, as thousands of years ago, must daily and hourly be fulfilled merely in order to sustain human life. Even when the sensuous world is reduced to a minimum, to a stick as with Saint Bruno[5] it presupposes the action of producing this stick. Therefore in any conception of history one has first of all to observe this fundamental fact in all its significance and all its implications and to accord it its due importance. It is well known that the Germans have never done this, and they have never, therefore, had an *earthly* basis for history and consequently never a historian. The French and the English, even if they have conceived the relation of this fact with so-called history only in an extremely one-sided fashion, especially since they remained in the toils of political ideology, have nevertheless made the first attempts to give the writing of history a materialistic basis by being the first to write histories of civil society, of commerce and industry.

The second point is that the satisfaction of the first need, the action of satisfying and the instrument of satisfaction which has been acquired, leads to new needs; and this creation of new needs is the first historical act. Here we recognise immediately the spiritual ancestry of the great historical wisdom of the Germans who, when they run out of positive material and when they can serve up neither theological nor political nor literary rubbish, assert that this is not history at all, but the "prehistoric age". They do not, however, enlighten us as to how we proceed from this nonsensical "prehistory" to history proper; although, on the other hand, in their historical speculation they seize upon this "prehistory" with especial eagerness because they imagine themselves safe there from interference on the part of "crude facts", and, at the same time, because there they can give full rein to their speculative impulse and set up and knock down hypotheses by the thousand.

The third circumstance which, from the very outset, enters into historical development, is that men, who daily re-create their own life, begin to make other men, to propagate their kind: the relation between man and woman, parents and children, the *family*. The family, which to begin with is the only social relation, becomes later, when increased needs create new social relations and the increased population new needs, a subordinate one (except in Germany), and must then be treated and analysed according to the existing empirical data, not according to "the concept of the family", as is the custom in Germany.

These three aspects of social activity are not of course to be taken as three different stages, but just as three aspects or, to make it clear to the Germans, three "moments", which have existed simultaneously since the dawn of history and the first men, and which still assert themselves in history today.

The production of life, both of one's own in labour and of fresh life in procreation, now appears as a twofold relation: on the one hand as a natural, on the other as a social relation — social in the sense that it denotes the co-operation of several individuals, no matter under what conditions, in what manner and to what end. It follows from this that a certain mode of production, or industrial stage, is always combined with a certain mode of co-operation, or social stage, and this mode of co-operation is itself a "productive force". Further, that the aggregate of productive forces accessible to men determines the condition of society, hence, the "history of humanity" must always be studied and treated in relation to the history of industry and exchange. But it is also clear that in Germany it is impossible to write this sort of history, because the Germans lack not only the necessary power of comprehension and the material but also the "sensuous certainty", for across the Rhine one cannot have any experience of these things since there history has stopped happening. Thus it is quite obvious from the start that there exists a materialist connection of men with one another, which is determined by their needs and their mode of production, and which is as old as men themselves. This connection is ever taking on new forms, and thus presents a "history" irrespective of the existence of any political or religious nonsense which would especially hold men together.

Only now, after having considered four moments, four aspects of primary historical relations, do we find that man also possesses "consciousness". But even from the outset this is not "pure" consciousness. The "mind" is from the outset afflicted with the curse of being "burdened" with matter, which here makes its appearance in the form of agitated layers of air, sounds, in short, of language. Language is as old as consciousness, language *is* practical, real consciousness that exists for other men as well, and only therefore does it also exist for me; language, like consciousness, only arises from the need, the necessity, of intercourse with other men. Where there exists a relationship, it exists for me: the animal does not "*relate*" itself to anything, it does not "*relate*" itself at all. For the animal its relation to others does not exist as a relation. Consciousness is, therefore, from the very beginning a social product, and remains so as long as men exist at all. Consciousness is at first, of course, merely consciousness concerning the *immediate* sensuous environment and consciousness of the limited connection with other persons and things outside the individual who is growing self-conscious. At the same time it is consciousness of nature, which first confronts men as a completely alien, all-powerful and unassailable force, with which men's relations are purely animal and by which they are overawed like beasts; it is thus a purely animal consciousness of nature (natural religion) precisely because nature is as yet hardly altered by history—on the other hand, it is man's consciousness of the necessity of associating with the individuals around him, the beginning of the consciousness that he is living in society at all. This beginning is as animal as social life itself at this stage. It is mere herd-consciousness, and at this point man is distinguished from sheep only by the fact that with him consciousness takes the place of instinct or that his instinct is a conscious one. This sheep-like or tribal consciousness receives its further development and extension through increased productivity, the increase of needs, and, what is fundamental to both of these, he increase of population. With these there develops the division of labour, which was originally nothing but the division of labour in the sexual act, then the division of labour which develops spontaneously or "naturally" by virtue of natural predisposition (e.g., physical strength), needs, accidents, etc., etc. Division of labour only becomes truly such from the moment when a division of material and mental labour appears. From this moment onwards consciousness *can* really flatter itself that it is something other than consciousness of existing practice, that it *really* represents something without representing something real; from now on consciousness is in a position to emancipate itself from the world and to proceed to the formation of "pure" theory, theology, philosophy, morality, etc., come into contradiction with the existing relations, this can only occur because existing social relations have come into contradiction with existing productive forces; moreover, in a particular national sphere of relations this can also occur through the contradiction, arising not within the national orbit, but between this national consciousness and the practice of other nations, i.e., between the national and the general consciousness of a nation (as is happening now in Germany); but since this contradiction appears to exist only as a contradiction within the national consciousness, it seems to this nation that the struggle too is confined to this national muck, precisely because this nation represents this muck as such.

Incidentally, it is quite immaterial what consciousness starts to do on its own: out of all this trash we get only the one inference that these three moments, the productive forces, the state of society and consciousness, can and must come into contradiction with one another, because the *division of labour* implies the possibility, may the fact, that intellectual and material activity. that enjoyment and labour, production and consumption, devolve on different individuals, and that the only possibility of their not coming into contradiction lies in negating in its turn the division of labour. It is self-evident, moreover, that "spectres", "bonds", "the higher being", "concept", "scruple", are merely idealist, speculative, mental expressions, the concepts apparently of the isolated individual, the mere images of very empirical fetters and limitations, within which move the mode of production of life, and the form of intercourse coupled with it.

[SOCIAL DIVISION OF LABOUR AND ITS CONSEQUENCES: PRIVATE PROPERTY, THE STATE, "ESTRANGEMENT" OF SOCIAL ACTIVITY]

The division of labour in which all these contradictions are implicit, and which in its turn is based on the natural division of labour in the family and the separation of society into individual families opposed to one another, simultaneously implies the *distribution*, and indeed the *unequal* distribution, both quantitative and qualitative, of labour and its products, hence property, the nucleus, the first form of which lies in the family, where wife and children are the slaves of the husband. This latent slavery in the family, though still very crude, is the first form of property, but even at this stage it corresponds perfectly to the definition of modern economists, who call it the power of disposing of the labour-power of others. Division of labour and private property are, after all, identical expressions: in the one the same thing is affirmed with reference to activity as is affirmed in the other with reference to the product of the activity.

Further, the division of labour also implies the contradiction between the interest of the separate individual or the individual family and the common interest of all individuals who have intercourse with one another. And indeed, this common interest does not exist merely in the imagination, as the "general interest", but first of all in reality, as the mutual interdependence of the individuals among whom the labour is divided.

Out of this very contradiction between the particular and the common interests, the common interest assumes an independent form as the *state*, which is divorced from the real individual and collective interests, and at the same time as an illusory community, always based, however, on the real ties existing in every family conglomeration and tribal conglomeration—such as flesh and blood, language, division of labour on a larger scale, and other interests—and especially, as we shall show later, on the classes, already implied by the division of labour, which in every such mass of men separate out, and one of which dominates all the others. It follows from this that all struggles within the state, the struggle between democracy, aristocracy, and monarchy, the struggle for the franchise, etc., etc., are merely the illusory forms—altogether the general interest is the illusory form of common interests—in which the real struggles of the different classes are fought out among one another (of this the German theoreticians have not the faintest inkling, although they have received a sufficient initiation into the subject in the *German-French Annals* and *The Holy Family*).[6] Further, it follows that every class which is aiming at domination, even when its domination, as is the case with the proletariat, leads to the abolition of the old form of society in its entirety and of domination in general, must first conquer political power in order to represent its interest in turn as the general interest, which in the first moment it is forced to do.

Just because individuals seek *only* their particular interest, which for them does not coincide with their common interest, the latter is asserted as an interest "alien" ["*fremd*"] to them, and "independent" of them, as in its turn a particular and distinctive "general" interest; or they themselves must remain within this discord, as in democracy. On the other hand, too, the *practical* struggle of these particular interests, which *actually* constantly run counter to the common and illusory common interests, necessitates *practical* intervention and restraint by the illusory "general" interest in the form of the state.

And finally, the division of labour offers us the first example of the fact that, as long as man remains in naturally evolved society, that is, as long as a cleavage exists between the particular and the common interest, as long, therefore, as activity is not voluntarily, but naturally, divided, man's own deed becomes an alien power opposed to him, which enslaves him instead of being controlled by him. For as soon as the division of labour comes into being, each man has a particular, exclusive sphere of activity, which is forced upon him and from which he cannot escape. He is a hunter, a fisherman, a shepherd, or a critical critic, and must remain so if he does not want to lose his means of livelihood; whereas in communist society, where nobody has one exclusive sphere of activity but each can become accomplished in any branch he wishes, society regulates the general production and thus makes it possible for me to do one thing today and another tomorrow, to hunt in the morning, fish in the afternoon, rear cattle in the evening, criticise after dinner, just as I have a mind, without ever becoming hunter, fisherman, shepherd or critic.

This fixation of social activity, this consolidation of what we ourselves produce into a material power above us, growing out of our control, thwarting our expectations, bringing to naught our calculations, is one of the chief factors in historical development up till now. The social power, i.e., the multiplied productive force, which arises through the co-operation of different individuals as it is caused by the division of labour, appears to these individuals, since their co-operation is not voluntary but has come about naturally, not as their own united power, but as an alien force existing outside them, of the origin and goal of which they are ignorant, which they thus are no longer able to control, which on the contrary passes through a peculiar series of phases and stages independent of the will and the action of man, nay even being the prime governor of these. How otherwise could for instance property have had a history at all, have taken on different forms, and landed property, for example, according to the different premises given, have proceeded in France from parcellation to centralisation in the hands of a few, in England from centralisation in the hands of a few to parcellation, as is actually the case today? Or how does it happen that trade, which after all is nothing more than the exchange of products of various individuals and countries, rules the whole world through the relation of supply and demand—a relation which, as an English economist says, hovers over the earth like the fate of the ancients, and with invisible hand allots fortune and misfortune to men, sets up empires and wrecks empires, causes nations to rise and to disappear— whereas with the abolition of the basis, private property, with the communistic regulation of production (and, implicit in this, the abolition of the alien attitude [*Fremdheit*] of men to their own product), the power of the relation of supply and demand is dissolved into nothing, and men once more gain control of exchange, production and the way they behave to one another?

[DEVELOPMENT OF THE PRODUCTIVE FORCES
AS A MATERIAL PREMISE OF COMMUNISM]

This "estrangement" [*"Entfremdung"*] (to use a term which will be comprehensible to the philosophers) can, of course, only be abolished given two *practical* premises. In order to become an "unendurable" power, i.e., a power against which men make a revolution, it must necessarily have rendered the great mass of humanity "propertyless", and moreover in contradiction to an existing world of wealth and culture; both these premises presuppose a great increase in productive power, a high degree of its development. And, on the other hand, this development of productive forces (which at the same time implies the actual empirical existence of men in their *world-historical*, instead of local, being) is an absolutely necessary practical premise, because without it privation, *want* is merely made general, and with *want* the struggle for necessities would begin again, and all the old filthy business would necessarily be restored; and furthermore, because only with this universal development of productive forces is a *universal* intercourse between men established, which on the one side produces in *all* nations simultaneously the phenomenon of the "propertyless" mass (universal competition), making each nation dependent on the revolutions of the others, and finally puts *world-historical*, empirically universal individuals in place of local ones. Without this, 1) communism could only exist as a local phenomenon; 2) the *forces* of intercourse themselves could not have developed as *universal* hence unendurable powers: they would have remained home-bred "conditions" surrounded by superstition; and 3) each extension of intercourse would abolish local communism. Empirically, communism is only possible as the act of the dominant peoples "all at once" and simultaneously which presupposes the universal development of productive forces and the world intercourse bound up with them.

Moreover, the mass of workers who are *nothing but workers*—labour-power on a mass scale cut off from capital or from even a limited satisfaction [of their needs] and, hence, as a result of competition their utterly precarious position, the no longer merely temporary loss of work as a secure source of life—presupposes the *world market*. The proletariat can thus only exist *world-historically*, just as communism, its activity, can only have a "world-historical" existence. World-historical existence of individuals, i.e., existence of individuals which is directly linked up with world history.

Communism is for us not a *state of affairs* which is to be established, an *ideal* to which reality [will] have to adjust itself. We call communism the *real* movement which abolishes the present state of things. The conditions of this movement result from the now existing premise.

The form of intercourse determined by the existing productive forces at all previous historical stages, and in its turn determining these, is *civil society*. The latter, as is clear from what we have said above, has as its premise and basis the simple family and the multiple, called the tribe, and the more precise definition of this society is given in our remarks above. Already here we see that this civil society is the true focus and theatre of all history, and how absurd is the conception of history held hitherto, which neglects the real relations and confines itself to spectacular historical events.

[CONCLUSIONS FROM THE MATERIALIST CONCEPTION OF HISTORY: HISTORY AS A CONTINUOUS PROCESS, HISTORY AS BECOMING WORLD HISTORY, THE NECESSITY OF COMMUNIST REVOLUTION]

History is nothing but the succession of the separate generations, each of which uses the materials, the capital funds, the productive forces handed down to it by all preceding generations, and thus, on the one hand, continues the traditional activity in completely changed circumstances and, on the other, modifies the old circumstances with a completely changed activity. This can be speculatively distorted so that later history is made the goal of earlier history, e.g., the goal ascribed to the discovery of America is to further the eruption of the French Revolution. Thereby history receives its own special goals and becomes "a person ranking with other persons" (to wit: "self-consciousness, criticism, the unique", etc.), while what is designated with the words "destiny", "goal" "germ", or "idea" of earlier history is nothing more than an abstraction from later history, from the active influence which earlier history exercises on later history.

The further the separate spheres, which act on one another, extend in the course of this development and the more the original isolation of the separate nationalities is destroyed by the advanced mode of production, by intercourse and by the natural division of labour between various nations arising as a result, the more history becomes world history. Thus, for instance, if in England a machine is invented which deprives countless workers of bread in India and China, and overturns the whole form of existence of these empires, this invention becomes a world-historical fact. Or again, take the case of sugar and coffee, which have proved their world-historical importance in the nineteenth century by the fact that the lack of these products, occasioned by the Napoleonic Continental System, caused the Germans to rise against Napoleon, and thus became the real basis of the glorious Wars of Liberation of 1813.[7] From this it follows that this transformation of history into world history is by no means a mere abstract act on the part of "self-consciousness", the world spirit, or of any other metaphysical spectre, but a quite material, empirically verifiable act, an act the proof of which every individual furnishes as he comes and goes, eats, drinks and clothes himself.

In history up to the present it is certainly likewise an empirical fact that separate individuals have, with the broadening of their activity into world-historical activity, become more and more enslaved under a power alien to them (a pressure which they have conceived of as a dirty trick on the part of the so-called world spirit, etc.), a power which has become more and more enormous and, in the last instance, turns out to be the *world market*. But it is just as empirically established that, by the overthrow of the existing state of society by the communist revolution (of which more below) and the abolition of private property which is identical with it, this power, which so baffles the German theoreticians, will be dissolved; and that then the liberation of each single individual will be accomplished in the measure in which history becomes wholly transformed into world history. From the above it is clear that the real intellectual wealth of the individual depends entirely on the wealth of his real connections. Only this will liberate the separate individuals from the various national and local barriers, bring them into practical connection with the production (including intellectual production) of the whole world and make it possible for them to acquire the capacity to enjoy this all-sided production of the whole earth (the creations of man). *All-round* dependence, this primary natural form of the *world-historical* co-operation of individuals, will be transformed by this communist revolution into the control and conscious mastery of these powers, which, born of the action of men on one another, have till now overawed and ruled men as powers completely alien to them. Now this view can be expressed again in a speculative-idealistic, i.e., fantastic, way as "self-generation of the species" ("society as the subject"), and thereby the consecutive series of interrelated individuals can be regarded as a single individual, which accomplishes the mystery of generating itself. In this context it is evident that individuals undoubtedly make *one another*, physically and mentally, but do not make themselves, either in the nonsense of Saint Bruno, or in the sense of the "unique", of the "made" man.

Finally, from the conception of history set forth by us we obtain these further conclusions: 1) In the development of productive forces there comes a stage when productive forces and means of intercourse are brought into being which, under the existing relations, only cause mischief, and are no longer productive but destructive forces (machinery and money); and connected with this a class is called forth which has to bear all the burdens of society without enjoying its advantages, which is ousted from society and forced into the sharpest contradiction to all other classes; a class which forms the majority of all members of society, and from which emanates the consciousness of the necessity of a fundamental revolution, the communist consciousness, which may, of course, arise among the other classes too through the contemplation of the situation of this class. 2) The conditions under which definite productive forces can be applied are the conditions of the rule of a definite class of society, whose social power, deriving from its property, has its *practical*-idealistic expression in each case in the form of the state and, therefore, every revolutionary struggle is directed against a class which till then has been in power. 3) In all previous revolutions the mode of activity always remained unchanged and it was only a question of a different distribution of this activity, a new distribution of labour to other persons, whilst the communist revolution is directed against the hitherto existing *mode* of activity, does away with *labour*, and abolishes the rule of all classes with the classes themselves, because it is carried through by the class which no longer counts as a class in society, which is not recognised as a class, and is in itself the expression of the dissolution of all classes, nationalities, etc., within present society; and 4) Both for the production on a mass scale of this communist consciousness, and for the success of the cause itself, the alteration of men on a mass scale is necessary, an alteration which can only take place in a practical movement, a *revolution*, the revolution is necessary, therefore, not only because the *ruling* class cannot be overthrown in any other way, but also because the class *overthrowing* it can only in a revolution succeed in ridding itself of all the muck of ages and become fitted to found society anew.

[THE RULING CLASS AND THE RULING IDEAS. HOW THE HEGELIAN CONCEPTION OF THE DOMINATION OF THE SPIRIT IN HISTORY AROSE]

The ideas of the ruling class are in every epoch the ruling ideas: i.e., the class which is the ruling *material* force of society is at the same time its ruling *intellectual* force. The class which has the means of material production at its disposal, consequently also controls the means of mental production, so that the ideas of those who lack the means of mental production are on the whole subject to it. The ruling ideas are nothing more than the ideal expression of the dominant material relations, the dominant material relations grasped as ideas; hence of the relations which make the one class the ruling one, therefore, the ideas of its dominance. The individuals composing the ruling class possess among other things consciousness, and therefore think. Insofar, therefore, as they rule as a class and determine the extent and compass of an historical epoch, it is self-evident that they do this in its whole range, hence among other things rule also as thinkers, as producers of ideas, and regulate the production and distribution of the ideas of their age: thus their ideas are the ruling ideas of the epoch. For instance, in an age and in a country where royal power, aristocracy and bourgeoisie are contending for domination and where, therefore, domination is shared, the doctrine of the separation of powers proves to be the dominant idea and is expressed as an "eternal law".

The division of labour, which we already saw above as one of the chief forces of history up till now, manifests itself also in the ruling class as the division of mental and material labour, so that inside this class one part appears as the thinkers of the class (its active, conceptive ideologists, who make the formation of the illusions of the class about itself their chief source of livelihood), while the others' attitude to these ideas and illusions is more passive and receptive, because they are in reality the active members of this class and have less time to make up illusions and ideas about themselves. Within this class this cleavage can even develop into a certain opposition and hostility between the two parts, but whenever a practical collision occurs in which the class itself is endangered they automatically vanish, in which case there also vanishes the appearance of the ruling ideas being not the ideas of the ruling class and having a power distinct from the power of this class. The existence of revolutionary ideas in a particular period presupposes the existence of a revolutionary class; about the premises of the latter sufficient has already been said above.

If now in considering the course of history we detach the ideas of the ruling class from the ruling class itself and attribute to them an independent existence, if we confine ourselves to saying that these or those ideas were dominant at a given time, without bothering ourselves about the conditions of production and the producers of these ideas, if we thus ignore the individuals and world conditions which are the source of the ideas, then we can say, for instance, that during the time the aristocracy was dominant, the concepts honour, loyalty, etc., were dominant, during the dominance of the bourgeoisie the concepts freedom, equality, etc. The ruling class itself on the whole imagines this to be so. This conception of history, which is common to all historians, particularly since the eighteenth century, will necessarily come up against the phenomenon that ever more abstract ideas hold sway, i.e., ideas which increasingly take on the form of universality. For each new class which puts itself in the place of one ruling before it is compelled, merely in order to carry through its aim, to present its interest as the common interest of all the members of society, that is, expressed in ideal form: it has to give its ideas the form of universality, and present them as the only rational, universally valid ones. The class making a revolution comes forward from the very start, if only because it is opposed to a *class*, not as a class but as the representative of the whole of society, as the whole mass of society confronting the one ruling class. It can do this because initially its interest really is as yet mostly connected with the common interest of all other non-ruling classes, because under the pressure of hitherto existing conditions its interest has not yet been able to develop as the particular interest of a particular class. Its victory, therefore, benefits also many individuals of other classes which are not winning a dominant position, but only insofar as it now enables these individuals to raise themselves into the ruling class. When the French bourgeoisie overthrew the rule of the aristocracy, it thereby made it possible for many proletarians to raise themselves above the proletariat, but only insofar as they became bourgeois. Every new class, therefore, achieves domination only on a broader basis than that of the class ruling previously; on the other hand the opposition of the non-ruling class to the new ruling class then develops all the more sharply and profoundly. Both these things determine the fact that the struggle to be waged against this new ruling class, in its turn, has as its aim a more decisive and more radical negation of the previous conditions of society than all previous classes which sought to rule could have.

This whole appearance, that the rule of a certain class is only the rule of certain ideas, comes to a natural end, of course, as soon as class rule in general ceases to be the form in which society is organised, that is to say, as soon as it is no longer necessary to represent a particular interest as general or the "general interest" as ruling.

Once the ruling ideas have been separated from the ruling individuals and, above all, from the relations which result from a given stage of the mode of production, and in this way the conclusion has been reached that history is always under the sway of ideas, it is very easy to abstract from these various ideas "the Idea", the thought, etc., as the dominant force in history, and thus to consider all these separate ideas and concepts as "forms of self-determination" of the Concept developing in history. It follows then naturally, too, that all the relations of men can be derived from the concept of man, man as conceived, the essence of man, Man. This has been done by speculative philosophy. Hegel himself confesses at the end of the *Philosophy of History* that he "has considered the progress of *the concept* only" and has represented in history the "true *theodicy.*"[8] Now one can go back again to the producers of "the concept", to the theorists, ideologists and philosophers, and one comes then to the conclusion that the philosophers, the thinkers as such have at all times been dominant in history: a conclusion, as we see already expressed by Hegel.

The whole trick of proving the hegemony of the spirit in history (hierarchy Stirner calls it) is thus confined to the following three attempts.

No. 1. One must separate the ideas of those ruling for empirical reasons, under empirical conditions and as corporeal individuals, from these rulers, and thus recognise the rule of ideas or illusions in history.

No. 2. One must bring an order into this rule of ideas, prove a mystical connection among the successive ruling ideas, which is managed by regarding them as "forms of self-determination of the concept" (this is possible because by virtue of their empirical basis these ideas are really connected with one another and because, conceived as *mere* ideas, they become self-distinctions, distinctions made by thought).

No. 3. To remove the mystical appearance of this "self-determining concept" it is changed into a person—"self-consciousness"—or, to appear thoroughly materialistic, into a series of persons, who represent the "concept" in history, into the "thinkers", the "philosophers", the ideologists, who again are understood as the manufacturers of history, as the "council of guardians", as the rulers. Thus the whole body of materialistic elements has been eliminated from history and now full rein can be given to the speculative steed.

This historical method which reigned in Germany, and especially the reason why, must be explained from its connection with the illusion of ideologists in general, e.g., the illusions of the jurists, politicians (including the practical statesmen), from the dogmatic dreamings and distortions of these fellows; this is explained perfectly easily from their practical position in life, their job, and the division of labour.

Whilst in ordinary life every shopkeeper is very well able to distinguish between what somebody professes to be and what he really is, our historiography has not yet won this trivial insight. It takes every epoch at its word and believes that everything it says and imagines about itself is true. . . .

[COMMUNISM]

Communism differs from all previous movements in that it overturns the basis of all earlier relations of production and intercourse, and for the first time consciously treats all naturally evolved premises as the creations of hitherto existing men, strips them of their natural character and subjugates them to the power of the united individuals. Its organisation is, therefore, essentially economic, the material production of the conditions of this unity; it turns existing conditions into conditions of unity. The reality which communism creates is precisely the true basis for rendering it impossible that anything should exist independently of individuals, insofar as reality is nevertheless only a product of the preceding intercourse of individuals. Thus the Communists in practice treat the conditions created up to now by production and intercourse as inorganic conditions, without, however, imagining that it was the plan or the destiny of previous generations to give them material, and without believing that these conditions were inorganic for the individuals creating them.

[PERSONAL INTERESTS AND CLASS INTERESTS]

How is it that personal interests always develop, against the will of individuals, into class interests, into common interests which acquire independent existence in relation to the individual persons, and in their independence assume the form of *general* interests? How is it that as such they come into contradiction with the actual individuals and in this contradiction, by which they are defined as *general* interests, they can be conceived by consciousness as *ideal* and even as religious, holy interests? How is it that in this process of private interests acquiring independent existence as class interests the personal behaviour of the individual is bound to be objectified [*sich versachlichen*], estranged [*sich entfremden*], and at the same time exists as a power independent of him and without him, created by intercourse, and is transformed into social relations, into a series of powers which determine and subordinate the individual, and which, therefore, appear in the imagination as "holy" powers? Had Sancho[9] understood the fact that within the framework of definite *modes of production*, which, of course, are not dependent on the will, alien [*fremde*] practical forces, which are independent not only of isolated individuals but even of all of them together, always come to stand above people—then he could be fairly indifferent as to whether this fact is presented in a religious form or distorted in the fancy of the egoist, above whom everything is placed in imagination, in such a way that he places nothing above himself. Sancho would then have descended from the realm of speculation into the realm of reality, from what people fancy to what they actually are, from what they imagine to how they act and are bound to act in definite circumstances. What seems to him a product of *thought*, he would have understood to be a product of *life*. He, would not then have arrived at the absurdity worthy of him—of explaining the division between personal and general interests by saying that people imagine this division *also* in a religious way and *seem* to themselves to be such and such, which is, however, only another word for "imagining" . . .

[SELF-ENJOYMENT, MORALITY AND HISTORICAL MATERIALISM]

Communism is quite incomprehensible to our saint because the communists do not oppose egoism to selflessness or selflessness to egoism, nor do they express this contradiction theoretically either in its sentimental or in its highflown ideological form; they rather demonstrate its material source, with which it disappears of itself. The communists do not preach *morality* at all, as Stirner does so extensively. They do not put to people the moral demand: love one another, do not be egoists, etc.; on the contrary, they are very well aware that egoism, just as much as selflessness, is in definite circumstances a necessary form of the self-assertion of individuals. Hence, the communists by no means want, as Saint Max believes, and as his loyal *Dottore Graziano* (Arnold Ruge) repeats after him (for which Saint Max calls him "an unusually cunning and politic mind",

Wigand, p. 192), to do away with the "private individual" for the sake of the "general", selfless man. That is a figment of the imagination concerning which both of them could already have found the necessary explanation in the *German French Annals*. Communist theoreticians, the only communists who have time to devote to the study of history, are distinguished precisely by the fact that they alone have *discovered* that throughout history the "general interest" is created by individuals who are defined as "private persons". They know that this contradiction is only a *seeming* one because one side of it, what is called the "general interest", is constantly being produced by the other side, private interest, and in relation to the latter it is by no means an independent force with an independent history—so that this contradiction is in practice constantly destroyed and reproduced. Hence it is not a question of the Hegelian "negative unity" of two sides of a contradiction, but of the materially determined destruction of the preceding materially determined mode of life of individuals, with the disappearance of which this contradiction together with its unity also disappears. . . .

The *philosophy* which preaches enjoyment is as old in Europe as the Cyrenaic school.[10] Just as in antiquity it was the *Greeks* who were the protagonists of this philosophy, so in modern times it is the *French*, and indeed for the same reason, because their temperament and their society made them most capable of enjoyment. The philosophy of enjoyment was never anything but the clever language of certain social circles who had the privilege of enjoyment. Apart from the fact that the manner and content of their enjoyment was always determined by the whole structure of the rest of society and suffered from all its contradictions, this philosophy became a mere *phrase* as soon as it began to lay claim to a universal character and proclaimed itself the outlook on life of society as a whole. It sank then to the level of edifying moralising, to a sophistical palliation of existing society, or it was transformed into its opposite, by declaring compulsory asceticism to be enjoyment.

In modern times the philosophy of enjoyment arose with the decline of feudalism and with the transformation of the feudal landed nobility into the pleasure-loving and extravagant nobles of the court under the absolute monarchy. Among these nobles this philosophy still has largely the form of a direct, naive outlook on life which finds expression in memoirs, poems, novels, etc. It only becomes a real philosophy in the hands of a few writers of the revolutionary bourgeoisie, who, on the one hand, participated in the culture and mode of life of the court nobility and, on the other hand, shared the more general outlook of the bourgeoisie, based on the more general conditions of existence of this class. This philosophy was, therefore, accepted by both classes, although from totally different points of view. Whereas among the nobility this language was restricted exclusively to its estate and to the conditions of life of this estate, it was given a generalised character by the bourgeoisie and addressed to every individual without distinction. The conditions of life of these individuals were thus disregarded and the theory of enjoyment thereby transformed into an insipid and hypocritical moral doctrine. When, in the course of further development, the nobility was overthrown and the bourgeoisie brought into conflict with its opposite, the proletariat, the nobility became devoutly religious, and the bourgeoisie solemnly moral and strict in its theories, or else succumbed to the above-mentioned hypocrisy, although the nobility in practice by no means renounced enjoyment, while among the bourgeoisie enjoyment even assumed an official, economic form—that of *luxury.*

It was only possible to discover the connection between the kinds of enjoyment open to individuals at any particular time and the class relations in which they live, and the conditions of production and intercourse which give rise to these relations, the narrowness of the hitherto existing forms of enjoyment, which were outside the actual content of the life of people and in contradiction to it, the connection between every philosophy of enjoyment and the enjoyment actually present and the hypocrisy of such a philosophy which treated all individuals without distinction—it was, of course, only possible to discover all this when it became possible to criticise the conditions of production and intercourse in the hitherto existing world, i.e., when the contradiction between the bourgeoisie and the proletariat had given rise to communist and socialist views. That shattered the basis of all morality, whether the morality of asceticism or of enjoyment.

Our insipid, moralising Sancho believes, of course, as his whole book shows, that it is merely a matter of a different morality, of what appears to him a new outlook on life, of "getting out of one's head" a few "fixed ideas", to make everyone happy and able to enjoy life. Hence the chapter on self-enjoyment could at most reproduce under a new label the same phrases and maxims which he had already so frequently had the "self-enjoyment" of preaching to us. This chapter has only one original feature, namely that he *deifies* and turns into philosophical German all enjoyment, by giving it the name *"self-enjoyment"*. While the French philosophy of enjoyment of the eighteenth century at least gave a witty description of the gay and audacious mode of life that then existed, Sancho's whole frivolity is limited to such expressions as "consuming" and "squandering", to images such as the "light" (it should read a candle) and to natural-scientific recollections which amount either to belletristic nonsense such as that the plant "imbibes the air of the ether" and that "song-birds swallow beetles", or else to wrong statements, for example, that a candle burns itself. On the other hand, here we again enjoy all the solemn seriousness of the statements against "the holy", which, we are told, in the guise of "vocation—designation—task" and "ideal" has hitherto spoiled people's self-enjoyment. For the rest, without dwelling on the more or less dirty forms in which the "self" in 'self-enjoyment" can be more than a mere phrase, we must once more as briefly as possible outline for the reader Sancho's machinations against the holy, with the insignificant modulations occurring in this chapter.

To recapitulate briefly, "vocation, designation, task, ideal" are either

1) the idea of the revolutionary tasks laid down for an oppressed class by the material conditions; or

2) mere idealistic paraphrases, or also the apt conscious expression of the individuals' modes of activity which owing to division of labour have assumed independent existence as various professions; or

3) the conscious expression of the necessity which at every moment confronts individuals, classes and nations to assert their position through some quite definite activity; or

4) the conditions of existence of the ruling class (as determined by the preceding development of production), ideally expressed in law, morality, etc., to which [conditions] the ideologists of that class more or less consciously give a sort of theoretical independence; they can be conceived by separate individuals of that class as vocation, etc., and are held up as a standard of life to the individuals of the oppressed class, partly as an embellishment or recognition of domination, partly as a moral means for this domination. It is to be noted here, as in general with ideologists, that they inevitably put the thing upside-down and regard their ideology both as the creative force and as the aim of all social relations, whereas it is only an expression and symptom of these relations. . . .

NOTES TO "THE GERMAN IDEOLOGY"

1. "Substance" is an allusion to David Friedrich Strauss; "self-consciousness", to Bruno Bauer; "species" and "man", to Ludwig Feuerbach; and "the unique" (*das Einzige*), to Max Stirner.
2. "Saint Max" is Max Stirner.
3. "Human" is an allusion to Feuerbach; "critical", to Bauer; and "egoistic", to Stirner.
4. The Licinian law was a Roman agrarian law, promulgated under the tribunes Licinius and Sextius in 367 B.C. It limited the amount of common land (*ager publicus*) a Roman citizen could hold at any one time to 500 *yugera* (about 309 acres).
5. "Saint Bruno" is Bruno Bauer. The allusion is to Bauer's article "Charakteristik Ludwig Feuerbachs," *Wigands Vierteljahrschrift* (Wigand's Quarterly) 3 (1845).
6. The allusion is to the articles by Marx and Engels in the *Deutsch-Französiche Jahrbücher* (German-French Annals) in 1843–1844 and to their first collaboration, *The Holy Family* (1844), a critique of Bruno Bauer and his associates.

7. The "Napoleonic Continental System" refers to Napoleon's attempt to ruin England economically by a shipping blockade and trade embargo. The embargo was imposed in 1807 and lasted until the failure of Napoleon's Russian campaign in 1812.
8. Hegel, *The Philosophy of History*, tr. J. Sibree, p. 457.
9. "Sancho" is Max Stirner.
10. A school of ancient Greek philosophy, founded early in the 4th Century B.C. by Aristippus of Cyrene, a pupil of Socrates. The Cyrenaics were ethical hedonists and skeptics on questions of religion.

Letter to P. V. Annenkov (1846) (*Excerpt*)

In December, 1846, Marx read Proudhon's book *The Philosophy of Poverty* (1846), an attempt to systematize the categories of political economy according to Hegelian philosophy, and incidentally to argue for his own economic proposals. Proudhon had first acquired his acquaintance with Hegelian philosophy through Marx, when the two had met two years earlier in Paris. Marx had become friends with the liberal Russian landowner Pavel Vassilyevich Annenkov (1812–1887) in Paris. Writing from Brussels on December 28, 1846, Marx gave Annenkov his first reactions to Proudhon's new book. Though Marx was soon to have a fuller say on the subject in his own polemic *The Poverty of Philosophy* (1847), the letter to Annenkov provides us with one of his most lucid statements of his newly developed materialist conception of history and its empirical assumptions. Translated from the French by I. Lasker.

My Dear Monsieur Annenkov,

You would long ago have received my answer to your letter of November 1 but for the fact that my bookseller only sent me Monsieur Proudhon's book, *The Philosophy of Poverty*, last week. I have gone through it in two days in order to be able to give you my opinion about it at once. As I have read the book very hurriedly, I cannot go into details but can only tell you the general impression it has made on me. If you wish I could go into details in a second letter.

I must frankly confess that I find the book on the whole bad, and very bad. You yourself laugh in your letter at the "patch of German philosophy" which M. Proudhon parades in this formless and pretentious work, but you suppose that the economic argument has not been infected by the philosophic poison. I too am very far from imputing the faults in the economic argument to M. Proudhon's philosophy. M. Proudhon does not give us a false criticism of political economy because he is the possessor of an absurd philosophic theory, but he gives us an absurd philosophic theory because he fails to understand the social system of today in its *engrènement*, to use a word which, like much else, M. Proudhon has borrowed from Fourier.

Why does M. Proudhon talk about God, about universal reason, about the impersonal reason of humanity which never errs, which has always been equal to itself throughout all the ages and of which one need only have the right consciousness in order to know the truth? Why does he resort to feeble Hegelianism to give himself the appearance of a bold thinker?

He himself provides you with the clue to this enigma. M. Proudhon sees in history a series of social developments; he finds progress realised in history; finally he finds that men, as individuals, did not know what they were doing and were mistaken about their own movement, that is to say, their social development seems at the first glance to be distinct, separate and independent of their individual development. He cannot explain these facts, and so the hypothesis of universal reason manifesting itself comes in very handy. Nothing is easier than to invent mystical causes, that is to say, phrases which lack common sense.

But when M. Proudhon admits that he understands nothing about the historical development of humanity—he admits this by using such high-sounding words as: Universal Reason, God, etc.—is he not implicitly and necessarily admitting that he is incapable of understanding *economic development*?

What is society, whatever its form may be? The product of men's reciprocal action. Are men free to choose this or that form of society? By no means. Assume a particular state of development in the productive faculties of man and you will get a particular form of commerce and consumption. Assume particular stages of development in production, commerce and consumption and you will have a corresponding social constitution, a corresponding organisation of the family, of orders or of classes, in a word, a corresponding civil society. Assume a particular civil society and you will get particular political conditions which are only the official expression of civil society. M. Proudhon will never understand this because he thinks he is doing something great by appealing from the state to civil society—that is to say, from the official résumé of society to official society.

It is superfluous to add that men are not free to choose *their productive forces*—which are the basis of all their history—for every productive force is an acquired force, the product of former activity. The productive forces are therefore the result of practical human energy; but this energy is itself conditioned by the circumstances in which men find themselves, by the productive forces already acquired, by the social form which exists before they do, which they do not create, which is the product of the preceding generation. Because of this simple fact that every succeeding generation finds itself in possession of the productive forces acquired by the previous generation, which serve it as the raw material for new production, a coherence arises in human history, a history of humanity takes shape which is all the more a history of humanity as the productive forces of man and therefore his social relations have been more developed. Hence it necessarily follows that the social history of men is never anything but the history of their individual development, whether they are conscious of it or not. Their material relations are the basis of all their relations. These material relations are only the necessary forms in which their material and individual activity is realised.

M. Proudhon mixes up ideas and things. Men never relinquish what they have won, but this does not mean that they never relinquish the social form in which they have acquired certain productive forces. On the contrary, in order that they may not be deprived of the result attained and forfeit the fruits of civilisation, they are obliged, from the moment when their mode of carrying on commerce no longer corresponds to the productive forces acquired, to change all their traditional social forms. I am using the word "commerce" here in its widest sense, as we use *Verkehr* in German. For example: the privileges, the institution of guilds and corporations, the regulatory regime of the Middle Ages, were social relations that alone corresponded to the acquired productive forces and to the social condition which had previously existed and from which these institutions had arisen. Under the protection of the regime of corporations and regulations, capital was accumulated, overseas trade was developed, colonies were founded. But the fruits of this men would have forfeited if they had tried to retain the forms under whose shelter these fruits had ripened. Hence burst two thunderclaps—the Revolutions of 1640 and 1688. All the old economic forms, the social relations corresponding to them, the political conditions which were the official expression of the old civil society, were destroyed in England. Thus the economic forms in which men produce, consume, and exchange, are *transitory and historical*. With the acquisition of new productive faculties, men change their mode of production and with the mode of production all the economic relations which are merely the necessary relations of this particular mode of production.

This is what M. Proudhon has not understood and still less demonstrated. M. Proudhon, incapable of following the real movement of history, produces a phantasmagoria which presumptuously claims to be dialectical. He does not feel it necessary to speak of the seventeenth, the eighteenth or the nineteenth century, for his history proceeds in the misty realm of imagination and rises far above space and time. In short, it is not history but old Hegelian junk, it is not profane history—a history of man—but sacred history—a history of ideas. From his point of view man is only the instrument of which the idea or the eternal reason makes use in order to unfold itself. The *evolutions* of which M. Proudhon speaks are understood to be evolutions such as are accomplished within the mystic womb of the absolute idea. If you tear the veil from this mystical language, what it comes to is that M. Proudhon is offering you the order in which economic categories arrange themselves inside his own mind. It will not require great exertion on my part to prove to you that it is the order of a very disorderly mind.

M. Proudhon begins his book with a dissertation on *value*, which is his pet subject. I will not enter on an examination of this dissertation today.

The series of economic evolutions of the eternal reason begins with *division of labour*. To M. Proudhon division of labour is a perfectly simple thing. But was not the caste regime also a particular division of labour? Was not the regime of the corporations another division of labour? And is not the division of labour under the system of manufacture, which in England begins in the middle of the seventeenth century and comes to an end in the last part of the eighteenth, also totally different from the division of labour in large-scale, modern industry?

M. Proudhon is so far from the truth that he neglects what even the profane economists attend to. When he talks about division of labour he does not feel it necessary to mention the world *market*. Good. Yet must not the division of labour in the fourteenth and fifteenth centuries, when there were still no colonies, when America did not as yet exist for Europe, and Eastern Asia only existed for her through the medium of Constantinople, have been fundamentally different from what it was in the seventeenth century when colonies were already developed?

And that is not all. Is the whole inner organisation of nations, are all their international relations anything else than the expression of a particular division of labour? And must not these change when the division of labour changes?

M. Proudhon has so little understood the problem of the division of labour that he never even mentions the separation of town and country, which took place in Germany, for instance, from the ninth to the twelfth century. Thus, to M. Proudhon, this separation is an eternal law since he knows neither its origin nor its development. All through his book he speaks as if this creation of a particular mode of production would endure until the end of time. All that M. Proudhon says about the division of labour is only a summary, and moreover a very superficial and incomplete summary, of what Adam Smith and a thousand others have said before him.

The second evolution is *machinery*. The connection between the division of labour and machinery is entirely mystical to M. Proudhon. Each kind of division of labour had its specific instruments of production. Between the middle of the seventeenth and the middle of the eighteenth century, for instance, people did not make everything by hand. They had instruments, and very complicated ones at that, such as looms, ships, levers, etc.

Thus there is nothing more absurd than to derive machinery from division of labour in general.

I may also remark, by the way, that M. Proudhon has understood very little the historical origin of machinery, but has still less understood its development. One can say that up to the year 1825—the period of the first general crisis—the demands of consumption in general increased more rapidly than production, and the development of machinery was a necessary consequence of the needs of the market. Since 1825, the invention and application of machinery has been simply the result of the war between workers and employers. But this is only true of England. As for the European nations, they were driven to adopt machinery owing to English competition both in their home markets and on the world market. Finally, in North America the introduction of machinery was due both to competition with other countries and to lack of hands, that is, to the disproportion between the population of North America and its industrial needs. From these facts you can see what sagacity Monsieur Proudhon develops when he conjures up the spectre of competition as the third evolution, the antithesis to machinery!

Lastly and in general, it is altogether absurd to make *machinery* an economic category alongside with division of labour, competition, credit, etc.

Machinery is no more an economic category than the ox which draws the plough. The *application* of machinery in the present day is one of the relations of our present economic system, but the way in which machinery is utilised is totally distinct from the machinery itself. Powder is powder whether used to wound a man or to dress his wounds.

M. Proudhon surpasses himself when he allows competition, monopoly, taxes or police, balance of trade, credit and property to develop inside his head in the order in which I have mentioned them. Nearly all credit institutions had been developed in England by the beginning of the eighteenth century, before the invention of machinery. Public credit was only a fresh method of increasing taxation and satisfying the new demands created by the rise of the bourgeoisie to power.

M. Proudhon surpasses himself when he allows competition, monopoly, taxes or police, balance of trade, credit and property to develop inside his head in the order in which I have mentioned them. Nearly all credit institutions had been developed in England by the beginning of the eighteenth century, before the invention of machinery. Public credit was only a fresh method of increasing taxation and satisfying the new demands created by the rise of the bourgeoisie to power.

Finally, the last category in M. Proudhon's system is constituted by *property*. In the real world, on the other hand, the division of labour and all M. Proudhon's other categories are social relations forming in their entirety what is today known as *property*; outside these relations bourgeois property is nothing but a metaphysical or juristic illusion. The property of a different epoch, feudal property, develops in a series of entirely different social relations. M. Proudhon, by establishing property as an independent relation, commits more than a mistake in method: he clearly shows that he has not grasped the bond which holds together all forms of *bourgeois* production, that he has not understood the *historical* and *transitory* character of the forms of production in a particular epoch. M. Proudhon, who does not regard our social institutions as historical products, who can understand neither their origin nor their development, can only produce dogmatic criticism of them.

M. Proudhon is therefore obliged to take refuge in a *fiction* in order to explain development. He imagines that division of labour, credit, machinery, etc., were all invented to serve his fixed idea, the idea of equality. His explanation is sublimely naïve. These things were invented in the interests of equality but unfortunately they turned against equality. This constitutes his whole argument. In other words, he makes a gratuitous assumption and then, as the actual development contradicts his fiction at every step, he concludes that there is a contradiction. He conceals from you the fact that the contradiction exists solely between his fixed ideas and the real movement.

Thus, M. Proudhon, mainly because he lacks the historical knowledge, has not perceived that as men develop their productive faculties, that is, as they live, they develop certain relations with one another and that the nature of these relations must necessarily change with the change and growth of the productive faculties. He has not perceived that *economic categories* are only *abstract expressions* of these actual relations and only remain true while these relations exist. He therefore falls into the error of the bourgeois economists, who regard these economic categories as eternal and not as historical laws which are only laws for a particular historical development, for a definite development of the productive forces. Instead, therefore, of regarding the political-economic categories as abstract expressions of the real, transitory, historic social relations, Monsieur Proudhon, thanks to a mystic inversion, sees in the real relations only embodiments of these abstractions. These abstractions themselves are formulas which have been slumbering in the heart of God the Father since the beginning of the world.

The Poverty of Philosophy (1847) (*Excerpts*)

By Marx's own account (p. 137), his polemic against Proudhon contains his first published expression of the materialist theory of history. *The Poverty of Philosophy*, a reply to Proudhon's *The Philosophy of Poverty* (1846), was written in Brussels. The following excerpts emphasize the role of the class struggle in this theory. Marx had especial reason to underscore this aspect of his theory in a polemic against Proudhon, owing to Proudhon's opposition (on proto-anarchist principles) to workers' combinations, strikes, and political activity as means of furthering working class interests. Translated from the French by Frida Knight.

[ECONOMIC CATEGORIES AND HISTORY]

Economic categories are only the theoretical expressions, the abstractions of the social relations of production. M. Proudhon, holding things upside down like a true philosopher, sees in actual relations nothing but the incarnation of these principles, of these categories, which were slumbering—so M. Proudhon the philosopher tells us—in the bosom of the "impersonal reason of humanity".

M. Proudhon the economist understands very well that men make cloth, linen or silk materials in definite relations of production. But what he has not understood is that these definite social relations are just as much produced by men as linen, flax, etc. Social relations are closely bound up with productive forces. In acquiring new productive forces men change their mode of production; and in changing their mode of production, in changing the way of earning their living, they change all their social relations. The hand-mill gives you society with the feudal lord; the steam-mill, society with the industrial capitalist.

The same men who establish their social relations in conformity with their material productivity, produce also principles, ideas and categories, in conformity with their social relations.

Thus these ideas, these categories, are as little eternal as the relations they express. They are *historical and transitory products*.

There is a continual movement of growth in productive forces, of destruction in social relations, of formation in ideas; the only immutable thing is the abstraction of movement—*mors immortalis*.[1]

[ECONOMISTS AS CLASS IDEOLOGUES]

Economists have a singular method of procedure. There are only two kinds of institutions for them, artificial and natural. The institutions of feudalism are artificial institutions, those of the bourgeoisie are natural institutions. In this they resemble the theologians, who likewise establish two kinds of religion. Every religion which is not theirs is an invention of men, while their own is an emanation from God. When the economists say that present-day relations—the relations of bourgeois production—are natural, they imply that these are the relations in which wealth is created and productive forces developed in conformity with the laws of nature. These relations therefore are themselves natural laws independent of the influence of time. They are eternal laws which must always govern society. Thus there has been history, but there is no longer any. There has been history, since there were the institutions of feudalism, and in these institutions of feudalism we find quite different relations of production from those of bourgeois society, which the economists try to pass off as natural and as such, eternal.

Feudalism also had its proletariat—serfage, which contained all the germs of the bourgeoisie. Feudal production also had two antagonistic elements which are likewise designated by the name of the *good side* and the *bad side* of feudalism, irrespective of the fact that it is always the bad side that in the end triumphs over the good side. It is the bad side that produces the movement which makes history, by providing a struggle. If, during the epoch of the domination of feudalism, the economists, enthusiastic over the knightly virtues, the beautiful harmony between rights and duties, the patriarchal life of the towns, the prosperous condition of domestic industry in the countryside, the development of industry organised into corporations, guilds and fraternities, in short, everything that constitutes the good side of feudalism, had set themselves the problem of eliminating everything that cast a shadow on this picture—serfdom, privileges, anarchy—what would have happened? All the elements which called forth the struggle would have been destroyed, and the development of the bourgeoisie nipped in the bud. One would have set oneself the absurd problem of eliminating history.

After the triumph of the bourgeoisie there was no longer any question of the good or the bad side of feudalism. The bourgeoisie took possession of the productive forces it had developed under feudalism. All the old economic forms, the corresponding civil relations, the political system which was the official expression of the old civil society, were smashed.

Thus feudal production, to be judged properly, must be considered as a mode of production founded on antagonism. It must be shown how wealth was produced within this antagonism, how the productive forces were developed at the same time as class antagonisms, how one of the classes, the bad side, the drawback of society, went on growing until the material conditions for its emancipation had attained full maturity. Is not this as good as saying that the mode of production, the relations in which productive forces are developed, are anything but eternal laws, but that they correspond to a definite development of men and of their productive forces, and that a change in men's productive forces necessarily brings about a change in their relations of production? As the main thing is not to be deprived of the fruits of civilisation, of the acquired productive forces, the traditional forms in which they were produced must be smashed. From this moment the revolutionary class becomes conservative.

The bourgeoisie begins with a proletariat which is itself a relic of the proletariat[1] of feudal times. In the course of its historical development, the bourgeoisie necessarily develops its antagonistic character, which at first is more or less disguised, existing only in a latent state. As the bourgeoisie develops, there develops in its bosom a new proletariat, a modern proletariat; there develops a struggle between the proletarian class and the bourgeois class, a struggle which, before being felt, perceived, appreciated, understood, avowed and proclaimed aloud by both sides, expresses itself, to start with, merely in partial and momentary conflicts, in subversive acts. Just as the *economists* are the scientific representatives of the bourgeois class, so the *socialists* and the *Communists* are the theoreticians of the proletarian class. So long as the proletariat is not yet sufficiently developed to constitute itself as a class, and consequently so long as the very struggle of the proletariat with the bourgeoisie has not yet assumed a political character, and the productive forces are not yet sufficiently developed in the bosom of the bourgeoisie itself to enable us to catch a glimpse of the material conditions necessary for the emancipation of the proletariat and for the formation of a new society, these theoreticians are merely utopians who, to meet the wants of the oppressed classes, improvise systems and go in search of a regenerating science. But in the measure that history moves forward, and with it the struggle of the proletariat assumes clearer outlines, they no longer need to seek science in their minds; they have only to take note of what is happening before their eyes and to become its mouthpiece. So long as they look for science and merely make systems, so long as they are at the beginning of the struggle, they see in poverty nothing but poverty, without seeing in it the revolutionary, subversive side, which will overthrow the old society. From the moment they see this side, science, which is produced by the historical movement and associating itself consciously with it, has ceased to be doctrinaire and has become revolutionary.)

[CLASS REVOLUTION]

The economists want the workers to remain in society as it is constituted and as it has been signed and sealed by them in their manuals.

The socialists[2] want the workers to leave the old society alone, the better to be able to enter the new society which they have prepared for them with so much foresight.

In spite of both of them, in spite of manuals and utopias, combination has not ceased for an instant to go forward and grow with the development and growth of modern industry. It has now reached such a stage, that the degree to which combination has developed in any country clearly marks the rank it occupies in the hierarchy of the world market. England, whose industry has attained the highest degree of development, has the biggest and best organised combinations.

In England they have not stopped at partial combinations which have no other objective than a passing strike, and which disappear with it. Permanent combinations have been formed, *trades unions*, which serve as bulwarks for the workers in their struggles with the employers. And at the present time all these local *trades unions* find a rallying point in the *National Association of United Trades*, the central committee of which is in London, and which already numbers 80,000 members. The organisation of these strikes, combinations, and *trades unions* went on simultaneously with the political struggles of the workers, who now constitute a large political party, under the name of *Chartists*.[3]

The first attempts of workers to *associate* among themselves always take place in the form of combinations.

Large-scale industry concentrates in one place a crowd of people unknown to one another. Competition divides their interests. But the maintenance of wages, this common interest which they have against their boss, unites them in a common thought of resistance—*combination*. Thus combination always has a double aim, that of stopping competition among the workers, so that they can carry on general competition with the capitalist. If the first aim of resistance was merely the maintenance of wages, combinations, at first isolated, constitute themselves into groups as the capitalists in their turn unite for the purpose of repression, and in face of always united capital, the maintenance of the association becomes more necessary to them than that of wages. This is so true that English economists are amazed to see the workers sacrifice a good part of their wages in favour of associations, which, in the eyes of these economists, are established solely in favour of wages. In this struggle—a veritable civil war—all the elements necessary for a coming battle unite and develop. Once it has reached this point, association takes on a political character.

Economic conditions had first transformed the mass of the people of the country into workers. The domination of capital has created for this mass a common situation, common interests. This mass is thus already a class as against capital, but not yet for itself. In the struggle, of which we have pointed out only a few phases, this mass becomes united, and constitutes itself as a class for itself. The interests it defends become class interests. But the struggle of class against class is a political struggle.

In the bourgeoisie we have two phases to distinguish: that in which it constituted itself as a class under the regime of feudalism and absolute monarchy, and that in which, already constituted as a class, it overthrew feudalism and monarchy to make society into a bourgeois society. The first of these phases was the longer and necessitated the greater efforts. This too began by partial combinations against the feudal lords.

Much research has been carried out to trace the different historical phases that the bourgeoisie has passed through, from the commune up to its constitution as a class.

But when it is a question of making a precise study of strikes, combinations and other forms in which the proletarians carry out before our eyes their organisation as a class, some are seized with real fear and others display a *transcendental* disdain.

An oppressed class is the vital condition for every society founded on the antagonism of classes. The emancipation of the oppressed class thus implies necessarily the creation of a new society. For the oppressed class to be able to emancipate itself it is necessary that the productive powers already acquired and the existing social relations should no longer be capable of existing side by side. Of all the instruments of production, the greatest productive power is the revolutionary class itself. The organisation of revolutionary elements as a class supposes the existence of all the productive forces which could be engendered in the bosom of the old society.

Does this mean that after the fall of the old society there will be a new class domination culminating in a new political power? No.

The condition for the emancipation of the working class is the abolition of all classes, just as the condition for the emancipation of the third estate, of the bourgeois order, was the abolition of all estates and all orders.[4]

The working class, in the course of its development, will substitute for the old civil society an association which will exclude classes and their antagonism, and there will be no more political power properly so-called, since political power is precisely the official expression of antagonism in civil society.

Meanwhile the antagonism between the proletariat and the bourgeoisie is a struggle of class against class, a struggle which carried to its highest expression is a total revolution. Indeed, is it at all surprising that a society founded on the *opposition* of classes should culminate in brutal *contradiction*, the shock of body against body, as its final denouement?

Do not say that social movement excludes political movement. There is never a political movement which is not at the same time social.

It is only in an order of things in which there are no more classes and class antagonisms that *social evolutions* will cease to be *political revolutions.* Till then, on the eve of every general reshuffling of society, the last word of social science will always be:

> Le combat ou la mort; la lutte sanguinaire ou le néant. C'est ainsi que la question est invinciblement posée.
>
> GEORGE SAND[5]

NOTES TO "THE POVERTY OF PHILOSOPHY"

1. The Latin phrase is an allusion to Lucretius' *On the Nature of Things*, 3: 882: *mortalem vitam mors immortalis ademit*—"mortal life has been usurped by death, the immortal."
2. "Socialists" in this passage refers to those who share the views of Proudhon about workers' combinations.
3. Chartism was a British working class political movement of the 1830's to the 1850's. It was named for "The People's Charter," a radical proposal for English political reform, submitted in the form of a bill to Parliament in May, 1838. The Charter called for universal manhood suffrage, annual parliamentary elections, secret ballot, equal constituencies, the abolition of property qualifications for MPs and the institution of salaries for MPs. Engels became a Chartist in the early 1840s.
4. "Estates here in the historical sense of the estates of feudalism, estates with definite and limited privileges. The revolution of the bourgeoisie abolished the estates and their privileges. Bourgeois society knows only *classes*. It was, therefore, absolutely in contradiction with history to describe the proletariat as the 'fourth estate' Note by Engels to the German edition of *The Poverty of Philosophy* (1885).
5. "Combat or death, bloody struggle or nothing. It is thus that the question is inevitably posed." George Sand, *Jean Ziska: An Episode from the Hussite War*, Introduction.

The Eighteenth Brumaire of Louis Bonaparte (1852) (*Excerpts*)

On November 9, 1799 (the eighteenth Brumaire, 1799, according to the calendar of the First French Republic), Napoleon Bonaparte's coup d'etat began the First French Empire. On December 2, 1851, Napoleon's nephew Louis Bonaparte staged another coup d'etat, ending the Second Republic and establishing the Second Empire, which was to last until the Franco-Prussian war of 1870. Marx had already given an account of the 1848 revolution in *The Class Struggles in France 1848–1850* (1850). Writing from exile in London between December, 1851, and March, 1852, *The Eighteenth Brumaire* is his account of Louis Bonaparte's coup and the events leading up to it. This is the most brilliant of all Marx's historical writings, and the principal text in which he attempts to apply the materialist conception of history to concrete political reality. Translated from the German by Ben Fowkes.

[REVOLUTIONARY CONSCIOUSNESS]

Hegel remarks somewhere that all the great events and characters of world history occur, so to speak, twice.[1] He forgot to add: the first time as tragedy, the second as farce. Caussidière in place of Danton, Louis Blanc in place of Robespierre, the Montagne of 1848–51 in place of the Montagne of 1793–5, the Nephew in place of the Uncle[2] And we can perceive the same caricature in the circumstances surrounding the second edition of the eighteenth Brumaire!

Men make their own history, but not of their own free will; not under circumstances they themselves have chosen but under the given and inherited circumstances with which they are directly confronted. The tradition of the dead generations weighs like a nightmare on the minds of the living. And, just when they appear to be engaged in the revolutionary transformation of themselves and their material surroundings, in the creation of something which does not yet exist, precisely in such epochs of revolutionary crisis they timidly conjure up the spirits of the past to help them; they borrow their names, slogans and costumes so as to stage the new world-historical scene in this venerable disguise and borrowed language. Luther put on the mask of the apostle Paul; the Revolution of 1789–1814 draped itself alternately as the Roman republic and the Roman empire; and the revolution of 1848 knew no better than to parody at some points 1789 and at others the revolutionary traditions of 1793–5. In the same way, the beginner who has learned a new language always retranslates it into his mother tongue: he can only be said to have appropriated the spirit of the new language and to be able to express himself in it freely when he can manipulate it without reference to the old, and when he forgets his original language while using the new one.

If we reflect on this process of world-historical necromancy, we see at once a salient distinction. Camille Desmoulins, Danton, Robespierre, Saint-Just and Napoleon, the heroes of the old French Revolution, as well as its parties and masses, accomplished the task of their epoch, which was the emancipation and establishment of modern *bourgeois* society, in Roman costume and with Roman slogans. The first revolutionaries smashed the feudal basis to pieces and struck off the feudal heads which had grown on it. Then came Napoleon. Within France he created the conditions which first made possible the development of free competition, the exploitation of the land by small peasant property, and the application of the unleashed productive power of the nation's industries. Beyond the borders of France he swept away feudal institutions so far as this was necessary for the provision on the European continent of an appropriate modern environment for the bourgeois society in France. Once the new social formation had been established, the antediluvian colossi disappeared along with the resurrected imitations of Rome—imitations of Brutus, Gracchus, Publicola, the tribunes, the senators, and Caesar himself. Bourgeois society in its sober reality had created its true interpreters and spokesmen in such people as Say, Cousin, Royer-Collard, Benjamin Constant and Guizot.[3] The real leaders of the bourgeois army sat behind office desks while the fathead Louis XVIII served as the bourgeoisie's political head. Bourgeois society was no longer aware that the ghosts of Rome had watched over its cradle, since it was wholly absorbed in the production of wealth and the peaceful struggle of economic competition. But unheroic as bourgeois society is, it still required heroism, self-sacrifice, terror, civil war, and battles in which whole nations were engaged, to bring it into the world. And its gladiators found in the stern classical traditions of the Roman republic the ideals, art forms and self-deceptions they needed in order to hide from themselves the limited bourgeois content of their struggles and to maintain their enthusiasm at the high level appropriate to great historical tragedy. A century earlier, in the same way but at a different stage of development, Cromwell and the English people had borrowed for their bourgeois revolution the language, passions and illusions of the Old Testament. When the actual goal had been reached,

when the bourgeois transformation of English society had been accomplished, Locke drove out Habakkuk.

In these revolutions, then, the resurrection of the dead served to exalt
the new struggles, rather than to parody the old, to exaggerate the given
task in the imagination, rather than to flee from solving it in reality, and
to recover the spirit of the revolution, rather than to set its ghost walking
again.

For it was only the ghost of the old revolution which walked in the
years from 1848 to 1851, from Marrast, the *républican en gants jaunes* who
disguised himself as old Bailly[4] right down to the adventurer who is now
hiding his commonplace and repulsive countenance beneath the iron
death-mask of Napoleon.

An entire people thought it had provided itself with a more powerful
motive force by means of a revolution; instead, it suddenly found itself
plunged back into an already dead epoch. It was impossible to mistake
this relapse into the past, for the old dates arose again, along with the
old chronology, the old names, the old edicts, long abandoned to the
erudition of the antiquaries, and the old minions of the law, apparently
long decayed. The nation might well appear to itself to be in the same
situation as that mad Englishman in Bedlam, who thought he was living
in the time of the pharaohs. He moaned every day about the hard work
he had to perform as a gold-digger in the Ethiopian mines, immured in
his subterranean prison, by the exiguous light of a lamp fixed on his own
head. The overseer of the slaves stood behind him with a long whip, and
at the exits was a motley assembly of barbarian mercenaries, who had no
common language and therefore understood neither the forced labourers
in the mines nor each other. 'And I, a freeborn Briton,' sighed the mad
Englishman, 'must bear all this to make gold for the old pharaohs.' 'To
pay the debts of the Bonaparte family,' sighed the French nation. As long
as he was in his right mind, the Englishman could not free himself of the
obsession of making gold. As long as the French were engaged in revolution, they could not free themselves of the memory of Napoleon. The
election of 10 December 1848 proved this.[5] They yearned to return from
the dangers of revolution to the fleshpots of Egypt, and 2 December 1851
was the answer. They have not merely acquired a caricature of the old
Napoleon, they have the old Napoleon himself, in the caricature form he
had to take in the middle of the nineteenth century.

The social revolution of the nineteenth century can only create its
poetry from the future, not from the past. It cannot begin its own work
until it has sloughed off all its superstitious regard for the past. Earlier
revolutions have needed world-historical reminiscences to deaden their
awareness of their own content. In order to arrive at its own content the
revolution of the nineteenth century must let the dead bury their dead.
Previously the phrase transcended the content; here the content transcends the phrase.

The February revolution was a surprise attack, it took the old society *unawares*. The people proclaimed this unexpected *coup de main* to be an historic deed, the opening of a new epoch. On 2 December the February revolution was conjured away by the sleight of hand of a cardsharper. It is no longer the monarchy that appears to have been overthrown but the liberal concessions extracted from it by a century of struggle. Instead of *society* conquering a new content for itself, it only seems that the *state* has returned to its most ancient form, the unashamedly simple rule of the military sabre and the clerical cowl. The answer to the *coup de main* of February 1848 was the *coup de tête* of December 1851. Easy come, easy go! However, the intervening period has not gone unused. Between 1848 and 1851 French society, using an abbreviated because revolutionary method, caught up on the studies and experiences which would in the normal or, so to speak, textbook course of development have had to precede the February revolution if it were to do more than merely shatter the surface. Society now appears to have fallen back behind its starting-point; but in reality it must first create the revolutionary starting-point, i.e. the situation, relations, and conditions necessary for the modern revolution to become serious.

Bourgeois revolutions, such as those of the eighteenth century, storm quickly from success to success. They outdo each other in dramatic effects; men and things seem set in sparkling diamonds and each day's spirit is ecstatic. But they are short-lived; they soon reach their apogee, and society has to undergo a long period of regret until it has learned to assimilate soberly the achievements of its period of storm and stress. Proletarian revolutions, however, such as those of the nineteenth century, constantly engage in self-criticism, and in repeated interruptions of their own course. They return to what has apparently already been accomplished in order to begin the task again; with merciless thoroughness they mock the inadequate, weak and wretched aspects of their first attempts; they seem to throw their opponent to the ground only to see him draw new strength from the earth and rise again before them, more colossal than ever; they shrink back again and again before the indeterminate immensity of their own goals, until the situation is created in which any retreat is impossible, and the conditions themselves cry out:

Hic Rhodus, hic salta! Here is the rose, dance here![6]

[CLASS IDEOLOGY]

Before we follow the parliamentary history any further, some remarks are necessary in order to avoid certain common delusions about the overall character of the epoch which lies before us. If we look at this in the fashion of the democrats, the issue during the period of the Legislative National Assembly was the same issue as in the period of the Constituent

Assembly: a simple struggle between republicans and royalists. However, the democrats sum up the whole course of development itself in *one* slogan: '*reaction*' —a night in which all cats are grey and which allows them to reel off their useless platitudes. And of course an initial inspection reveals the party of Order to be a conglomeration of different royalist fractions, which not only intrigue against each other to raise their own pretender to the throne and exclude the pretender of the opposing fraction, but also unite together in a common hatred of the 'republic' and in common attacks on it. The Montagne for its part appears as the representative of the 'republic' in opposition to this royalist conspiracy. The party of Order appears to be constantly engaged in a 'reaction' directed, neither more nor less than in Prussia, against the press, the right of association, and similar things, and which is accomplished, as in Prussia, by means of the brutal police interventions of the bureaucracy, the *gendarmerie*, and the courts. The Montagne for its part is just as continually engaged in fighting off these attacks and in this way defending the 'rights of man', more or less in the same way as every so-called people's party has done for a century and a half. But this superficial appearance veils the *class struggle* and the peculiar physiognomy of this period, and it vanishes on a closer examination of the situation and the parties.

As we have said, Legitimists and Orleanists formed the two great fractions of the party of Order. Was it nothing but the *fleur de-lis* and the tricolour, the House of Bourbon and the House of Orleans, the different shades of royalism, which held the fractions fast to their pretenders and apart from each other? Was it their royalist creed at all? Under the Bourbons, *big landed property* had ruled, with its priests and lackeys; under the July monarchy, it had been high finance, large-scale industry, large-scale trade, i.e., *capital*, with its retinue of advocates, professors and fine speechmakers. The legitimate monarchy was simply the political expression of the immemorial domination of the lords of the soil, just as the July monarchy was only the political expression of the usured rule of the bourgeois parvenus. It was therefore not so-called principles which kept these fractions divided, but rather their material conditions of existence, two distinct sorts of property; it was the old opposition between town and country, the old rivalry between capital and landed property. Who would deny that at the same time old memories, personal enmities, fears and hopes, prejudices and illusions, sympathies and antipathies, convictions, articles of faith and principles bound them to one or the other royal house? A whole superstructure of different and specifically formed feelings, illusions, modes of thought and views of life arises on the basis of the different forms of property, of the social conditions of existence. The whole class creates and forms these out of its material foundations and the corresponding social relations. The single individual, who derives these feelings, etc. through tradition and upbringing, may well imagine that they form the real determinants and the starting-point of his activity. The Orleanist and Legitimist fractions each tried to make out to their opponents and themselves that they were divided by their adherence to the two royal houses; facts later proved that it was rather the division between their interests which forbade the unification of the royal houses. A distinction is made in private life between what a man thinks and says of himself and what he really is and does. In historical struggles one must make a still sharper distinction between the phrases and fantasies of the parties and their real organization and real interests, between their conception of themselves and what they really are. Orleanists and Legitimists found themselves side by side in the republic, making equal claims. Each side wanted to secure the *restoration* of its *own* royal house against the other; this had no other meaning than that each of the *two great interests* into which the bourgeoisie is divided—landed property and capital—was endeavouring to restore its own supremacy and the subordination of the other interest. We refer to the two interests of the bourgeoisie because big landed property in fact has been completely bourgeoisified by the development of modern society, despite its feudal coquetry and racial pride. The Tories in England long imagined they were enthusiastic about the monarchy, the church, and the beauties of the old English constitution, until the day of danger wrung from them the confession that they were only enthusiastic about *ground rent*.[7]

The members of the royalist coalition intrigued against each other outside parliament: in the press, at Ems, and at Claremont.[8] Behind the scenes they dressed up again in their old Orleanist and Legitimist liveries and went back to their old tournaments. But on the public stage, in their grand national performances as a great parliamentary party, they put off their respective royal houses with mere bows and adjourned the restoration of the monarchy to an indefinite point in the future. They did their real business as the *party of Order*, i.e., under a *social* and not a *political* title, as representatives of the bourgeois world order, not as knights of errant princesses, as the bourgeois class against other classes, not as royalists against republicans. And as the party of Order they ruled over the other classes of society more harshly and with less restriction than ever they could under the Restoration or the July monarchy. This was only possible given the governmental form of the parliamentary republic, for the two great subdivisions of the French bourgeoisie could only unite under this form, thus placing on the agenda the rule of their class instead of the regime of a privileged fraction of it. If, nevertheless, as the party of Order, they also insulted the republic and expressed their abhorrence of it, this did not happen merely as a result of royalist memories. They realized instinctively that although the republic made their political rule complete it simultaneously undermined its social foundation, since they had now to confront the subjugated classes and contend with them without mediation, without being concealed by the Crown, without the possibility of diverting the national attention by their secondary conflicts amongst themselves and with the monarchy. It was a feeling of weakness which caused them to recoil when faced with the pure conditions of their own class rule and to yearn for the return of the previous forms of this rule, which were less complete, less developed, and, precisely for that reason, less dangerous. But whenever the royalists in coalition came into conflict with the pretender who confronted them, with Bonaparte, whenever they thought the executive power was endangering their parliamentary omnipotence, whenever, in other words, they had to produce the political title-deeds of their domination, they came forward as *republicans*, not *royalists*, from the Orleanist Thiers, who warned the National Assembly that the republic divided them least, to the Legitimist Berryer, who, on 2 December 1851, swathed in the tricoloured sash, harangued the people assembled in front of the town hall of the tenth *arrondissement* as a tribune speaking in the name of the republic. Admittedly a mocking echo called back to him: *Henri V! Henri V!*[9]

The petty bourgeoisie and the workers had formed their own coalition, the so-called *social-democratic* party, in opposition to the coalition of the bourgeoisie. The petty bourgeoisie saw that they had done badly out of the June days. Their material interests were in danger, and the counter-revolution called into question the democratic guarantees which were supposed to secure the assertion of those interests. They therefore drew closer to the workers. Their parliamentary representatives, on the other hand, the Montagne, had improved their position. After being pushed aside during the dictatorship of the bourgeois republicans, they had reconquered their lost popularity in the latter half of the session of the Constituent Assembly by their struggle with Bonaparte and the royalist ministers. They had concluded an alliance with the socialist leaders, celebrated in February 1849 with banquets of reconciliation. A joint programme was drafted, joint election committees were set up, and joint candidates put forward. The social demands of the proletariat lost their revolutionary point and gained a democratic twist, while the democratic claims of the petty bourgeoisie were stripped of their purely political form and had their socialist point emphasized. In this way arose *social-democracy*. Apart from some working-class extras, and a few members of the socialist sects, the new Montagne, the result of this combination, contained the same elements as the old Montagne, but more of them. However, it had changed along with the class it represented in the course of historical development. The peculiar character of social-democracy can be summed up in the following way: democratic republican institutions are demanded as a means of softening the antagonism between the two extremes of capital and wage labour and transforming it into harmony, not of superseding both of them. However varied the measures proposed for achieving this goal, however much it may be edged with more or less revolutionary conceptions, its content remains the same. This content is the reformation of society by democratic means, but a reformation within the boundaries set by the petty bourgeoisie. Only one must not take the narrow view that the petty bourgeoisie explicitly sets out to assert its egoistic class interests. It rather believes that the *particular* conditions of its liberation are the only *general* conditions within which modern society can be saved and the class struggle avoided. Nor indeed must one imagine that the democratic representatives are all *shopkeepers* or their enthusiastic supporters. They may well be poles apart from them in their education and their individual situation. What makes them representatives of the petty bourgeoisie is the fact that their minds are restricted by the same barriers which the petty bourgeoisie fails to overcome in real life, and that they are therefore driven in theory to the same problems and solutions to which material interest and social situation drive the latter in practice. This is the general relationship between the *political and literary representatives* of a class and the class which they represent.

[THE ECONOMIC BASIS OF LOUIS BONAPARTE'S RULE]

The executive power possesses an immense bureaucratic and military organization, an ingenious and broadly based state machinery, and an army of half a million officials alongside the actual army, which numbers a further half million. This frightful parasitic body, which surrounds the body of French society like a caul and stops up all its pores, arose in the time of the absolute monarchy, with the decay of the feudal system, which it helped to accelerate. The seignorial privileges of the landowners and towns were transformed into attributes of the state power, the feudal dignitaries became paid officials, and the variegated medieval pattern of conflicting plenary authorities became the regulated plan of a state authority characterized by a centralization and division of labour reminiscent of a factory. The task of the first French revolution was to destroy all separate local, territorial, urban and provincial powers in order to create the civil unity of the nation. It had to carry further the centralization that the absolute monarchy had begun, but at the same time it had to develop the extent, the attributes and the number of underlings of the governmental power. Napoleon perfected this state machinery. The Legitimist and July monarchies only added a greater division of labour, which grew in proportion to the creation of new interest groups, and therefore new material for state administration, by the division of labour within bourgeois society. Every *common* interest was immediately detached from society, opposed to it as a higher, *general* interest, torn away from the self-activity of the individual members of society and made a subject for governmental activity, whether it was a bridge, a schoolhouse, the communal property of a village community, or the railways, the national wealth and the national university of France. Finally, the parliamentary republic was compelled in its struggle against the revolution to strengthen by means of repressive measures the resources and centralization of governmental power. All political upheavals perfected this machine instead of smashing it. The parties that strove in turn for mastery regarded possession of this immense state edifice as the main booty for the victor.

However, under the absolute monarchy, during the first French revolution, and under Napoleon, bureaucracy was only the means of preparing the class rule of the bourgeoisie. Under the Restoration, Louis Philippe, and the parliamentary republic, on the other hand, it was the instrument of the ruling class, however much it strove for power in its own right.

Only under the second Bonaparte does the state seem to have attained a completely autonomous position. The state machine has established itself so firmly *vis-à-vis* civil society that the only leader it needs is the head of the Society of 10 December, an adventurer who has rushed in from abroad and been chosen as leader by a drunken soldiery, which he originally bought with liquor and sausages, and to which he constantly has to throw more sausages. This explains the shamefaced despair, the feeling of terrible humiliation and degradation which weighs upon France's breast and makes her catch her breath. France feels dishonoured.

But the state power does not hover in mid-air. Bonaparte represents a class, indeed he represents the most numerous class of French society, the *small peasant proprietors*.

Just as the Bourbons were the dynasty of big landed property and the Orleans the dynasty of money, so the Bonapartes are the dynasty of the peasants, i.e., of the mass of the French people. The chosen hero of the peasantry is not the Bonaparte who submitted to the bourgeois parliament but the Bonaparte who dispersed it. For three years the towns succeeded in falsifying the meaning of the election of 10 December and swindling the peasants out of the restoration of the empire. The election of 10 December 1848 was completed only with the coup d'état of 2 December 1851.

The small peasant proprietors form an immense mass, the members of which live in the same situation but do not enter into manifold relationships with each other. Their mode of operation isolates them instead of bringing them into mutual intercourse. This isolation is strengthened by the wretched state of France's means of communication and by the poverty of the peasants. Their place of operation, the smallholding, permits no division of labour in its cultivation, no application of science and therefore no diversity of development, variety of talent, or wealth of social relationships. Each individual peasant family is almost self-sufficient; it directly produces the greater part of its own consumption and therefore obtains its means of life more through exchange with nature than through intercourse with society. The smallholding, the peasant, and the family; next door, another smallholding, another peasant, and another family. A bunch of these makes up a village, and a bunch of villages makes up a department. Thus the great mass of the French nation is formed by the simple addition of isomorphous magnitudes, much as potatoes in a sack form a sack of potatoes. In so far as millions of families live under economic conditions of existence that separate their mode of life, their interests and their cultural formation from those of the other classes and bring them into conflict with those classes, they form a class. In so far as these small peasant proprietors are merely connected on a local basis, and the identity of their interests fails to produce a feeling of community, national links, or a political organization, they do not form a class. They are therefore incapable of asserting their class interest in their own name, whether through a parliament or through a convention. They cannot represent themselves; they must be represented. Their representative must appear simultaneously as their master, as an authority over them, an unrestricted governmental power that protects them from the other classes and sends them rain and sunshine from above. The political influence of the small peasant proprietors is therefore ultimately expressed in the executive subordinating society to itself.

Historical tradition produced the French peasants' belief that a miracle would occur, that a man called Napoleon would restore all their glory. And an individual turned up who pretended to be that man, because he bore the name of Napoleon, thanks to the stipulation of the Code Napoléon that *'la récherche de la paternité est interdite'*. After twenty years of vagabondage and a series of grotesque adventures the prophecy was fulfilled and the man became Emperor of the French. The nephew's obsession was realized, because it coincided with the obsession of the most numerous class of the French people.

But the objection will be made: What about the peasant risings in half of France, the army's murderous forays against them, and their imprisonment and transportation *en masse*?

Since Louis XIV, France has experienced no corresponding persecution of the peasants 'for demagogic practices'.

This point should be clearly understood: the Bonaparte dynasty represents the conservative, not the revolutionary peasant: the peasant who wants to consolidate the condition of his social existence, the smallholding, not the peasant who strikes out beyond it. It does not represent the country people who want to overthrow the older order by their own energies, in alliance with the towns, but the precise opposite, those who are gloomily enclosed within this old order and want to see themselves and their smallholdings saved and given preferential treatment by the ghost of the Empire. It represents the peasant's superstition, not his enlightenment; his prejudice, not his judgement; his past, not his future; his modern Vendée, not his modern Cevennes.[10]

NOTES TO "THE EIGHTEENTH BRUMAIRE OF LOUIS BONAPARTE"

1. The passage Marx seems to have in mind is the following: "In all periods of the world a political revolution is sanctioned in men's opinions, when it repeats itself. Thus Napoleon was twice defeated, and the Bourbons twice expelled." Hegel, *The Philosophy of History*, tr. J. Sibree, p. 313.
2. Georges Jacques Danton (1759–1794), leader of the right wing of the Jacobin party in the French Revolution of 1789, guillotined in 1794; Maximilien Robespierre (1758–1794), Jacobin and leader of the French revolutionary government (1793–1794), guillotined in 1794; Marc Caussidière (1808–1861), active in the French revolution of 1848, exiled to England after the June insurrection; Louis Blanc (1811–1882), socialist member of the Provisional Government in the French revolution of 1848. Marx is drawing a parallel between the French Revolutions of 1789 and 1848: Caussidière is to Danton, as Louis Blanc is to Robespierre, as Louis Napoleon (the Nephew) is to Napoleon I (the Uncle). The Montagne was in both revolutions a democratic faction (so named because its seats in the Legislative Assembly were above those of the other groups); Marx sees the Montagne of 1848 as a representative of petty bourgeois class interests.
3. Jean-Baptiste Say (1767–1832), a French political economist and popularizer of the theories of Adam Smith; Victor Cousin (1792–1867), a French philosopher and political moderate, who was French Minister of Education in 1840; Pierre-Paul Royer-Collard (1763–1845), a political theorist and politician under the Restoration and July monarchy, a defender of moderate constitutional monarchy; Benjamin Constant (1767–1830), French liberal politician, philosopher and novelist, a leading opponent of the Bourbon Restoration in the 1820s; Francois Pierre Guillaume Guizot (1787–1874), French historian and statesman, active in the Second Republic, precursor of Marx's view that the key to modern political history is the struggle of economic classes.
4. Armand Marrast (1801–1852), French republican politician, editor of the newspaper *Le National*, member of the Provisional Government, mayor of Paris and President of the Constituent Assembly during the Second Republic (1848–1849); Jean Sylvain Bailly (1736–1793), a leader of the constitutionalist faction in the first French Revolution, guillotined in 1793.
5. Louis Bonaparte was elected President of the French Republic on December 10, 1848.
6. The quotation is from one of Aesop's fables, a reply to a braggart who claimed he had once made an immense leap in Rhodes. It signifies a challenge to one who claims to be equal to some demanding task. But *Rhodos* can mean either "Rhodes" or "rose," and *salta* can mean either "jump" or "dance." In the Preface to *The Philosophy of Right*, Hegel used these puns to suggest that the real task confronting philosophy of the state is to show people "the rose in the cross of

the present," the substance of rational actuality hidden beneath the defects of transitory political reality, so that they may find satisfaction in the state as it is. Marx is now putting the same puns to a different use, suggesting that the proletariat rejoices in the world-historical challenge set for it by its historic mission.

7. In 1846, the Corn Laws (protectionist measures benefitting landed interests in England) were abolished. The Tory party thereupon changed its name to the Protectionist Party, and campaigned for some years on the single issue of restoring the Corn Laws, which would have the effect of keeping ground rents high.

8. Ems, near Wiesbaden, was the residence of the comte de Chambord, the Legitimist claimant to the French throne; Claremont, near London, was the residence of the Orleanist monarch Louis Philippe since his overthrow in 1848.

9. Adolphe Thiers (1797–1877), French historian and Orleanist statesman, later President of the Third Republic which suppressed the Paris Commune; Pierre Antoine Berryer (1790–1868), Legitimist politician; Henri V: Henri Charles d'Artois, comte de Cambord, grandson of Charles X and Legitimist claimant to the throne. The point of the "echo" is that the Legitimist Berryer was an unconvincing republican at best.

10. Vendee, in Brittany, was the cite of a royalist peasant revolt during the first French revolution; Cevennes was the region of southern France where in 1702 there was a rising of Protestants in behalf of freedom of conscience and against feudal tithes. Marx's point is that Louis Bonaparte appeals to the reactionary, not to the progressive, peasant.

Toward a Critique of Political Economy: Preface (1859) (*Complete*)

After nearly a decade spent in London, studying the political economy of modern capitalism under the most adverse circumstances, Marx finally published his first book on the subject in 1859. Its Preface contains a valuable account of the development of his thought to that point and a succinct summary of the materialist conception of history. Translated from the German by S. W. Ryazanskaya, translation edited by Maurice Dobb.

I examine the system of bourgeois economy in the following order: *capital, landed property, wage-labour; the State, foreign trade, world market.* The economic conditions of existence of the three great classes into which modern bourgeois society is divided are analysed under the first three headings; the interconnection of the other three headings is self-evident. The first part of the first book, dealing with Capital, comprises the following chapters: 1. The commodity; 2. Money or simple circulation; 3. Capital in general. The present part consists of the first two chapters. The entire material lies before me in the form of monographs, which were written not for publication but for self-clarification at widely separated periods; their remoulding into an integrated whole according to the plan I have indicated will depend upon circumstances.

A general introduction[1], which I had drafted, is omitted, since on further consideration it seems to me confusing to anticipate results which still have to be substantiated, and the reader who really wishes to follow me will have to decide to advance from the particular to the general. A few brief remarks regarding the course of my study of political economy may, however, be appropriate here.

Although I studied jurisprudence, I pursued it as a subject subordinated to philosophy and history. In the year 1842–43, as editor of the *Rheinische Zeitung*, I first found myself in the embarrassing position of having to discuss what is known as material interests. The deliberations of the Rhenish Landtag on forest thefts and the division of landed property; the official polemic started by Herr von Schaper, then Oberpräsident of the Rhine Province, against the *Rheinische Zeitung* about the condition of the

Moselle peasantry, and finally the debates on free trade and protective tariffs caused me in the first instance to turn my attention to economic questions. On the other hand, at that time when good intentions "to push forward" often took the place of factual knowledge, an echo of French socialism and communism, slightly tinged by philosophy, was noticeable in the *Rheinische Zeitung*. I objected to this dilettantism, but at the same time frankly admitted in a controversy with the *Allgemeine Augsburger Zeitung* that my previous studies did not allow me to express any opinion on the content of the French theories. When the publishers of the *Rheinische Zeitung* conceived the illusion that by a more compliant policy on the part of the paper it might be possible to secure the abrogation of the death sentence passed upon it, I eagerly grasped the opportunity to withdraw from the public stage to my study.[2]

The first work which I undertook to dispel the doubts assailing me was a critical re-examination of the Hegelian philosophy of law; the introduction to this work being published in the *Deutsch-Französische Jahrbücher* issued in Paris in 1844.[3] My inquiry led me to the conclusion that neither legal relations nor political forms could be comprehended whether by themselves or on the basis of a so-called general development of the human mind, but that on the contrary they originate in the material conditions of life, the totality of which Hegel, following the example of English and French thinkers of the eighteenth century, embraces within the term "civil society"; that the anatomy of this civil society, however, has to be sought in political economy. The study of this, which I began in Paris, I continued in Brussels, where I moved owing to an expulsion order issued by M. Guizot.[4] The general conclusion at which I arrived and which, once reached, became the guiding principle of my studies can be summarised as follows. In the social production of their existence, men inevitably enter into definite relations, which are independent of their will, namely relations of production appropriate to a given stage in the development of their material forces of production. The totality of these relations of production constitutes the economic structure of society, the real foundation, on which arises a legal and political superstructure and to which correspond definite forms of social consciousness. The mode of production of material life conditions the general process of social, political and intellectual life. It is not the consciousness of men that determines their existence, but their social existence that determines their consciousness. At a certain stage of development, the material productive forces of society come into conflict with the existing relations of production or—this merely expresses the same thing in legal terms—with the property relations within the framework of which they have operated hitherto. From forms of development of the productive forces these relations turn into their fetters. Then begins an era of social revolution. The changes in the economic foundation lead sooner or later to the transformation of the whole immense superstructure. In studying such transformations it is always necessary to distinguish between the material transformation of the economic conditions of production, which can be determined with the precision of natural science, and the legal, political, religious, artistic or philosophic—in short, ideological forms in which men become conscious of this conflict and fight it out. Just as one does not judge an individual by what he thinks about himself, so one cannot judge such a period of transformation by its consciousness, but, on the contrary, this consciousness must be explained from the contradictions of material life, from the conflict existing between the social forces of production and the relations of production. No social order is ever destroyed before all the productive forces for which it is sufficient have been developed, and new superior relations of production never replace older ones before the material conditions for their existence have matured within the framework of the old society. Mankind thus inevitably sets itself only such tasks as it is able to solve, since closer examination will always show that the problem itself arises only when the material conditions for its solution are already present or at least in the course of formation. In broad outline, the Asiatic, ancient, feudal and modern bourgeois modes of production may be designated as epochs marking progress in the economic development of society. The bourgeois mode of production is the last antagonistic form of the social process of production—antagonistic not in the sense of individual antagonism but of an antagonism that emanates from the individuals' social conditions of existence—but the productive forces developing within bourgeois society create also the material conditions for a solution of this antagonism. The prehistory of human society accordingly closes with this social formation.

Frederick Engels, with whom I maintained a constant exchange of ideas by correspondence since the publication of his brilliant essay on the critique of economic categories[5] (printed in the *Deutsch-Französische Jahrbücher*), arrived by another road (compare his *Lage der arbeitenden Klasse in England*[6]) at the same result as I, and when in the spring of 1845 he too came to live in Brussels, we decided to set forth together our conception as opposed to the ideological one of German philosophy, in fact to settle accounts with our former philosophical conscience. The intention was carried out in the form of a critique of post-Hegelian philosophy.[7] The manuscript, two large octavo volumes, had long ago reached the publishers in Westphalia when we were informed that owing to changed circumstances it could not be printed. We abandoned the manuscript to the gnawing criticism of the mice all the more willingly since we had achieved our main purpose—self-clarification. Of the scattered works in which at that time we presented one or another aspect of our views to the public, I shall mention only the *Manifesto of the Communist Party*, jointly written by Engels and myself, and a *Discours sur le libre échange*, which I myself published. The salient points of our conception were first outlined

in an academic, although polemical, form in my *Misère de la philosophie*
. . . , this book which was aimed at Proudhon appeared in 1847. The
publication of an essay on *Wage-Labour*[8] written in German in which I
combined the lectures I had held on this subject at the German Workers'
Association in Brussels, was interrupted by the February Revolution and
my forcible removal from Belgium in consequence.

The publication of the *Neue Rheinische Zeitung*[9] in 1848 and 1849 and
subsequent events cut short my economic studies, which I could only
resume in London in 1850. The enormous amount of material relating to
the history of political economy assembled in the British Museum, the
fact that London is a convenient vantage point for the observation of
bourgeois society, and finally the new stage of development which this
society seemed to have entered with the discovery of gold in California
and Australia, induced me to start again from the very beginning and to
work carefully through the new material. These studies led partly of their
own accord to apparently quite remote subjects on which I had to spend
a certain amount of time. But it was in particular the imperative necessity
of earning my living which reduced the time at my disposal. My collaboration, continued now for eight years, with the *New York Tribune*,[10] the
leading Anglo-American newspaper, necessitated an excessive fragmentation of my studies, for I wrote only exceptionally newspaper correspondence in the strict sense. Since a considerable part of my contributions
consisted of articles dealing with important economic events in Britain
and on the Continent, I was compelled to become conversant with practical detail which, strictly speaking, lie outside the sphere of political
economy.

This sketch of the course of my studies in the domain of political
economy is intended merely to show that my views—no matter how they
may be judged and how little they conform to the interested prejudices
of the ruling classes—are the outcome of conscientious research carried
on over many years. At the entrance to science, as at the entrance to hell,
the demand must be made:

> *Qui si convien lasciare ogni sospetto*
> *Ogni viltà convien che qui sia morta.*[11]
> KARL MARX

NOTES TO "TOWARD A CRITIQUE OF POLITICAL ECONOMY: PREFACE"

1. This introduction is included in the *Grundrisse*.
2. Marx edited the *Rheinische Zeitung* from April, 1842 until March, 1843. The
   Augsburger Allgemeine Zeitung was a reactionary newspaper to whose criticisms
   of French utopian communism Marx replied in an 1843 article.

3. The article referred to is "Toward a Critique of Hegel's *Philosophy of Right*: Introduction," above, pp. 23–35.
4. Francois Pierre Guillaume Guizot (1787–1874), French historian and statesman, active in the Second Republic, precursor of Marx's view that the key to modern political history is the struggle of economic classes.
5. Friedrich Engels, "Outlines of a Critique of Political Economy," *German-French Annals* (1844).
6. Friedrich Engels, *The Condition of the Working Class in England* (1845).
7. Marx and Engels, *The German Ideology* (1845–1846).
8. Marx, *Wage Labor and Capital* (1847).
9. The *Neue Rheinische Zeitung* was the radical newspaper Marx edited in Cologne during the revolution of 1848–1849.
10. Marx served as European correspondent for Horace Greeley's *New York Tribune* throughout the 1850s, writing articles for £1 apiece.

11.   "Here must be abandoned all distrust,
       All cowardice must here be dead.
               —Dante, *The Divine Comedy.*
                        Inferno 3:13

III

Communism and the
Working Class Movement

(1848–1875)

Marx and Engels
Manifesto of the Communist Party (1848)
(*Complete*)

In 1836 some German workers living in Paris formed a secret conspiratorial organization called "The League of the Just". Engels was invited to join the organization in 1843, but refused. In 1847 Marx and Engels, then living in Brussels, were approached again, but this time asked to help refound the League and to prepare a statement of principles for it. At a congress in London in 1847, the name was changed to "the Communist League" and the secret, conspiratorial intent of the organization was repudiated. Engels drafted a statement of principles and even a catechism for the League, but Marx is thought to have done most of the writing of the *Communist Manifesto*, first published in London in February, 1848, on the eve of the Paris Revolution (a French translation was available in time to influence the June insurrection). The League lasted until 1850, but the *Manifesto* has gone through countless editions in many languages, and its influence is perhaps unequalled by any other comparable political document of modern times. The reasons for this are not far to seek. The *Communist Manifesto* is a masterpiece of popular political writing; at the same time, it is the single most comprehensive statement of the Marxian theory of the modern class struggle and the definitive call to arms of the revolutionary working class. The text printed here follows the English edition of 1888.

A spectre is haunting Europe—the spectre of Communism. All the Powers of old Europe have entered into a holy alliance to exorcise this spectre: Pope and Czar, Metternich and Guizot, French Radicals and German police-spies.

Where is the party in opposition that has not been decried as Communistic by its opponents in power? Where the Opposition that has not hurled back the branding reproach of Communism, against the more advanced opposition parties, as well as against its reactionary adversaries?

Two things result from this fact:

I. Communism is already acknowledged by all European Powers to be itself a Power.

II. It is high time that Communists should openly, in the face of the whole world, publish their views, their aims, their tendencies, and meet this nursery tale of the Spectre of Communism with a Manifesto of the party itself.

To this end, Communists of various nationalities have assembled in London, and sketched the following Manifesto, to be published in the English, French, German, Italian, Flemish and Danish languages.

I
BOURGEOIS AND PROLETARIANS[a]

The history of all hitherto existing society[b] is the history of class struggles.

Freeman and slave, patrician and plebeian, lord and serf, guild-master[c] and journeyman, in a word, oppressor and oppressed, stood in constant opposition to one another, carried on an uninterrupted, now hidden, now open fight, a fight that each time ended, either in a revolutionary reconstitution of society at large, or in the common ruin of the contending classes.

In the earlier epochs of history, we find almost everywhere a complicated arrangement of society into various orders, a manifold gradation of social rank. In ancient Rome we have patricians, knights, plebeians, slaves; in the Middle Ages, feudal lords, vassals, guild-masters, journeymen, apprentices, serfs; in almost all of these classes, again, subordinate gradations.

The modern bourgeois society that has sprouted from the ruins of feudal society has not done away with class antagonisms. It has but established new classes, new conditions of oppression, new forms of struggle in place of the old ones.

Our epoch, the epoch of the bourgeoisie, possesses, however, this distinctive feature: it has simplified the class antagonisms. Society as a whole

[a] By bourgeoisie is meant the class of modern Capitalists, owners of the means of social production and employers of wage-labour. By proletariat, the class of modern wage-labourers who, having no means of production of their own, are reduced to selling their labour-power in order to live. [*Note by Engels to the English edition of 1888.*]

[b] That is, all *written* history. In 1847, the pre-history of society, the social organization existing previous to recorded history, was all but unknown. Since then, Haxthausen discovered common ownership of land in Russia, Maurer proved it to be the social foundation from which all Teutonic races started in history, and by and by village communities were found to be, or to have been the primitive form of society everywhere from India to Ireland. The inner organisation of this primitive Communistic society was laid bare, in its typical form, by Morgan's crowning discovery of the true nature of the *gens* and its relation to the *tribe*. With the dissolution of these primeval communities society begins to be differentiated into separate and finally antagonistic classes. I have attempted to retrace this process of dissolution in *Der Ursprung der Familie, des Privateigenthums und des Staats*, 2nd edition, Stuttgart, 1886. [*Note by Engels to the English edition of 1888, and—less the last sentence—to the German edition of 1890.*]

[c] Guild-master, that is, a full member of a guild, a master within, not a head of a guild. [*Note by Engels to the English edition of 1888.*]

is more and more splitting up into two great hostile camps, into two great classes directly facing each other: Bourgeoisie and Proletariat.

From the serfs of the Middle Ages sprang the chartered burghers of the earliest towns. From these burgesses the first elements of the bourgeoisie were developed.

The discovery of America, the rounding of the Cape, opened up fresh ground for the rising bourgeoisie. The East-Indian and Chinese markets, the colonisation of America, trade with the colonies, the increase in the means of exchange and in commodities generally, gave to commerce, to navigation, to industry, an impulse never before known, and thereby, to the revolutionary element in the tottering feudal society, a rapid development.

The feudal system of industry, under which industrial production was monopolised by closed guilds now no longer sufficed for the growing wants of the new markets. The manufacturing system took its place. The guild-masters were pushed on one side by the manufacturing middle class; division of labour between the different corporate guilds vanished in the face of division of labour in each single workshop.

Meantime the markets kept ever growing, the demand ever rising. Even manufacture no longer sufficed. Thereupon, steam and machinery revolutionised industrial production. The place of manufacture was taken by the giant, Modern Industry, the place of the industrial middle class, by industrial millionaires, the leaders of whole industrial armies, the modern bourgeois.

Modern industry has established the world market, for which the discovery of America paved the way. This market has given an immense development to commerce, to navigation, to communication by land. This development has, in its turn, reacted on the extension of industry; and in proportion as industry, commerce, navigation, railways extended, in the same proportion the bourgeoisie developed, increased its capital, and pushed into the background every class handed down from the Middle Ages.

We see, therefore, how the modern bourgeoisie is itself the product of a long course of development, of a series of revolutions in the modes of production and of exchange.

Each step in the development of the bourgeoisie was accompanied by a corresponding political advance of that class. An oppressed class under the sway of the feudal nobility an armed and self-governing association in the medieval commune[d]; here independent urban republic (as in Italy

---

[d] "Commune" was the name taken, in France, by the nascent towns even before they had conquered from their feudal lords and masters local self-government and political rights as the "Third Estate". Generally speaking, for the economical development of the bourgeoisie, England is here taken as the typical country; for its political development, France. [*Note by Engels to the English edition of 1888.*]

and Germany), there taxable "third estate" of the monarchy (as in France), afterwards, in the period of manufacture proper, serving either the semi-feudal or the absolute monarchy as a counterpoise against the nobility, and, in fact, cornerstone of the great monarchies in general, the bourgeoisie has at last, since the establishment of Modern Industry and of the world market, conquered for itself, in the modern representative State, exclusive political sway. The executive of the modern State is but a committee for managing the common affairs of the whole bourgeoisie.

The bourgeoisie, historically, has played a most revolutionary part.

The bourgeoisie, wherever it has got the upper hand, has put an end to all feudal, patriarchal, idyllic relations. It has pitilessly torn asunder the motely feudal ties that bound man to his "natural superiors", and has left remaining no other nexus between man and man than naked self-interest, than callous "cash payment". It has drowned the most heavenly ecstasies of religious fervour, of chivalrous enthusiasm, of philistine sentimentalism, in the icy water of egotistical calculation. It has resolved personal worth into exchange value, and in place of the numberless indefeasible chartered freedoms, has set up that single, unconscionable freedom—Free Trade. In one word, for exploitation, veiled by religious and political illusions, it has substituted naked, shameless, direct, brutal exploitation.

The bourgeoisie has stripped of its halo every occupation hitherto honoured and looked up to with reverent awe. It has converted the physician, the lawyer, the priest, the poet, the man of science, into its paid wage-labourers.

The bourgeoisie has torn away from the family its sentimental veil, and has reduced the family relation to a mere money relation.

The bourgeoisie has disclosed how it came to pass that the brutal display of vigour in the Middle Ages, which Reactionists so much admire, found its fitting complement in the most slothful indolence. It has been the first to show what man's activity can bring about. It has accomplished wonders far surpassing Egyptian pyramids, Roman aqueducts, and Gothic cathedrals; it has conducted expeditions that put in the shade all former Exoduses of nations and crusades.

The bourgeoisie cannot exist without constantly revolutionising the instruments of production, and thereby the relations of production, and with them the whole relations of society. Conservation of the old modes of production in unaltered form, was, on the contrary, the first condition of existence for all earlier industrial classes. Constant revolutionising of production, uninterrupted disturbance of all social conditions, everlasting uncertainty and agitation distinguish the bourgeois epoch from all earlier ones. All fixed, fast-frozen relations, with their train of ancient and venerable prejudices and opinions, are swept away, all new-formed ones become antiquated before they can ossify. All that is solid melts into air, all that is holy is profaned, and man is at last compelled to face with sober senses, his real conditions of life, and his relations with his kind.

The need of a constantly expanding market for its products chases the bourgeoisie over the whole surface of the globe. It must nestle, everywhere, settle everywhere, establish connexions everywhere.

The bourgeoisie has through its exploitation of the world market given a cosmopolitan character to production and consumption in every country. To the great chagrin of Reactionists, it has drawn from under the feet of industry the national ground on which it stood. All old-established national industries have been destroyed or are daily being destroyed. They are dislodged by new industries, whose introduction becomes a life and death question for all civilised nations, by industries that no longer work up indigenous raw material, but raw material drawn from the remotest zones; industries whose products are consumed, not only at home, but in every quarter of the globe. In place of the old wants, satisfied by the productions of the country, we find new wants, requiring for their satisfaction the products of distant lands and climes. In place of the old local and national seclusion and self-sufficiency, we have intercourse in every direction, universal inter-dependence of nations. And as in material, so also in intellectual production. The intellectual creations of individual nations become common property. National one-sidedness and narrow-mindedness become more and more impossible, and from the numerous national and local literatures, there arises a world literature.

The bourgeoisie, by the rapid improvement of all instruments of production, by the immensely facilitated means of communication, draws all, even the most barbarian, nations into civilisation. The cheap prices of its commodities are the heavy artillery with which it batters down all Chinese walls, with which it forces the barbarians' intensely obstinate hatred of foreigners to capitulate. It compels all nations, on pain of extinction, to adopt the bourgeois mode of production; it compels them to introduce what it calls civilisation into their midst, i.e., to become bourgeois themselves. In one word, it creates a world after its own image.

The bourgeoisie has subjected the country to the rule of the towns. It has created enormous cities, has greatly increased the urban population as compared with the rural, and has thus rescued a considerable part of the population from the idiocy of rural life. Just as it has made the country dependent on the towns, so it has made barbarian and semi-barbarian countries dependent on the civilised ones, nations of peasants on nations of bourgeois, the East on the West.

The bourgeoisie keeps more and more doing away with the scattered state of the population, of the means of production, and of property. It has agglomerated population, centralised means of production, and has concentrated property in a few hands. The necessary consequence of this was political centralisation. Independent, or but loosely connected provinces with separate interests, laws, governments and systems of taxation, became lumped together into one nation, with one government, one code of laws, one national class-interest, one frontier and one customs-tariff.

The bourgeoisie, during its rule of scarce one hundred years, has created more massive and more colossal productive forces than have all preceding generations together. Subjection of Nature's forces to man, machinery, application of chemistry to industry and agriculture, steam-navigation, railways, electric telegraphs, clearing of whole continents for cultivation, canalisation of rivers, whole populations conjured out of the ground—what earlier century had even a presentiment that such productive forces slumbered in the lap of social labour?

We see then: the means of production and of exchange, on whose foundation the bourgeoisie built itself up, were generated in feudal society. At a certain stage in the development of these means of production and of exchange, the conditions under which feudal society produced and exchanged, the feudal organization of agriculture and manufacturing industry, in one word, the feudal relations of property became no longer compatible with the already developed productive forces; they became so many fetters. They had to be burst asunder; they were burst asunder.

Into their place stepped free competition, accompanied by a social and political constitution adapted to it, and by the economical and political sway of the bourgeois class.

A similar movement is going on before our own eyes. Modern bourgeois society with its relations of production, of exchange and of property, a society that has conjured up such gigantic means of production and of exchange, is like the sorcerer, who is no longer able to control the powers of the nether world whom he has called up by his spells. For many a decade past the history of industry and commerce is but the history of the revolt of modern productive forces against modern conditions of production, against the property relations that are the conditions for the existence of the bourgeoisie and of its rule. It is enough to mention the commercial crises that by their periodical return put on its trial, each time more threateningly, the existence of the entire bourgeois society. In these crises a great part not only of the existing products, but also of the previously created productive forces, are periodically destroyed. In these crises there breaks out an epidemic that, in all earlier epochs, would have seemed an absurdity—the epidemic of over-production. Society suddenly finds itself put back into a state of momentary barbarism; it appears as if a famine, a universal war of devastation had cut off the supply of every means of subsistence; industry and commerce seem to be destroyed; and why? Because there is too much civilisation, too much means of subsistence, too much industry, too much commerce. The productive forces at the disposal of society no longer tend to further the development of the conditions of bourgeois property; on the contrary, they have become too powerful for these conditions, by which they are fettered, and so soon as they overcome these fetters, they bring disorder into the whole of bourgeois society, endanger the existence of bourgeois property. The conditions of bourgeois society are too narrow to comprise the wealth created by them. And how does the bourgeoisie get over these crises? On the one hand by enforced destruction of a mass of productive forces; on the other, by the conquest of new markets, and by the more thorough exploitation of the old ones. That is to say, by paving the way for more extensive and more destructive crises, and by diminishing the means whereby crises are prevented.

The weapons with which the bourgeoisie felled feudalism to the ground are now turned against the bourgeoisie itself.

But not only has the bourgeoisie forged the weapons that bring death to itself; it has also called into existence the men who are to wield those weapons—the modern working class—the proletarians.

In proportion as the bourgeoisie, i.e., capital, is developed, in the same proportion is the proletariat, the modern working class, developed—a class of labourers, who live only so long as they find work, and who find work only so long as their labour increases capital. These labourers, who must sell themselves piecemeal, are a commodity, like every other article of commerce, and are consequently exposed to all the vicissitudes of competition, to all the fluctuations of the market.

Owing to the extensive use of machinery and to division of labour, the work of the proletarians has lost all individual character, and, consequently, all charm for the workman. He becomes an appendage of the machine, and it is only the most simple, most monotonous and most easily acquired knack, that is required of him. Hence, the cost of production of a workman is restricted, almost entirely, to the means of subsistence that he requires for his maintenance, and for the propagation of his race. But the price of a commodity, and therefore also of labour, is equal to its cost of production. In proportion, therefore, as the repulsiveness of the work increases, the wage decreases. Nay more, in proportion as the use of machinery and division of labour increases, in the same proportion the burden of toil also increases, whether by prolongation of the working hours by increase of the work exacted in a given time or by increased speed of the machinery, etc.

Modern industry has converted the little workshop of the patriarchal master into the great factory of the industrial capitalist. Masses of labourers, crowded into the factory, are organized like soldiers. As privates of the industrial army they are placed under the command of a perfect hierarchy of officers and sergeants. Not only are they slaves of the bourgeois class, and of the bourgeois State; they are daily and hourly enslaved by the machine, by the overlooker, and, above all, by the individual bourgeois manufacturer himself. The more openly this despotism proclaims gain to be its end and aim, the more petty, the more hateful and the more embittering it is.

The less the skill and exertion of strength implied in manual labour, in other words, the more modern industry becomes developed, the more is the labour of men superseded by that of women. Differences of age and sex have no longer any distinctive social validity for the working class. All are instruments of labour, more or less expensive to use, according to their age and sex.

No sooner is the exploitation of the labourer by the manufacturer, so far, at an end, and he receives his wages in cash, than he is set upon by the other portions of the bourgeoisie, the landlord, the shopkeeper, the pawnbroker, etc.

The lower strata of the middle class—the small tradespeople, shopkeepers. and retired tradesmen generally, the handicraftsmen and peasants—all these sink gradually into the proletariat, partly because their diminutive capital does not suffice for the scale on which Modern Industry is carried on, and is swamped in the competition with the large capitalists, partly because their specialised skill is rendered worthless by new methods of production. Thus the proletariat is recruited from all classes of the population.

The proletariat goes through various stages of development. With its birth begins its struggle with the bourgeoisie. At first the contest is carried on by individual labourers, then by the workpeople of a factory, then by the operatives of one trade, in one locality, against the individual bourgeois who directly exploits them. They direct their attacks not against the bourgeois conditions of production, but against the instruments of production themselves; they destroy imported wares that compete with their labour, they smash to pieces machinery, they set factories ablaze, they seek to restore by force the vanished status of the workman of the Middle Ages.

At this stage the labourers still form an incoherent mass scattered over the whole country, and broken up by their mutual competition. If anywhere they unite to form more compact bodies, this is not yet the consequence of their own active union, but of the union of the bourgeoisie, which class, in order to attain its own political ends, is compelled to set the whole proletariat in motion, and is moreover yet, for a time, able to do so. At this stage, therefore, the proletarians do not fight their enemies, but the enemies of their enemies, the remnants of absolute monarchy, the landowners, the non-industrial bourgeois, the petty bourgeoisie. Thus the whole historical movement is concentrated in the hands of the bourgeoisie; every victory so obtained is a victory for the bourgeoisie.

But with the development of industry the proletariat not only increases in number; it becomes concentrated in greater masses, its strength grows, and it feels that strength more. The various interests and conditions of life within the ranks of the proletariat are more and more equalised, in proportion as machinery obliterates all distinctions of labour, and nearly everywhere reduces wages to the same low level. The growing competition among the bourgeois, and the resulting commercial crises, make the wages of the workers ever more fluctuating. The unceasing improvement of machinery, ever more rapidly developing, makes their livelihood more and more precarious; the collisions between individual workmen and individual bourgeois take more and more the character of collisions between two classes. Thereupon the workers begin to form combinations (Trade Unions) against the bourgeois; they club together in order to keep up the rate of wages; they found permanent associations in order to make provision beforehand for these occasional revolts. Here and there the contest breaks out into riots.

Now and then the workers are victorious, but only for a time. The real fruit of their battles lies, not in the immediate result, but in the ever-expanding union of the workers. This union is helped on by the improved means of communication that are created by modern industry and that place the workers of different localities in contact with one another. It was just this contact that was needed to centralise the numerous local struggles, all of the same character, into one national struggle between classes. But every class struggle is a political struggle. And that union, to attain which the burghers of the Middle Ages, with their miserable highways, required centuries, the modern proletarians, thanks to railways, achieve in a few years.

This organisation of the proletarians into a class, and consequently into a political party, is continually being upset again by the competition between the workers themselves. But it ever rises up again, stronger, firmer, mightier. It compels legislative recognition of particular interests of the workers, by taking advantage of the divisions among the bourgeoisie itself. Thus the ten-hours' bill in England was carried.[1]

Altogether collisions between the classes of the old society further, in many ways, the course of development of the proletariat. The bourgeoisie finds itself involved in a constant battle. At first with the aristocracy; later on, with those portions of the bourgeoisie itself, whose interests have become antagonistic to the progress of industry; at all times, with the bourgeoisie of foreign countries. In all these battles it sees itself compelled to appeal to the proletariat, to ask for its help, and thus, to drag it into the political arena. The bourgeoisie itself, therefore, supplies the proletariat with its own elements of political and general education, in other words, it furnishes the proletariat with weapons for fighting the bourgeoisie.

Further, as we have already seen, entire sections of the ruling classes are, by the advance of industry, precipitated into the proletariat, or are at least threatened in their conditions of existence. These also supply the proletariat with fresh elements of enlightenment and progress.

Finally, in times when the class struggle nears the decisive hour, the process of dissolution going on within the ruling class, in fact within the whole range of old society, assumes such a violent, glaring character, that a small section of the ruling class cuts itself adrift, and joins the revolutionary class, the class that holds the future in its hands. Just as, therefore, at an earlier period, a section of the nobility went over to the bourgeoisie, so now a portion of the bourgeoisie goes over to the proletariat, and in particular, a portion of the bourgeois ideologists, who have raised themselves to the level of comprehending theoretically the historical movement as a whole.

Of all the classes that stand face to face with the bourgeoisie today, the proletariat alone is a really revolutionary class. The other classes decay and finally disappear in the face of Modern Industry; the proletariat is its special and essential product.

The lower middle class, the small manufacturer, the shopkeeper, the artisan, the peasant, all these fight against the bourgeoisie, to save from extinction their existence as fractions of the middle class. They are therefore not revolutionary, but conservative. Nay more, they are reactionary, for they try to roll back the wheel of history. If by chance they are revolutionary, they are so only in view of their impending transfer into the proletariat, they thus defend not their present, but their future interests, they desert their own standpoint to place themselves at that of the proletariat.

The "dangerous class", the social scum, that passively rotting mass thrown off by the lowest layers of old society may, here and there, be swept into the movement by a proletarian revolution; its conditions of life, however, prepare it far more for the part of a bribed tool of reactionary intrigue.

In the conditions of the proletariat, those of old society at large are already virtually swamped. The proletarian is without property; his relation to his wife and children has no longer anything in common with the bourgeois family relations; modern industrial labour, modern subjection to capital, the same in England as in France, in America as in Germany, has stripped him of every trace of national character. Law, morality, religion, are to him so many bourgeois prejudices, behind which lurk in ambush just as many bourgeois interests.

All the preceding classes that got the upper hand, sought to fortify their already acquired status by subjecting society at large to their conditions of appropriation. The proletarians cannot become masters of the productive forces of society, except by abolishing their own previous mode of appropriation, and thereby also every other previous mode of appropriation. They have nothing of their own to secure and to fortify; their mission is to destroy all previous securities for, and insurances of, individual property.

All previous historical movements were movements of minorities, or in the interest of minorities. The proletarian movement is the self-conscious independent movement of the immense majority, in the interest of the immense majority. The proletariat, the lowest stratum of our present society, cannot stir, cannot raise itself up, without the whole superincumbent strata of official society being sprung into the air.

Though not in substance, yet in form, the struggle of the proletariat with the bourgeoisie is at first a national struggle. The proletariat of each country must, of course, first of all settle matters with its own bourgeoisie.

In depicting the most general phases of the development of the proletariat, we traced the more or less veiled civil war, raging within existing society, up to the point where that war breaks out into open revolution, and where the violent overthrow of the bourgeoisie lays the foundation for the sway of the proletariat.

Hitherto, every form of society has been based, as we have already seen, on the antagonism of oppressing and oppressed classes. But in order to oppress a class, certain conditions must be assured to it under which it can, at least, continue its slavish existence. The serf, in the period of serfdom, raised himself to membership in the commune, just as the petty bourgeois, under the yoke of feudal absolutism, managed to develop into a bourgeois. The modern labourer, on the contrary, instead of rising with the progress of industry, sinks deeper and deeper below the conditions of existence of his own class. He becomes a pauper, and pauperism develops more rapidly than population and wealth. And here it becomes evident, that the bourgeoisie is unfit any longer to be the ruling class in society, and to impose its conditions of existence upon society as an over-riding law. It is unfit to rule because it is incompetent to assure an existence to its slave within his slavery, because it cannot help letting him sink into such a state, that it has to feed him, instead of being fed by him. Society can no longer live under this bourgeoisie, in other words, its existence is no longer compatible with society.

The essential condition for the existence, and for the sway of the bourgeois class, is the formation and augmentation of capital; the condition for capital is wage-labour. Wage-labour rests exclusively on competition between the labourers. The advance of industry, whose involuntary promoter is the bourgeoisie, replaces the isolation of the labourers, due to competition, by their revolutionary combination, due to association. The development of Modern Industry, therefore, cuts from under its feet the very foundation on which the bourgeoisie produces and appropriates products. What the bourgeoisie, therefore, produces, above all, is its own grave-diggers. Its fall and the victory of the proletariat are equally inevitable.

II
PROLETARIANS AND COMMUNISTS

In what relation do the Communists stand to the proletarians as a whole?

The Communists do not form a separate party opposed to other working-class parties.

They have no interests separate and apart from those of the proletariat as a whole.

They do not set up any sectarian principles of their own, by which to shape and mould the proletarian movement.

The Communists are distinguished from the other working-class parties by this only: 1. In the national struggles of the proletarians of the different countries, they point out and bring to the front the common interests of the entire proletariat, independently of all nationality. 2. In the various stages of development which the struggle of the working class against the bourgeoisie has to pass through, they always and everywhere represent the interests of the movement as a whole.

The Communists, therefore, are on the one hand, practically, the most advanced and resolute section of the working-class parties of every country, that section which pushes forward all others; on the other hand, theoretically, they have over the great mass of the proletariat the advantage of clearly understanding the line of march, the conditions, and the ultimate general results of the proletarian movement.

The immediate aim of the Communists is the same as that of all the other proletarian parties: formation of the proletariat into a class, overthrow of the bourgeois supremacy, conquest of political power by the proletariat.

The theoretical conclusions of the Communists are in no way based on ideas or principles that have been invented, or discovered by this or that would-be universal reformer.

They merely express, in general terms, actual relations springing from an existing class struggle, from a historical movement going on under our very eyes. The abolition of existing property relations is not at all a distinctive feature of Communism.

All property relations in the past have continually been subject to historical change consequent upon the change in historical conditions.

The French Revolution, for example, abolished feudal property in favour of bourgeois property.

The distinguishing feature of Communism is not the abolition of property generally, but the abolition of bourgeois property. But modern bourgeois private property is the final and most complete expression of the system of producing and appropriating products, that is based on class antagonisms, on the exploitation of the many by the few.

In this sense, the theory of the Communists may be summed up in the single sentence: Abolition of private property.

We Communists have been reproached with the desire of abolishing the right of personally acquiring property as the fruit of a man's own labour, which property is alleged to be the groundwork of all personal freedom, activity and independence.

Hard-won, self-acquired, self-earned property! Do you mean the property of the petty artisan and of the small peasant, a form of property that preceded the bourgeois form? There is no need to abolish that; the development of industry has to a great extent already destroyed it, and is still destroying it daily.

Or do you mean modern bourgeois private property?

But does wage-labour create any property for the labourer? Not a bit. It creates capital, i.e., that kind of property which exploits wage-labour, and which cannot increase except upon condition of begetting a new supply of wage-labour for fresh exploitation. Property, in its present form, is based on the antagonism of capital and wage-labour. Let us examine both sides of this antagonism.

To be a capitalist is to have not only a purely personal, but a social *status* in production. Capital is a collective product, and only by the united action of many members, nay, in the last resort, only by the united action of all members of society, can it be set in motion.

Capital is, therefore, not a personal, it is a social power.

When, therefore, capital is converted into common property, into the property of all members of society, personal property is not thereby transformed into social property. It is only the social character of the property that is changed. It loses its class character.

Let us now take wage-labour.

The average price of wage-labour is the minimum wage, i.e., that quantum of the means of subsistence, which is absolutely requisite to keep the labourer in bare existence as a labourer. What, therefore, the wage-labourer appropriates by means of his labour, merely suffices to prolong and reproduce a bare existence. We by no means intend to abolish this personal appropriation of the products of labour, an appropriation that is made for the maintenance and reproduction of human life, and that leaves no surplus wherewith to command the labour of others. All that we want to do away with is the miserable character of this appropriation, under which the labourer lives merely to increase capital, and is allowed to live only in so far as the interest of the ruling class requires it.

In bourgeois society, living labour is but a means to increase accumulated labour. In Communist society, accumulated labour is but a means to widen, to enrich, to promote the existence of the labourer.

In bourgeois society, therefore, the past dominates the present; in Communist society, the present dominates the past. In bourgeois society capital is independent and has individuality, while the living person is dependent and has no individuality.

And the abolition of this state of things is called by the bourgeois abolition of individuality and freedom! And rightly so. The abolition of bourgeois individuality, bourgeois independence, and bourgeois freedom is undoubtedly aimed at.

By freedom is meant, under the present bourgeois conditions of production, free trade, free selling and buying.

But if selling and buying disappears, free selling and buying disappears also. This talk about free selling and buying, and all the other "brave words" of our bourgeoisie about freedom in general, have a meaning, if any, only in contrast with restricted selling and buying, with the fettered traders of the Middle Ages, but have no meaning when opposed to the Communistic abolition of buying and selling, of the bourgeois conditions of production, and of the bourgeoisie itself.

You are horrified at our intending to do away with private property. But in your existing society, private property is already done away with for nine-tenths of the population; its existence for the few is solely due to its non-existence in the hands of those nine-tenths. You reproach us, therefore, with intending to do away with a form of property, the necessary condition for whose existence is the non-existence of any property for the immense majority of society.

In one word, you reproach us with intending to do away with your property. Precisely so; that is just what we intend.

From the moment when labour can no longer be converted into capital, money, or rent, into a social power capable of being monopolised, i.e., from the moment when individual property can no longer be transformed into bourgeois property, into capital, from that moment, you say, individuality vanishes.

You must, therefore, confess that by "individual" you mean no other person than the bourgeois, than the middle-class owner of property. This person must, indeed, be swept out of the way, and made impossible.

Communism deprives no man of the power to appropriate the products of society; all that it does is to deprive him of the power to subjugate the labour of others by means of such appropriation.

It has been objected that upon the abolition of private property all work will cease, and universal laziness will overtake us.

According to this, bourgeois society ought long ago to have gone to the dogs through sheer idleness; for those of its members who work, acquire nothing, and those who acquire anything, do not work. The whole of this objection is but another expression of the tautology: that there can no longer be any wage-labour when there is no longer any capital.

All objections urged against the Communistic mode of producing and appropriating material products, have, in the same way, been urged against the Communistic modes of producing and appropriating intellectual products. Just as, to the bourgeois, the disappearance of class property is the disappearance of production itself, so the disappearance of class culture is to him identical with the disappearance of all culture.

That culture, the loss of which he laments, is, for the enormous majority, a mere training to act as a machine.

But don't wrangle with us so long as you apply, to our intended abolition of bourgeois property, the standard of your bourgeois notions of freedom, culture, law, etc. Your very ideas are but the outgrowth of the conditions of your bourgeois production and bourgeois property, just as your jurisprudence is but the will of your class made into a law for all, a will, whose essential character and direction are determined by the economical conditions of existence of your class.

The selfish misconception that induces you to transform into eternal laws of nature and of reason, the social forms springing from your present mode of production and form of property—historical relations that rise and disappear in the progress of production—this misconception you share with every ruling class that has preceded you. What you see clearly in the case of ancient property, what you admit in the case of feudal property, you are of course forbidden to admit in the case of your own bourgeois form of property.

Abolition of the family! Even the most radical flare up at this infamous proposal of the Communists.

On what foundation is the present family, the bourgeois family, based? On capital, on private gain. In its completely developed form this family exists only among the bourgeois. But this state of things finds its complement in the practical absence of the family among the proletarians, and in public prostitution.

The bourgeois family will vanish as a matter of course when its complement vanishes, and both will vanish with the vanishing of capital.

Do you charge us with wanting to stop the exploitation of children by their parents? To this crime we plead guilty.

But, you will say, we destroy the most hallowed of relations, when we replace home education by social.

And your education! Is not that also social, and determined by the social conditions under which you educate, by the intervention, direct or indirect, of society, by means of schools, etc. The Communists have not invented the intervention of society in education; they do but seek to alter the character of that intervention, and to rescue education from the influence of the ruling class.

The bourgeois clap-trap about the family and education, about the hallowed co-relation of parent and child, becomes all the more disgusting, the more, by the action of Modern Industry, all family ties among the proletarians are torn asunder, and their children transformed into simple articles of commerce and instruments of labour.

But your Communists would introduce community of women, screams the whole bourgeoisie in chorus.

The bourgeois sees in his wife a mere instrument of production. He hears that the instruments of production are to be exploited in common, and, naturally, can come to no other conclusion than that the lot of being common to all will likewise fall to the women.

He has not even a suspicion that the real point aimed at is to do away with the status of women as mere instruments of production.

For the rest, nothing is more ridiculous than the virtuous indignation of our bourgeois at the community of women which, they pretend, is to be openly and officially established by the Communists. The Communists have no need to introduce community of women; it has existed almost from time immemorial.

Our bourgeois, not content with having the wives and daughters of their proletarians at their disposal, not to speak of common prostitutes, take the greatest pleasure in seducing each other's wives.

Bourgeois marriage is in reality a system of wives in common and thus, at the most, what the Communists might possibly be reproached with, is that they desire to introduce, in substitution for a hypocritically concealed, an openly legalised community of women. For the rest, it is self-evident that the abolition of the present system of production must bring with it the abolition of the community of women springing from that system, i.e., of prostitution both public and private.

The Communists are further reproached with desiring to abolish countries and nationality.

The working men have no country. We cannot take from them what they have not got. Since the proletariat must first of all acquire political supremacy, must rise to be the leading class of the nation, must constitute itself *the* nation, it is so far, itself national, though not in the bourgeois sense of the word.

National differences and antagonisms between peoples are daily more and more vanishing, owing to the development of the bourgeoisie, to freedom of commerce, to the world market, to uniformity in the mode of production and in the conditions of life corresponding thereto.

The supremacy of the proletariat will cause them to vanish still faster. United action, of the leading civilised countries at least, is one of the first conditions for the emancipation of the proletariat.

In proportion as the exploitation of one individual by another is put an end to, the exploitation of one nation by another will also be put an end to. In proportion as the antagonism between classes within the nation vanishes, the hostility of one nation to another will come to an end.

The charges against Communism made from a religious, a philosophical, and, generally, from an ideological standpoint, are not deserving of serious examination.

Does it require deep intuition to comprehend that man's ideas, views and conceptions, in one word, man's consciousness, changes with every change in the conditions of his material existence, in his social relations and in his social life?

What else does the history of ideas prove, than that intellectual production changes its character in proportion as material production is changed? The ruling ideas of each age have ever been the ideas of its ruling class.

When people speak of ideas that revolutionise society, they do but express the fact, that within the old society, the elements of a new one have been created, and that the dissolution of the old ideas keeps even pace with the dissolution of the old conditions of existence.

When the ancient world was in its last throes, the ancient religions were overcome by Christianity. When Christian ideas succumbed in the 18th century to rationalist ideas, feudal society fought its death battle with the then revolutionary bourgeoisie. The ideas of religious liberty and freedom of conscience merely gave expression to the sway of free competition within the domain of knowledge.

"Undoubtedly," it will be said, "religious, moral, philosophical and juridical ideas have been modified in the course of historical development. But religion, morality, philosophy, political science, and law, constantly survived this change.

"There are, besides, eternal truths, such as Freedom, Justice, etc., that are common to all states of society. But Communism abolishes eternal truths, it abolishes all religion and all morality, instead of constituting them on a new basis; it therefore acts in contradiction to all past historical experience."

What does this accusation reduce itself to? The history of all past society has consisted in the development of class antagonisms, antagonisms that assumed different forms at different epochs.

But whatever form they may have taken, one fact is common to all past ages, *viz.*, the exploitation of one part of society by the other. No wonder, then, that the social consciousness of past ages, despite all the multiplicity and variety it displays, moves within certain common forms, or general ideas, which cannot completely vanish except with the total disappearance of class antagonisms.

The Communist revolution is the most radical rupture with traditional property relations; no wonder that its development involves the most radical rupture with traditional ideas.

But let us have done with the bourgeois objections to Communism.

We have seen above, that the first step in the revolution by the working class is to raise the proletariat to the position of ruling class, to win the battle of democracy.

The proletariat will use its political supremacy to wrest, by degrees, all capital from the bourgeoisie, to centralise all instruments of production in the hands of the State, i.e., of the proletariat organised as the ruling class; and to increase the total of productive forces as rapidly as possible.

Of course, in the beginning, this cannot be effected except by means of despotic inroads on the rights of property, and on the conditions of bourgeois production; by means of measures, therefore, which appear economically insufficient and untenable, but which, in the course of the movement, outstrip themselves, necessitate further inroads upon the old social order, and are unavoidable as a means of entirely revolutionising the mode of production.

These measures will of course be different in different countries.

Nevertheless in the most advanced countries, the following will be pretty generally applicable:

1. Abolition of property in land and application of all rents of land to public purposes.

2. A heavy progressive or graduated income tax.

3. Abolition of all right of inheritance.

4. Confiscation of the property of all emigrants and rebels.

5. Centralisation of credit in the hands of the State, by means of a national bank with State capital and an exclusive monopoly.

6. Centralisation of the means of communication and transport in the hands of the State.

7. Extension of factories and instruments of production owned by the State; the bringing into cultivation of waste-lands, and the improvement of the soil generally in accordance with a common plan.

8. Equal liability of all to labour. Establishment of industrial armies, especially for agriculture.

9. Combination of agriculture with manufacturing industries; gradual abolition of the distinction between town and country, by a more equable distribution of the population over the country.

10. Free education for all children in public schools. Abolition of children's factory labour in its present form. Combination of education with industrial production etc., etc.

When, in the course of development, class distinctions have disappeared, and all production has been concentrated in the hands of a vast association of the whole nation, the public power will lose its political character. Political power, properly so called, is merely the organised power of one class for oppressing another. If the proletariat during its contest with the bourgeoisie is compelled, by the force of circumstances, to organise itself as a class, if, by means of a revolution, it makes itself the ruling class, and, as such, sweeps away by force the old conditions of production, then it will, along with these conditions, have swept away the conditions for the existence of class antagonisms and of classes generally, and will thereby have abolished its own supremacy as a class.

In place of the old bourgeois society, with its classes and class antagonisms, we shall have an association, in which the free development of each is the condition for the free development of all.

III
SOCIALIST AND COMMUNIST LITERATURE

1. Reactionary Socialism

a. Feudal Socialism

Owing to their historical position, it became the vocation of the aristocracies of France and England to write pamphlets against modern bourgeois society. In the French revolution of July 1830, and in the English reform agitation, these aristocracies again succumbed to the hateful upstart. Thenceforth, a serious political contest was altogether out of question. A literary battle alone remained possible. But even in the domain of literature the old cries of the restoration period had become impossible.[a]

In order to arouse sympathy, the aristocracy were obliged to lose sight, apparently, of their own interests, and to formulate their indictment against the bourgeoisie in the interest of the exploited working class alone. Thus the aristocracy took their revenge by singing lampoons on their new master, and whispering in his ears sinister prophecies of coming catastrophe.

In this way arose feudal Socialism; half lamentation, half lampoon; half echo of the past, half menace of the future; at times, by its bitter, witty and incisive criticism, striking the bourgeoisie to the very heart's core; but always ludicrous in its effect, through total incapacity to comprehend the march of modern history.

The aristocracy, in order to rally the people to them, waved the proletarian alms-bag in front for a banner. But the people, so often as it joined them, saw on their hindquarters the old feudal coats of arms, and deserted with loud and irreverent laughter.

One section of the French Legitimists and "Young England"[2] exhibited this spectacle.

In pointing out that their mode of exploitation was different to that of the bourgeoisie, the feudalists forget that they exploited under circumstances and conditions that were quite different, and that are now antiquated. In showing that, under their rule, the modern proletariat never existed, they forget that the modern bourgeoisie is the necessary offspring of their own form of society.

For the rest, so little do they conceal the reactionary character of their criticism that their chief accusation against the bourgeoisie amounts to this, that under the bourgeois *régime* a class is being developed, which is destined to cut up root and branch the old order of society.

What they upbraid the bourgeoisie with is not so much that it creates a proletariat, as that it creates a *revolutionary* proletariat.

In political practice, therefore, they join in all coercive measures against the working class; and in ordinary life, despite their high-falutin' phrases, they stoop to pick up the golden apples dropped from the tree of industry and to barter truth, love, and honour for traffic in wool, beetroot-sugar, and potato spirits.[b]

---

[a] Not the English Restoration 1660 to 1689, but the French Restoration 1814 to 1830. *Note by Engels to the English edition of 1888.*]

[b] This applies chiefly to Germany where the landed aristocracy and squirearchy have large portions of their estates cultivated for their own account by stewards, and are, moreover, extensive beetroot-sugar manufacturers and distillers of potato spirits. The wealthier British aristocracy are, as yet, rather above that; but they, too, know how to make up for declining rents by lending their names to floaters of more or less shady joint-stock companies. [*Note by Engels to the English edition of 1888.*]

As the parson has ever gone hand in hand with the landlord, so has Clerical Socialism with Feudal Socialism.

Nothing is easier than to give Christian asceticism a Socialist tinge. Has not Christianity declaimed against private property, against marriage, against the State? Has it not preached in the place of these, charity and poverty, celibacy and mortification of the flesh, monastic life and Mother Church? Christian Socialism is but the holy water with which the priest consecrates the heart-burnings of the aristocrat.

b. Petty-Bourgeois Socialism

The feudal aristocracy was not the only class that was ruined by the bourgeoisie, not the only class whose conditions of existence pined and perished in the atmosphere of modern bourgeois society. The medieval burgesses and the small peasant proprietors were the precursors of the modern bourgeoisie. In those countries which are but little developed, industrially and commercially, these two classes still vegetate side by side with the rising bourgeoisie.

In countries where modern civilisation has become fully developed, a new class of petty bourgeois has been formed, fluctuating between proletariat and bourgeoisie and ever renewing itself as a supplementary part of bourgeois society. The individual members of this class, however, are being constantly hurled down into the proletariat by the action of competition, and, as modern industry develops, they even see the moment approaching when they will completely disappear as an independent section of modern society, to be replaced, in manufacturers, agriculture and commerce, by overlookers, bailiffs and shopmen.

In countries like France, where the peasants constitute far more than half of the population, it was natural that writers who sided with the proletariat against the bourgeoisie, should use, in their criticism of the bourgeois *régime*, the standard of the peasant and petty bourgeois, and from the standpoint of these intermediate classes should take up the cudgels for the working class. Thus arose petty-bourgeois Socialism. Sismondi was the head of this school, not only in France but also in England.[3]

This school of Socialism dissected with great acuteness the contradictions in the conditions of modern production. It laid bare the hypocritical apologies of economists. It proved, incontrovertibly, the disastrous effects of machinery and division of labour; the concentration of capital and land in a few hands; over-production and crises; it pointed out the inevitable ruin of the petty bourgeois and peasant, the misery of the proletariat, the anarchy in production, the crying inequalities in the distribution of wealth, the industrial war of extermination between nations, the dissolution of old moral bonds, of the old family relations, of the old nationalities.

In its positive aims, however, this form of Socialism aspires either to restoring the old means of production and of exchange, and with them the old property relations, and the old society, or to cramping the modern means of production and of exchange, within the framework of the old property relations that have been, and were bound to be, exploded by those means. In either case, it is both reactionary and Utopian.

Its last words are: corporate guilds for manufacture; patriarchal relations in agriculture.

Ultimately, when stubborn historical facts had dispersed all intoxicating effects of self-deception, this form of Socialism ended in a miserable fit of the blues.

c. German, or "True", Socialism

The Socialist and Communist literature of France, a literature that originated under the pressure of a bourgeoisie in power, and that was the expression of the struggle against this power, was introduced into Germany at a time when the bourgeoisie, in that country, had just begun its contest with feudal absolutism.

German philosophers, would-be philosophers, and *beaux esprits*, eagerly seized on this literature, only forgetting, that when these writings immigrated from France into Germany, French social conditions had not immigrated along with them. In contact with German social conditions, this French literature lost all its immediate practical significance, and assumed a purely literary aspect. Thus, to the German philosophers of the Eighteenth Century, the demands of the first French Revolution were nothing more than the demands of "Practical Reason"[4] in general, and the utterance of the will of the revolutionary French bourgeoisie signified in their eyes the laws of pure Will, of Will as it was bound to be, of true human Will generally.

The work of the German *literati* consisted solely in bringing the new French ideas into harmony with their ancient philosophical conscience, or rather, in annexing the French ideas without deserting their own philosophic point of view.

This annexation took place in the same way in which a foreign language is appropriated, namely, by translation.

It is well known how the monks wrote silly lives of Catholic Saints *over* the manuscripts on which the classical works of ancient heathendom had been written. The German *literati* reversed this process with the profane French literature. They wrote their philosophical nonsense beneath the French original. For instance, beneath the French criticism of the economic functions of money, they wrote "Alienation of Humanity", and beneath the French criticism of the bourgeois State they wrote, "Dethronement of the Category of the General", and so forth.

The introduction of these philosophical phrases at the back of the French historical criticisms they dubbed "Philosophy of Action", "True Socialism", "German Science of Socialism", "Philosophical Foundation of Socialism", and so on.

The French Socialist and Communist literature was thus completely emasculated. And, since it ceased in the hands of the German to express the struggle of one class with the other, he felt conscious of having overcome "French one-sidedness" and of representing, not true requirements, but the requirements of Truth; not the interests of the proletariat, but the interests of Human Nature, of Man in general, who belongs to no class, has no reality, who exists only in the misty realm of philosophical fantasy.

This German Socialism, which took its schoolboy task so seriously and solemnly, and extolled its poor stock-in-trade in such mounte-bank fashion, meanwhile gradually lost its pedantic innocence.

The fight of the German, and, especially, of the Prussian bourgeoisie, against feudal aristocracy and absolute monarchy, in other words, the liberal movement, became more earnest.

By this, the long wished-for opportunity was offered to "True" Socialism of confronting the political movement with the Socialist demands, of hurling the traditional anathemas against liberalism, against representative government, against bourgeois competition, bourgeois freedom of the press, bourgeois legislation, bourgeois liberty and equality, and of preaching to the masses that they had nothing to gain, and everything to lose, by this bourgeois movement. German Socialism forgot, in the nick of time, that the French criticism, whose silly echo it was, presupposed the existence of modern bourgeois society, with its corresponding economic conditions of existence, and the political constitution adapted thereto, the very things whose attainment was the object of the pending struggle in Germany.

To the absolute governments, with their following of parsons, professors, country squires and officials, it served as a welcome scarecrow against the threatening bourgeoisie.

It was a sweet finish after the bitter pills of floggings and bullets with which these same governments, just at that time, dosed the German working-class risings.

While this "True" Socialism thus served the governments as a weapon for fighting the German bourgeoisie, it, at the same time, directly represented a reactionary interest, the interest of the German Philistines. In Germany the *petty-bourgeois* class, a relic of the sixteenth century, and since then constantly cropping up again under various forms, is the real social basis of the existing state of things.

To preserve this class is to preserve the existing state of things in Germany. The industrial and political supremacy of the bourgeoisie threatens it with certain destruction; on the one hand, from the concentration of capital; on the other, from the rise of a revolutionary proletariat. "True" Socialism appeared to kill these two birds with one stone. It spread like an epidemic.

The robe of speculative cobwebs, embroidered with flowers of rhetoric, steeped in the dew of sickly sentiment, this transcendental robe in which the German Socialists wrapped their sorry "eternal truths", all skin and bone, served to wonderfully increase the sale of their goods amongst such a public.

And on its part, German Socialism recognised, more and more, its own calling as the bombastic representative of the petty-bourgeois Philistine.

It proclaimed the German nation to be the model nation, and the German petty Philistine to be the typical man. To every villainous meanness of this model man it gave a hidden, higher, Socialistic interpretation, the exact contrary of its real character. It went to the extreme length of directly opposing the "brutally destructive" tendency of Communism, and of proclaiming its supreme and impartial contempt of all class struggles. With very few exceptions, all the so-called Socialist and Communist publications that now (1847) circulate in Germany belong to the domain of this foul and enervating literature.^c

2. Conservative, or Bourgeois, Socialism

A part of the bourgeoisie is desirous of redressing social grievances, in order to secure the continued existence of bourgeois society.

To this section belong economists, philanthropists, humanitarians, improvers of the condition of the working class, organisers of charity, members of societies for the prevention of cruelty to animals, temperance fanatics, hole-and-corner reformers of every imaginable kind. This form of Socialism has, moreover, been worked out into complete systems.

We may cite Proudhon's *Philosophie de la Misère* as an example of this form.

The Socialistic bourgeois want all the advantages of modern social conditions without the struggles and dangers necessarily resulting therefrom. They desire the existing state of society minus its revolutionary and disintegrating elements. They wish for a bourgeoisie without a proletariat. The bourgeoisie naturally conceives the world in which it is supreme to be the best; and bourgeois Socialism develops this comfortable conception into various more or less complete systems. In requiring the proletariat to carry out such a system, and thereby to march straightway into the social New Jerusalem, it but requires in reality, that the proletariat should remain within the bounds of existing society, but should cast away all its hateful ideas concerning the bourgeoisie.

A second and more practical, but less systematic, form of this Socialism sought to depreciate every revolutionary movement in the eyes of the working class, by showing that no mere political reform, but only a change in the material conditions of existence, in economical relations, could be

---

^c The revolutionary storm of 1848 swept away this whole shabby tendency and cured its protagonists of the desire to dabble further in Socialism. The chief representative and classical type of this tendency is Herr Karl Grün. [*Note by Engels to the German edition of 1890.*]

of any advantage to them. By changes in the material conditions of existence, this form of Socialism, however, by no means understands abolition of the bourgeois relations of production, an abolition that can be effected only by a revolution, but administrative reforms, based on the continued existence of these relations; reforms, therefore, that in no respect affect the relations between capital and labour, but, at the best, lessen the cost, and simplify the administrative work, of bourgeois government.

Bourgeois Socialism attains adequate expression, when, and only when, it becomes a mere figure of speech.

Free trade: for the benefit of the working class. Protective duties: for the benefit of the working class. Prison Reform for the benefit of the working class. This is the last word and the only seriously meant word of bourgeois Socialism.

It is summed up in the phrase: the bourgeois is a bourgeois—for the benefit of the working class.

3. Critical-Utopian Socialism and Communism

We do not here refer to that literature which, in every great modern revolution, has always given voice to the demands of the proletariat, such as the writings of Babeuf[5] and others.

The first direct attempts of the proletariat to attain its own ends, made in times of universal excitement, when feudal society was being overthrown, these attempts necessarily failed, owing to the then undeveloped state of the proletariat, as well as to the absence of the economic conditions for its emancipation, conditions that had yet to be produced, and could be produced by the impending bourgeois epoch alone. The revolutionary literature that accompanied these first movements of the proletariat had necessarily a reactionary character. It inculcated universal asceticism and social levelling in its crudest form.

The Socialist and Communist systems properly so called, those of Saint-Simon, Fourier, Owen and others,[6] spring into existence in the early undeveloped period, described above, of the struggle between proletariat and bourgeoisie (see Section I. Bourgeois and Proletarians).

The founders of these systems see, indeed, the class antagonisms, as well as the action of the decomposing elements in the prevailing form of society. But the proletariat, as yet in its infancy offers to them the spectacle of a class without any historical initiative or any independent political movement.

Since the development of class antagonism keeps even pace with the development of industry, the economic situation, as they find it, does not as yet offer to them the material conditions for the emancipation of the proletariat. They therefore search after a new social science, after new social laws, that are to create these conditions.

Historical action is to yield to their personal inventive action, historically created conditions of emancipation to fantastic ones, and the gradual, spontaneous class organisation of the proletariat to an organisation of society specially contrived by these inventors. Future history resolves itself, in their eyes, into the propaganda and the practical carrying out of their social plans.

In the formation of their plans they are conscious of caring chiefly for the interests of the working class, as being the most suffering class. Only from the point of view of being the most suffering class does the proletariat exist for them.

The undeveloped state of the class struggle, as well as their own surroundings, causes Socialists of this kind to consider themselves far superior to all class antagonisms. They want to improve the condition of every member of society, even that of the most favoured. Hence, they habitually appeal to society at large, without distinction of class; nay, by preference, to the ruling class. For how can people, when once they understand their system, fail to see in it the best possible plan of the best possible state of society?

Hence, they reject all political, and especially all revolutionary, action; they wish to attain their ends by peaceful means, and endeavour, by small experiments, necessarily doomed to failure, and by the force of example, to pave the way for the new social Gospel.

Such fantastic pictures of future society, painted at a time when the proletariat is still in a very undeveloped state and has but a fantastic conception of its own position, correspond with the first instinctive yearnings of that class for a general reconstruction of society.

But these Socialist and Communist publications contain also a critical element. They attack every principle of existing society. Hence they are full of the most valuable materials for the enlightenment of the working class. The practical measures proposed in them—such as the abolition of the distinction between town and country, of the family, of the carrying on of industries for the account of private individuals, and of the wage system, the proclamation of social harmony, the conversion of the functions of the State into a mere superintendence of production, all these proposals point solely to the disappearance of class antagonisms which were, at that time, only just cropping up, and which, in these publications, are recognised in their earliest indistinct and undefined forms only. These proposals, therefore, are of a purely Utopian character.

The significance of Critical-Utopian Socialism and Communism bears an inverse relation to historical development. In proportion as the modern class struggle develops and takes definite shape, this fantastic standing apart from the contest, these fantastic attacks on it, lose all practical value and all theoretical justification. Therefore, although the originators of these systems were, in many respects, revolutionary, their disciples have, in every case, formed mere reactionary sects. They hold fast by the original views of their masters, in opposition to the progressive historical development of the proletariat. They, therefore, endeavour, and that consistently, to deaden the class struggle and to reconcile the class antagonisms. They still dream of experimental realisation of their social Utopias, of founding isolated "phalanstères", of establishing "Home Colonies", of setting up a "Little Icaria"*d* duodecimo editions of the New Jerusalem— and to realise all these castles in the air, they are compelled to appeal to the feelings and purses of the bourgeois. By degrees they sink into the category of the reactionary [or] conservative Socialists depicted above, differing from these only by more systematic pedantry, and by their fanatical and superstitious belief in the miraculous effects of their social science.

They, therefore, violently oppose all political action on the part of the working class; such action, according to them, can only result from blind unbelief in the new Gospel.

The Owenites in England, and the Fourierists in France, respectively oppose the Chartists and the *Réformistes.*[7]

IV

POSITION OF THE COMMUNISTS IN RELATION TO THE VARIOUS EXISTING OPPOSITION PARTIES

Section II has made clear the relations of the Communists to the existing working-class parties, such as the Chartists in England and the Agrarian Reformers in America.

The Communists fight for the attainment of the immediate aims, for the enforcement of the momentary interests of the working class; but in the movement of the present, they also represent and take care of the future of that movement. In France the Communists ally themselves with the Social-Democrats,*e* against the conservative and radical bourgeoisie, reserving, however, the right to take up a critical position in regard to phrases and illusions traditionally handed down from the great Revolution.

In Switzerland they support the Radicals, without losing sight of the

---

d Phalanstères were Socialist colonies on the plan of Charles Fourier; *Icaria* was the name given by Cabet to his Utopia and, later on, to his American Communist colony. [*Note by Engels to the English edition of 1888.*]

"Home Colonies" were what Owen called his Communist model societies. *Phalanstères* was the name of the public palaces planned by Fourier. *Icaria* was the name given to the Utopian land of fancy, whose Communist institutions Cabet portrayed. [*Note by Engels to the German edition of 1890.*]

e The party then represented in Parliament by Ledru-Rollin, in literature by Louis Blanc, in the daily press by the *Réforme.* The name of Social-Democracy signified, with these its inventors, a section of the Democratic or Republican party more or less tinged with Socialism. [*Note by Engels to the English edition of 1888.*]

The party in France which at that time called itself Socialist-Democratic was represented in political life by Ledru-Rollin and in literature by Louis Blanc; thus it differed immeasurably from present-day German Social-Democracy. [*Note by Engels to the German edition of 1890.*]

fact that this party consists of antagonistic elements, partly of Democratic Socialists, in the French sense, partly of radical bourgeois.

In Poland they support the party that insists on an agrarian revolution as the prime condition for national emancipation, that party which fomented the insurrection of Cracow in 1846.

In Germany they fight with the bourgeoisie whenever it acts in a revolutionary way, against the absolute monarchy, the feudal squirearchy, and the petty bourgeoisie.

But they never cease, for a single instant, to instil into the working class the clearest possible recognition of the hostile antagonism between bourgeoisie and proletariat, in order that the German workers may straightway use, as so many weapons against the bourgeoisie, the social and political conditions that the bourgeoisie must necessarily introduce along with its supremacy, and in order that, after the fall of the reactionary classes in Germany, the fight against the bourgeoisie itself may immediately begin.

The Communists turn their attention chiefly to Germany, because that country is on the eve of a bourgeois revolution that is bound to be carried out under more advanced conditions of European civilisation, and with a much more developed proletariat, than that of England was in the seventeenth, and of France in the eighteenth century, and because the bourgeois revolution in Germany will be but the prelude to an immediately following proletarian revolution.

In short, the Communists everywhere support every revolutionary movement against the existing social and political order of things.

In all these movements they bring to the front, as the leading question in each, the property question, no matter what its degree of development at the time.

Finally, they labour everywhere for the union and agreement of the democratic parties of all countries.

The Communists disdain to conceal their views and aims. They openly declare that their ends can be attained only by the forcible overthrow of all existing social conditions. Let the ruling classes tremble at a Communistic revolution. The proletarians have nothing to lose but their chains. They have a world to win.

WORKING MEN OF ALL COUNTRIES, UNITE!

NOTES TO "MANIFESTO OF THE COMMUNIST PARTY"

1. The Ten Hours Act limited the working day of women and children in textile factories to ten hours. It was proposed to Parliament in 1846 by the British philanthropist Anthony Ashley Cooper, Seventh Earl of Shaftesbury (1801–1885), and it passed on June 8, 1847. After its passage, Lord Shaftesbury left

the Tories and became a Whig. Enforcement of the Act, however, was sporadic and intermittent at best.

2. "Young England" was a group of British Conservatives formed in the early 1840s. It attempted to enlist the working class in support of the landed aristocracy's struggle against the bourgeoisie.

3. Jean Charles Leonard Sismondi (1773–1842), Swiss political economist whose criticisms of capitalism Marx frequently quotes with favor.

4. "Practical Reason"—an allusion to Immanuel Kant's moral philosophy.

5. Francois Noel Babeuf (1760–1797), French revolutionary communist.

6. Charles Fourier (1772–1837), French communist; Henri Saint-Simon (1760–1825), French socialist; Robert Owen (1771–1858), British socialist and founder of utopian communities.

7. Chartism was a British working class political movement of the 1830s to the 1850s. It was named for "The People's Charter," a radical proposal for English political reform, submitted in the form of a bill to Parliament in May, 1838. The Charter called for universal manhood suffrage, annual parliamentary elections, secret ballot, equal constituencies, the abolition of property qualifications for MPs and the institution of salaries for MPs. (Engels became a Chartist in the early 1840s.) *Reformistes* were adherents to the French newspaper *La Reforme*, published in Paris between 1843 and 1850; they were republicans who advocated democratic reforms in the French political system.

The Civil War in France (1871)
(*Excerpt*)

The Second Empire of Louis Bonaparte, Emperor Napoleon III, fell with the French defeat by Bismarck's Prussian army in September, 1870. Early in 1871, the workers of the city of Paris, who had been starving under Prussian siege for four months, overthrew the government and—to the horror of civilized Europe—established a Commune. The Commune held sway in the capital from March to May of 1871, when it was forcibly suppressed by the newly founded Third Republic, based in Versailles. During the "Bloody Week" of May 21–28, the Communards executed sixty-four hostages, including Georges Darboy, Archbishop of Paris; the Versailles government, displaying respectable society's righteous indignation toward acts of terrorism in typical fashion, responded by summarily executing large but indeterminate numbers of its prisoners.

Marx celebrated the defeated Commune in a long address to the General Council of the First International in London on May 30, 1871. He saw the Commune as a sign that the workers, though still unripe to rule, were capable of giving a foretaste of future proletarian society. It was in this spirit that he described the functioning of the Commune in Part III of his address, which is excerpted here. It emphasizes less what the Commune did than what it would have done; less what it was, than what it was to have become. It perhaps provides us, more than any other Marxian text, with a depiction of what Marx thought the "dictatorship of the proletariat" would be like. Noteworthy is Marx's praise for democratic institutions, with decentralization, demilitarization and the elimination of state bureaucracy. But equally noteworthy is his cautionary admonition that the working class "has no ideals to realize," and his indication that the goals of the movement will change as it passes "through a series of historic processes, transforming circumstances and men."

Marx's support for the Commune was an unpopular stand. It probably contributed to the demise of the First International five years later. The original of Marx's address was in English.

III

On the dawn of 18 March, Paris arose to the thunderburst of '*Vive la Commune!*' What is the Commune, that sphinx so tantalizing to the bourgeois mind? 'The proletarians of Paris,' said the Central Committee in its manifesto of 18 March,

> amidst the failures and treasons of the ruling classes, have under-
> stood that the hour has struck for them to save the situation by
> taking into their own hands the direction of public affairs. . . . They
> have understood that it is their imperious duty and their absolute
> right to render themselves masters of their own destinies, by seizing
> upon the governmental power.

But the working class cannot simply lay hold of the ready-made state machinery, and wield it for its own purposes.

The centralized state power, with its ubiquitous organs of standing army, police, bureaucracy, clergy, and judicature—organs wrought after the plan of a systematic and hierarchic division of labour—originates from the days of absolute monarchy, serving nascent middle-class society as a mighty weapon in its struggles against feudalism. Still, its development remained clogged by all manner of medieval rubbish, seignorial rights, local privileges, municipal and guild monopolies and provincial constitutions. The gigantic broom of the French revolution of the eighteenth century swept away all these relics of bygone times, thus clearing simultaneously the social soil of its last hindrances to the superstructure of the modern state edifice raised under the First Empire, itself the offspring of the coalition wars of old semi-feudal Europe against modern France. During the subsequent regimes the government, placed under parliamentary control—that is, under the direct control of the propertied classes—became not only a hotbed of huge national debts and crushing taxes; with its irresistible allurements of place, pelf, and patronage, it became not only the bone of contention between the rival factions and adventurers of the ruling classes; but its political character changed simultaneously with the economic changes of society. At the same pace at which the progress of modern industry developed, widened, intensified the class antagonism between capital and labour, the state power assumed more and more the character of the national power of capital over labour, of a public force organized for social enslavement, of an engine of class despotism. After every revolution marking a progressive phase in the class struggle, the purely repressive character of the state power stands out in bolder and bolder relief. The revolution of 1830, resulting in the transfer of government from the landlords to the capitalists, transferred it from the more remote to the more direct antagonists of the working men. The bourgeois republicans, who, in the name of the revolution of February

[1848], took the state power, used it for the June massacres, in order to convince the working class that 'social' republic meant the republic ensuring their social subjection, and in order to convince the royalist bulk of the bourgeois and landlord class that they might safely leave the cares and emoluments of government to the bourgeois 'republicans'. However, after their one heroic exploit of June, the bourgeois republicans had, from the front, to fall back to the rear of the 'party of Order'—a combination formed by all the rival fractions and fractions of the appropriating class in their now openly declared antagonism to the producing classes. The proper form of their joint-stock government was the *parliamentary republic*, with Louis Bonaparte for its President. Theirs was a regime of avowed class terrorism and deliberate insult toward the 'vile multitude'. If the parliamentary republic, as M. Thiers[1] said, 'divided them' (the different fractions of the ruling class) 'least', it opened an abyss between that class and the whole body of society outside their spare ranks. The restraints by which their own divisions had under former regimes still checked the state power, were removed by their union; and in view of the threatening upheaval of the proletariat, they now used that state power mercilessly and ostentatiously as the national war-engine of capital against labour. In their uninterrupted crusade against the producing masses they were, however, bound not only to invest the executive with continually increased powers of repression, but at the same time to divest their own parliamentary stronghold—the National Assembly—one by one, of all its own means of defence against the executive. The executive, in the person of Louis Bonaparte, turned them out. The natural offspring of the 'party-of-Order' republic was the Second Empire.

The Empire, with the coup d'état for its certificate of birth, universal suffrage for its sanction, and the sword for its sceptre, professed to rest upon the peasantry, the large mass of producers not directly involved in the struggle of capital and labour. It professed to save the working class by breaking down parliamentarism, and, with it, the undisguised subserviency of government to the propertied classes. It professed to save the propertied classes by upholding their economic supremacy over the working class; and, finally, it professed to unite all classes by reviving for all the chimera of national glory. In reality, it was the only form of government possible at a time when the bourgeoisie had already lost, and the working class had not yet acquired, the faculty of ruling the nation. It was acclaimed throughout the world as the saviour of society. Under its sway, bourgeois society, freed from political cares, attained a development unexpected even by itself. Its industry and commerce expanded to colossal dimensions; financial swindling celebrated cosmopolitan orgies; the misery of the masses was set off by a shameless display of gorgeous, meretricious and debased luxury. The state power, apparently soaring high above society, was at the same time itself the greatest scandal of that society and the very hotbed of all its corruptions. Its own rottenness, and the rottenness of the society it had saved, were laid bare by the bayonet of Prussia, herself eagerly bent upon transferring the supreme seat of that regime from Paris to Berlin. Imperialism is, at the same time, the most prostitute and the ultimate form of the state power which nascent middle-class society had commenced to elaborate as a means of its own emancipation from feudalism, and which full-grown bourgeois society had finally transformed into a means for the enslavement of labour by capital.

The direct antithesis to the Empire was the Commune. The cry of 'social republic', with which the revolution of February was ushered in by the Paris proletariat, did but express a vague aspiration after a republic that was not only to supersede the monarchical form of class rule, but class rule itself. The Commune was the positive form of that republic.

Paris, the central seat of the old governmental power, and, at the same time, the social stronghold of the French working class, had risen in arms against the attempt of Thiers and the Rurals to restore and perpetuate that old governmental power bequeathed to them by the Empire. Paris could resist only because, in consequence of the siege, it had got rid of the army, and replaced it by a National Guard, the bulk of which consisted of working men. This fact was now to be transformed into an institution. The first decree of the Commune, therefore, was the suppression of the standing army, and the substitution for it of the armed people.

The Commune was formed of the municipal councillors, chosen by universal suffrage in the various wards of the town, responsible and revocable at short terms. The majority of its members were naturally working men, or acknowledged representatives of the working class. The Commune was to be a working, not a parliamentary body, executive and legislative at the same time. Instead of continuing to be the agent of the central government, the police was at once stripped of its political attributes, and turned into the responsible and at all times revocable agent of the Commune. So were the officials of all other branches of the administration. From the members of the Commune downwards, the public service had to be done at *workmen's wages*. The vested interests and the representation allowances of the high dignitaries of state disappeared along with the high dignitaries themselves. Public functions ceased to be the private property of the tools of the central government. Not only municipal administration, but the whole initiative hitherto exercised by the state was laid into the hands of the Commune.

Having once got rid of the standing army and the police, the physical force elements of the old government, the Commune was anxious to break the spiritual force of repression, the 'parson-power', by the disestablishment and disendowment of all churches as proprietary bodies. The priests were sent back to the recesses of private life, there to feed upon the alms of the faithful in imitation of their predecessors, the apostles.

The whole of the educational institutions were opened to the people gratuitously, and at the same time cleared of all interference of church and state. Thus, not only was education made accessible to all, but science itself freed from the fetters which class prejudice and governmental force had imposed upon it.

The judicial functionaries were to be divested of that sham independence which had but served to mask their abject subserviency to all succeeding governments to which, in turn, they had taken, and broken, the oaths of allegiance. Like the rest of public servants, magistrates and judges were to be elective, responsible, and revocable.

The Paris Commune was, of course, to serve as a model to all the great industrial centres of France. The communal regime once established in Paris and the secondary centres, the old centralized government would in the provinces, too, have to give way to the self-government of the producers. In a rough sketch of national organization which the Commune had no time to develop, it states clearly that the commune was to be the political form of even the smallest country hamlet, and that in the rural districts the standing army was to be replaced by a national militia, with an extremely short term of service. The rural communes of every district were to administer their common affairs by an assembly of delegates in the central town, and these district assemblies were again to send deputies to the national delegation in Paris, each delegate to be at any time revocable and bound by the *mandat impératif* (formal instructions) of his constituents. The few but important functions which still would remain for a central government were not to be suppressed, as has been intentionally mis-stated, but were to be discharged by Communal, and therefore strictly responsible agents. The unity of the nation was not to be broken, but, on the contrary, to be organized by the Communal constitution and to become a reality by the destruction of the state power which claimed to be the embodiment of that unity independent of, and superior to, the nation itself, from which it was but a parasitic excrescence. While the merely repressive organs of the old governmental power were to be amputated, its legitimate functions were to be wrested from an authority usurping pre-eminence over society itself, and restored to the responsible agents of society. Instead of deciding once in three or six years which member of the ruling class was to misrepresent the people in parliament, universal suffrage was to serve the people, constituted in communes, as individual suffrage serves every other employer in the search for the workmen and managers in his business. And it is well known that companies, like individuals, in matters of real business generally know how to put the right man in the right place, and, if they for once make a mistake, to redress it promptly. On the other hand, nothing could be more foreign to the spirit of the Commune than to supersede universal suffrage by hierarchic investiture.

It is generally the fate of completely new historical creations to be mistaken for the counterpart of older and even defunct forms of social life, to which they may bear a certain likeness. Thus, this new Commune, which breaks the modern state power, has been mistaken for a reproduction of the medieval communes, which first preceded, and afterwards became the substratum of, that very state power. The Communal constitution has been mistaken for an attempt to break up into a federation of small states, as dreamt of by Montesquieu and the Girondins,[2] that unity of great nations which, if originally brought about by political force, has now become a powerful coefficient of social production. The antagonism of the Commune against the state power has been mistaken for an exaggerated form of the ancient struggle against over-centralization. Peculiar historical circumstances may have prevented the classical development, as in France, of the bourgeois form of government, and may have allowed, as in England, to complete the great central state organs by corrupt vestries, jobbing councillors, and ferocious poor-law guardians in the towns, and virtually hereditary magistrates in the counties. The Communal constitution would have restored to the social body all the forces hitherto absorbed by the state parasite feeding upon, and clogging the free movement of, society. By this one act it would have initiated the regeneration of France. The provincial French middle class saw in the Commune an attempt to restore the sway their order had held over the country under Louis Philippe, and which, under Louis Napoleon, was supplanted by the pretended rule of the country over the towns. In reality, the Communal constitution brought the rural producers under the intellectual lead of the central towns of their districts, and these secured to them, in the working men, the natural trustees of their interests. The very existence of the Commune involved, as a matter of course, local municipal liberty, but no longer as a check upon the, now superseded, state power. It could only enter into the head of a Bismarck, who, when not engaged on his intrigues of blood and iron, always likes to resume his old trade, so befitting his mental calibre, of contributor to *Kladderadatsch* (the Berlin *Punch*), it could only enter into such a head, to ascribe to the Paris Commune aspirations after that caricature of the old French municipal organization of 1791, the Prussian municipal constitution which degrades the town governments to mere secondary wheels in the police machinery of the Prussian state.

The Commune made that catchword of bourgeois revolutions, cheap government, a reality, by destroying the two greatest sources of expenditure—the standing army and state functionarism. Its very existence presupposed the non-existence of monarchy, which, in Europe at least, is the normal incumbrance and indispensable cloak of class rule. It supplied the republic with the basis of really democratic institutions. But neither cheap government nor the 'true republic' was its ultimate aim; they were its mere concomitants.

The multiplicity of interpretations to which the Commune has been subjected, and the multiplicity of interests which construed it in their favour, show that it was a thoroughly expansive political form, while all previous forms of government had been emphatically repressive. Its true secret was this. It was essentially a working-class government, the produce of the struggle of the producing against the appropriating class, the political form at last discovered under which to work out the economical emancipation of labour.

Except on this last condition, the Communal constitution would have been an impossibility and a delusion. The political rule of the producer cannot coexist with the perpetuation of his social slavery. The Commune was therefore to serve as a lever for uprooting the economical foundations upon which rests the existence of classes, and therefore of class rule. With labour emancipated, every man becomes a working man, and productive labour ceases to be a class attribute.

It is a strange fact. In spite of all the tall talk and all the immense literature, for the last sixty years, about emancipation of labour, no sooner do the working men anywhere take the subject into their own hands with a will, than up rises at once all the apologetic phraseology of the mouth-pieces of present society with its two poles of capital and wage slavery (the landlord now is but the sleeping partner of the capitalist), as if capitalist society was still in its purest state of virgin innocence, with its antagonisms still undeveloped, with its delusions still unexploded, with its prostitute realities not yet laid bare. The Commune, they exclaim, intends to abolish property, the basis of all civilization! Yes, gentlemen, the Commune intended to abolish that class property which makes the labour of the many the wealth of the few. It aimed at the expropriation of the expropriators. It wanted to make individual property a truth by transforming the means of production, land and capital, now chiefly the means of enslaving and exploiting labour, into mere instruments of free and associated labour. But this is communism, 'impossible' communism! Why, those members of the ruling classes who are intelligent enough to perceive the impossibility of continuing the present system—and they are many—have become the obtrusive and full-mouthed apostles of cooperative production. If cooperative production is not to remain a sham and a snare; if it is to supersede the capitalist system; if united cooperative societies are to regulate national production upon a common plan, thus taking it under their own control, and putting an end to the constant anarchy and periodical convulsions which are the fatality of capitalist production—what else, gentlemen, would it be but communism, 'possible' communism?

The working class did not expect miracles from the Commune. They have no ready-made utopias to introduce *par décret du peuple*. They know that in order to work out their own emancipation, and along with it that higher form to which present society is irresistibly tending by its own economical agencies, they will have to pass through long struggles, through a series of historic processes, transforming circumstances and men. They have no ideals to realize, but to set free the elements of the new society with which old collapsing bourgeois society itself is pregnant. In the full consciousness of their historic mission, and with the heroic resolve to act up to it, the working class can afford to smile at the coarse invective of the gentlemen's gentlemen with the pen and inkhorn, and at the didactic patronage of well-wishing bourgeois doctrinaires, pouring forth their ignorant platitudes and sectarian crotchets in the oracular tone of scientific infallibility.

When the Paris Commune took the management of the revolution in its own hands; when plain working men for the first time dared to infringe upon the governmental privilege of their 'natural superiors', and, under circumstances of unexampled difficulty, performed their work modestly, conscientiously, and efficiently—performed it at salaries the highest of which barely amounted to one fifth of what, according to high scientific authority,[3] is the minimum required for a secretary to a certain metropolitan school board—the old world writhed in convulsions of rage at the sight of the red flag, the symbol of the republic of labour, floating over the Hôtel de Ville.

And yet, this was the first revolution in which the working class was openly acknowledged as the only class capable of social initiative, even by the great bulk of the Paris middle class—shop-keepers, tradesmen, merchants—the wealthy capitalists alone excepted. The Commune had saved them by a sagacious settlement of that ever-recurring cause of dispute among the middle classes themselves—the debtor and creditor accounts.[4] The same portion of the middle class, after they had assisted in putting down the working men's insurrection of June 1848, had been at once unceremoniously sacrificed to their creditors by the then Constituent Assembly.[5] But this was not their only motive for now rallying round the working class. They felt that there was but one alternative—the Commune, or the Empire—under whatever name it might reappear. The Empire had ruined them economically by the havoc it made of public wealth, by the wholesale financial swindling it fostered, by the props it lent to the artificially accelerated centralization of capital, and the concomitant expropriation of their own ranks. It had suppressed them politically, it had shocked them morally by its orgies, it had insulted their Voltaireanism by handing over the education of their children to the *frères ignorantins*,[6] it had revolted their national feeling as Frenchmen by precipitating them headlong into a war which left only one equivalent for the ruins it made—the disappearance of the Empire. In fact, after the exodus from Paris of the high Bonapartist and capitalist *bohème*, the true middle-class party of Order came out in the shape of the 'Union Républicaine',[7] enrolling themselves under the colours of the Commune and defending it against the wilful misconstruction of Thiers. Whether the gratitude of this great body of the middle class will stand the present severe trial, time must show.

The Commune was perfectly right in telling the peasants that 'its victory was their only hope'.[8] Of all the lies hatched at Versailles and re-echoed by the glorious European penny-a-liner, one of the most tremendous was that the Rurals represented the French peasantry. Think only of the love of the French peasant for the men to whom, after 1815, he had to pay the milliard of indemnity![9] In the eyes of the French peasant, the very existence of a great landed proprietor is in itself an encroachment on his conquests of 1789. The bourgeois, in 1848, had burdened his plot of land with the additional tax of forty-five cents in the franc;[10] but then he did so in the name of the revolution; while now he had fomented a civil war against the revolution, to shift on to the peasant's shoulders the chief load of the five milliards of indemnity to be paid to the Prussian. The Commune, on the other hand, in one of its first proclamations, declared that the true originators of the war would be made to pay its cost. The Commune would have delivered the peasant of the blood tax,[11] would have given him a cheap government, transformed his present blood-suckers, the notary, advocate, executor, and other judicial vampires, into salaried communal agents, elected by, and responsible to, himself. It would have freed him of the tyranny of the *garde champêtre*, the gendarme, and the prefect; would have put enlightenment by the schoolmaster in the place of stultification by the priest. And the French peasant is, above all, a man of reckoning. He would find it extremely reasonable that the pay of the priest, instead of being extorted by the tax-gatherer, should only depend upon the spontaneous action of the parishioners' religious instincts. Such were the great immediate boons which the rule of the Commune—and that rule alone—held out to the French peasantry. It is, therefore, quite superfluous here to expatiate upon the more complicated but vital problems which the Commune alone was able, and at the same time compelled, to solve in favour of the peasant, *viz.*, the hypothecary debt, lying like an incubus upon his parcel of soil, the *prolétariat foncier* (the rural proletariat), daily growing upon it, and his expropriation from it enforced, at a more and more rapid rate, by the very development of modern agriculture and the competition of capitalist farming.

The French peasant had elected Louis Bonaparte President of the Republic; but the party of Order created the Empire. What the French peasant really wants he commenced to show in 1849 and 1850, by opposing his *maire* to the government's prefect, his schoolmaster to the government's priest, and himself to the government's gendarme. All the laws made by the party of Order in January and February 1850[12] were avowed measures of repression against the peasant. The peasant was a Bonapartist, because the great Revolution, with all its benefits to him, was, in his eyes, personified in Napoleon. This delusion, rapidly breaking down under the Second Empire (and in its very nature hostile to the Rurals), this prejudice of the past, how could it have withstood the appeal of the Commune to the living interests and urgent wants of the peasantry?

The Rurals—this was, in fact, their chief apprehension—knew that three months' free communication of Communal Paris with the provinces would bring about a general rising of the peasants, and hence their anxiety to establish a police blockade around Paris, so as to stop the spread of the rinderpest.[13]

If the Commune was thus the true representative of all the healthy elements of French society, and therefore the truly national government, it was, at the same time, as a working men's government, as the bold champion of the emancipation of labour, emphatically international. Within sight of the Prussian army, that had annexed to Germany two French provinces, the Commune annexed to France the working people all over the world.

The Second Empire had been the jubilee of cosmopolitan blackleg-ism, the rakes of all countries rushing in at its call for a share in its orgies and in the plunder of the French people. Even at this moment the right hand of Thiers is Ganesco, the foul Wallachian, and his left hand is Markovsky, the Russian spy.[14] The Commune admitted all foreigners to the honour of dying for an immortal cause. Between the foreign war lost by their treason, and the civil war fomented by their conspiracy with the foreign invader, the bourgeoisie had found the time to display their patriotism by organizing police-hunts upon the Germans in France. The Commune made a German working man its Minister of Labour.[15] Thiers, the bourgeoisie, the Second Empire, had continually deluded Poland by loud professions of sympathy, while in reality betraying her to, and doing the dirty work of, Russia. The Commune honoured the heroic sons of Poland by placing them at the head of the defenders of Paris.[16] And, to broadly mark the new era of history it was conscious of initiating, under the eyes of the conquering Prussians, on the one side, and of the Bonapartist army, led by Bonapartist generals, on the other, the Commune pulled down that colossal symbol of martial glory, the Vendôme column.[17]

The great social measure of the Commune was its own working existence. Its special measures could but betoken the tendency of a government of the people by the people. Such were the abolition of the nightwork of journeymen bakers; the prohibition, under penalty, of the employers' practice to reduce wages by levying upon their work-people fines under manifold pretexts—a process in which the employer combines in his own person the parts of legislator, judge, and executor, and filches the money to boot. Another measure of this class was the surrender to associations of workmen, under reserve of compensation, of all closed workshops and factories, no matter whether the respective capitalists had absconded or preferred to strike work.

The financial measures of the Commune, remarkable for their sagacity and moderation, could only be such as were compatible with the state of a besieged town. Considering the colossal robberies committed upon the city of Paris by the great financial companies and contractors, under the protection of Haussmann[18] the Commune would have had an incomparably better title to confiscate their property than Louis Napoleon had against the Orleans family. The Hohenzollern[19] and the English oligarchs, who both have derived a good deal of their estates from church plunder, were, of course, greatly shocked at the Commune clearing but 8,000 francs out of secularization.

While the Versailles government, as soon as it had recovered some spirit and strength, used the most violent means against the Commune; while it put down the free expression of opinion all over France, even to the forbidding of meetings of delegates from the large towns; while it subjected Versailles and the rest of France to an espionage far surpassing that of the Second Empire; while it burned by its gendarme inquisitors all papers printed at Paris, and sifted all correspondence from and to Paris; while in the National Assembly the most timid attempts to put in a word for Paris were howled down in a manner unknown even to the *Chambre introuvable* of 1816; with the savage warfare of Versailles outside, and its attempts at corruption and conspiracy inside Paris—would the Commune not have shamefully betrayed its trust by affecting to keep up all the decencies and appearances of liberalism as in a time of profound peace? Had the government of the Commune been akin to that of M. Thiers, there would have been no more occasion to suppress party-of-Order papers at Paris than there was to suppress Communal papers at Versailles.

It was irritating indeed to the Rurals that at the very same time they declared the return to the church to be the only means of salvation for France, the infidel Commune unearthed the peculiar mysteries of the Picpus nunnery, and of the Church of Saint Laurent.[20] It was a satire upon M. Thiers that, while he showered grand crosses upon the Bonapartist generals in acknowledgement of their mastery in losing battles, signing capitulations, and turning cigarettes at Wilhelmshöhe,[21] the Commune dismissed and arrested its generals whenever they were suspected of neglecting their duties. The expulsion from, and arrest by, the Commune of one of its members[22] who had slipped in under a false name, and had undergone at Lyons six days' imprisonment for simple bankruptcy, was it not a deliberate insult hurled at the forger, Jules Favre,[23] then still the Foreign Minister of France, still selling France to Bismarck, and still dictating his orders to that paragon government of Belgium? But indeed the Commune did not pretend to infallibility, the invariable attribute of all governments of the old stamp. It published its doings and sayings, it initiated the public into all its shortcomings.

In every revolution there intrude, at the side of its true agents, men of a different stamp; some of them survivors of and devotees to past revolutions, without insight into the present movement, but preserving popular influence by their known honesty and courage, or by the sheer force of tradition; others mere bawlers, who, by dint of repeating year after year the same set of stereotyped declamations against the government of the day, have sneaked into the reputation of revolutionists of the first water. After 18 March, some such men did also turn up, and in some cases contrived to play pre-eminent parts. As far as their power went, they hampered the real action of the working class, exactly as men of that sort have hampered the full development of every previous revolution. They are an unavoidable evil: with time they are shaken off; but time was not allowed to the Commune.

Wonderful, indeed, was the change the Commune had wrought in Paris! No longer any trace of the meretricious Paris of the Second Empire. No longer was Paris the rendezvous of British landlords, Irish absentees, American ex-slaveholders and shoddy men, Russian ex-serfowners, and Wallachian boyards. No more corpses at the morgue, no nocturnal burglaries, scarcely any robberies; in fact, for the first time since the days of February 1848 the streets of Paris were safe, and that without any police of any kind. 'We', said a member of the Commune, 'hear no longer of assassination, theft and personal assault; it seems indeed as if the police had dragged along with it to Versailles all its conservative friends.'

The *cocottes* had refound the scent of their protectors—the absconding men of family, religion, and, above all, of property. In their stead, the real women of Paris showed again at the surface—heroic, noble, and devoted, like the women of antiquity. Working, thinking, fighting, bleeding Paris—almost forgetful, in its incubation of a new society, of the cannibals at its gates radiant in the enthusiasm of its historic initiative!

Opposed to this new world at Paris, behold the old world at Versailles—that assembly of the ghouls of all defunct regimes, Legitimists and Orleanists, eager to feed upon the carcass of the nation—with a tail of antediluvian republicans, sanctioning, by their presence in the Assembly, the slaveholders' rebellion, relying for the maintenance of their parliamentary republic upon the vanity of the senile mountebank at its head, and caricaturing 1789 by holding their ghastly meetings in the Jeu de Paume.[24] There it was, this Assembly, the representative of everything dead in France, propped up to the semblance of life by nothing but the swords of the generals of Louis Bonaparte. Paris all truth, Versailles all lie; and that lie vented through the mouth of Thiers.

Thiers tells a deputation of the mayors of the Seine-et-Oise, 'You may rely upon my word, which I have *never* broken!'

He tells the Assembly itself that it was 'the most freely elected and most liberal Assembly France ever possessed'; he tells his motley soldiery that it was 'the admiration of the world, and the finest army France ever possessed'; he tells the provinces that the bombardment of Paris by him was a myth: 'If some cannon-shots have been fired, it is not the deed of the army of Versailles, but of some insurgents trying to make believe that they are fighting, while they dare not show their faces.'

He again tells the provinces that 'of Versailles does not bombard Paris, but only cannonades it'.

He tells the Archbishop of Paris that the pretended executions and reprisals (!) attributed to the Versailles troops were all moonshine. He tells Paris that he was only anxious 'to free it from the hideous tyrants who oppress it', and that, in fact, the Paris of the Commune was 'but a handful of criminals'.

The Paris of M. Thiers was not the real Paris of the 'vile multitude', but a phantom Paris, the Paris of the *francs-fileurs*,[25] the Paris of the boulevards, male and female—the rich, the capitalist, the gilded, the idle Paris, now thronging with its lackeys, its blacklegs, its literary *bohéme* and its *cocottes* at Versailles, Saint-Denis, Rueil, and Saint-Germain; considering the civil war but an agreeable diversion, eyeing the battle going on through telescopes, counting the rounds of cannon, and swearing by their own honour, and that of their prostitutes, that the performance was far better got up than it used to be at the Porte Saint Martin. The men who fell were really dead; the cries of the wounded were cries in good earnest; and, besides, the whole thing was so intensely historical.

This is the Paris of M. Thiers, as the emigration of Coblenz was the France of M. de Calonne.[26]

NOTES TO "THE CIVIL WAR IN FRANCE" (Excerpt)

1. Adolphe Thiers (1797–1877), Orleanist deputy in the Second Republic (1849–1851) and President of the Third Republic (1871–1873).
2. The Girondins were the party of the Right in the French National Convention of 1792, in opposition to the democratic Left, the Montagne (which included the Jacobins). The Girondins favored a republican federation as the form of government for France. The party was so called because its leading members came from Bordeaux (department of the Gironde).
3. Marx's note to the 1871 German edition indicates that Thomas Henry Huxley is meant.
4. On April 16, the Commune declared a moratorium on all war debts and a cancellation of interest payments.

5. An allusion to the rejection of the *concordats a l'amiable* on August 22, 1848. The *concordats* were a proposal, made in June, 1848, to extend the period of payment to debtors who could show that their insolvency was due to the commercial stagnation occasioned by the revolution. Their rejection in August was a direct result of the refusal of the petty bourgeoisie to side with the working class on the issue of amnesty for the June insurgents. The rejection of the *concordats* caused the financial ruin of a large section of the petty bourgeoisie.

6. The "Ignorant Brothers" is the actual name of a religious order, but Marx is using it more generally to refer to the clerical influence on French education during the Second Empire.

7. The *Union Republicaine* (whose actual name was *Alliance Republicaine des Departements*) was a petty bourgeois group of provincial representatives in Paris who were loyal to the Commune.

8. The Commune made an appeal "to the rural workers" at the end of April, 1871.

9. In 1825, the Bourbon restoration government granted compensation amounting to a billion (a milliard) francs to large landowners expropriated during the first French Revolution. The cost of the compensation fell heavily on the peasantry.

10. In 1848 the Provisional Government dealt with its growing deficit by imposing a 45-centime-per-franc surcharge on the peasant's property tax.

11. "the blood tax", military conscription.

12. These laws provided for dictatorial control of the Parisian government over provincial prefects, soldiers, mayors, and schoolteachers.

13. "Rinderpest"- cattle-plague; here, the spirit of revolution.

14. Gregory Ganesco (1830–1877), French publicist, a Rumanian native, supporter first of the Second Empire and then of the Thiers government; Markovsky was Tsarist agent in France who became an official in Thiers' government.

15. The head of the Labor and Exchange Commission under the Commune was Leo Frankel (1844–1896), Hungarian by birth, a member of the General Council of the First International.

16. Jaroslaw Dombrowski (1836–1871), Polish revolutionary democrat, had been active in the movement to liberate Poland from Russian domination in 1863–1864; exiled to France, he led the army of the Commune and was killed in its defense; Walery Wroblewski (1836–1908), also a veteran of the Polish revolt, was a general in the army of the Commune, a member of the General Council of the First International, and its Corresponding Secretary for Poland (1871–1872).

17. The Vendôme column, fashioned out of melted-down cannon, was erected in 1806–1810 to commemorate Napoleon's victories in the German campaign. It was pulled down on May 16, 1871, but restored by the Third Republic after its defeat of the Commune.

18. Eugene Georges Haussmann (1809–1891), Bonapartist politician who directed work on the reconstruction of Paris under the Third Republic.

19. The Hohenzollerns were the Prussian royal family from the amalgamation of Brandenburg with the Duchy of Prussia under Friedrich Wilhelm I in 1618 until the defeat of Wilhelm II in 1918.

20. In the Picpus nunnery, the Commune found instruments of torture and evidence that nuns had been incarcerated in cells. In the Church of Saint Laurent a secret cemetry was discovered, attesting to the murders committed there. The findings were published in the newspaper *Mot d'Ordre* on May 5, 1871.

21. Wilhelmshöhe was the castle where Louis Bonaparte and the captured French generals were imprisoned.
22. Stanislas Blanchet (b. 1833) (real name Pourille) was a French monk and agent provocateur, exposed and arrested by the Commune.
23. Jules Favre (1809–1880), Foreign Minister of the Third Republic (1870–1871); negotiated the capitulation of Paris with Prussia.
24. The Jeu de Paume is the famous tennis court where the Third Estate met in June, 1789 and took an oath to demand a constitution of Louis XVI.
25. *francs-fileurs*, literally, "those who freely walk along"; a pun on *franc-tireur*, a sniper or guerilla (literally, "one who fires freely").
26. During the first French Revolution, Charles Alexandre de Calonne (1734–1832) headed a counterrevolutionary government in exile in Koblenz, on the Rhine, a center for French monarchist emigrés.

Critique of the
Gotha Program (1875)
(*Complete*)

In May of 1875, a congress was held in Gotha to unite the two German
working class parties, the Social Democratic Workers' Party (SDAP) and
the General German Workers' Union (ADAV) into the Socialist Workers'
Party of Germany (SAPD, later SPD). The SDAP (also called the
"Eisenachers") was led by Wilhelm Liebknecht (1826–1800) and August
Bebel (1840–1913), associates of Marx; the ADAV was led by followers of
Ferdinand Lassalle (1825–1864), who had combined working class
politics with advocacy of German unification under Prussian rule. Marx
had been sent a draft of the unity program for the congress, and on May
5 he conveyed his views on it to Wilhelm Bracke (1842–1880), who had
been a member of the ADAV until 1869, when he transferred his allegiance
to the Eisenachers. Marx criticized Lassallean elements in the proposal,
especially its appeals to "equal rights" and "distributive justice," its
emphasis on political remedies, and its tendencies toward Prussian
statism. Despite his objections, the program was adopted with few
amendments on May 27, 1875. Marx's notes were published by Engels
in the form of a pamphlet in 1891, when the SAPD met in Erfurt to draft
a new program. *Critique of the Gotha Program* is Marx's fullest statement
concerning working class demands and goals. The text printed here is
based on Marx's manuscript of 1875; translated from the German by
Joris de Bres.

MARGINAL NOTES ON THE PROGRAMME
OF THE GERMAN WORKERS' PARTY

I

1. Labour is the source of all wealth and culture, *and since* useful
   labour can only be performed in and through society, all members
   of society have an equal right to the undiminished proceeds of
   labour.

First part of the paragraph: 'Labor is the source of all wealth and culture'.
   Labour is *not the source* of all wealth. Nature is just as much the source
of use-values (and surely these are what make up material wealth!) as

labour. Labour is itself only the manifestation of a force of nature, human labour power. This phrase can be found in any children's primer; it is correct in so far as it is *assumed* that labour is performed with the objects and instruments necessary to it. A socialist programme, however, cannot allow such bourgeois formulations to silence the *conditions* which give them the only meaning they possess. Man's labour only becomes a source of use-values, and hence also of wealth, if his relation to nature, the primary source of all instruments and objects of labour, is one of ownership from the start, and if he treats it as belonging to him. There is every good reason for the bourgeoisie to ascribe *supernatural creative power* to labour, for when a man has no property other than his labour power it is precisely labour's dependence on nature that forces him, in all social and cultural conditions, to be the slave of other men who have taken the objective conditions of labour into their own possession. He needs their permission to work, and hence their permission to live.

Let us now leave this sentence as it stands, or rather hobbles. What sort of conclusion would one have expected? Obviously the following: 'Since labour is the source of all wealth, it follows that no one in society can appropriate wealth except as the product of labour. Thus, if a person does not work himself, he must live off the labour of others, and his culture, too, must be acquired at the cost of other people's labour.'

Instead of this the words '*and since*' are used to tack on a second proposition so that a conclusion can be drawn from this one rather than the first.

Second part of the paragraph: 'Useful labour can only be performed in and through society'.

According to the first proposition, labour was the source of all wealth and culture, so that a society could not exist without labour. Now we are told the opposite: 'useful' labour cannot exist without society.

One could just as well have said that it is only in society that useless labour, or even labour harmful to the community, can become a line of business, and that only in society is it possible to live from idleness, etc., etc. —in short, one could have copied down the whole of Rousseau.

And what is 'useful' labour? Surely simply labour which brings the desired useful result. A savage—and man was a savage after he ceased to be an ape—who kills an animal with a stone, gathers fruit, etc., is performing 'useful' labour.

Thirdly: the conclusion: 'And since useful labour can only be performed in and through society, all members of society have an equal right to the undiminished proceeds of labour.'

A beautiful conclusion! If useful labour can only be performed in and through society then the proceeds of labour belong to society—even if the individual worker only receives as much of them as is not required for the maintenance of the 'condition' of labour, society.

In fact, this sentence is not new: it has been used in all periods by the *champions of the existing state of society.* First come the claims of the government and all that goes with it, since it is the social organ for the maintenance of social order; then come the claims of the various kinds of private property, since the various kinds of private property form the foundations of society, etc. Hollow phrases such as these can clearly be twisted and turned at will.

The first and second parts of the paragraph would have some intelligible connection only if worded as follows: 'Labour becomes the source of all wealth and culture only when it is social labour,' or, which comes to the same thing, only 'in and through society'.

This proposition is indisputably correct, for although isolated labour (given its material conditions) can also create use-values, it cannot create either wealth or culture.

But this other proposition is equally indisputable: 'The social development of labour, and thus its development as a source of wealth and culture, proceeds in equal proportion to the development of poverty and destitution among the workers and of wealth and culture among the non-workers.'

Up to the present day all history has been governed by this law. What was needed here, therefore, was not generalizations about 'labour' and 'society' but concrete proof that in present capitalist society the material etc. conditions have finally been created which enable and compel the worker to break this historical curse.

In fact, however, the sole purpose of this paragraph, a mess both in style and content, is to inscribe the Lassallean catchword of 'the undiminished proceeds of labour' as a slogan at the top of the party banner. I shall return to the 'proceeds of labour', 'equal right', etc. below, where the same things reappear in a somewhat different form.

> 2. In present society the capitalist class has a monopoly of the instruments of labour; the resultant dependence of the working class is the cause of misery and servitude in all its forms.

This sentence has been lifted from the Rules of the International but is incorrect in this 'improved' version.[1]

In present society the instruments of labour are the monopoly of the landowners (the monopoly of landed property is even the basis of the monopoly of capital) *and* of the capitalists. Neither class of monopolists is mentioned by name in the relevant passage of the Rules of the International. This text speaks of the *'monopolizer of the means of labour, that is, the sources of life'*; the addition of the 'sources of life' is adequate indication that land and soil are included under the instruments of labour.

The amendment was made because Lassalle, for reasons now generally known, *only* attacked the capitalist class and not the landowners. In Eng-

land, the capitalist generally does not even own the land and soil on which
his factory stands.

> 3. For the emancipation of labour the instruments of labour must be
> elevated to the common property of society and the whole of labour
> must be regulated on a cooperative basis, with a just distribution
> of the proceeds of labour.

'The instruments of labour must be elevated to common property'!
This is probably meant to mean 'converted into common property'. But
this just incidentally.

What are the 'proceeds of labour'? Are they the product of labour or
its value? And in the latter case, is it the total value of the product or
only that part of its value which labour has created over and above the
value of the means of production consumed?

'Proceeds of labour' is a loose notion, used by Lassalle in place of
definite economic concepts.

What is 'just' distribution?

Does not the bourgeoisie claim that the present system of distribution
is 'just'? And given the present mode of production is it not, in fact, the
only 'just' system of distribution? Are economic relations regulated by
legal concepts of right or is the opposite not the case, that legal relations
spring from economic ones? Do not the socialist sectarians themselves
have the most varied notions of 'just' distribution?

To discover what we are meant to understand by the phrase 'just distribution' as used here we must take the opening paragraph and this one
together. The latter presupposes a society in which 'the instruments of
labour are common property and the whole of labour is regulated on a
cooperative basis' and from the opening paragraph we learn that 'all members of society have an equal right to the undiminished proceeds of
labour'.

'All members of society'? Including people who do not work? Then
what remains of the 'undiminished proceeds of labour'? Only the working
members of society? Then what remains of the 'equal right' of all members of society?

'All members of society' and 'equal right', however, are obviously mere
phrases. The heart of the matter is that in this communist society every
worker is supposed to receive the 'undiminished' Lassallean 'proceeds
of labour'.

If we start by taking 'proceeds of labour' to mean the product of labour,
then the cooperative proceeds of labour are the *total social product*.

From this the following must now be deducted:

Firstly: cover to replace the means of production used up.

Secondly: an additional portion for the expansion of production.

Thirdly: a reserve or insurance fund in case of accidents, disruption caused by natural calamities, etc.

These deductions from the 'undiminished proceeds of labour' are an economic necessity and their magnitude will be determined by the means and forces available. They can partly be calculated by reference to probability, but on no account by reference to justice.

There remains the other part of the total product, designed to serve as means of consumption.

But before this is distributed to individuals the following further deductions must be made:

Firstly: the general costs of all administration not directly appertaining to production.

This part will, from the outset, be very significantly limited in comparison with the present society. It will diminish commensurately with the development of the new society.

Secondly: the amount set aside for needs communally satisfied, such as schools, health services, etc.

This part will, from the outset, be significantly greater than in the present society. It will grow commensurately with the development of the new society.

Thirdly: a fund for people unable to work, etc., in short, for what today comes under so-called official poor relief.

Only now do we come to that 'distribution' which, under the influence of the Lassalleans, is the only thing considered by this narrow-minded programme, namely that part of the means of consumption which is distributed among the individual producers within the cooperative.

The 'undiminished proceeds of labour' have meanwhile already been quietly 'diminished', although as a member of society the producer still receives, directly or indirectly, what is withheld from him as a private individual.

Just as the phrase 'undiminished proceeds of labour' has vanished, the phrase 'proceeds of labour' now disappears altogether.

Within the cooperative society based on common ownership of the means of production the producers do not exchange their products; similarly, the labour spent on the products no longer appears *as the value* of these products, possessed by them as a material characteristic, for now, in contrast to capitalist society, individual pieces of labour are no longer merely indirectly, but directly, a component part of the total labour. The phrase 'proceeds of labour', which even today is too ambiguous to be of any value, thus loses any meaning whatsoever.

We are dealing here with a communist society, not as it has *developed* on its own foundations, but on the contrary, just as it *emerges* from capitalist society. In every respect, economically, morally, intellectually, it is thus still stamped with the birth-marks of the old society from whose womb it has emerged. Accordingly, the individual producer gets back from society—after the deductions—exactly what he has given it. What he has given it is his individual quantum of labour. For instance, the social working day consists of the sum of the individual hours of work. The individual labour time of the individual producer thus constitutes his contribution to the social working day, his share of it. Society gives him a certificate stating that he has done such and such an amount of work (after the labour done for the communal fund has been deducted), and with this certificate he can withdraw from the social supply of means of consumption as much as costs an equivalent amount of labour. The same amount of labour he has given to society in one form, he receives back in another.

Clearly, the same principle is at work here as that which regulates the exchange of commodities as far as this is an exchange of equal values. Content and form have changed because under the new conditions no one can contribute anything except his labour and conversely nothing can pass into the ownership of individuals except individual means of consumption. The latter's distribution among individual producers, however, is governed by the same principle as the exchange of commodity equivalents: a given amount of labour in one form is exchanged for the same amount in another.

Hence *equal right* is here still—in principle—a *bourgeois right*, although principle and practice are no longer at loggerheads, while the exchange of equivalents in commodity exchange only exists *on the average* and not in the individual case.

In spite of such progress this *equal right* still constantly suffers a bourgeois limitation. The right of the producers is *proportional* to the labour they do; the equality consists in the fact that measurement is *by the same standard*, labour. One person, however, may be physically and intellectually superior to another and thus be able to do more labour in the same space of time or work for a longer period. To serve as a measure labour must therefore be determined by duration or intensity, otherwise it ceases to be a standard. This *equal* right is an unequal right for unequal labour. It does not acknowledge any class distinctions, because everyone is just a worker like everyone else, but it gives tacit recognition to a worker's individual endowment and hence productive capacity as natural privileges. *This right is thus in its content one of inequality, just like any other right.* A right can by its nature only consist in the application of an equal standard, but unequal individuals (and they would not be different individuals if they were not unequal) can only be measured by the same standard if they are looked at from the same aspect, if they are grasped from one *particular* side, e.g., if in the present case they are regarded *only as workers* and nothing else is seen in them, everything else is ignored. Further: one worker is married, another is not; one has more children than another, etc., etc. Thus, with the same work performance and hence the same share of the social consumption fund, one will in fact be receiving more than another, one will be richer than another, etc. If all these defects were to be avoided rights would have to be unequal rather than equal.

Such defects, however, are inevitable in the first phase of communist society, given the specific form in which it has emerged after prolonged birth-pangs from capitalist society. Right can never rise above the economic structure of a society and its contingent cultural development.

In a more advanced phase of communist society, when the enslaving subjugation of individuals to the division of labour, and thereby the antithesis between intellectual and physical labour, have disappeared; when labour is no longer just a means of keeping alive but has itself become a vital need; when the all-round development of individuals has also increased their productive powers and all the springs of cooperative wealth flow more abundantly—only then can society wholly cross the narrow horizon of bourgeois right and inscribe on its banner: From each according to his abilities, to each according to his needs![2]

If I have dealt at some length with the 'undiminished proceeds of labour' on the one hand, and 'equal right' and 'just distribution' on the other, it is in order to show the criminal nature of what is being attempted: on the one hand, our party is to be forced to re-accept as dogmas ideas which may have made some sense at a particular time but which are now only a load of obsolete verbal rubbish; on the other hand, the realistic outlook instilled in our party at the cost of immense effort, but now firmly rooted in it, is to be perverted by means of ideological, legal and other humbug so common among the democrats and the French socialists.

Quite apart from the points made so far, it was a mistake anyway to lay the main stress on so-called *distribution* and to make it into the central point.

The distribution of the means of consumption at any given time is merely a consequence of the distribution of the conditions of production themselves; the distribution of the latter, however, is a feature of the mode of production itself. The capitalist mode of production, for example, rests on the fact that the material conditions of production are in the hands of non-workers in the form of property in capital and land, while the masses are only in possession of their personal condition of production, labour power. If the elements of production are distributed in this way, the present distribution of the means of consumption follows automatically. If the material conditions of production were the cooperative property of the workers themselves a different distribution of the means of consumption from that of today would follow of its own accord. Vulgar socialists (and from them, in turn, a section of the democrats) have followed the bourgeois economists in their consideration and treatment of distribution as something independent of the mode of production and hence in the presentation of socialism as primarily revolving around the question of distribution. Why go back a step when the real state of affairs has been laid bare?

> 4. The emancipation of labour must be the work of the working
> class, in relation to which all other classes are *a single reactionary*
> *mass*.

The first strophe is an 'improved' version of the preamble to the Rules of the International. There it is said: 'The emancipation of the working classes must be conquered by the working classes themselves'; here, in contrast, 'the working class' has to emancipate—what?—labour. Understand who may.

In compensation, however, the antistrophe is a Lassallean quote of the purest ilk: 'in relation to which (the working class) all other classes are *a single reactionary mass*'.

In the Communist Manifesto it is said, 'Of all the classes that stand face to face with the bourgeoisie today, the proletariat alone is a *really revolutionary class*. The other classes decay and finally disappear in the face of modern industry; the proletariat is its special and essential product.'

The bourgeoisie is here conceived of as a revolutionary class—as the bringer of large-scale industry—in relation to the feudal lords and the lower middle class, who want to retain all the social positions created by obsolete modes of production. These do not, therefore, form a single reactionary mass *together with the bourgeoisie*.

On the other hand the proletariat is revolutionary in relation to the bourgeoisie because it has itself sprung up on the ground of large-scale industry; it is struggling to divest production of its capitalist character, which the bourgeoisie seeks to perpetuate. The Manifesto adds, however, that the lower middle class is becoming revolutionary 'in view of (its) impending transfer into the proletariat'.

From this point of view, therefore, it is once again nonsense to say that in relation to the working class it 'forms a single reactionary mass', 'together with the bourgeoisie' and with the feudal lords to boot.

At the last elections, did we proclaim to the artisans, small manufacturers, etc. and *peasants*: In relation to us you, together with the bourgeoisie and the feudal lords, form a single reactionary mass?

Lassalle knew the Communist Manifesto by heart, just as his faithful followers know his own gospels. The reason for such gross falsification can thus only be that he wanted to extenuate his alliance with the absolutist and feudal opponents of the bourgeoisie.

In the above paragraph, moreover, this oracular utterance is dragged in by the scruff of its neck, without any connection to the bowdlerized quote from the Rules of the International. It is therefore simply an impertinence to include it here and one that will by no means displease Herr Bismarck — a cheap swipe typical of Berlin's would-be Marat.[3]

> 5. The working class must initially work for its emancipation *within the framework of the present-day national state*, conscious that the necessary result of its efforts, common to the workers of all civilized countries, will be the international brotherhood of peoples.

In contrast to the Communist Manifesto and all earlier forms of socialism, Lassalle approached the workers' movement from the narrowest national point of view. His approach is followed here — and this after the work of the International!

It is perfectly self-evident that in order to be at all capable of struggle the working class must organize itself *as a class* at home and that the domestic sphere must be the immediate arena for its struggle. To this extent its class struggle is national, not in content, but as the Communist Manifesto says, 'in form'. But the 'framework of the present-day national state', e.g., the German Reich, is itself in turn economically 'within the framework of the world market' and politically 'within the framework of the system of states'. Any businessman will tell you that German trade is at the same time foreign trade, and the greatness of Herr Bismarck lies exactly in the *international* orientation of his policy.

And to what is the internationalism of the German workers' party reduced? To the consciousness that the result of their efforts 'will be *the international brotherhood of peoples*' — a phrase borrowed from the bourgeois League of Peace and Freedom[4] and which is intended to pass as an equivalent for the international brotherhood of the working classes in the joint struggle against the ruling classes and their governments. Not a word, therefore, of the *international role* of the German working class! And this is how it is meant to challenge its own bourgeoisie, which is already fraternally linked with the bourgeoisie in all other countries, and Herr Bismarck's international policy of conspiracy!

In fact, the programme's commitment to internationalism is *infinitely smaller* even than that of the free trade party. The latter also claims that the result of its efforts will be the 'international brotherhood of peoples'. It is also *doing* something, however, to internationalize trade and is certainly not content with the mere consciousness that all peoples are carrying on trade at home.

The international activity of the working classes is not in any way dependent on the existence of the International Working Men's Association. This was only the first attempt to create a central organ for such activity; an attempt which will be of lasting success because of the impetus it gave but which could not be continued in its *initial historical form* following the fall of the Paris Commune.

Bismarck's *Norddeutsche* was perfectly right when it declared, to the satisfaction of its master, that the German workers' party had renounced internationalism in its new programme.[5]

II

> Starting from these basic principles, the German workers' party will strive, by all legal means, for a *free state and* a socialist society; the abolition of the wage system *together with* the *iron law of wages*, and of exploitation in every form; the removal of all social and political inequality.

I will come back to the 'free' state below.

So, in future, the German workers' party will have to believe in Lassalle's 'iron law of wages'! To prevent it from being lost, the programme goes through the nonsense of speaking of the 'abolition of the wage system' (which should read 'the system of wage labour') '*together with* the iron law of wages'. If I abolish wage labour I naturally abolish all its laws as well, whether they are made of iron or sponge. Lassalle's attack on wage labour, however, revolves almost exclusively around this so-called law. As proof, therefore, that the Lassallean sect has come out on top, the 'wage system' must be abolished '*together with* the iron law of wages', and never without it.

It is common knowledge that Lassalle contributed nothing to the 'iron law of wages' expect the word 'iron', which he pilfered from Goethe's 'great, eternal, iron laws'. The word 'iron' is a label by which the true believers can recognize each other. But if I take the law with Lassalle's stamp on it and thus in the way he meant it, then I must also take it with his supporting arguments. And what do I get? As Lange showed only a short time after Lassalle's death, the Malthusian theory of population (preached by Lange himself).[6] But if this theory is right, then I *cannot* abolish the law, even by abolishing wage labour a hundred times over, for this law then governs not only the system of wage labour but *all* social systems. This, precisely, has been the basis of economists' proofs, for fifty years or more, that socialism cannot abolish poverty, which has its basis in nature, but can only *generalize* it, distributing it simultaneously over the whole surface of society.

But all that is beside the main point. *Quite apart* from the *false* Lassallean formulation of the law, the really outrageous step back consists in the following:

Since Lassalle's death the scientific insight has made headway in our party that wages are not what they *appear* to be, namely the value or price of labour, but only a disguised form of the *value or price of labour power*. Thereby the whole of the former bourgeois conception of wages was thrown overboard once and for all, as well as all criticisms of it, and it became clear that the wage labourer is only allowed to work for his own livelihood, i.e., *to live*, if he works a certain amount of time without pay for the capitalist (and thus also for the latter's fellow consumers of surplus value); that the whole capitalist system of production turns on the prolongation of this free labour through the extension of the working day and through the development of productivity, the increasing intensification of labour power, etc.; and that the system of wage labour is consequently a system of slavery, increasing in severity commensurately with the development of the social productive forces of labour, irrespective of whether the worker is then better or worse paid. And now, after this insight has gained more and more ground in our party, there comes this return to the dogmas of Lassalle, even though people must be aware that Lassalle *knew nothing* of the true nature of wages and that he followed the bourgeois economists in mistaking the appearance of the matter for its essence.

It is as if, among slaves who have finally got behind the secret of slavery and broken out in rebellion, one slave, still the prisoner of obsolete ideas, were to write in the programme of the rebellion: Slavery must be abolished because the provisioning of slaves in the slave system cannot exceed a certain low maximum!

The mere fact that the representatives of our party were capable of making such a monstrous attack on an insight which has gained wide acceptance among the mass of the party is surely sufficient proof of the criminal levity and complete lack of conscience with which they set to work on the formulation of the compromise programme.

Instead of the unspecific closing phrase of the paragraph, 'the removal of all social and political inequality', it should have been said that with the abolition of class distinctions all forms of social and political inequality will disappear of their own accord.

III

> The German workers' party, *in order to pave the way for the solution of the social question*, demands the creation of producers' cooperatives with state aid under the democratic control of the working people. These producers' cooperatives are *to be called into being* for industry and agriculture to such an extent *that the socialist organization of the whole of labour will arise out of them*.

After Lassalle's 'iron law of wages', the prophet's remedy! The way is 'paved' for it in a suitably dignified manner! The existing class struggle is discarded in favour of the hack phrase of a newspaper scribbler—'*the social question'*, for the solution of which one 'paves the way'. Instead of being the result of the revolutionary process of social transformation in society, the 'socialist organization of the whole of labour' 'arises' from 'state aid' to producers' cooperatives which the *state*, not the workers, is to 'call into being'. The notion that state loans can be used for the construction of a new society as easily as they can for the construction of a new railway is worthy of Lassalle's imagination!

A last remnant of shame induces them to put 'state aid' — 'under the democratic control of the working people'.

Firstly, the 'working people' in Germany are mainly peasants, and not proletarians.

Secondly, 'democratic' translates as 'by the rule of the people'. But what does 'control by the rule of the people of the working people' mean? Particularly in the case of a working people which in presenting the state with demands such as these is expressing its full awareness of the fact that it neither rules nor is mature enough to rule!

It would be superfluous to begin to criticize here a recipe which Buchez concocted under Louis Philippe *in opposition* to the French socialists and which was accepted by the reactionary workers of the *Atelier*.[7] The most offensive fact is not that this wonder cure has been included in the programme but that there has been a general retreat from the standpoint of a class movement to that of a sectarian one.

The workers' desire to create the conditions for cooperative production on a social and, by beginning at home, at first on a national scale, means nothing beyond that they are working to revolutionize the present conditions of production; it has nothing in common with the creation of cooperative societies with state aid! As far as the present cooperative societies are concerned, they are *only* valuable if they are independent creations of the workers, and not the protégés either of governments or of the bourgeoisie.

IV

I come now to the democratic section.

A. The free basis of the state.

According to Section II, the first thing that the German workers' party strives for is 'a free state'.

A free state — what does that mean?

It is by no means the goal of workers who have discarded the narrow mentality of humble subjects to make the state 'free'. In the German Reich the 'state' has almost as much 'freedom' as in Russia. Freedom consists in converting the state from an organ superimposed on society into one thoroughly subordinate to it; and even today state forms are more or less free depending on the degree to which they restrict the 'freedom of the state'.

The German workers' party—at least if it adopts this programme—thus shows that its socialist values do not even go skin-deep, for instead of treating existing society (and the same holds good for any future one) as the *basis* of the existing *state* (or future state in the case of future society), it treats the state as an independent entity with its own 'intellectual, ethical and liberal foundations'.

And what of the wild misuse made in the programme of the words 'present state' and 'present society', or the even more riotous misconception of the state to which it addresses its demands?

The 'present society' is capitalist society, which exists in all civilized countries, freed in varying degrees from the admixture of medievalism, modified in varying degrees by the particular historical development of each country, and developed to a varying degree. In contrast to this, the 'present state' changes with each country's border. It differs between the Prusso-German empire and Switzerland, between England and the United States. '*The* present state' is thus a fiction.

Nevertheless, the various states of the various civilized countries, despite their motley diversity of form, do have this in common: they all stand on the ground of modern bourgeois society although the degree of capitalist development varies. They thus also share certain essential characteristics. In this sense one can speak of 'present states' in contrast to the future when their present root, bourgeois society, will have died off.

The question then arises: What transformation will the state undergo in a communist society? In other words, what social functions will remain that are analogous to the present functions of the state? This question can only be answered scientifically and even a thousandfold combination of the word 'state' and the word 'people' will not bring us a flea-hop nearer the problem.

Between capitalist and communist society lies a period of revolutionary transformation from one to the other. There is a corresponding period of transition in the political sphere and in this period the state can only take the form of a *revolutionary dictatorship of the proletariat*.

The programme, however, does not deal either with this or with the future public affairs of communist society.

There is nothing in its political demands beyond the old and generally familiar democratic litany: universal suffrage, direct legislation, popular justice, a people's army, etc. They merely echo the bourgeois People's Party[8] or the League of Peace and Freedom. All these demands, unless exaggerated into fantastic dreams, have already been *realized*. It is just that the state to which they belong does not lie within the borders of the German Reich but in Switzerland, the United States, etc. This kind of 'state of the future' is a '*present state*', although it exists outside the 'framework' of the German Empire.

One thing has been forgotten, however. The German workers' party expressly declares that it acts within the 'present national state'. This means their own state, the Prusso-German empire. (Most of its demands would be meaningless if this were not so, for one can only demand what one has not already got.) Under these circumstances the main point should not have been forgotten, which is that all these pretty little gewgaws depend on the recognition of the so-called sovereignty of the people and are hence only appropriate in a *democratic republic.*

Although they lack the courage—and wisely so, for the circumstances demand caution—to call for a democratic republic after the manner of the French workers' programmes under Louis Philippe and Louis Napoleon, it was wrong to resort to the subterfuge which is neither 'honest'[9] nor decent of making demands which are only feasible in a democratic repub-lic, and to address these demands to a state which is no more than a military despotism and a police state, bureaucratically carpentered, embel-lished with parliamentary forms and disguised by an admixture of feudalism although already under the influence of the bourgeoisie, and then to assure this same state into the bargain that they imagine they can impose these demands on it 'by legal means'.

Even vulgar democrats, who see the millennium in the democratic republic and who have no inkling that it is precisely in this final state form of bourgeois society that the class struggle must be fought to a conclusion, even they tower mountains above this kind of democratism which keeps within the bounds of what is allowed by the police and disallowed by logic.

The fact that the 'state' here stands for the government machine or for the state in so far as it forms through the division of labour a special organism separate from society is shown by the following words: 'The German workers' party demands *as the economic basis of* the state: a single progressive income tax, etc.' Taxes provide the economic basis of the government machinery and of nothing else. In the state of the future, already existing in Switzerland, this demand has been pretty well realized. Income tax presupposes varied sources of income for varied social classes, and hence capitalist society. It is thus not surprising that the Liverpool Financial Reformers, a bourgeois group led by Gladstone's brother, are putting forward the same demands as this programme.

B. The German workers' party demands as the intellectual and ethical basis of the state:

1. Universal and *equal elementary education* by the state. Universal com-pulsory school attendance. Free tuition.

'*Equal elementary education*'? What are we meant to understand by these words? Is it believed that in our present society (and this is all we have to deal with here) education can be *equal* for all classes? Or is it demanded that the upper classes ought also to be reduced to the modicum of education—the elementary school—which is all that is compatible with the economic conditions of both wage-labourers and peasants?

'Universal compulsory school attendance. Free tuition.' The first of these exists even in Germany, and the second, in the case of elementary schools, in Switzerland and the United States. If in some states of the latter higher institutions of learning are also 'free', this in fact only means that the upper classes can defray the costs of their education out of the general taxpayer's pocket. Incidentally, the same is true of the 'free administration of justice' demanded under A/5. Criminal justice can be had free anywhere; civil justice is almost exclusively concerned with property conflicts and is hence almost exclusively the concern of the propertied classes. Should their cases be paid for out of public funds?

The paragraph on schools at least ought to have demanded technical schools (theoretical and practical) in combination with elementary schooling.

The idea of *elementary education by the state* is completely objectionable. Specifying the means available to elementary schools, the qualification of teaching staff, the subjects to be taught, etc. by a general law, as is done in the United States, and having state inspectors to supervise the observance of these regulations, is something quite different from appointing the state as educator of the people! Rather, government and church should alike be excluded from all influence on the schools. Indeed, in the Prusso-German Empire of all places, (and the lame excuse that one is speaking of a future state is no way out; we have already seen what that means), it is inversely the state that could do with a rude education by the people.

Despite its democratic clang, the whole programme is thoroughly infested with the Lassallean sect's servile belief in the state, or, what is no better, by a democratic faith in miracles, or rather, it is a compromise between these two sorts of faith in miracles, both equally far removed from socialism.

'*Freedom of science*', says one paragraph of the Prussian Constitution. Then why here?

'*Freedom of conscience*'! If one should want, in this era of the *Kulturkampf*,[10] to remind the liberals of their old catchwords, then surely it should only have been done in this form: Everyone should be free to relieve himself religiously as well as physically without the police sticking their noses in. But at this point the workers' party ought to have expressed its awareness that bourgeois 'freedom of conscience' only means the toleration of every possible kind of *religious freedom of conscience*, while its own goal is rather the liberation of the conscience from all religious spookery. But it chooses not to go further than the 'bourgeois' level.

I have now come to the end, for the appendix which now follows is not a *characteristic* part of the programme. I can thus be very brief here.

2. Normal working day.

In no other country has a workers' party restricted itself to such a vague demand. The length of the working day considered normal in the given circumstances has always been specified.

3. The restriction of female labour and the prohibition of child labour.

The standardization of the working day must anyway result in the restriction of female labour as far as this refers to the length of the working day, breaks, etc. Otherwise, the reference can only be to the exclusion of women from branches of labour which are specifically unhealthy for the female body or morally objectionable to the female sex. If this is what was meant, it should have been stated.

'*Prohibition of child labour*'! It was absolutely essential to give an *age-limit* here.

The *general prohibition* of child labour is incompatible with the existence of large-scale industry. It is thus only an empty, pious wish.

Its implementation—if possible—would be a reactionary step. With strict regulation of working hours according to age and with other precautionary measures to protect the children, the early combination of productive labour with education is one of the most powerful means for the transformation of present society.

4. State supervision of industry in the factory, workshop and home.

In the case of the Prusso-German state there should certainly have been a demand that inspectors be removable only by a court of law; that every worker should be able to take inspectors to court for neglect of duty; and that inspectors should only be recruited from the medical profession.

5. Regulation of prison labour.

A pretty demand in a general workers' programme. In any case, it ought to have been made clear that there was no wish to see prisoners handled like animals for fear of competition, and especially no intention to deprive them of their only means of improvement, productive labour. Surely at least this much could have been expected from socialists.

6. An effective liability law.

What is meant by an 'effective' liability law should have been stated.

It could be noted in passing that, in speaking of the normal working day, the section of the factory laws relating to health regulations, safety measures, etc. has been overlooked. The liability law would only come into operation when these regulations were infringed.

In short, this appendix, too, is distinguished by its slovenly editing. *Dixi et salvavi animam meam.*[11]

NOTES TO "CRITIQUE OF THE GOTHA PROGRAM"

1. The relevant section of the Rules reads as follows: "The economical subjection of the man of labor to the monopolizer of the means of labor, that is, the sources of life, lies at the bottom of servitude in all its forms, of all social misery, mental degradation, and political dependence" (*The First International*

and After, edited by David Fernbach. New York: Vintage Books, 1974), p. 82). Marx perceives the revision as a deliberate exclusion by the Lassalleans of landowners from those specified as "monopolizers of the means of labor".

2. This slogan, so often attributed to Marx on the basis of this text, was actually being quoted by him. Its real author is now disputed, but in 1875 the slogan was generally attributed to Louis Blanc (1811–1882), member of the Provisional Government in the French Revolution of 1848.

3. Jean-Paul Marat (1743–1793), outspoken French publicist and Jacobin revolutionary, persecuted and eventually assassinated by the Girondins, and thereafter regarded as a martyr by the Left. "Berlin's would-be Marat" is apparently a reference to Wilhelm Hasselmann (b. 1844), prominent figure in the ADAV and editor of the Lassallean paper *Neuer Sozial-Demokrat* (1871–1875); he remained a member of the SAPD, and was expelled from Bismark's Germany in 1880.

4. The League of Peace and Freedom was a democratically oriented political organization which represented bourgeois rather than proletarian interests. Mikhail Bakunin (1814–1876), Marx's rival within the First International, worked within it until 1868, when the working class orientation of his secret International Brotherhood became clear to the League's members.

5. This claim was made in the March 20, 1875 issue of the *Norddeutsche Allgemeine Zeitung*.

6. Friedrich Albert Lange (1828–1875), neo-Kantian philosopher, author of *The Workers' Question in its Significance for Present and Future* (1865). Engels criticized this book's reliance on Malthus and low opinion of Hegel in a letter to Lange of March 29, 1865.

7. *L'Atelier* was a monthly journal published in the 1840s, influenced by the "Christian Socialism" of the French writer Philippe Buchez (1796–1865).

8. The People's Party was a south-German democratic party of petty bourgeois class affiliation.

9. "honest" was a nickname of the Eisenachers (the SDAP).

10. *Kulturkampf* = "cultural struggle," the name for Bismarck's repressive anti-Catholic policies of the 1870s.

11. *Dixi et salvavi animam meam* = "I have spoken and saved my soul."

IV
Capital
(1867–1883)

Capital (1867)
(*Selections*)

The first volume of Marx's *Capital: A Critique of Political Economy*, was finally published in May, 1867. The remainder of the work was left unfinished at Marx's death, but his drafts were edited and published by Engels: Volume 2 in 1885 and Volume 3 in 1894. *Capital* has the reputation of being a difficult work, but after the opening exposition of value (about which Marx warns us himself in the Preface) there is nothing very abstract or obscure about its argument. Marx's style is polished, often witty; and the book is copiously documented from Marx's extensive readings in political economy and history.

Marx regarded *Capital* as the chief accomplishment of his life. On April 30, 1867, shortly before the publication of Volume 1, he wrote of its composition to his friend Siegfried Meyer (1840–1872) in New York: "I was constantly hovering on the edge of the grave. Hence I had to make use of *every* moment when I was able to work to complete my book, to which I have sacrificed health, happiness and family. . . . I laugh at the so-called "practical" men with their wisdom. If one chose to be an ox, one could of course turn one's back on the sufferings of mankind and look after one's own skin. But I should have really regarded myself as *impractical* if I had pegged out without completely finishing my book, at least in manuscript."

The following selections from *Capital* are all drawn from Volume 1. Emphasis is on Marx's exposition of his theory of value as socially necessary labor time, his theory of surplus-value, and his account of the historical tendency of capitalist accumulation. Translated from the German by Ben Fowkes.

Preface to the First Edition

This work, whose first volume I now submit to the public, forms the continuation of my book *Zur Kritik der Politischen Ökonomie*, published in 1859. The long pause between the first part and the continuation is due to an illness of many years' duration, which interrupted my work again and again.

The substance of that earlier work is summarized in the first chapter of this volume. This is done not merely for the sake of connectedness and completeness. The presentation is improved. As far as circumstances in any way permit, many points only hinted at in the earlier book are here worked out more fully, while, conversely, points worked out fully there are only touched upon in this volume. The sections on the history of the theories of value and of money are now, of course, left out altogether. However, the reader of the earlier work will find new sources relating to the history of those theories in the notes to the first chapter.

Beginnings are always difficult in all sciences. The understanding of the first chapter, especially the section that contains the analysis of commodities, will therefore present the greatest difficulty. I have popularized the passages concerning the substance of value and the magnitude of value as much as possible.*ᵃ* The value-form, whose fully developed shape is the money-form, is very simple and slight in content. Nevertheless, the human mind has sought in vain for more than 2,000 years to get to the bottom of it, while on the other hand there has been at least an approximation to a successful analysis of forms which are much richer in content and more complex. Why? Because the complete body is easier to study than its cells. Moreover, in the analysis of economic forms neither microscopes nor chemical reagents are of assistance. The power of abstraction must replace both. But for bourgeois society, the commodity-form of the product of labour, or the value-form of the commodity, is the economic cell-form. To the superficial observer, the analysis of these forms seems to turn upon minutiae. It does in fact deal with minutiae, but so similarly does microscopic anatomy.

With the exception of the section on the form of value, therefore, this volume cannot stand accused on the score of difficulty. I assume, of

---

ᵃ This is the more necessary, in that even the section of Ferdinand Lassalle's work against Schulze-Delitzsch in which he professes to give 'the intellectual quintessence' of my explanations on these matters, contains important mistakes. If Ferdinand Lassalle has borrowed almost literally from my writings, and without any acknowledgement, all the general theoretical propositions in his economic works, for example those on the historical character of capital, on the connection between the relations of production and the mode of production, etc., etc., even down to the terminology created by me, this may perhaps be due to purposes of propaganda. I am of course not speaking here of his detailed working-out and application of these propositions, which I have nothing to do with.[1]

course, a reader who is willing to learn something new and therefore to think for himself.

The physicist either observes natural processes where they occur in their most significant form, and are least affected by disturbing influences, or, wherever possible, he makes experiments under conditions which ensure that the process will occur in its pure state. What I have to examine in this work is the capitalist mode of production, and the relations of production and forms of intercourse [*Verkehrsverhältnisse*] that correspond to it. Until now, their *locus classicus* has been England. This is the reason why England is used as the main illustration of the theoretical developments I make. If, however, the German reader pharisaically shrugs his shoulders at the condition of the English industrial and agricultural workers, or optimistically comforts himself with the thought that in Germany things are not nearly so bad, I must plainly tell him: *De te fabula narratur!*[2]

Intrinsically, it is not a question of the higher or lower degree of development of the social antagonisms that spring from the natural laws of capitalist production. It is a question of these laws themselves, of these tendencies winning their way through and working themselves out with iron necessity. The country that is more developed industrially only shows, to the less developed, the image of its own future.

But in any case, and apart from all this, where capitalist production has made itself fully at home amongst us,[3] for instance in the factories properly so called, the situation is much worse than in England, because the counterpoise of the Factory Acts is absent. In all other spheres, and just like the rest of Continental Western Europe, we suffer not only from the development of capitalist production, but also from the incompleteness of that development. Alongside the modern evils, we are oppressed by a whole series of inherited evils, arising from the passive survival of archaic and outmoded modes of production, with their accompanying train of anachronistic social and political relations. We suffer not only from the living, but from the dead. *Le mort saisit le vif!*[4]

The social statistics of Germany and the rest of Continental Western Europe are, in comparison with those of England, quite wretched. But they raise the veil just enough to let us catch a glimpse of the Medusa's head behind it. We should be appalled at our own circumstances if, as in England, our governments and parliaments periodically appointed commissions of inquiry into economic conditions; if these commissions were armed with the same plenary powers to get at the truth; if it were possible to find for this purpose men as competent, as free from partisanship and respect of persons as are England's factory inspectors, her medical reporters on public health, her commissioners of inquiry into the exploitation of women and children, into conditions of housing and nourishment, and so on. Perseus wore a magic cap so that the monsters he hunted down might not see him. We draw the magic cap down over our own eyes and ears so as to deny that there are any monsters.

Let us not deceive ourselves about this. Just as in the eighteenth century the American War of Independence sounded the tocsin for the European middle class, so in the nineteenth century the American Civil War did the same for the European working class. In England the process of transformation is palpably evident. When it has reached a certain point, it must react on the Continent. There it will take a form more brutal or more humane, according to the degree of development of the working class itself. Apart from any higher motives, then, the most basic interests of the present ruling classes dictate to them that they clear out of the way all the legally removable obstacles to the development of the working class. For this reason, among others, I have devoted a great deal of space in this volume to the history, the details, and the results of the English factory legislation. One nation can and should learn from others. Even when a society has begun to track down the natural laws of its movement—and it is the ultimate aim of this work to reveal the economic law of motion of modern society—it can neither leap over the natural phases of its development nor remove them by decree. But it can shorten and lessen the birth-pangs.

To prevent possible misunderstandings, let me say this. I do not by any means depict the capitalist and the landowner in rosy colours. But individuals are dealt with here only in so far as they are the personifications of economic categories, the bearers [*Träger*] of particular class-relations and interests. My standpoint, from which the development of the economic formation of society is viewed as a process of natural history, can less than any other make the individual responsible for relations whose creature he remains, socially speaking, however much he may subjectively raise himself above them.

In the domain of political economy, free scientific inquiry does not merely meet the same enemies as in all other domains. The peculiar nature of the material it deals with summons into the fray on the opposing side the most violent, sordid and malignant passions of the human breast, the Furies of private interest. The Established Church, for instance, will more readily pardon an attack on thirty-eight of its thirty-nine articles than on one thirty-ninth of its income. Nowadays atheism itself is a *culpa levis*,[b] as compared with the criticism of existing property relations. Nevertheless, even here there is an unmistakable advance. I refer, as an example, to the Blue Book published within the last few weeks: 'Correspondence with Her Majesty's Missions Abroad, Regarding Industrial Questions and Trades' Unions'. There the representatives of the English Crown in foreign countries declare in plain language that in Germany, in France, in short in all the civilized states of the European Continent, a radical change in the existing relations between capital and labour is as

_____

[b] 'Venial sin'.

evident and inevitable as in England. At the same time, on the other side of the Atlantic Ocean, Mr. Wade, Vice-President of the United States, has declared in public meetings that, after the abolition of slavery, a radical transformation in the existing relations of capital and landed property is on the agenda. These are signs of the times, not to be hidden by purple mantles or black cassocks. They do not signify that tomorrow a miracle will occur. They do show that, within the ruling classes themselves, the foreboding is emerging that the present society is no solid crystal, but an organism capable of change, and constantly engaged in a process of change.

The second volume of this work will deal with the process of the circulation of capital (Book II) and the various forms of the process of capital in its totality (Book III), while the third and last volume (Book IV) will deal with the history of the theory.[5]

I welcome every opinion based on scientific criticism. As to the prejudices of so-called public opinion, to which I have never made concessions, now, as ever, my maxim is that of the great Florentine:

'*Segui il tuo corso, e lascia dir le genti.*'[6]

Karl Marx

London, 25 July 1867

Part One
Commodities and Money

Chapter 1
The Commodity

I. THE TWO FACTORS OF THE COMMODITY: USE-VALUE AND VALUE (SUBSTANCE OF VALUE, MAGNITUDE OF VALUE)

The wealth of societies in which the capitalist mode of production prevails appears as an 'immense collection of commodities'[c]; the individual commodity appears as its elementary form. Our investigation therefore begins with the analysis of the commodity.

The commodity is, first of all, an external object, a thing which through its qualities satisfies human needs of whatever kind. The nature of these needs, whether they arise, for example, from the stomach, or the imagi-

---

[c] Karl Marx, *Zur Kritik der Politischen Ökonomie*, Berlin, 1859, p. 3 [English translation, p. 27].

nation, makes no difference.*d* Nor does it matter here how the thing satisfies man's need, whether directly as a means of subsistence, i.e. an object of consumption, or indirectly as a means of production.

Every useful thing, for example, iron, paper, etc., may be looked at from the two points of view of quality and quantity. Every useful thing is a whole composed of many properties; it can therefore be useful in various ways. The discovery of these ways and hence of the manifold uses of things is the work of history.*e* So also is the invention of socially recognized standards of measurement for the quantities of these useful objects. The diversity of the measures for commodities arises in part from the diverse nature of the objects to be measured, and in part from convention.

The usefulness of a thing makes it a use-value.*f* But this usefulness does not dangle in mid-air. It is conditioned by the physical properties of the commodity, and has no existence apart from the latter. It is therefore the physical body of the commodity itself, for instance iron, corn, a diamond, which is the use-value or useful thing. This property of a commodity is independent of the amount of labour required to appropriate its useful qualities. When examining use-values, we always assume we are dealing with definite quantities, such as dozens of watches, yards of linen, or tons of iron. The use-values of commodities provide the material for a special branch of knowledge, namely the commercial knowledge of commodities.*g* Use-values are only realized [*verwirklicht*] in use or in consumption. They constitute the material content of wealth, whatever its social form may be. In the form of society to be considered here they are also the material bearers [*Träger*] of . . . exchange-value.

Exchange-value appears first of all as the quantitative relation, the proportion, in which use-values of one kind exchange for use-values of another kind.*h* This relation changes constantly with time and place.

---

d 'Desire implies want; it is the appetite of the mind, and as natural as hunger to the body. . . . The greatest number (of things) have their value from supplying the wants of the mind' (Nicholas Barbon,[7] *A Discourse on Coining the New Money Lighter. In Answer to Mr Locke's Considerations etc.*, London, 1696, pp. 2, 3).

e 'Things have an intrinsick vertue' (this is Barbon's special term for use-value) 'which in all places have the same vertue; as the loadstone to attract iron' (op. cit., p. 6). The magnet's property of attracting iron only became useful once it had led to the discovery of magnetic polarity.

f 'The natural worth of anything consists in its fitness to supply the necessities, or serve the conveniences of human life' (John Locke, 'Some Considerations on the Consequences of the Lowering of Interest' (1691), in *Works*, London, 1777, Vol. 2, p. 28). In English writers of the seventeenth century we still often find the word 'worth' used for use-value and 'value' for exchange-value. This is quite in accordance with the spirit of a language that likes to use a Teutonic word for the actual thing, and a Romance word for its reflection.

g In bourgeois society the legal fiction prevails that each person, as a buyer, has an encyclopedic knowledge of commodities.

h Value consists in the exchange relation between one thing and another, between a given amount of one product and a given amount of another' (Le Trosne, *De l'intérêt social*, in *Physiocrates*, ed. Daire, Paris, 1846, p. 889).

Hence exchange-value appears to be something accidental and purely relative, and consequently an intrinsic value, i.e., an exchange-value that is inseparably connected with the commodity, inherent in it, seems a contradiction in terms.*ⁱ* Let us consider the matter more closely.

A given commodity, a quarter of wheat for example, is exchanged for *x* boot-polish, *y* silk or *z* gold, etc. In short, it is exchanged for other commodities in the most diverse proportions. Therefore the wheat has many exchange values instead of one. But *x* boot-polish, *y* silk or *z* gold, etc., each represent the exchange-value of one quarter of wheat. Therefore *x* boot-polish, *y* silk, *z* gold, etc., must, as exchange-values, be mutually replaceable or of identical magnitude. It follows from this that, firstly, the valid exchange-values of a particular commodity express something equal, and secondly, exchange-value cannot be anything other than the mode of expression, the 'form of appearance' of a content distinguishable from it.

Let us now take two commodities, for example corn and iron. Whatever their exchange relation may be, it can always be represented by an equation in which a given quantity of corn is equated to some quantity of iron, for instance 1 quarter of corn = *x* cwt of iron. What does this equation signify? It signifies that a common element of identical magnitude exists in two different things, in 1 quarter of corn and similarly in *x* cwt of iron. Both are therefore equal to a third thing, which in itself is neither the one nor the other. Each of them, so far as it is exchange-value, must therefore be reducible to this third thing.

A simple geometrical example will illustrate this. In order to determine and compare the areas of all rectilinear figures we split them up into triangles. Then the triangle itself is reduced to an expression totally different from its visible shape: half the product of the base and the altitude. In the same way the exchange values of commodities must be reduced to a common element, of which they represent a greater or a lesser quantity.

This common element cannot be a geometrical, physical, chemical or other natural property of commodities. Such properties come into consideration only to the extent that they make the commodities useful, i.e., turn them into use-values. But clearly, the exchange relation of commodities is characterized precisely by its abstraction from their use-values. Within the exchange relation, one use-value is worth just as much as another, provided only that it is present in the appropriate quantity. Or, as old Barbon says: 'One sort of wares are as good as another, if the value be equal. There is no difference or distinction in things of equal value . . . One hundred pounds worth of lead or iron, is of as great a value as one hundred pounds worth of silver and gold.'*ʲ*

ⁱ Nothing can can have an intrinsick value' (N. Barbon, op. cit., p. 6); or as Butler says:
      '*The value of a thing*
      Is just as much as it will bring.'[8]
ʲ N. Barbon, op. cit., pp. 53 and 7.

As use-values, commodities differ above all in quality, while as exchange-values they can only differ in quantity, and therefore do not contain an atom of use-value.

If then we disregard the use-value of commodities, only one property remains, that of being products of labour. But even the product of labour has already been transformed in our hands. If we make abstraction from its use-value, we abstract also from the material constituents and forms which make it a use-value. It is no longer a table, a house, a piece of yarn or any other useful thing. All its sensuous characteristics are extinguished. Nor is it any longer the product of the labour of the joiner, the mason or the spinner, or of any other particular kind of productive labour. With the disappearance of the useful character of the products of labour, the useful character of the kinds of labour embodied in them also disappears; this in turn entails the disappearance of the different concrete forms of labour. They can no longer be distinguished, but are all together reduced to the same kind of labour, human labour in the abstract.

Let us now look at the residue of the products of labour. There is nothing left of them in each case but the same phantom-like objectivity; they are merely congealed quantities of homogeneous human labour, i.e., of human labour-power expended without regard to the form of its expenditure. All these things now tell us is that human labour-power has been expended to produce them, human labour is accumulated in them. As crystals of this social substance, which is common to them all, they are values—commodity values [*Warenwerte*].

We have seen that when commodities are in the relation of exchange, their exchange-value manifests itself as something totally independent of their use-value. But if we abstract from their use-value, there remains their value, as it has just been defined. The common factor in the exchange relation, or in the exchange-value of the commodity, is therefore its value. The progress of the investigation will lead us back to exchange-value as the necessary mode of expression, or form of appearance, of value. For the present, however, we must consider the nature of value independently of its form of appearance [*Erscheinungsform*].

A use-value, or useful article, therefore, has value only because abstract human labour is objectified [*vergegenständlicht*] or materialized in it. How, then, is the magnitude of this value to be measured? By means of the quantity of the 'value-forming substance', the labour, contained in the article. This quantity is measured by its duration, and the labour-time is itself measured on the particular scale of hours, days etc.

It might seem that if the value of a commodity is determined by the quantity of labour expended to produce it, it would be the more valuable the more unskilful and lazy the worker who produced it, because he would need more time to complete the article. However, the labour that forms the substance of value is equal human labour, the expenditure of identical human labour-power. The total labour-power of society, which is manifested in the values of the world of commodities, counts here as one homogeneous mass of human labour-power, although composed of innumerable individual units of labour-power. Each of these units is the same as any other, to the extent that it has the character of a socially average unit of labour-power and acts as such, i.e., only needs, in order to produce a commodity, the labour time which is necessary on an average, or in other words is socially necessary. Socially necessary labour-time is the labour-time required to produce any use-value under the conditions of production normal for a given society and with the average degree of skill and intensity of labour prevalent in that society. The introduction of power-looms into England, for example, probably reduced by one half the labour required to convert a given quantity of yarn into woven fabric. In order to do this, the English hand-loom weaver in fact needed the same amount of labour-time as before; but the product of his individual hour of labour now only represented half an hour of social labour, and consequently fell to one half its former value.

What exclusively determines the magnitude of the value of any article is therefore the amount of labour socially necessary, or the labour-time socially necessary for its production.[k] The individual commodity counts here only as an average sample of its kind.[l] Commodities which contain equal quantities of labour, or which can be produced in the same time, have therefore the same value. The value of a commodity is related to the value of any other commodity as the labour-time necessary for the production of the one is related to the labour-time necessary for the production of the other. 'As exchange-values, all commodities are merely definite quantities of *congealed labour-time.*'[m]

The value of a commodity would therefore remain constant, if the labour-time required for its production also remained constant. But the latter changes with every variation in the productivity of labour. This is determined by a wide range of circumstances; it is determined amongst other things by the workers' average degree of skill, the level of development of science and its technological application, the social organization

---

[k] 'The value of them' (the necessaries of life) 'when they are exchanged the one for another, is regulated by the quantity of labour necessarily required, and commonly taken in producing them' (*Some Thoughts on the Interest of Money in General, and Particularly in the Publick Funds*, London, pp. 36, 37).[9] This remarkable anonymous work of the eighteenth century bears no date. However, it is clear from its contents that it appeared in the reign of George II, about 1739 or 1740.

[l] Properly speaking, all products of the same kind form a single mass, and their price is determined in general and without regard to particular circumstances' (Le Trosne, op. cit., p. 893).

[m] Karl Marx, op. cit., p. 6 [English translation, p. 30].

of the process of production, the extent and effectiveness of the means of production, and the conditions found in the natural environment. For example, the same quantity of labour is present in eight bushels of corn in favourable seasons and in only four bushels in unfavourable seasons. The same quantity of labour provides more metal in rich mines than in poor. Diamonds are of very rare occurrence on the earth's surface, and hence their discovery costs, on an average, a great deal of labour-time. Consequently much labour is represented in a small volume. Jacob questions whether gold has ever been paid for at its full value.[10] This applies still more to diamonds. According to Eschwege, the total produce of the Brazilian diamond mines for the eighty years ending in 1823 still did not amount to the price of 1 1/2 years' average produce of the sugar and coffee plantations of the same country,[11] although the diamonds represented much more labour, therefore more value. With richer mines, the same quantity of labour would be embodied in more diamonds, and their value would fall. If man succeeded, without much labour, in transforming carbon into diamonds, their value might fall below that of bricks. In general, the greater the productivity of labour, the less the labour-time required to produce an article, the less the mass of labour crystallized in that article, and the less its value. Inversely, the less the productivity of labour, the greater the labour-time necessary to produce an article, and the greater its value. The value of a commodity, therefore, varies directly as the quantity, and inversely as the productivity, of the labour which finds its realization within the commodity. (Now we know the *substance* of value. It is *labour*. We know the *measure of its magnitude*. It is *labour-time*. The *form*, which stamps *value* as *exchange-value*, remains to be analysed. But before this we need to develop the characteristics we have already found somewhat more fully.)[12]

A thing can be a use-value without being a value. This is the case whenever its utility to man is not mediated through labour. Air, virgin soil, natural meadows, unplanted forests, etc. fall into this category. A thing can be useful, and a product of human labour, without being a commodity. He who satisfies his own need with the product of his own labour admittedly creates use-values, but not commodities. In order to produce the latter, he must not only produce use-values, but use-values for others, social use-values. (And not merely for others. The medieval peasant produced a corn-rent for the feudal lord and a corn-tithe for the priest; but neither the corn-rent nor the corn-tithe became commodities simply by being produced for others. In order to become a commodity, the product must be transferred to the other person, for whom it serves as a use-value, through the medium of exchange.[13] Finally, nothing can be a value without being an object of utility. If the thing is useless, so is the labour contained in it; the labour does not count as labour, and therefore creates no value.

2. THE DUAL CHARACTER OF THE LABOUR EMBODIED IN COMMODITIES

Initially the commodity appeared to us as an object with a dual character, possessing both use-value and exchange-value. Later on it was seen that labour, too, has a dual character: in so far as it finds its expression in value, it no longer possesses the same characteristics as when it is the creator of use-values. I was the first to point out and examine critically this twofold nature of the labour contained in commodities.[*] As this point is crucial to an understanding of political economy, it requires further elucidation.

Let us take two commodities, such as a coat and 10 yards of linen, and let the value of the first be twice the value of the second, so that, if 10 yards of linen $= W$, the coat $= 2W$.

The coat is a use-value that satisfies a particular need. A specific kind of productive activity is required to bring it into existence. This activity is determined by its aim, mode of operation, object, means and result. We use the abbreviated expression 'useful labour' for labour whose utility is represented by the use-value of its product, or by the fact that its product is a use-value. In this connection we consider only its useful effect.

As the coat and the linen are qualitatively different use-values, so also are the forms of labour through which their existence is mediated—tailoring and weaving. If the use-values were not qualitatively different, hence not the products of qualitatively different forms of useful labour, they would be absolutely incapable of confronting each other as commodities. Coats cannot be exchanged for coats, one use-value cannot be exchanged for another of the same kind.

The totality of heterogeneous use-values or physical commodities reflects a totality of similarly heterogeneous forms of useful labour, which differ in order, genus, species and variety: in short, a social division of labour. This division of labour is a necessary condition for commodity production, although the converse does not hold; commodity production is not a necessary condition for the social division of labour. Labour is socially divided in the primitive Indian community, although the products do not thereby become commodities. Or, to take an example nearer home, labour is systematically divided in every factory, but the workers do not bring about this division by exchanging their individual products. Only the products of mutually independent acts of labour, performed in isolation, can confront each other as commodities.

To sum up, then: the use-value of every commodity contains useful labour, i.e. productive activity of a definite kind, carried on with a definite

[*] Karl Marx, op, cit., pp. 12, 13, and passim [English translation, pp. 41, 42].

aim. Use-values cannot confront each other as commodities unless the useful labour contained in them is qualitatively different in each case. In a society whose products generally assume the form of commodities, i.e. in a society of commodity producers, this qualitative difference between the useful forms of labour which are carried on independently and privately by individual producers develops into a complex system, a social division of labour.

It is moreover a matter of indifference whether the coat is worn by the tailor or by his customer. In both cases it acts as a use-value. So, too, the relation between the coat and the labour that produced it is not in itself altered when tailoring becomes a special trade, an independent branch of the social division of labour. Men made clothes for thousands of years, under the compulsion of the need for clothing, without a single man ever becoming a tailor. But the existence of coats, of linen, of every element of material wealth not provided in advance by nature, had always to be mediated through a specific productive activity appropriate to its purpose, a productive activity that assimilated particular natural materials to particular human requirements. Labour, then, as the creator of use-values, as useful labour, is a condition of human existence which is independent of all forms of society; it is an eternal natural necessity which mediates the metabolism between man and nature, and therefore human life itself.

Use-values like coats, linen, etc., in short, the physical bodies of commodities, are combinations of two elements, the material provided by nature, and labour. If we subtract the total amount of useful labour of different kinds which is contained in the coat, the linen, etc., a material substratum is always left. This substratum is furnished by nature without human intervention. When man engages in production, he can only proceed as nature does herself, i.e. he can only change the form of the materials.⁰ Furthermore, even in this work of modification he is constantly helped by natural forces. Labour is therefore not the only source of material wealth, i.e., of the use-values it produces. As William Petty says, labour is the father of material wealth, the earth is its mother.[14]

Let us now pass from the commodity as an object of utility to the value of commodities.

⁰ All the phenomena of the universe, whether produced by the hand of man or indeed by the universal laws of physics, are not to be conceived of as acts of creation but solely as a reordering of matter. Composition and separation are the only elements found by the human mind whenever it analyses the notion of reproduction; and so it is with the reproduction of value' (use-value, although Verri himself, in this polemic against the Physiocrats, is not quite certain of the kind of value he is referring to) 'and wealth, whether earth, air and water are turned into corn in the fields, or the secretions of an insect are turned into silk by the hand of man, or some small pieces of metal are arranged together to form a repeating watch' (Pietro Verri, *Meditazioni sulla economia politica*—first printed in 1771—in Custodi's edition of the Italian economists, *Parte moderna*, Vol. 15, pp. 21, 22).

We have assumed that the coat is worth twice as much as the linen. But this is merely a quantitative difference, and does not concern us at the moment. We shall therefore simply bear in mind that if the value of a coat is twice that of 10 yards of linen, 20 yards of linen will have the same value as a coat. As values, the coat and the linen have the same substance, they are the objective expressions of homogeneous labour. But tailoring and weaving are qualitatively different forms of labour. There are, however, states of society in which the same man alternately makes clothes and weaves. In this case, these two different modes of labour are only modifications of the labour of the same individual and not yet fixed functions peculiar to different individuals, just as the coat our tailor makes today, and the pair of trousers he makes tomorrow, require him only to vary his own individual labour. Moreover, we can see at a glance that in our capitalist society a given portion of labour is supplied alternately in the form of tailoring and in the form of weaving, in acordance with changes in the direction of the demand for labour. This change in the form of labour may well not take place without friction, but it must take place.

If we leave aside the determinate quality of productive activity and therefore the useful character of the labour, what remains is its quality of being an expenditure of human labour-power. Tailoring and weaving, although they are qualitatively different productive activities, are both a productive expenditure of human brains, muscles, nerves, hands etc., and in this sense both human labour. They are merely two different forms of the expenditure of human labour-power. Of course, human labour-power must itself have attained a certain level of development before it can be expended in this or that form. But the value of a commodity represents human labour pure and simple, the expenditure of human labour in general. And just as, in civil society, a general or a banker plays a great part but man as such plays a very mean part, *p* so, here too, the same is true of human labour. It is the expenditure of simple labour-power, i.e., of the labour-power possessed in his bodily organism by every ordinary man, on the average, without being developed in any special way. *Simple average labour*, it is true, varies in character in different countries and at different cultural epochs, but in a particular society it is given. More complex labour counts only as *intensified*, or rather *multiplied* simple labour, so that a smaller quantity of complex labour is considered equal to a larger quantity of simple labour. Experience shows that this reduction is constantly being made. A commodity may be the outcome of the most complicated labour, but through its *value* it is posited as equal to the product of simple labour, hence it represents only a specific quantity of

p Cf. Hegel, *Philosophie des Rechts*, Berlin, 1840, p. 250, § 190.[15]

simple labour.⁹ The various proportions in which different kinds of labour are reduced to simple labour as their unit of measurement are established by a social process that goes on behind the backs of the producers; these proportions therefore appear to the producers to have been handed down by tradition. In the interests of simplification, we shall henceforth view every form of labour-power directly as simple labour-power; by this we shall simply be saving ourselves the trouble of making the reduction.

Just as, in viewing the coat and the linen as values, we abstract from their different use-values, so, in the case of the labour represented by those values, do we disregard the difference between its useful forms, tailoring and weaving. The use-values coat and linen are combinations of, on the one hand, productive activity with a definite purpose, and, on the other, cloth and yarn; the values coat and linen, however, are merely congealed quantities of homogeneous labour. In the same way, the labour contained in these values does not count by virtue of its productive relation to cloth and yarn, but only as being an expenditure of human labour-power. Tailoring and weaving are the formative elements in the use-values coat and linen, precisely because these two kinds of labour are of different qualities; but only in so far as abstraction is made from their particular qualities, only in so far as both possess the same quality of being human labour, do tailoring and weaving form the substance of the values of the two articles mentioned.

Coats and linen, however, are not merely values in general, but values of definite magnitude, and, following our assumption, the coat is worth twice as much as the 10 yards of linen. Why is there this difference in value? Because the linen contains only half as much labour as the coat, so that labour-power had to be expended twice as long to produce the second as to produce the first.

While, therefore, with reference to use-value, the labour contained in a commodity counts only qualitatively, with reference to value it counts only quantitatively, once it has been reduced to human labour pure and simple. In the former case it was a matter of the 'how' and the 'what' of labour, in the latter of the 'how much', of the temporal duration of labour. Since the magnitude of the value of a commodity represents nothing but the quantity of labour embodied in it, it follows that all commodities, when taken in certain proportions, must be equal in value.

If the productivity of all the different sorts of useful labour required, let us say, for the production of a coat remains unchanged, the total value of the coats produced will increase along with their quantity. If one coat represents x days' labour, two coats will represent $2x$ days' labour, and so

⁹ The reader should note that we are not speaking here of the wages or value the worker receives for (e.g.) a day's labour, but of the value of the commodity in which his day of labour is objectified. At this stage of our presentation, the category of wages does not exist at all.

on. But now assume that the duration of the labour necessary for the production of a coat is doubled or halved. In the first case, one coat is worth as much as two coats were before; in the second case two coats are only worth as much as one was before; in the second case two coats are only worth as much as one was before, although in both cases one coat performs the same service, and the useful labour contained in it remains of the same quality. One change has taken place, however: a change in the quantity of labour expended to produce the article.

In itself, an increase in the quantity of use-values constitutes an increase in material wealth. Two coats will clothe two men, one coat will only clothe one man, etc. Nevertheless, an increase in the amount of material wealth may correspond to a simultaneous fall in the magnitude of its value. This contradictory movement arises out of the twofold character of labour. By 'productivity' of course, we always mean the productivity of concrete useful labour; in reality this determines only the degree of effectiveness of productive activity directed towards a given purpose within a given period of time. Useful labour becomes, therefore, a more or less abundant source of products in direct proportion as its productivity rises or falls. As against this, however, variations in productivity have no impact whatever on the labour itself represented in value. As productivity is an attribute of labour in its concrete useful form, it naturally ceases to have any bearing on that labour as soon as we abstract from its concrete useful form. The same labour, therefore, performed for the same length of time, always yields the same amount of value, independently of any variations in productivity. But it provides different quantities of use-values during equal periods of time; more, if productivity rises; fewer, if it falls. For this reason, the same change in productivity which increases the fruitfulness of labour, and therefore the amount of use-values produced by it, also brings about a reduction in the value of this increased total amount, if it cuts down the total amount of labour-time necessary to produce the use-values. The converse also holds.

On the one hand, all labour is an expenditure of human labour-power, in the physiological sense, and it is in this quality of being equal, or abstract, human labour that it forms the value of commodities. On the other hand, all labour is an expenditure of human labour-power in a particular form and with a definite aim, and it is in this quality of being concrete useful labour that it produces use-values.[r]

[r] In order to prove that 'labour alone is the ultimate and real standard by which the value of all commodities can at all times and places be estimated and compared', Adam Smith[16] says this: 'Equal quantities of labour, at all times and places, must have the same value for the labourer. In his ordinary state of health, strength and activity; in the ordinary degree of his skill and dexterity, he must always lay down the same portion of his ease, his liberty, and his happiness' (*Wealth of Nations*, Bk I, Ch. 5). On the one hand, Adam Smith here (but not everywhere) confuses his determination of value by the quantity of labour expended in the production of commodities with the determination of the values of commodities by

4. THE FETISHISM OF THE COMMODITY AND ITS SECRET

A commodity appears at first sight an extremely obvious, trivial thing. But its analysis brings out that it is a very strange thing, abounding in metaphysical subtleties and theological niceties. So far as it is a use-value, there is nothing mysterious about it, whether we consider it from the point of view that by its properties it satisfies human needs, or that it first takes on these properties as the product of human labour. It is absolutely clear that, by his activity, man changes the forms of the materials of nature in such a way as to make them useful to him. The form of wood, for instance, is altered if a table is made out of it. Nevertheless the table continues to be wood, an ordinary, sensuous thing. But as soon as it emerges as a commodity, it changes into a thing which transcends sensuousness. It not only stands with its feet on the ground, but, in relation to all other commodities, it stands on its head, and evolves out of its wooden brain grotesque ideas, far more wonderful than if it were to begin dancing of its own free will.*

The mystical character of the commodity does not therefore arise from its use-value. Just as little does it proceed from the nature of the determinants of value. For in the first place, however varied the useful kinds of labour, or productive activities, it is a physiological fact that they are functions of the human organism, and that each such function, whatever may be its nature or its form, is essentially the expenditure of human brain, nerves, muscles and sense organs. Secondly, with regard to the foundation of the quantitative determination of value, namely the duration of that expenditure or the quantity of labour, this is quite palpably different from its quality. In all situations, the labour-time it costs to produce the means of subsistence must necessarily concern mankind,

---

the value of labour, and therefore endeavours to prove that equal quantities of labour always have the same value. On the other hand, he has a suspicion that, in so far as labour manifests itself in the value of commodities, it only counts as an expenditure of labour-power; but then again he views this expenditure merely as the sacrifice of rest, freedom and happiness, not as also man's normal life-activity. Of course, he has the modern wage-labourer in mind. Adam Smith's anonymous predecessor, cited in note *K* is much nearer the mark when he says: 'One man has employed himself a week in providing this necessary of life . . . and he that gives him some other in exchange, cannot make a better estimate of what is a proper equivalent, than by computing what cost him just as much labour and time: which in effect is no more than exchanging one man's labour in one thing for a time certain, for another man's labour in another thing for the same time' (*Some Thoughts on the Interest of Money in General etc., p. 39*). [Note by Engels to the fourth German edition:] The English language has the advantage of possessing two separate words for these two different aspects of labour. Labour which creates use-values and is qualitatively determined is called 'work' as opposed to 'labour'; labour which creates value and is only measured quantitatively is called 'labour', as opposed to 'work'.

s One may recall that China and the tables began to dance when the rest of the world appeared to be standing still—*pour encourager les autres.*[17]

although not to the same degree at different stages of development.[r] And finally, as soon as men start to work for each other in any way, their labour also assumes a social form.

Whence, then, arises the enigmatic character of the product of labour, as soon as it assumes the form of a commodity? Clearly, it arises from this form itself. The equality of the kinds of human labour takes on a physical form in the equal objectivity of the products of labour as values; the measure of the expenditure of human labour-power by its duration takes on the form of the magnitude of the value of the products of labour; and finally the relationships between the producers, within which the social characteristics of their labours are manifested, take on the form of a social relation between the products of labour.

The mysterious character of the commodity-form consists therefore simply in the fact that the commodity reflects the social characteristics of men's own labour as objective characteristics of the products of labour themselves, as the socio-natural properties of these things. Hence it also reflects the social relation of the producers to the sum total of labour as a social relation between objects, a relation which exists apart from and outside the producers. Through this substitution, the products of labour become commodities, sensuous things which are at the same time supra-sensible or social. In the same way, the impression made by a thing on the optic nerve is perceived not as a subjective excitation of that nerve but as the objective form of a thing outside the eye. In the act of seeing, of course, light is really transmitted from one thing, the external object, to another thing, the eye. It is a physical relation between physical things. As against this, the commodity-form, and the value-relation of the products of labour within which it appears, have absolutely no connection with the physical nature of the commodity and the material [*dinglich*] relations arising out of this. It is nothing but the definite social relation between men themselves which assumes here, for them, the fantastic form of a relation between things. In order, therefore, to find an analogy we must take flight into the misty realm of religion. There the products of the human brain appear as autonomous figures endowed with a life of their own, which enter into relations both with each other and with the human race. So it is in the world of commodities with the products of men's hands. I call this the fetishism which attaches itself to the products of labour as soon as they are produced as commodities, and is therefore inseparable from the production of commodities.

As the foregoing analysis has already demonstrated, this fetishism of

---

[r] Among the ancient Germans the size of a piece of land was measured according to the labour of a day; hence the acre was called *Tagwerk*, *Tagwanne* (*jurnale*, or *terra jurnalis*, or *diornalis*), *Mannwerk*, *Mannskraft*, *Mannsmaad*, *Mannshauet*, etc. See Georg Ludwig von Maurer, *Einleitung zur Geschichte der Mark-, Hof-, usw. Verfassung*, Munich, 1854, p. 129 ff.

the world of commodities arises from the peculiar social character of the labour which produces them.

Objects of utility become commodities only because they are the products of the labour of private individuals who work independently of each other. The sum total of the labour of all these private individuals forms the aggregate labour of society. Since the producers do not come into social contact until they exchange the products of their labour, the specific social characteristics of their private labours appear only within this exchange. In other words, the labour of the private individual manifests itself as an element of the total labour of society only through the relations which the act of exchange establishes between the products, and, through their mediation, between the producers. To the producers, therefore, the social relations between their private labours appear as what they are, i.e., they do not appear as direct social relations between persons in their work, but rather as material [*dinglich*] relations between persons and social relations between things.

It is only by being exchanged that the products of labour acquire a socially uniform objectivity as values, which is distinct from their sensuously varied objectivity as articles of utility. This division of the product of labour into a useful thing and a thing possessing value appears in practice only when exchange has already acquired a sufficient extension and importance to allow useful things to be produced for the purpose of being exchanged, so that their character as values has already to be taken into consideration during production. From this moment on, the labour of the individual producer acquires a twofold social character. On the one hand, it must, as a definite useful kind of labour, satisfy a definite social need, and thus maintain its position as an element of the total labour, as a branch of the social division of labour, which originally sprang up spontaneously. On the other hand, it can satisfy the manifold needs of the individual producer himself only in so far as every particular kind of useful private labour can be exchanged with, i.e., counts as the equal of, every other kind of useful private labour. Equality in the full sense between different kinds of labour can be arrived at only if we abstract from their real inequality, if we reduce them to the characteristic they have in common, that of being the expenditure of human labour-power, of human labour in the abstract. The private producer's brain reflects this twofold social character of his labour only in the forms which appear in practical intercourse, in the exchange of products. Hence the socially useful character of his private labour is reflected in the form that the product of labour has to be useful to others, and the social character of the equality of the various kinds of labour is reflected in the form of the common character, as values, possessed by these materially different things, the products of labour.

Men do not therefore bring the products of their labour into relation with each other as values because they see these objects merely as the material integuments of homogeneous human labour. The reverse is true: by equating their different products to each other in exchange as values, they equate their different kinds of labour as human labour. They do this without being aware of it." Value, therefore, does not have its description branded on its forehead; it rather transforms every product of labour into a social hieroglyphic. Later on, men try to decipher the hieroglyphic, to get behind the secret of their own social product: for the characteristic which objects of utility have of being values is as much men's social product as is their language. The belated scientific discovery that the products of labour, in so far as they are values, are merely the material expressions of the human labour expended to produce them, marks an epoch in the history of mankind's development, but by no means banishes the semblance of objectivity possessed by the social characteristics of labour. Something which is only valid for this particular form of production, the production of commodities, namely the fact that the specific social character of private labours carried on independently of each other consists in their equality as human labour, and, in the product, assumes the form of the existence of value, appears to those caught up in the relations of commodity production (and this is true both before and after the above-mentioned scientific discovery) to be just as ultimately valid as the fact that the scientific dissection of the air into its component parts left the atmosphere itself unaltered in its physical configuration.

What initially concerns producers in practice when they make an exchange is how much of some other product they get for their own; in what proportions can the products be exchanged? As soon as these proportions have attained a certain customary stability, they appear to result from the nature of the products, so that, for instance, one ton of iron and two ounces of gold appear to be equal in value, in the same way as a pound of gold and a pound of iron are equal in weight, despite their different physical and chemical properties. The value character of the products of labour becomes firmly established only when they act as magnitudes of value. These magnitudes vary continually, independently of the will, foreknowledge and actions of the exchangers. Their own movement within society has for them the form of a movement made by things, and these things, far from being under their control, in fact control them. The production of commodities must be fully developed before the scientific conviction emerges, from experience itself, that all the different kinds of private labour (which are carried on independently of each other, and yet, as spontaneously developed branches of the social division of labour, are

---

" Therefore, when Galiani[18] said: Value is a relation between persons ('*La Ricchezza è una ragione tra due persone*') he ought to have added: a relation concealed beneath a material shell. (Galiani, *Della Moneta*, p. 221, Vol. 3 of Custodi's collection entitled *Scrittori classici italiani di economia politica, Parte moderna*, Milan, 1803.)

in a situation of all-round dependence on each other) are continually being reduced to the quantitative proportions in which society requires them. The reason for this reduction is that in the midst of the accidental and ever-fluctuating exchange relations between the products, the labour-time socially necessary to produce them asserts itself as a regulative law of nature. In the same way, the law of gravity asserts itself when a person's house collapses on top of him.^{v} The determination of the magnitude of value by labour-time is therefore a secret hidden under the apparent movements in the relative values of commodities. Its discovery destroys the semblance of the merely accidental determination of the magnitude of the value of the products of labour, but by no means abolishes that determination's material form.

Reflection on the forms of human life, hence also scientific analysis of those forms, takes a course directly opposite to their real development. Reflection begins *post festum*,[19] and therefore with the results of the process of development ready to hand. The forms which stamp products as commodities and which are therefore the preliminary requirements for the circulation of commodities, already possess the fixed quality of natural forms of social life before man seeks to give an account, not of their historical character, for in his eyes they are immutable, but of their content and meaning. Consequently, it was solely the analysis of the prices of commodities which led to the determination of the magnitude of value, and solely the common expression of all commodities in money which led to the establishment of their character as values. It is however precisely this finished form of the world of commodities—the money form—which conceals the social character of private labour and the social relations between the individual workers, by making those relations appear as relations between material objects, instead of revealing them plainly. If I state that coats or boots stand in a relation to linen because the latter is the universal incarnation of abstract human labour, the absurdity of the statement is self-evident. Nevertheless, when the producers of coats and boots bring these commodities into a relation with linen, or with gold or silver (and this makes no difference here), as the universal equivalent, the relation between their own private labour and the collective labour of society appears to them in exactly this absurd form.

The categories of bourgeois economics consist precisely of forms of this kind. They are forms of thought which are socially valid, and therefore objective, for the relations of production belonging to this historically determined mode of social production, i.e., commodity production. The whole mystery of commodities, all the magic and necromancy that sur-

---

^{v} What are we to think of a law which can only assert itself through periodic crises? It is just a natural law which depends on the lack of awareness of the people who undergo it' (Friedrich Engels, *Umrisse zu einer Kritik der Nationalökonomie*, in the *Deutsch-Französische Jahrbücher*, edited by Arnold Ruge and Karl Marx, Paris, 1844).

rounds the products of labour on the basis of commodity production, vanishes therefore as soon as we come to other forms of production.

As political economists are fond of Robinson Crusoe stories,[w] let us first look at Robinson on his island. Undemanding though he is by nature, he still has needs to satisfy, and must therefore perform useful labours of various kinds: he must make tools, knock together furniture, tame llamas, fish, hunt and so on. Of his prayers and the like, we take no account here, since our friend takes pleasure in them and sees them as recreation. Despite the diversity of his productive functions, he knows that they are only different forms of activity of one and the same Robinson, hence only different modes of human labour. Necessity itself compels him to divide his time with precision between his different functions. Whether one function occupies a greater space in his total activity than another depends on the magnitude of the difficulties to be overcome in attaining the useful effect aimed at. Our friend Robinson Crusoe learns this by experience, and having saved a watch, ledger, ink and pen from the shipwreck, he soon begins, like a good Englishman, to keep a set of books. His stock-book contains a catalogue of the useful objects he possesses, of the various operations necessary for their production, and finally of the labour-time that specific quantities of these products have on average cost him. All the relations between Robinson and these objects that form his self-created wealth are here so simple and transparent that even Mr Sedley Taylor[21] could understand them. And yet those relations contain all the essential determinants of value.

Let us now transport ourselves from Robinson's island, bathed in light, to medieval Europe, shrouded in darkness. Here, instead of the independent man, we find everyone dependent—serfs and lords, vassals and suzerains, laymen and clerics. Personal dependence characterizes the social relations of material production as much as it does the other spheres of life based on that production. But precisely because relations of personal dependence form the given social foundation, there is no need for labour and its products to assume a fantastic form different from their reality. They take the shape, in the transactions of society, of services in kind and payments in kind. The natural form of labour, its particularity— and not, as in a society based on commodity production, its universality—is here its immediate social form. The corvée can be measured by time just as well as the labour which produces commodities, but every serf knows

---

[w] Even Ricardo has his Robinson Crusoe stories. 'Ricardo makes his primitive fisherman and primitive hunter into owners of commodities who immediately exchange their fish and game in proportion to the labour-time which is materialized in these exchange-values. On this occasion he slips into the anachronism of allowing the primitive fisherman and hunter to calculate the value of their implements in accordance with the annuity tables used on the London Stock Exchange in 1817. Apart from bourgeois society, the "parallelograms of Mr Owen" seem to have been the only form of society Ricardo was acquainted with' (Karl Marx, *Zur Kritik etc.*, pp. 38–9)[20] [English translation, p.60].

that what he expends in the service of his lord is a specific quantity of his own personal labour-power. The tithe owed to the priest is more clearly apparent than his blessing. Whatever we may think, then, of the different roles in which men confront each other in such a society, the social relations between individuals in the performance of their labour appear at all events as their own personal relations, and are not disguised as social relations between things, between the products of labour.

For an example of labour in common, i.e., directly associated labour, we do not need to go back to the spontaneously developed form which we find at the threshold of the history of all civilized peoples.[x] We have one nearer to hand in the patriarchal rural industry of a peasant family which produces corn, cattle, yarn, linen and clothing for its own use. These things confront the family as so many products of its collective labour, but they do not confront each other as commodities. The different kinds of labour which create these products—such as tilling the fields, tending the cattle, spinning, weaving and making clothes—are already in their natural form social functions; for they are functions of the family, which, just as much as a society based on commodity production, possesses its own spontaneously developed division of labour. The distribution of labour within the family and the labour-time expended by the individual members of the family, are regulated by differences of sex and age as well as by seasonal variations in the natural conditions of labour. The fact that the expenditure of the individual labour-powers is measured by duration appears here, by its very nature, as a social characteristic of labour itself, because the individual labour-powers, by their very nature, act only as instruments of the joint labour-power of the family.

Let us finally imagine, for a change, an association of free men, working with the means of production held in common, and expending their many different forms of labour-power in full self-awareness as one single social labour force. All the characteristics of Robinson's labour are repeated here, but with the difference that they are social instead of individual. All Robinson's products were exclusively the result of his own personal labour and they were therefore directly objects of utility for him personally. The total product of our imagined association is a social product. One part of this product serves as fresh means of production and remains easy to penetrate. But when we come to more concrete forms, even this appear-

---

[x] 'A ridiculous notion has spread abroad recently that communal property in its natural, spontaneous form is specifically Slav, indeed exclusively Russian. In fact, it is the primitive form that we can prove to have existed among Romans, Teutons and Celts, and which indeed still exists to this day in India, in a whole range of diverse patterns, albeit sometimes only as remnants. A more exact study of the Asiatic, and specifically of the Indian form of communal property would indicate the way in which different forms of spontaneous, primitive communal property give rise to different forms of its dissolution. Thus the different original types of Roman and Germanic private property can be deduced from the different forms of Indian communal property' (Karl Marx, *Zur Kritik, etc.*, p. 10).

ance of simplicity vanishes. must therefore be divided amongst them. The way this division is made will vary with the particular kind of social organization of production and the corresponding level of social development attained by the producers. We shall assume, but only for the sake of a parallel with the production of commodities, that the share of each individual producer in the means of subsistence is determined by his labour-time. Labour-time would in that case play a double part. Its apportionment in accordance with a definite social plan maintains the correct proportion between the different functions of labour and the various needs of the associations. On the other hand, labour-time also serves as a measure of the part taken by each individual in the common labour, and of his share in the part of the total product destined for individual consumption. The social relations of the individual producers, both towards their labour and the products of their labour, are here transparent in their simplicity, in production as well as in distribution.

For a society of commodity producers, whose general social relation of production consists in the fact that they treat their products as commodities, hence as values, and in this material [*sachlich*] form bring their individual, private labours into relation with each other as homogeneous human labour, Christianity with its religious cult of man in the abstract, more particularly in its bourgeois development, i.e., in Protestantism, Deism, etc., is the most fitting form of religion. In the ancient Asiatic, Classical-antique, and other such modes of production, the transformation of the product into a commodity, and therefore men's existence as producers of commodities, plays a subordinate role, which however increases in importance as these communities approach nearer and nearer to the stage of their dissolution. Trading nations, properly so called, exist only in the interstices of the ancient world, like the gods of Epicurus in the *intermundia*[22] or Jews in the pores of Polish society. Those ancient social organisms of production are much more simple and transparent than those of bourgeois society. But they are founded either on the immaturity of man as an individual, when he has not yet torn himself loose from the umbilical cord of his natural species-connection with other men, or on direct relations of dominance and servitude. They are conditioned by a low stage of development of the productive powers of labour and correspondingly limited relations between men within the process of creating and reproducing their material life, hence also limited relations between man and nature. These real limitations are reflected in the ancient worship of nature, and in other elements of tribal religions. The religious reflections of the real world can, in any case, vanish only when the practical relations of everyday life between man and man, and man and nature, generally present themselves to him in a transparent and rational form. The veil is not removed from the countenance of the social life-process, i.e., the process of material production, until it becomes production by freely associated men, and stands under their conscious and planned control. This, however, requires that society possess a material foundation, or a series of material conditions of existence, which in their turn are the natural and spontaneous product of a long and tormented historical development.

Political economy has indeed analysed value and its magnitude, however incompletely,[y] and has uncovered the content concealed within these forms. But it has never once asked the question why this content has assumed that particular form, that is to say, why labour is expressed in value, and why the measurement of labour by its duration is expressed in the magnitude of the value of the product.[z] These formulas, which bear the unmistakable stamp of belonging to a social formation in which the process of production has mastery over man, instead of the opposite, appear to the political economists' bourgeois consciousness to be as much a self-evident and nature-imposed necessity as productive labour itself. Hence the pre-bourgeois forms of the social organization of production are treated by political economy in much the same way as the Fathers of the Church treated pre-Christian religions.[aa]

[y] The insufficiency of Ricardo's analysis of the magnitude of value—and his analysis is by far the best—will appear from the third and fourth books of this work[23] As regards value in general, classical political economy in fact nowhere distinguishes explicitly and with a clear awareness between labour as it appears in the value of a product, and the same labour as it appears in the product's use-value. Of course the distinction is made in practice, since labour is treated sometimes from its quantitative aspect, and at other times qualitatively. But it does not occur to the economists that a purely quantitative distinction between the kinds of labour presupposes their qualitative unity or equality, and therefore their reduction to abstract human labour. For instance, Ricardo declares that he agrees with Destutt de Tracy when the latter says: 'As it is certain that our physical and moral faculties are alone our original riches, the employment of those faculties, labour of some kind, is our original treasure, and it is always from this employment that all those things are created which we call riches. . . . It is certain too, that all those things only represent the labour which has created them, and if they have a value, or even two distinct values, they can only derive them from that' (the value)—of the labour from which they emanate' (Ricardo, *The Principles of Political Economy*, 3rd edn, London, 1821, p. 334).[24] We would here only point out that Ricardo imposes his own more profound interpretation on the words of Destutt. Admittedly Destutt does say that all things which constitute wealth 'represent the labour which has created them', but, on the other hand, he also says that they acquire their 'two different values' (use-value and exchange-value) from 'the value of labour'. He thus falls into the commonplace error of the vulgar economists, who assume the value of one commodity (here labour) in order in turn to use it to determine the values of other commodities. But Ricardo reads him as if he had said that labour (not the value of labour) is represented both in use-value and in exchange-value. Nevertheless, Ricardo himself makes so little of the dual character of the labour represented in this twofold way that he is forced to spend the whole of his chapter 'Value and Riches, their Distinctive Properties' on a laborious examination of the trivialities of a J. B. Say. And at the end he is therefore quite astonished to find that while Destutt agrees with him that labour is the source of value, he nevertheless also agrees with Say about the concept of value.[25]

[z] It is one of the chief failings of classical political economy that it has never succeeded, by means of its analysis of commodities, and in particular of their value, in discovering the form of value which in fact turns value into exchange-value. Even its best representatives, Adam Smith and Ricardo, treat the form of value as something of indifference, something

The degree to which some economists are misled by the fetishism attached to the world of commodities, or by the objective appearance of the social characteristics of labour, is shown, among other things, by the dull and tedious dispute over the part played by nature in the formation of exchange-value. Since exchange-value is a definite social manner of expressing the labour bestowed on a thing, it can have no more natural content than has, for example, the rate of exchange.

As the commodity-form is the most general and the most undeveloped form of bourgeois production, it makes its appearance at an early date, though not in the same predominant and therefore characteristic manner as nowadays. Hence its fetish character is still relatively easy to penetrate. But when we come to more concrete forms, even this appearance of simplicity vanishes. Where did the illusions of the Monetary System come from? The adherents of the Monetary System did not see god and silver as representing money as a social relation of production, but in the form of natural objects with peculiar social properties. And what of modern political economy, which looks down so disdainfully on the Monetary System? Does not its fetishism become quite palpable when it deals with capital? How long is it since the disappearance of the Physiocratic illusion that ground rent grow out of the soil, not out of society?

---

external to the nature of the commodity itself. The explanation for this is not simply that their attention is entirely absorbed by the analysis of the magnitude of value. It lies deeper. The value-form of the product of labour is the most abstract, but also the most universal form of the bourgeois mode of production; by that fact it stamps the bourgeois mode of production as a particular kind of social production of a historical and transitory character. If then we make the mistake of treating it as the external natural form of social production, we necessarily over-look the specificity of the value-form, and consequently of the commodity-form together with its further developments, the money form, the capital form, etc. We therefore find that economists who are entirely agreed that labour-time is the measure of the magnitude of value, have the strangest and most contradictory ideas about money, that is, about the universal equivalent in its finished form. This emerges sharply when they deal with banking, where the commonplace definitions of money will no longer hold water. Hence there has arisen in opposition to the classical economists a restored Mercantilist System (Ganilh etc.), which sees in value only the social form, or rather its insubstantial semblance. Let me point out once and for all that by classical political economy I mean all the economists who, since the time of W. Petty, have investigated the real internal framework [*Zusammenhang*] of bourgeois relations of production, as opposed to the vulgar economists who only flounder around within the apparent framework of those relations, ceaselessly ruminate on the materials long since provided by scientific political economy, and seek there plausible explanations of the crudest phenomena for the domestic purposes of the bourgeoisie. Apart from this, the vulgar economists confine themselves to systematizing in a pedantic way, and proclaiming for everlasting truths, the banal and complacent notions held by the bourgeois agents of production about their own world, which is to them the best possible one.

aa 'The economists have a singular way of proceeding. For them, there are only two kinds of institutions, artificial and natural. The institutions of feudalism are artificial institutions, those of the bourgeoisie are natural institutions. In this they resemble the theologians, who likewise establish two kinds of religion. Every religion which is not heirs is an invention of men, while their own is an emanation of God . . . Thus there has been history, but there

But, to avoid anticipating, we will content ourselves here with one more example relating to the commodity-form itself. If commodities could speak, they would say this: our use-value may interest men, but it does not belong to us as objects. What does belong to us as objects, however, is our value. Our own intercourse. as commodities proves it. We relate to each other merely as exchange-values. Now listen how those commodities speak through the mouth of the economist:

'Value (i.e. exchange-value) is a property of things, riches (i.e., use-value) of man. Value, in this sense, necessarily implies exchanges, riches do not.'*bb*

'Riches (use-value) are the attribute of man, value is the attribute of commodities. A man or a community is rich, a pearl or a diamond is valuable . . . A pearl or a diamond is valuable as a pearl or diamond.'*cc*

So far no chemist has ever discovered exchange-value either in a pearl or a diamond. The economists who have discovered this chemical substance, and who lay special claim to critical acumen, nevertheless find that the use-value of material objects belongs to them independently of their material properties, while their value, on the other hand, forms a

---

is no longer any' (Karl Marx, *Misère de la philosophie. Réponse à la philosophie de la misère de M. Proudhon*, 1847, p. 113). Truly comical is M. Bastiat, who imagines that the ancient Greeks and Romans lived by plunder alone. For if people live by plunder for centuries there must, after all, always be something there to plunder; in other words, the objects of plunder must be continually reproduced. It seems, therefore, that even the Greeks and the Romans had a process of production, hence an economy, which constituted the material basis of their world as much as the bourgeois economy constitutes that of the present-day world. Or perhaps Bastiat means that a mode of production based on the labour of slaves is based on a system of plunder? In that case he is on dangerous ground. If a giant thinker like Aristotle could err in his evaluation of slave-labour, why should a dwarf economist like Bastiat be right in his evaluation of wage-labour? I seize this opportunity of briefly refuting an objection made by a German-American publication to my work *Zur Kritik der Politischen Ökonomie*, 1859. My view is that each particular mode of production, and the relations of production corresponding to it at each given moment, in short 'the economic structure of society', is 'the real foundation, on which arises a legal and political superstructure and to which correspond definite forms of social consciousness', and that 'the mode of production of material life conditions the general process of social, political and intellectual life'.[26] In the opinion of the German-American publication this is all very true for our own times, in which material interests are preponderant, but not for the Middle Ages, dominated by Catholicism, nor for Athens and Rome, dominated by politics. In the first place, it strikes us as odd that anyone should suppose that these well-worn phrases about the Middle Ages and the ancient world were unknown to anyone else. One thing is clear: the Middle Ages could not live on Catholicism, nor could the ancient world on politics. On the contrary, it is the manner in which they gained their livelihood which explains why in one case politics, in the other case Catholicism, played the chief part. For the rest, one needs no more than a slight acquaintance with, for example, the history of the Roman Republic, to be aware that its secret history is the history of landed property. And then there is Don Quixote, who long ago paid the penalty for wrongly imagining that knight errantry was compatible with all economic forms of society.

bb *Observations on Some Verbal Disputes in Pol. Econ., Particularly Relating to Value, and to Supply and Demand*, London, 1821, p. 16.

cc S. Bailey, op. cit., p. 165.

part of them as objects. What confirms them in this view is the peculiar circumstances that the use-value of a thing is realized without exchange, i.e., in the direct relation between the thing and man, while, inversely, its value is realized only in exchange, i.e., in a social process. Who would not call to mind at this point the advice given by the good Dogberry to the night-watchman Seacoal?[27]

'To be a well-favoured man is the gift of fortune; but reading and writing comes by nature.'[dd]

Part Two
Transformation of Money into Capital

Chapter 6
The Sale and Purchase of Labour-Power

The change in value of the money which has to be transformed into capital cannot take place in the money itself, since in its function as means of purchase and payment it does no more than realize [*realisieren*] the price of the commodity it buys or pays for, while, when it sticks to its own peculiar form, it petrifies into a mass of value of constant magnitude[ee] Just as little can this change originate in the second act of circulation, the resale of the commodity, for this act merely converts the commodity from its natural form back into its money-form. The change must therefore take place in the commodity which is brought in the first act of circulation, M-C, but not in its value, for it is equivalents which are being exchanged, and the commodity is paid for at its full value. The change can therefore originate only in the actual use-value of the commodity, i.e. in its consumption. In order to extract value out of the consumption of a commodity, our friend the money-owner must be lucky enough to find within the sphere of circulation, on the market, a commodity whose use-value possesses the peculiar property of being a source of value, whose actual consumption is therefore itself an objectification [*Vergegenständlichung*] of

---

[dd] Both the author of *Observations etc.*, and S. Bailey accuse Ricardo of converting exchange-value from something relative into something absolute. The reverse is true. He has reduced the apparent relativity which these things (diamonds, pearls, etc.) possess to the true relation hidden behind the appearance, namely their relativity as mere expressions of human labour. If the followers of Ricardo answer Bailey somewhat rudely, but by no means convincingly, this is because they are unable to find in Ricardo's own works any elucidation of the inner connection between value and the form of value, or exchange-value.

[ee] 'In the form of money . . . capital is productive of no profit' (Ricardo, *Principles of Political Economy*, p. 267).

labour, hence a creation of value. The possessor of money does find such a special commodity on the market: the capacity for labour [*Arbeitsvermögen*], in other words labour-power [*Arbeitskraft*].

We mean by labour-power, or labour-capacity, the aggregate of those mental and physical capabilities existing in the physical form, the living personality, of a human being, capabilities which he sets in motion whenever he produces a use-value of any kind.

But in order that the owner of money may find labour-power on the market as a commodity, various conditions must first be fulfilled. In and for itself, the exchange of commodities implies no other relations of dependence than those which result from its own nature. On this assumption, labour-power can appear on the market as a commodity only if, and in so far as, its possessor, the individual whose labour-power it is, offers it for sale or sells it as a commodity. In order that its possessor may sell it as a commodity, he must have it at his disposal, he must be the free proprietor of his own labour-capacity, hence of his person.*ff* He and the owner of money meet in the market, and enter into relations with each other on a footing of equality as owners of commodities, with the sole difference that one is a buyer, the other a seller; both are therefore equal in the eyes of the law. For this relation to continue, the proprietor of labour-power must always sell it for a limited period only, for if he were to sell it in a lump, once and for all, he would be selling himself, converting himself from a free man into a slave, from an owner of a commodity into a commodity. He must constantly treat his labour-power as his own property, his own commodity, and he can do this only by placing it at the disposal of the buyer, i.e., handing it over to the buyer for him to consume, for a definite period of time, temporarily. In this way he manages both to alienate [*veräussern*] his labour-power and to avoid renouncing his rights of ownership over it.*gg*

The second essential condition which allows the owner of money to

---

ff In encyclopedias of classical antiquity one can read such nonsense as this: In the ancient world capital was fully developed, 'except for the absence of the free worker and of a system of credit'. Mommsen too, in his *History of Rome*, commits one blunder after another in this respect.[28]

gg Hence legislation in various countries fixes a maximum length for labour contracts. Wherever free labour is the rule, the law regulates the conditions for terminating this contract. In some states, particularly in Mexico (and before the American Civil War in the territories taken by the United States from Mexico, as also in practice in the Danubian Principalities until Cuza's *coup d'etat*[29]), slavery is hidden under the form of peonage. By means of advances repayable in labour, which are handed down from generation to generation, not only the individual worker, but also his family, become in fact the property of other persons and their families. Juarez abolished peonage, but the so-called Emperor Maximilian re-established it by a decree which was aptly denounced in the House of Representatives in Washington as a decree for the re-introduction of slavery into Mexico. 'Single products of my particular physical and mental skill and of my power to act I can alienate to someone else and I can give him the use of my abilities for a restricted period, because, on the strength of this restriction, my abilities acquire an external relation to the totality and universality of my being. By alienating the whole of my time, as crystallized find labour-power in the market as a commodity is this, that the possessor of labour-power, instead of being able to sell commodities in which his labour has been objectified, must rather be compelled to offer for sale as a commodity that very labour-power which exists only in his living body.

In order that a man may be able to sell commodities other than his labour-power, he must of course possess means of production, such as raw materials, instruments of labour, etc. No boots can be made without leather. He requires also the means of subsistence. Nobody—not even a practitioner of *Zukunftsmusik*[30]—can live on the products of the future, or on use-values whose production has not yet been completed; just as on the first day of his appearance on the world's stage, man must still consume every day, before and while he produces. If products are produced as commodities, they must be sold after they have been produced, and they can only satisfy the producer's needs after they have been sold. The time necessary for sale must be counted as well as the time of production.

For the transformation of money into capital, therefore, the owner of money must find the free worker available on the commodity-market; and this worker must be free in the double sense that as a free individual he can dispose of his labour-power as his own commodity, and that, on the other hand, he has no other commodity for sale, i.e., he is rid of them, he is free of all the objects needed for the realization [*Verwirklichung*] of his labour-power.

Why this free worker confronts him in the sphere of circulation is a question which does not interest the owner of money, for he finds the labour-market in existence as a particular branch of the commodity-market. And for the present it interests us just as little. We confine ourselves to the fact theoretically, as he does practically. One thing, however, is clear: nature does not produce on the one hand owners of money or commodities, and on the other hand men possessing nothing but their own labour-power. This relation has no basis in natural history, nor does it have a social basis common to all periods of human history. It is clearly the result of a past historical development, the product of many economic revolutions, of the extinction of a whole series of older formations of social production.

The economic categories already discussed similarly bear a historical imprint. Definite historical conditions are involved in the existence of the product as a commodity. In order to become a commodity, the product must cease to be produced as the immediate means of subsistence of the producer himself. Had we gone further, and inquired under what circumstances all, or even the majority of products take the form of commodities, we should have found that this only happens on the basis of one particular

---

in my work, and everything I produced, I would be making into another's property the substance of my being, my universal activity and actuality, my personality' (Hegel, *Philosophie des Rechts*, Berlin, 1840, p. 104, § 67).

mode of production, the capitalist one. Such an investigation, however, would have been foreign to the analysis of commodities. The production and circulation of commodities can still take place even though the great mass of the objects produced are intended for the immediate require-ments of their producers, and are not turned into commodities, so that the process of social production is as yet by no means dominated in its length and breadth by exchange-value. The appearance of products as commodities requires a level of development of the division of labour within society such that the separation of use-value from exchange-value, a separation which first begins with barter, has already been completed. But such a degree of development is common to many economic forma-tions of society [*ökonomische Gesellschaftsformationen*], with the most diverse historical characteristics.

If we go on to consider money, its existence implies that a definite stage in the development of commodity exchange has been reached. The various forms of money (money as the mere equivalent of commodities, money as means of circulation, money as means of payment, money as hoard, or money as world currency) indicate very different levels of the process of social production, according to the extent and relative prepon-derance of one function or the other. Yet we know by experience that a relatively feeble development of commodity circulation suffices for the creation of all these forms. It is otherwise with capital. The historical conditions of its existence are by no means given with the mere circulation of money and commodities. It arises only when the owner of the means of production and subsistence finds the free worker available, on the market, as the seller of his own labour-power. And this one historical pre-condition comprises a world's history. Capital, therefore, announces from the outset a new epoch in the process of social production.[hh]

This peculiar commodity, labour-power, must now be examined more closely, Like all other commodities it has a value.[ii] How is that value determined?

The value of labour-power is determined, as in the case of every other commodity, by the labour-time necessary for the production, and con-sequently also the reproduction, of this specific article. In so far as it has value, it represents no more than a definite quantity of the average social labour objectified in it. Labour-power exists only as a capacity of the living individual. Its production consequently presupposes his existence. Given the existence of the individual, the production of labour-power consists in his reproduction of himself or his maintenance. For his maintenance

[hh] The capitalist epoch is therefore characterized by the fact that labour-power, in the eyes of the worker himself, takes on the form of a commodity which is his property; his labour consequently takes on the form of wage-labour. On the other hand, it is only from this moment that the commodity-form of the products of labour becomes universal.

[ii] 'The value or worth of a man, is as of all other things his price—that is to say, so much as would be given for the use of his power' (T. Hobbes, *Leviathan*, in *Works*, ed. Molesworth, London, 1839–44, Vol. 3, p. 76).

he requires a certain quantity of the means of subsistence. Therefore the labour-time necessary for the production of labour-power is the same as that necessary for the production of those means of subsistence; in other words, the value of labour-power is the value of the means of subsistence necessary for the maintenance of its owner. However, labour-power becomes a reality only by being expressed; it is activated only through labour. But in the course of this activity, i.e., labour, a definite quantity of human muscle, nerve, brain, etc. is expended, and these things have to be replaced. Since more is expended, more must be received.*jj* If the owner of labour-power works today, tomorrow he must again be able to repeat the same process in the same conditions as regards health and strength. His means of subsistence must therefore be sufficient to maintain him in his normal state as a working individual. His natural needs, such as food, clothing, fuel and housing vary according to the climatic and other physical peculiarities of his country. On the other hand, the number and extent of his so-called necessary requirements, as also the manner in which they are satisfied, are themselves products of history, and depend therefore to a great extent on the level of civilization attained by a country; in particular they depend on the conditions in which, and consequently on the habits and expectations with which, the class of free workers has been formed.*kk* In contrast, therefore, with the case of other commodities, the determination of the value of labour-power contains a historical and moral element. Nevertheless, in a given country at a given period, the average amount of the means of subsistence necessary for the worker is a known *datum*.

The owner of labour-power is mortal. If then his appearance in the market is to be continuous, and the continuous transformation of money into capital assumes this, the seller of labour-power must perpetuate himself 'in the way that every living individual perpetuates himself, by procreation'.*ll* The labour-power withdrawn from the market by wear and tear, and by death, must be continually replaced by, at the very least, an equal amount of fresh labour-power. Hence the sum of means of subsistence necessary for the production of labour-power must include the means necessary for the worker's replacements, i.e., his children, in order that this race of peculiar commodity-owners may perpetuate its presence on the market.*mm*

---

jj In ancient Rome, therefore, the *villicus*, as the overseer of the agricultural slaves, received 'more meagre fare than working slaves, because his work was lighter' (T. Mommsen, *Römische Geschichte*, 1856, p. 810).

kk Cf. W.T. Thornton, *Over-Population and Its Remedy*, London, 1846.

ll Petty.

mm Its' (labour's) 'natural price . . . consists in such a quantity of necessaries and comforts of life, as, from the nature of the climate, and the habits of the country, are necessary to support the labourer, and to enable him to rear such a family as may preserve, in the market, an undiminished supply of labour' (R. Torrens, *An Essay on the External Corn Trade*, London, 1815, p. 62). The word labour is here wrongly used for labour-power.

In order to modify the general nature of the human organism in such a way that it acquires skill and dexterity in a given branch of industry, and becomes labour-power of a developed and specific kind, a special education or training is needed, and this in turn costs an equivalent in commodities of a greater or lesser amount. The costs of education vary according to the degree of complexity of the labour-power required. These expenses (exceedingly small in the case of ordinary labour-power) form a part of the total value spent in producing it.

The value of labour-power can be resolved into the value of a definite quantity of the means of subsistence. It therefore varies with the value of the means of subsistence, i.e. with the quantity of labour-time required to produce them.

Some of the means of subsistence, such as food and fuel, are consumed every day, and must therefore be replaced every day. Others, such as clothes and furniture, last for longer periods and need to be replaced only at longer intervals. Articles of one kind must be bought or paid for every day, others every week, others every quarter and so on. But in whatever way the sum total of these outlays may be spread over the year, they must be covered by the average income, taking one day with another. If the total of the commodities required every day for the production of labour-power $= A$, and of those required every week $= B$, and of those required every quarter $= C$, and so on, the daily average of these commodities $=$
$$\frac{365A + 52B + 4C + \ldots}{365}$$
Suppose that this mass of commodities required for the average day contains 6 hours of social labour, then every day half a day of average social labour is objectified in labour-power, or in other words half a day of labour is required for the daily production of labour-power. This quantity of labour forms the value of a day's labour-power, or the value of the labour-power reproduced every day. If half a day of average social labour is present in 3 shillings, then 3 shillings is the price corresponding to the value of a day's labour-power. If its owner therefore offers it for sale at 3 shillings a day, its selling price is equal to its value, and according to our original assumption the owner of money, who is intent on transforming his 3 shillings into capital, pays this value.

The ultimate or minimum limit of the value of labour-power is formed by the value of the commodities which have to be supplied every day to the bearer of labour-power, the man, so that he can renew his life-process. That is to say, the limit is formed by the value of the physically indispensable means of subsistence. If the price of labour-power falls to this minimum, it falls below its value, since under such circumstances it can be maintained and developed only in a crippled state, and the value of every commodity is determined by the labour-time required to provide it in its normal quality.

It is an extraordinarily cheap kind of sentimentality which declares that this method of determining the value of labour-power, a method prescribed by the very nature of the case, is brutal, and which laments with Rossi in this matter: 'To conceive capacity for labour (*puissance de travail*) in abstraction from the worker's means of subsistence during the production process is to conceive a phantom (*être de raison*). When we speak of labour, or capacity for labour, we speak at the same time of the worker and his means of subsistence, of the worker and his wages.'[nn] When we speak of capacity for labour, we do not speak of labour, any more than we speak of digestion when we speak of capacity for digestion. As is well known, the latter process requires something more than a good stomach. When we speak of capacity for labour, we do not abstract from the necessary means of subsistence. On the contrary, their value is expressed in its value. If his capacity for labour remains unsold, this is of no advantage to the worker. He will rather feel it to be a cruel nature-imposed necessity that his capacity for labour has required for its production a definite quantity of the means of subsistence, and will continue to require this for its reproduction. Then like Sismondi, he will discover that 'the capacity for labour . . . is nothing unless it is sold'.[oo]

One consequence of the peculiar nature of labour-power as a commodity is this, that it does not in reality pass straight away into the hands of the buyer on the conclusion of the contract between buyer and seller. Its value, like that of every other commodity, is already determined before it enters into circulation, for a definite quantity of social labour has been spent on the production of the labour-power. But its use-value consists in the subsequent exercise of that power. The alienation [*Veräusserung*] of labour-power and its real manifestation [*Äusserung*]; i.e., the period of its existence as a use-value, do not coincide in time. But in those cases in which the formal alienation by sale of the use-value of a commodity is not simultaneous with its actual transfer to the buyer, the money of the buyer serves as means of payment.[pp]

In every country where the capitalist mode of production prevails, it is the custom not to pay for labour-power until it has been exercised for the period fixed by the contract, for example, at the end of each week. In all cases, therefore, the worker advances the use-value of his labour-power to the capitalist. He lets the buyer consume it before he receives payment of the price. Everywhere the worker allows credit to the capitalist. That this credit is no mere fiction is shown not only by the

[nn] Rossi, *Cours d'économie politique*, Brussels, 1842, pp. 370–71.

[oo] Sismondi, *Nouvelles Principes etc.*, Vol. 1, p. 113.

[pp] 'All labour is paid after it has ceased' (*An Inquiry into Those Principles, Respecting the Nature of Demand, etc.*, p. 104). 'The system of commercial credit had to start at the moment when the worker, the prime creator of products, could, thanks to his savings, wait for his wages until the end of the week, the fortnight, the month, the quarter, etc.' (C. Ganilh, *Des systèmes de l'économie politique*, 2nd edn, Paris, 1821, Vol. 1, p. 150).

occasional loss of the wages the worker has already advanced, when a capitalist goes bankrupt,[qq] but also by a series of more long-lasting consequences.[rr]

Whether money serves as a means of purchase or a means of payment, this does not alter the nature of the exchange of commodities. The price of the labour-power is fixed by the contract, although it is not realized till later, like the rent of a house. The labour-power is sold, although it is paid for only at a later period. It will therefore be useful, if we want to conceive the relation in its pure form, to presuppose for the moment that the possessor of labour-power, on the occasion of each sale, immediately receives the price stipulated in the contract.

[qq] 'The worker lends his industry,' says Storch. But he slyly adds to this the statement that the worker 'risks nothing', except 'the loss of his wages . . . . The worker does not hand over anything of a material nature' (Storch, *Cours d'économie politique*, St Petersburg, 1815, Vol. 2, pp. 36–7).

[rr] One example. In London there are two sorts of bakers, the 'full priced', who sell bread at its full value, and the 'undersellers', who sell it at less than its value. The latter class comprises more than three-quarters of the total number of bakers (p. xxxii in the Report of H. S. Tremenheere, the commissioner appointed to examine 'the grievances complained of by the journeymen bakers', etc., London, 1862). The undersellers, almost without exception, sell bread adulterated with alum, soap, pearl-ash, chalk, Derbyshire stone-dust and other similar agreeable, nourishing and wholesome ingredients. (See the above-cited Blue Book, as also the report of the select committee of 1855 on the adulteration of food, and Dr Hassall's *Adulterations Detected*, 2nd edn, London, 1861.) Sir John Gordon stated before the committee of 1855 that 'in consequence of these adulterations, the poor man, who lives on two pounds of bread a day, does not now get one-fourth part of nourishing matter, let alone the deleterious effects on his health'. Tremenheere states (op. cit., p. xlviii) as the reason why a 'very large part of the working class', although well aware of this adulteration, nevertheless accept the alum, stone-dust, etc. as part of their purchase, that it is for them 'a matter of necessity to take from their baker or from the chandler's shop such bread as they choose to supply'. As they are not paid their wages before the end of the week, they in their turn are unable 'to pay for the bread consumed by their families during the week, before the end of the week', and Tremenheere adds on the evidence of witnesses, 'it is notorious that bread composed of those mixtures is made expressly for sale in this manner'. 'In many English agricultural districts' (and still more in Scottish) 'wages are paid fortnightly and even monthly; with such long intervals between the payments, the agricultural labourer is obliged to buy on credit. . . . He must pay higher prices, and is in fact tied to the shop which gives him credit. Thus at Horningham in Wilts., for example, where the wages are monthly, the same flour that he could buy elsewhere at 1s. 10d. per stone, costs him 2s. 4d. per stone' (*Public Health, Sixth Report* of the Medical Officer of the Privy Council, etc., 1864, p. 264). 'The block-printers of Paisley and Kilmarnock' (Western Scotland) 'enforced in 1833 by a strike the reduction of the period of payment from monthly to fortnightly' (*Reports of the Inspectors of Factories . . . 31 October* 1853, p. 34). As a further nice development from the credit given by the workers to the capitalist, we may refer to the method adopted by many English coal-owners whereby the worker is not paid till the end of the month, and in the meantime receives sums on account from the capitalist, often in goods for which the miner is obliged to pay more than the market price (truck system). 'It is a common practice with the coal masters to pay once a month, and advance cash to their workmen at the end of each intermediate week. The cash is given in the shop' (i.e., the tommy-shop which belongs to the master); 'the men take it on one side and lay it out on the other' (*Children's Employment Commission, Third Report*, London, 1864, p. 38, n. 192).

We now know the manner of determining the value paid by the owner of money to the owner of this peculiar commodity, labour-power. The use-value which the former gets in exchange manifests itself only in the actual utilization, in the process of the consumption of the labour-power. The money-owner buys everything necessary for this process, such as raw material, in the market, and pays the full price for it. The process of the consumption of labour-power is at the same time the production process of commodities and of surplus-value. The consumption of labour-power is completed, as in the case of every other commodity, outside the market or the sphere of circulation. Let us therefore, in company with the owner of money and the owner of labour-power, leave this noisy sphere, where everything takes place on the surface and in full view of everyone, and follow them into the hidden abode of production, on whose threshold there hangs the notice 'No admittance except on business'. Here we shall see, not only how capital produces, but how capital is itself produced. The secret of profit-making must at last be laid bare.

The sphere of circulation or commodity exchange, within whose boundaries the sale and purchase of labour-power goes on, is in fact a very Eden of the innate rights of man. It is the exclusive realm of Freedom, Equality, Property and Bentham. Freedom, because both buyer and seller of a commodity, let us say of labour-power, are determined only by their own free will. They contract as free persons, who are equal before the law. Their contract is the final result in which their joint will finds a common legal expression. Equality, because each enters into relation with the other, as with a simple owner of commodities, and they exchange equivalent for equivalent. Property, because each disposes only of what is his own. And Bentham, because each looks only to his own advantage. The only force bringing them together, and putting them into relation with each other, is the selfishness, the gain and the private interest of each. Each pays heed to himself only, and no one worries about the others. And precisely for that reason, either in accordance with the pre-established harmony of things, or under the auspices of an omniscient providence, they all work together to their mutual advantage, for the common weal, and in the common interest.

When we leave this sphere of simple circulation or the exchange of commodities, which provides the 'free-trader *vulgaris*' with his views, his concepts and the standard by which he judges the society of capital and wage-labour, a certain change takes place, or so it appears, in the physiognomy of our *dramatis personae*. He who was previously the money-owner now strides out in front as a capitalist; the possessor of labour-power follows as his worker. The one smirks self-importantly and is intent on business; the other is timid and holds back, like someone who has brought his own hide to market and now has nothing else to expect but—a tanning.

Part Three
The Production of Absolute Surplus-Value

Chapter 7
The Labour Process and the Valorization Process

1. THE LABOUR PROCESS

The use of labour-power is labour itself. The purchaser of labour-power consumes it by setting the seller of it to work. By working, the latter becomes in actuality what previously he only was potentially, namely labour-power in action, a worker. In order to embody his labour in commodities, he must above all embody it in use-values, things which serve to satisfy needs of one kind or another. Hence what the capitalist sets the worker to produce is a particular use-value, a specific article. The fact that the production of use-values, or goods, is carried on under the control of a capitalist and on his behalf does not alter the general character of that production. We shall therefore, in the first place, have to consider the labour process independently of any specific social formation.

Labour is, first of all, a process between man and nature, a process by which man, through his own actions, mediates, regulates and controls the metabolism between himself and nature. He confronts the materials of nature as a force of nature. He sets in motion the natural forces which belong to his own body, his arms, legs, head and hands, in order to appropriate the materials of nature in a form adapted to his own needs. Through this movement he acts upon external nature and changes it, and in this way he simultaneously changes his own nature. He develops the potentialities slumbering within nature, and subjects the play of its forces to his own sovereign power. We are not dealing here with those first instinctive forms of labour which remain on the animal level. An immense interval of time separates the state of things in which a man brings his labour-power to market for sale as a commodity from the situation when human labour had not yet cast off its first instinctive form. We presuppose labour in a form in which it is an exclusively human characteristic. A spider conducts operations which resemble those of the weaver, and a bee would put many a human architect to shame by the construction of its honeycomb cells. But what distinguishes the worst architect from the best of bees is that the architect builds the cell in his mind before he constructs it in wax. At the end of every labour process, a result emerges which had already been conceived by the worker at the beginning, hence already existed ideally. Man not only effects a change of form in the materials of nature; he also realizes [*verwirklicht*] his own purpose in those materials. And this is a purpose he is conscious of, it determines the mode of his activity with the rigidity of a law, and he must subordinate his will to it. This subordination is no mere momentary act. Apart from the exertion of the working organs, a purposeful will is required for the entire duration of the work. This means close attention. The less he is attracted by the nature of the work and the way in which it has to be accomplished, and the less, therefore, he enjoys it as the free play of his own physical and mental powers, the closer his attention is forced to be.

The simple elements of the labour process are (1) purposeful activity, that is work itself, (2) the object on which that work is performed, and (3) the instruments of that work.

The land (and this, economically speaking, includes water) in its original state in which it supplies[ss] man with necessaries or means of subsistence ready to hand is available without any effort on his part as the universal material for human labour. All those things which labour merely separates from immediate connection with their environment are objects of labour spontaneously provided by nature, such as fish caught and separated from their natural element, namely water, timber felled in virgin forests, and ores extracted from their veins. If, on the other hand, the object of labour has, so to speak, been filtered through previous labour, we call it raw material. For example, ore already extracted and ready for washing. All raw material is an object of labour [*Arbeitsgegenstand*], but not every object of labour is raw material; the object of labour counts as raw material only when it has already undergone some alteration by means of labour.

An instrument of labour is a thing, or a complex of things, which the worker interposes between himself and the object of his labour and which serves as a conductor, directing his activity onto that object. He makes use of the mechanical, physical and chemical properties of some substances in order to set them to work on other substances as instruments of his power, and in accordance with his purposes.[tt] Leaving out of consideration such ready-made means of subsistence as fruits, in gathering which a man's bodily organs alone serve as the instruments of his labour, the object the worker directly takes possession of is not the object of labour but its instrument. Thus nature becomes one of the organs of his activity, which he annexes to his own bodily organs, adding stature to himself in

---

[ss] 'The earth's spontaneous productions being in small quantity, quite independent of man, appear, as it were, to be furnished by Nature, in the same way as a small sum is given to a young man, in order to put him in a way of industry, and of making his fortune' (James Steuart, *Principles of Political Economy*, Dublin, 1770, Vol. 1, p. 116).

[tt] 'Reason is as cunning as it is powerful. Cunning may be said to lie in the intermediative action which, while it permits the objects to follow their own bent and act upon one another till they waste away, and does not itself directly interfere in the process, is nevertheless only working out its own aims' (Hegel, *Enzyklopädie, Erster Theil, Die Logik*, Berlin, 1840, p. 382) [§ 209, Addition. English translation: *Hegel's Logic*, tr. W. V. Wallace (revised by J. N. Findlay), Oxford, 1975, pp. 272–3].

spite of the Bible. As the earth is his original larder, so too it is his original tool house. It supplies him, for instance, with stones for throwing, grinding, pressing, cutting, etc. The earth itself is an instrument of labour, but its use in this way, in agriculture, presupposes a whole series of other instruments and a comparatively high stage of development of labour-power.*uu* As soon as the labour process has undergone the slightest development, it requires specially prepared instruments. Thus we find stone implements and weapons in the oldest caves. In the earliest period of human history, domesticated animals, i.e. animals that have undergone modification by means of labour, that have been bred specially, play the chief part as instruments of labour along with stones, wood, bones and shells, which have also had work done on them.*vv* The use and construction of instruments of labour, although present in germ among certain species of animals, is characteristic of the specifically human labour process, and Franklin therefore defines man as 'a tool-making animal'. Relics of bygone instruments of labour possess the same importance for the investigation of extinct economic formations of society as do fossil bones for the determination of extinct species of animals. It is not what is made but how, and by what instruments of labour, that distinguishes different economic epochs.*ww* Instruments of labour not only supply a standard of the degree of development which human labour has attained, but they also indicate the social relations within which men work. Among the instruments of labour, those of a mechanical kind, which, taken as a whole, we may call the bones and muscles of production, offer much more decisive evidence of the character of a given social epoch of production than those which, like pipes, tubs, baskets, jars etc., serve only to hold the materials for labour, and may be given the general denotation of the vascular system of production. The latter first begins to play an important part in the chemical industries.*xx*

In a wider sense we may include among the instruments of labour, in addition to things through which the impact of labour on its object is mediated, and which therefore, in one way or another, serve as conductors

---

uu In his otherwise miserable work *Théorie de l'économie politique*, Paris, 1815, Ganilh enumerates in a striking manner in opposition to the Physiocrats* the long series of labour processes which form the presupposition for agriculture properly so called.

*For the Physiocrats, the productivity of labour appeared as a *gift of nature, a productive power of nature* . . . Surplus-value therefore appeared as a *gift of nature*' (*Theories of Surplus-Value*, Part 1, pp. 49–51).

vv In his *Réflexions sur la formation et la distribution des richesses* (1766), Turgot gives a good account of the importance of domesticated animals for the beginnings of civilization.

ww The least important commodities of all for the technological comparison of different epochs of production are articles of real luxury.

xx The writers of history have so far paid very little attention to the development of material production, which is the basis of all social life, and therefore of all real history. But prehistoric times at any rate have been classified on the basis of the investigations of natural science, rather than so-called historical research. Prehistory has been divided, according to the materials used to make tools and weapons, into the Stone Age, the Bronze Age and the Iron Age.

of activity, all the objective conditions necessary for carrying on the labour process. These do not enter directly into the process, but without them it is either impossible for it to take place, or possible only to a partial extent. Once again, the earth itself is a universal instrument of this kind, for it provides the worker with the ground beneath his feet and a 'field of employment' for his own particular process. Instruments of this kind, which have already been mediated through past labour, include workshops, canals, roads, etc.

In the labour process, therefore, man's activity, *via* the instruments of labour, effects an alteration in the object of labour which was intended from the outset. The process is extinguished in the product. The product of the process is a use-value, a piece of natural material adapted to human needs by means of a change in its form. Labour has become bound up in its object: labour has been objectified, the object has been worked on. What on the side of the worker appeared in the form of unrest [*Unruhe*] now appears, on the side of the product, in the form of being [*Sein*], as a fixed, immobile characteristic. The worker has spun, and the product is a spinning.

If we look at the whole process from the point of view of its result, the product, it is plain that both the instruments and the object of labour are means of production[yy] and that the labour itself is productive labour.[zz]

Although a use-value emerges from the labour process, in the form of a product, other use-values, products of previous labour, enter into it as means of production. The same use-value is both the product of a previous process, and a means of production in a later process. Products are therefore not only results of labour, but also its essential conditions.

With the exception of the extractive industries, such as mining, hunting, fishing (and agriculture, but only in so far as it starts by breaking up virgin soil), where the material for labour is provided directly by nature, all branches of industry deal with raw material, i.e. an object of labour which has already been filtered through labour, which is itself already a product of labour. An example is seed in agriculture. Animals and plants which we are accustomed to consider as products of nature, may be, in their present form, not only products of, say, last year's labour, but the result of a gradual transformation continued through many generations under human control, and through the agency of human labour. As regards the instruments of labour in particular, they show traces of the labour of past ages, even to the most superficial observer, in the great majority of cases.

Raw material may either form the principal substance of a product, or

---

[yy] It appears paradoxical to assert that uncaught fish, for instance, are a means of production in the fishing industry. But hitherto no one has discovered the art of catching fish in waters that contain none.

[zz] This method of determining what is productive labour, from the standpoint of the simple labour process, is by no means sufficient to cover the capitalist process of production.

it may enter into its formation only as an accessory. An accessory may be consumed by the instruments of labour, such as coal by a steam-engine, oil by a wheel, hay by draft-horses, or it may be added to the raw material in order to produce some physical modification of it, as chlorine is added to unbleached linen, coal to iron, dye to wool, or again it may help to accomplish the work itself, as in the case of the materials used for heating and lighting workshops. The distinction between principal substance and accessory vanishes in the chemical industries proper, because there none of the raw material re-appears, in its original composition, in the substance of the product.*aaa*

Every object possesses various properties, and is thus capable of being applied to different uses. The same product may therefore form the raw material for very different labour processes. Corn, for example, is a raw material for millers, starch-manufacturers, distillers and cattle-breeders. It also enters as raw material into its own production in the shape of seed; coal both emerges from the mining industry as a product and enters into it as a means of production.

Again, a particular product may be used as both instrument of labour and raw material in the same process. Take, for instance, the fattening of cattle, where the animal is the raw material, and at the same time an instrument for the production of manure.

A product, though ready for immediate consumption, may nevertheless serve as raw material for a further product, as grapes do when they become the raw material for wine. On the other hand, labour may release its product in such a form that it can only be used as raw material. Raw material in this condition, such as cotton, thread and yarn, is called semi-manufactured, but should rather be described as having been manufactured up to a certain level. Although itself already a product, this raw material may have to go through a whole series of different processes, and in each of these it serves as raw material, changing its shape constantly, until it is precipitated from the last process of the series in finished form, either as means of subsistence or as instrument of labour.

Hence we see that whether a use-value is to be regarded as raw material, as instrument of labour or as product is determined entirely by its specific function in the labour process, by the position it occupies there: as its position changes, so do its determining characteristics.

Therefore, whenever products enter as means of production into new labour processes, they lose their character of being products and function only as objective factors contributing to living labour. A spinner treats spindles only as a means for spinning, and flax as the material he spins. Of course it is impossible to spin without material and spindles; and

---

aaa Storch distinguishes between raw material ('*matière*') and accessory materials ('*matériaux*'). Cherbuliez describes accessories as '*matières instrumentales*'.[31]

therefore the availability of these products is presupposed at the beginning of the spinning operation. But in the process itself, the fact that they are the products of past labour is as irrelevant as, in the case of the digestive process, the fact that bread is the product of the previous labour of the farmer, the miller and the baker. On the contrary, it is by their imperfections that the means of production in any process bring to our attention their character of being the products of past labour. A knife which fails to cut, a piece of thread which keeps on snapping, forcibly remind us of Mr A, the cutler, or Mr. B, the spinner. In a successful product, the role played by past labour in mediating its useful properties has been extinguished.

A machine which is not active in the labour process is useless. In addition, it falls prey to the destructive power of natural processes. Iron rusts; wood rots. Yarn with which we neither weave nor knit is cotton wasted. Living labour must seize on these things, awaken them from the dead, change them from merely possible into real and effective use-values. Bathed in the fire of labour, appropriated as part of its organism, and infused with vital energy for the performance of the functions appropriate to their concept and to their vocation in the process, they are indeed consumed, but to some purpose, as elements in the formation of new use-values, new products, which are capable of entering into individual consumption as means of subsistence or into a new labour process as means of production.

If then, on the one hand, finished products are not only results of the labour process, but also conditions of its existence, their induction into the process, their contact with living labour, is the sole means by which they can be made to retain their character of use-values, and be realized.

Labour uses up its material elements, its objects and its instruments. It consumes them, and is therefore a process of consumption. Such productive consumption is distinguished from individual consumption by this, that the latter uses up products as means of subsistence for the living individual; the former, as means of subsistence for labour, i.e. for the activity through which the living individual's labour-power manifests itself. Thus the product of individual consumption is the consumer himself; the result of productive consumption is a product distinct from the consumer.

In so far then as its instruments and its objects are themselves products, labour consumes products in order to create products, or in other words consumes one set of products by turning them into means of production for another set. But just as the labour process originally took place only between man and the earth (which was available independently of any human action), so even now we still employ in the process many means of production which are provided directly by nature and do not represent any combination of natural substances with human labour.

The labour process, as we have just presented it in its simple and abstract elements, is purposeful activity aimed at the production of use-values. It is an appropriation of what exists in nature for the requirements of man. It is the universal condition for the metabolic interaction [*Stoffwechsel*] between man and nature, the everlasting nature-imposed condition of human existence, and it is therefore independent of every form of that existence, or rather it is common to all forms of society in which human beings live. We did not, therefore, have to present the worker in his relationship with other workers; it was enough to present man and his labour on one side, nature and its materials on the other. The taste of porridge does not tell us who grew the oats, and the process we have presented does not reveal the conditions under which it takes place, whether it is happening under the slave-owner's brutal lash or the anxious eye of the capitalist, whether Cincinnatus[32] undertakes it in tilling his couple of acres, or a savage, when he lays low a wild beast with a stone.*bbb*

Let us now return to our would-be capitalist. We left him just after he had purchased, in the open market, all the necessary factors of the labour process; its objective factors, the means of production, as well as its personal factor, labour-power. With the keen eye of an expert, he has selected the means of production and the kind of labour-power best adapted to his particular trade, be it spinning, bootmaking or any other kind. He then proceeds to consume the commodity, the labour-power he has just bought, i.e. he causes the worker, the bearer of that labour-power, to consume the means of production by his labour. The general character of the labour process is evidently not changed by the fact that the worker works for the capitalist instead of for himself; moreover, the particular methods and operations employed in bootmaking or spinning are not immediately altered by the intervention of the capitalist. He must begin by taking the labour-power as he finds it in the market, and consequently he must be satisfied with the kind of labour which arose in a period when there were as yet no capitalists. The transformation of the mode of production itself which results from the subordination of labour to capital can only occur later on, and we shall therefore deal with it in a later chapter.

The labour process, when it is the process by which the capitalist consumes labour-power, exhibits two characteristic phenomena.

First, the worker works under the control of the capitalist to whom his labour belongs; the capitalist takes good care that the work is done in a

---

bbb By a wonderful feat of logical acumen, Colonel Torrens has discovered, in this stone of the savage, the origin of capital. 'In the first stone which the savage flings at the wild animal he pursues, in the first stick that he seizes to strike down the fruit which hangs above his reach, we see the appropriation of one article for the purpose of aiding in the acquisition of another, and thus discover the origin of capital' (R. Torrens, *An Essay on the Production of Wealth*, etc., pp. 70–71). No doubt this 'first stick' [*Stock*] would also explain why 'stock' in English is synonymous with capital.

proper manner, and the means of production are applied directly to the purpose, so that the raw material is not wasted, and the instruments of labour are spared, i.e. only worn to the extent necessitated by their use in the work.

Secondly, the product is the property of the capitalist and not that of the worker, its immediate producer. Suppose that a capitalist pays for a day's worth of labour-power; then the right to use that power for a day belongs to him, just as much as the right to use any other commodity, such as a horse he had hired for the day. The use of a commodity belongs to its purchaser, and the seller of labour-power, by giving his labour, does no more, in reality, than part with the use-value he has sold. From the instant h steps into the workshop, the use-value of his labour-power and therefore also its use, which is labour, belongs to the capitalist. By the purchase of labour-power, the capitalist incorporates labour, as a living agent of fermentation, into the lifeless constituents of the product, which also belong to him. From his point of view, the labour process is nothing more than the consumption of the commodity purchased, i.e., of labour-power; but he can consume this labour-power only by adding the means of production to it. The labour process is a process between things the capitalist has purchased, things which belong to him. Thus the product of this process belongs to him just as much as the wine which is the product of the process of fermentation going on in his cellar.[ccc]

2. THE VALORIZATION PROCESS

The product—the property of the capitalist—is a use-value, as yarn, for example, or boots. But although boots are, to some extent, the basis of social progress, and our capitalist is decidedly in favour of progress, he does not manufacture boots for their own sake. Use-value is certainly not *la chose qu'on aime pour lui-même*[33] in the production of commodities. Use-values are produced by capitalists only because and in so far as they the material substratum of exchange-value, are the bearers of exchange-

[ccc] 'Products are appropriated before they are transformed into capital; this transformation does not withdraw them from that appropriation' (Cherbuliez, *Richesse on pauvreté*, Paris, 1841, p. 54). 'The proletarian, by selling his labour for a definite quantity of the means of subsistence (*approvisionnement*) renounces all claim to a share in the product. The products continue to be appropriated as before: this is in no way altered by the bargain we have mentioned. The product belongs exclusively to the capitalist, who supplied the raw materials and the *approvisionnement*. This follows rigorously from the law of appropriation, a law whose fundamental principle was the exact opposite, namely that every worker has an exclusive right to the ownership of what he produces' (ibid., p. 58). 'When the labourers receive wages for their labour . . . the capitalist is then the owner not of the capital only' (i.e., the means of production) 'but of the labour also. If what is paid as wages is included, as it commonly is, in the term capital, it is absurd to talk of labour separately from capital. The word capital as thus employed includes labour and capital both' (James Mill, *Elements of Political Economy*, London, 1821, pp. 70–71).

value. Our capitalist has two objectives: in the first place, he wants to produce a use-value which has exchange-value, i.e., an article destined to be sold, a commodity; and secondly he wants to produce a commodity greater in value than the sum of the values of the commodities used to produce it, namely the means of production and the labour-power he purchased with his good money on the open market. His aim is to produce not only a use-value, but a commodity; not only use-value, but value; and not just value, but also surplus-value.

It must be borne in mind that we are now dealing with the production of commodities, and that up to this point we have considered only one aspect of the process. Just as the commodity itself is a unity formed of use-value and value, so the process of production must be a unity, composed of the labour process and the process of creating value [*Wertbildungsprozess*].

Let us now examine production as a process of creating value.

We know that the value of each commodity is determined by the quantity of labour materialized in its use-value, by the labour-time socially necessary to produce it. This rule also holds good in the case of the product handed over to the capitalist as a result of the labour-process. Assuming this product to be yarn, our first step is to calculate the quantity of labour objectified in it.

For spinning the yarn, raw material is required; suppose in this case 10 lb. of cotton. We have no need at present to investigate the value of this cotton, for our capitalist has, we will assume, bought it at its full value, say 10 shillings. In this price the labour required for the production of the cotton is already expressed in terms of average social labour. We will further assume that the wear and tear of the spindle, which for our present purpose may represent all other instruments of labour employed, amounts to the value of 2 shillings. If then, twenty-four hours of labour, or two working days, are required to produce the quantity of gold represented by 12 shillings, it follows first of all that two days of labour are objectified in the yarn.

We should not let ourselves be misled by the circumstance that the cotton has changed its form and the worn-down portion of the spindle has entirely disappeared. According to the general law of value, if the value of 40 lb. of yarn = the value of 40 lb. of cotton the value of a whole spindle, i.e., if the same amount of labour-time is required to produce the commodities on either side of this equation, then 10 lb. of yarn are an equivalent for 10 lb. of cotton, together with a quarter of a spindle. In the case we are considering, the same amount of labour-time is represented in the 10 lb. of yarn on the one hand, and in the 10 lb. of cotton and the fraction of a spindle on the other. It is therefore a matter of indifference whether value appears in cotton, in a spindle or in yarn: its amount remains the same. The spindle and cotton, instead of resting quietly side by side, join together in the process, their forms are altered, and they are turned into yarn; but their value is no more affected by this fact than it would be if they had been simply exchanged for their equivalent in yarn.

The labour-time required for the production of the cotton, the raw material of the yarn, is part of the labour necessary to produce the yarn, and is therefore contained in the yarn. The same applies to the labour embodied in the spindle without whose wear and tear the cotton could not be spun.*ddd*

Hence in determining the value of the yarn, or the labour-time required for its production, all the special processes carried on at various times and in different places which were necessary, first to produce the cotton and the wasted portion of the spindle, and then with the cotton and the spindle to spin the yarn, may together be looked on as different and successive phases of the same labour process. All the labour contained in the yarn is past labour; and it is a matter of no importance that the labour expended to produce its constituent elements lies further back in the past than the labour expended on the final process, the spinning. The former stands, as it were, in the pluperfect, the latter in the perfect tense but this does not matter. If a definite quantity of labour, say thirty days, is needed to build a house, the total amount of labour incorporated in the house is not altered by the fact that the work of the last day was done twenty-nine days later than that of the first. Therefore the labour contained in the raw material and instruments of labour can be treated just as if it were labour expended in an earlier stage of the spinning process, before the labour finally added in the form of actual spinning.

The values of the means of production which are expressed in the price of 12 shillings (the cotton and the spindle) are therefore constituent parts of the value of the yarn, i.e., of the value of the product.

Two conditions must nevertheless be fulfilled. First, the cotton and the spindle must genuinely have served to produce a use-value; they must in the present case become yarn. Value is independent of the particular use-value by which it is borne, but a use-value of some kind has to act as its bearer. Second, the labour-time expended must not exceed what is necessary under the given social conditions of production. Therefore, if no more than 1 lb. of cotton is needed to spin 1 lb. of yarn, no more than this weight of cotton may be consumed in the production of 1 lb. of yarn. The same is true of the spindle. If the capitalist has a foible for using golden spindles instead of steel ones, the only labour that counts for anything in the value of the yarn remains that which would be required to produce a steel spindle, because no more is necessary under the given social conditions.

We now know what part of the value of the yarn is formed by the means

---

ddd 'Not only the labour applied immediately to commodities affects their value, but the labour also which is bestowed on the implements, tools, and buildings with which such labour is assisted' (Ricardo, op. cit., p. 16).

of production, namely the cotton and the spindle. It is 12 shillings, i.e., the materialization of two days of labour. The next point to be considered is what part of the value of the yarn is added to the cotton by the labour of the spinner.

We have now to consider this labour from a standpoint quite different from that adopted for the labour process. There we viewed it solely as the activity which has the purpose of changing cotton into yarn; there, the more appropriate the work was to its purpose, the better the yarn, other circumstances remaining the same. In that case the labour of the spinner was specifically different from other kinds of productive labour, and this difference revealed itself both subjectively in the particular purpose of spinning, and objectively in the special character of its operations, the special nature of its means of production, and the special use-value of its product. For the operation of spinning, cotton and spindles are a necessity, but for making rifled cannon they would be of no use whatever. Here, on the contrary, where we consider the labour of the spinner only in so far as it creates value, i.e., is a source of value, that labour differs in no respect from the labour of the man who bores cannon, or (what concerns us more closely here) from the labour of the cotton-planter and the spindle-maker which is realized in the means of production of the yarn. It is solely by reason of this identity that cotton planting, spindle-making and spinning are capable of forming the component parts of one whole, namely the value of the yarn, differing only quantitatively from each other. Here we are no longer concerned with the quality, the character and the content of the labour, but merely with its quantity. And this simply requires to be calculated. We assume that spinning is simple labour, the average labour of a given society. Later it will be seen that the contrary assumption would make no difference.

During the labour process, the worker's labour constantly undergoes a transformation, from the form of unrest [*Unruhe*] into that of being [*Sein*], from the form of motion [*Bewegung*] into that of objectivity [*Gegenständlichkeit*]. At the end of one hour, the spinning motion is represented in a certain quantity of yarn; in other words, a definite quantity of labour, namely that of one hour, has been objectified in the cotton. We say labour, i.e., the expenditure of his vital force by the spinner, and not spinning labour, because the special work of spinning counts here only in so far as it is the expenditure of labour-power in general, and not the specific labour of the spinner.

In the process we are now considering it is of extreme importance that no more time be consumed in the work of transforming the cotton into yarn than is necessary under the given social conditions. If under normal, i.e., average social conditions of production, x pounds of cotton are made into y pounds of yarn by one hour's labour, then a day's labour does not count as 12 hours' labour unless $12x$ lb. of cotton have been made into

12y lb. of yarn; for only socially necessary labour-time counts towards the creation of value.

Not only the labour, but also the raw material and the product now appear in quite a new light, very different from that in which we viewed them in the labour process pure and simple. Now the raw material merely serves to absorb a definite quantity of labour. By being soaked in labour, the raw material is in fact changed into yarn, because labour-power is expended in the form of spinning and added to it; but the product, the yarn, is now nothing more than a measure of the labour absorbed by the cotton. If in one hour 1⅔ lb. of cotton can be spun into 1⅔ lb. of yarn, then 10 lb. of yarn indicate the absorption of 6 hours of labour. Definite quantities of product, quantities which are determined by experience, now represent nothing but definite quantities of labour, definite masses of crystallized labour-time. They are now simply the material shape taken by a given number of hours or days of social labour.

The fact that the labour is precisely the labour of spinning, that its material is cotton, its product yarn, is as irrelevant here as it is that the object of labour is itself already a product, hence already raw material. If the worker, instead of spinning, were to be employed in a coal-mine, the object on which he worked would be coal, which is present in nature; nevertheless, a definite quantity of coal, when extracted from its seam, would represent a definite quantity of absorbed labour.

We assumed, on the occasion of its sale, that the value of a day's labour-power was 3 shillings, and that 6 hours of labour was incorporated in that sum; and consequently that this amount of labour was needed to produce the worker's average daily means of subsistence. If now our spinner by working for one hour, can convert 1⅔ lb. of cotton into 1⅔ lb. of yarn,*eee* it follows that in 6 hours he will convert 10 lb. of cotton into 10 lb. of yarn. Hence, during the spinning process, the cotton absorbs 6 hours of labour. The same quantity of labour is also embodied in a piece of gold of the value of 3 shillings. A value of 3 shillings, therefore, is added to the cotton by the labour of spinning.

Let us now consider the total value of the product, the 10 lb. of yarn. Two and a half days of labour have been objectified in it. Out of this, two days were contained in the cotton and the worn-down portion of the spindle, and half a day was absorbed during the process of spinning. This two and a half days of labour is represented by a piece of gold of the value of 15 shillings. Hence 15 shillings is an adequate price for the 10 lb. of yarn, and the price of 1 lb. is 1s. 6d.

Our capitalist stares in astonishment. The value of the product is equal to the value of the capital advanced. The value advanced has not been valorized, no surplus-value has been created, and consequently money

_____

eee These figures are entirely arbitrary.

has not been transformed into capital. The price of the yarn is 15 shillings, and 15 shillings were spent in the open market on the constituent elements of the product or, what amounts to the same thing, on the factors of the labour process; 10 shillings were paid for the cotton, 2 shillings for the wear of the spindle and 3 shillings for the labour-power. The swollen value of the yarn is of no avail, for it is merely the sum of the values formerly existing in the cotton, the spindle and the labour-power: out of such a simple addition of existing values, no surplus-value can possibly arise.*fff* These values are now all concentrated in one thing; but so they were in the sum of 15 shillings, before it was split up into three parts by the purchase of the commodities.

In itself this result is not particularly strange. The value of one pound of yarn is 1s. 6d., and our capitalist would therefore have to pay 15 shillings for 10 lb. of yarn on the open market. It is clear that whether a man buys his house ready built, or has it built for him, neither of these operations will increase the amount of money laid out on the house.

Our capitalist, who is at home in vulgar economics, may perhaps say that he advanced his money with the intention of making more money out of it. The road to hell is paved with good intentions, and he might just as well have intended to make money without producing at all.*ggg* He makes threats. He will not be caught napping again. In future he will buy the commodities in the market, instead of manufacturing them himself. But if all his brother capitalists were to do the same, where would he find his commodities on the market? And he cannot eat his money. He recites the catechism: 'Consider my abstinence. I might have squandered the 15 shillings, but instead I consumed it productively and made yarn with it.' Very true; and as a reward he is now in possession of good yarn instead of a bad conscience. As for playing the part of a miser, it would never do for him to relapse into such bad ways; we have already seen what such asceticism leads to. Besides, where there is nothing, the king has lost his rights; whatever the merits of his abstinence there is no money there to recompense him, because the value of the product is merely the sum of the values thrown into the process of production. Let him therefore console himself with the reflection that virtue is its own

---

fff This is the fundamental proposition which forms the basis of the doctrine of the Physiocrats that all non-agricultural labour is unproductive. For the professional economist it is irrefutable. 'This method of adding to one particular object the value of numerous others' (for example adding the living costs of the weaver to the flax) 'of as it were heaping up various values in layers on top of one single value, has the result that this value grows to the same extent. . . . The expression "addition" gives a very clear picture of the way in which the price of a manufactured product is formed; this price is only the sum of a number of values which have been consumed, and it is arrived at by adding them together; however, addition is not the same as multiplication' (Mercier de la Rivière, op. cit., p. 599).

ggg Thus from 1844 to 1847 he withdrew part of his capital from productive employment in order to throw it away in railway speculations; and so also, during the American Civil War, he closed his factory and turned the workers onto the street in order to gamble on the Liverpool cotton exchange.

reward. But no, on the contrary, he becomes insistent. The yarn is of no use to him, he says. He produced it in order to sell it. In that case let him sell it, or, easier still, let him in future produce only things he needs himself, a remedy already prescribed by his personal physician MacCulloch as being of proven efficacy against an epidemic of over-production. Now our capitalist grows defiant. 'Can the worker produce commodities out of nothing, merely by using his arms and legs? Did I not provide him with the materials through which, and in which alone, his labour could be embodied? And as the greater part of society consists of such impecunious creatures, have I not rendered society an incalculable service by providing my instruments of production, my cotton and my spindle, and the worker too, for have I not provided him with the means of subsistence? Am I to be allowed nothing in return for all this service?' But has the worker not performed an equivalent service in return, by changing his cotton and his spindle into yarn? In any case, here the question of service does not arise.*hhh* A service is nothing other than the useful effect of a use-value, be it that of a commodity, or that of the labour.*iii* But here we are dealing with exchange-value. The capitalist paid to the worker a value of 3 shillings, and the worker gave him back an exact equivalent in the value of 3 shillings he added to the cotton: he gave him value for value. Our friend, who has up till now displayed all the arrogance of capital, suddenly takes on the unassuming demeanour of one of his own workers, and exclaims: 'Have I myself not worked? Have I not performed the labour of superintendence, of overseeing the spinner? And does not this labour, too, create value?' The capitalist's own overseer and manager shrug their shoulders. In the meantime, with a hearty laugh, he recovers his composure. The whole litany he has just recited was simply meant to pull the wool over our eyes. He himself does not care two pence for it. He leaves this and all similar subterfuges and conjuring tricks to the professors of political economy, who are paid for it. He himself is a practical man, and although he does not always consider what he says outside his business, within his business he knows what he is doing.

---

hhh 'Let whoever wants to do so extol himself, put on finery and adorn himself [but pay no heed and keep firmly to the scriptures]. . . . Whoever takes more or better than he gives, that is usury and does not signify a service but a wrong done to his neighbour, as when one steals and robs. Not everything described as a service and a benefit to one's neighbour is in fact a service and a benefit. An adulteress and an adulterer do each other a great service and pleasure. A horseman does great service to a robber by helping him to rob on the highway, and attack the people and the land. The papists do our people a great service in that they do not drown, burn, or murder them all, or let them rot in prison, but let some live and drive them out or take from them what they have. The devil himself does his servants a great, inestimable service. . . . To sum up: the world is full of great, excellent daily services and good deeds' (Martin Luther, *An die Pfarrherrn, wider den Wucher zu predigen. Vermanung*, Wittenberg, 1540).

iii In *Zur Kritik der politischen Ökonomie*, p. 14 I make the following remark on this point: 'It is easy to understand what "service" the category "service" must render to economists like J. B. Say and F. Bastiat.'

Let us examine the matter more closely. The value of a day's labour-power amounts to 3 shillings, because on our assumption half a day's labour is objectified in that quantity of labour-power, i.e. because the means of subsistence required every day for the production of labour-power cost half a day's labour. But the past labour embodied in the labour-power and the living labour it can perform, and the daily cost of maintaining labour-power and its daily expenditure in work, are two totally different things. The former determines the exchange-value of the labour-power, the latter is its use-value. The fact that half a day's labour is necessary to keep the worker alive during 24 hours does not in any way prevent him from working a whole day. Therefore the value of labour-power, and the value which that labour-power valorizes [*verwertet*] in the labour-process, are two entirely different magnitudes; and this difference was what the capitalist had in mind when he was purchasing the labour-power. The useful quality of labour-power, by virtue of which it makes yarn or boots, was to the capitalist merely the necessary condition for his activity; for in order to create value labour must be expended in a useful manner. What was really decisive for him was the specific use-value which this commodity possesses of being a source not only of value, but of more value than it has itself. This is the specific service the capitalist expects from labour-power, and in this transaction he acts in accordance with the eternal laws of commodity-exchange. In fact, the seller of labour-power, like the seller of any other commodity, realizes [*realisiert*] its exchange-value, and alienates [*veräussert*] its use-value. He cannot take the one without giving the other. The use-value of labour-power, in other words labour, belongs just as little to its seller as the use-value of oil after it has been sold belongs to the dealer who sold it. The owner of the money has paid the value of a day's labour-power; he therefore has the use of it for a day, a day's labour belongs to him. On the one hand the daily sustenance of labour-power costs only half a day's labour, while on the other hand the very same labour-power can remain effective, can work, during a whole day, and consequently the value which its use during one day creates is double what the capitalist pays for that use; this circumstance is a piece of good luck for the buyer, but by no means an injustice towards the seller.[34]

Our capitalist foresaw this situation, and that was the cause of his laughter. The worker therefore finds, in the workshop, the means of production necessary for working not just 6 but 12 hours. If 10 lb. of cotton could absorb 6 hours' labour, and become 10 lb. of yarn, now 20 lb. of cotton will absorb 12 hours' labour and be changed into 20 lb. of yarn. Let us examine the product of this extended labour-process. Now five days of labour are objectified in this 20 lb. of yarn; four days are due to the cotton and the lost steel of the spindle, the remaining day has been absorbed by the cotton during the spinning process. Expressed in gold, the labour of five days is 30 shillings. This is therefore the price of the 20 lb. of yarn, giving, as before, 1s. 6d. as the price of 1 lb. But the sum of the values of the commodities thrown into the process amounts to 27 shillings. The value of the yarn is 30 shillings. Therefore the value of the product is one-ninth greater than the value advanced to produce it; 27 shillings have turned into 30 shillings; a surplus-value of 3 shillings has been precipitated. The trick has at last worked: money has been transformed into capital.

Every condition of the problem is satisfied, while the laws governing the exchange of commodities have not been violated in any way. Equivalent has been exchanged for equivalent. For the capitalist as buyer paid the full value for each commodity, for the cotton, for the spindle and for the labour-power. He then did what is done by every purchaser of commodities: he consumed their use-value. The process of consuming labour-power, which was also the process of producing commodities, resulted in 20 lb. of yarn, with a value of 30 shillings. The capitalist, formerly a buyer, now returns to the market as a seller. He sells his yarn at 1s. 6d. a pound, which is its exact value. Yet for all that he withdraws 3 shillings more from circulation than he originally threw into it. This whole course of events, the transformation of money into capital, both takes place and does not take place in the sphere of circulation. It takes place through the mediation of circulation because it is conditioned by the purchase of the labour-power in the market; it does not take place in circulation because what happens there is only an introduction to the valorization process, which is entirely confined to the sphere of production. And so 'everything is for the best in the best of all possible worlds'.[35]

By turning his money into commodities which serve as the building materials for a new product, and as factors in the labour process, by incorporating living labour into their lifeless objectivity, the capitalist simultaneously transforms value, i.e., past labour in its objectified and lifeless form, into capital, value which can perform its own valorization process, an animated monster which begins to 'work', 'as if its body were by love possessed'.[36]

If we now compare the process of creating value with the process of valorization, we see that the latter is nothing but the continuation of the former beyond a definite point. If the process is not carried beyond the point where the value paid by the capitalist for the labour-power is replaced by an exact equivalent, it is simply a process of creating value; but if it is continued beyond that point, it becomes a process of valorization.

If we proceed further, and compare the process of creating value with the labour process, we find that the latter consists in the useful labour which produces use-values. Here the movement of production is viewed qualitatively, with regard to the particular kind of article produced, and in accordance with the purpose and content of the movement. But if it is viewed as a value-creating process the same labour process appears only quantitatively. Here it is a question merely of the time needed to do the work, of the period, that is, during which the labour-power is usefully expended. Here the commodities which enter into the labour process no longer count as functionally determined and material elements on which labour-power acts with a given purpose. They count merely as definite quantities of objectified labour. Whether it was already contained in the means of production, or has just been added by the action of labour-power, that labour counts only according to its duration. It amounts to so many hours, or days, etc.

Moreover, the time spent in production counts only in so far as it is socially necessary for the production of a use-value. This has various consequences. First, the labour-power must be functioning under normal conditions. If a self-acting mule is the socially predominant instrument of labour for spinning, it would be impermissible to supply the spinner with a spinning-wheel. The cotton too must not be such rubbish as to tear at every other moment, but must be of suitable quality. Otherwise the spinner would spend more time than socially necessary in producing his pound of yarn, and in this case the excess of time would create neither value nor money. But whether the objective factors of labour are normal or not does not depend on the worker, but rather on the capitalist. A further condition is that the labour-power itself must be of normal effectiveness. In the trade in which it is being employed, it must possess the average skill, dexterity and speed prevalent in that trade, and our capitalist took good care to buy labour-power of such normal quality. It must be expended with the average amount of exertion and the usual degree of intensity; and the capitalist is as careful to see that this is done, as he is to ensure that his workmen are not idle for a single moment. He has bought the use of the labour-power for a definite period, and he insists on his rights. He has no intention of being robbed. Lastly—and for this purpose our friend has a penal code of his own—all wasteful consumption of raw material or instruments of labour is strictly forbidden, because what is wasted in this way represents a superfluous expenditure of quantities of objectified labour, labour that does not count in the product or enter into its value.*jjj*

---

jjj This is one of the circumstances which make production based on slavery more expensive. Under slavery, according to the striking expression employed in antiquity, the worker is distinguishable only as *instrumentum vocale* from an animal, which is *instrumentum semi-vocale*, and from a lifeless implement, which is *instrumentum mutum*.[37] But he himself takes care to let both beast and implement feel that he is none of them, but rather a human being. He gives himself the satisfaction of knowing that he is different by treating the one with brutality and damaging the other *con amore*. Hence the economic principle, universally applied in this mode of production, of employing only the rudest and heaviest implements, which are difficult to damage owing to their very clumsiness. In the slave states bordering on the Gulf of Mexico, down to the date of the Civil War, the only ploughs to be found

We now see that the difference between labour, considered on the one hand as producing utilities, and on the other hand as creating value, a difference which we discovered by our analysis of a commodity, resolves itself into a distinction between two aspects of the production process.

The production process, considered as the unity of the labour process and the process of creating value, is the process of production of commodities; considered as the unity of the labour process and the process of valorization, it is the capitalist process of production, or the capitalist form of the production of commodities.

We stated on a previous page that in the valorization process it does not in the least matter whether the labour appropriated by the capitalist is simple labour of average social quality, or more complex labour, labour with a higher specific gravity as it were. All labour of a higher, or more complicated, character than average labour is expenditure of labour-power of a more costly kind, labour-power whose production has cost more time and labour than unskilled or simple labour-power, and which therefore has a higher value. This power being of higher value, it expresses itself in labour of a higher sort, and therefore becomes objectified, during an equal amount of time, in proportionally higher values. Whatever difference in skill there may be between the labour of a spinner and that of a jeweller, the portion of his labour by which the jeweller merely replaces the value of his own labour-power does not in any way differ in quality from the additional portion by which he creates surplus-value. In both cases, the surplus-value results only from a quantitative excess of labour, from a lengthening of one and the same labour-process: in the one case, the process of making jewels, in the other, the process of making yarn.*kkk*

---

were those constructed on the old Chinese model, which turned up the earth like a pig or a mole, instead of making furrows. Cf. J. E. Cairnes, *The Slave Power*, London, 1862, pp. 46 ff. In his *Seaboard Slave States*, Olmsted says, among other things, 'I am here shown tools that no man in his senses, with us, would allow a labourer, for whom he was paying wages, to be encumbered with; and the excessive weight and clumsiness of which, I would judge, would make work at least ten per cent greater than with those ordinarily used with us. And I am assured that, with the careless and clumsy treatment they always must get from the slaves, anything lighter or less rude could not be furnished them with good economy, and that such tools as we constantly give our labourers and find our profit in giving them, would not last a day in a Virginia cornfield—much lighter and more free from stones though it be than ours. So, too, when I ask why mules are so universally substituted for horses on the farm, the first reason given, and confessedly the most conclusive one, is that horses are always soon foundered or crippled by them, while mules will bear cudgelling, or lose a meal or two now and then, ad not be materially injured, and they do not take cold or get sick, if neglected or overworked. But I do not need to go further than to the window of the room in which I am writing, to see at almost any time, treatment of cattle that would ensure the immediate discharge of the driver by almost any farmer owning them in the North.'[38]

kkk The distinction between higher and simple labour, 'skilled labour' and 'unskilled labour', rests in part on pure illusion or, to say the least, on distinctions that have long since ceased to be real, and survive only by virtue of a traditional convention; and in part on the

Part Six
Wages

Chapter 19
The Transformation of the Value (and Respectively the Price) of Labour-Power into Wages

On the surface of bourgeois society the worker's wage appears as the price of labour, as a certain quantity of money that is paid for a certain quantity of labour. Thus people speak of the value of labour, and call its expression in money its necessary or natural price. On the other hand they speak of the market prices of labour, i.e., prices which oscillate above or below its necessary price.

But what is the value of a commodity? The objective form of the social labour expended in its production. And how do we measure the quantity of this value? By the quantity of the labour contained in it. How then is the value, e.g., of a 12-hour working day to be determined? By the 12 working hours contained in a working day of 12 hours, which is an absurd tautology.*///*

---

helpless condition of some sections of the working class, a condition that prevents them from exacting equally with the rest the value of their labour-power. Accidental circumstances here play so great a part that these two forms of labour sometimes change places. Where, for instance, the physique of the working class has deteriorated and is, relatively speaking, exhausted, which is the case in all countries where capitalist production is highly developed, the lower forms of labour, which demand great expenditure of muscle, are in general considered as higher forms, compared with much more delicate forms of labour; the latter sink down to the level of simple labour. Take as an example the labour of a bricklayer, which in England occupies a much higher level than that of a damask-weaver. Again, although the labour of a fustian-cutter demands greater bodily exertion, and is at the same time unhealthy, it counts only as simple labour. Moreover, we must not imagine that so-called 'skilled' labour forms a large part of the whole of the nation's labour. Laing estimates that in England (and Wales) the livelihood of 11,300,000 people depends on unskilled labour. If from the total population of 18,000,000 living at the time when he wrote, we deduct 1,000,000 for the 'genteel population', 1,500,000 for paupers, vagrants, criminals and prostitutes, and 4,650,000 who compose the middle class, there remain the above-mentioned 11,000,000. But in his middle class he includes people who live on the interest of small investments, officials, men of letters, artists, schoolmasters and the like, and in order to swell the number he also includes in these 4,650,000 the better paid portion of the 'factory workers'! The bricklayers, too, figure amongst these 'high-class workers' (S. Laing, *National Distress etc.*, London, 1844). 'The great class who have nothing to give for food but ordinary labour, are the great bulk of the people' (James Mill, in the article 'Colony', *Supplement to the Encyclopaedia Britannica*, 1831).

/// 'Mr Ricardo, ingeniously enough, avoids a difficulty which, on a first view, threatens to encumber his doctrine, that value depends on the quantity of labour employed in production. If this principle is rigidly adhered to, it follows that the value of labour depends on the quantity of labour employed in producing it—which is evidently absurd. By a dexterous turn, therefore, Mr Ricardo makes the value of labour depend on the quantity of labour required to produce wages; or, to give him the benefit of his own language, he maintains that the value of labour is to be estimated by the quantity of labour required to produce

In order to be sold as a commodity in the market, labour must at all events exist before it is sold. But if the worker were able to endow it with an independent existence, he would be selling a commodity, and not labour. *mmm*

Apart from these contradictions, a direct exchange of money, i.e., of objectified labour, with living labour, would either supersede the law of value, which only begins to develop freely on the basis of capitalist production, or supersede capitalist production itself, which rests directly on wage-labour. The working day of 12 hours is represented in a monetary value of, for example, 6 shillings. There are two alternatives. Either equivalents are exchanged, and then the worker receives 6 shillings for 12 hours of labour; the price of his labour would be equal to the price of his product. In that case he produces no surplus-value for the buyer of his labour, the 6 shillings are not transformed into capital, and the basis of capitalist production vanishes. But it is precisely on that basis that he sells his labour and that his labour is wage-labour. Or else he receives, in return for 12 hours of labour, less than 6 shillings, i.e., less than 12 hours of labour. 12 hours of labour are exchanged for 10, 6, etc. hours of labour. But to equate unequal quantities in this way does not just do away with the determination of value. Such a self-destructive contradiction cannot be in any way even enunciated or formulated as a law. *nnn*

It is no use deducing the exchange of more labour against less from the differences in form in each case, one piece of labour being objectified, the other living. *ooo* In fact, this way out is even more absurd because the value of a commodity is determined not by the quantity of labour actually objectified in it, but by the quantity of living labour necessary to produce it. A commodity represents, say, 6 working hours. If an invention is made

---

wages; by which he means the quantity of labour required to produce the money or commodities given to the labourer. This is similar to saying, that the value of cloth is estimated, not by the quantity of labour bestowed on the production of the silver, for which the cloth is exchanged' ([S. Bailey,] *A Critical Dissertation on the Nature, etc., of Value*, pp. 50–51).

mmm If you call labour a commodity, it is not like a commodity which is first produced in order to exchange, and then brought to market where it must exchange with other commodities according to the respective quantities of each which there may be in the market at the time; labour is created the moment it is brought to market; nay, it is brought to market before it is created' (*Observations on Certain Verbal Disputes, etc.*, pp. 75–6).

nnn 'Treating labour as a commodity, and capital, the produce of labour, as another, then, if the value of these two commodities were regulated by equal quantities of labour, a given amount of labour would . . . exchange for that quantity of capital which had been produced by the same amount of labour; antecedent labour would . . . exchange for the same amount as present labour. But the value of labour in relation to other commodities . . . is not determined by equal quantities of labour' (E. G. Wakefield, in his edition of Adam Smith's *Wealth of Nations*, Vol. 1, London, 1835, pp. 230, 231, n.).

ooo 'It was necessary to reach an agreement' (yet another edition of the contrat social!) 'that every time completed labour was exchanged for labour still to be performed, the latter' (the capitalist) 'would receive a higher value than the former' (the worker). Simonde (i.e., Sismondi), *De la richesse commerciale* (Vol. 1, Geneva, 1803, p. 37).[39]

by which it can be produced in 3 hours, the value, even of the commodity already produced, falls by half. It now represents 3 hours of socially necessary labour instead of the 6 formerly required. It is therefore the quantity of labour required to produce it, not the objectified form of that labour, which determines the amount of the value of a commodity.

It is not labour which directly confronts the possessor of money on the commodity-market, but rather the worker. What the worker is selling is his labour-power. As soon as his labour actually begins, it has already ceased to belong to him; it can therefore no longer be sold by him. Labour is the substance, and the immanent measure of value, but it has no value itself.*ppp*

In the expression 'value of labour', the concept of value is not only completely extinguished, but inverted, so that it becomes its contrary. It is an expression as imaginary as the value of the earth. These imaginary expressions arise, nevertheless, from the relations of production themselves. They are categories for the forms of appearance of essential relations. That in their appearance things are often presented in an inverted way is something fairly familiar in every science, apart from political economy.*qqq*

Classical political economy borrowed the category 'price of labour' from everyday life without further criticism, and then simply asked the question, how is this price determined? It soon recognized that changes in the relation between demand and supply explained nothing, with regard to the price of labour or any other commodity, except those changes themselves, i.e., the oscillations of the market price above or below a certain mean. If demand and supply balance, the oscillation of prices ceases, all other circumstances remaining the same. But then demand and supply also cease to explain anything. The price of labour, at the moment when demand and supply are in equilibrium, is its natural price, determined

---

ppp 'Labour the exclusive standard of value . . . the creator of all wealth, no commodity' (Thomas Hodgskin, *Popular Political Economy*, p. 186).

qqq On the other hand, the attempt to explain such expressions as merely poetic license only shows the impotence of the analysis. Hence, in answer to Proudhon's phrase, 'Labour is said to *have value* not as a commodity itself, but in view of the values which it is supposed potentially to contain. The value of labour is a figurative expression', etc., I have remarked 'In labour as a commodity, which is a grim reality, he' (Proudhon) 'sees nothing but a grammatical ellipsis. Thus the whole of existing society, founded on labour as a commodity, is henceforth founded on a poetic license, a figurative expression. If society wants to "eliminate all the drawbacks" that assail it, well, let it eliminate all the ill-sounding terms, change the language; and to this end it has only to apply to the *Académie* for a new edition of its dictionary' (Karl Marx, *Misère de la philosophie*, pp. 34–5) [*The Poverty of Philosophy*, pp. 49–50]. It is naturally still more convenient to understand by value nothing at all. Then one can without difficulty subsume everything under this category. Thus, for instance, J. B. Say asks 'What is value?' Answer: 'It is what a thing is worth.' What is price? 'The value of a thing expressed in money.' And why has 'labour on the land . . . a value?' 'Because a price is put upon it.' Therefore value is what a thing is worth, and the land has its 'value' because its value is 'expressed in money'. This is, anyhow, a very simple way of explaining the why and wherefore of things.[40]

independently of the relation of demand and supply. It was therefore found that the natural price was the object which actually had to be analysed. Or a longer period of oscillation in the market price was taken, for example a year, and the oscillations were found to cancel each other out, leaving a mean average quantity, a constant magnitude. This naturally had to be determined otherwise than by its own mutually compensatory variations. This price, which ultimately predominates over the accidental market prices of labour and regulates them, this 'necessary price' (according to the Physiocrats) or 'natural price' of labour (according to Adam Smith) can only be its value expressed in money, as with all other commodities. In this way, the political economists believed they could penetrate to the value of labour through the medium of the accidental prices of labour. As with other commodities, this value was then further determined by the cost of production. But what is the cost of production . . . of the *worker*, i.e., the cost of producing or reproducing the worker himself? The political economists unconsciously substituted this question for the original one, for the search after the cost of production of labour as such turned in a circle, and did not allow them to get any further forward at all. Therefore what they called the 'value of labour' is in fact the value of labour-power, as it exists in the personality of the worker, and it is as different from its function, labour, as a machine is from the operations it performs. Because they were concerned with the difference between the market price of labour and its so-called value, with the relation of this value to the rate of profit and to the values of the commodities produced by means of labour, etc., they never discovered that the course of the analysis had led not only from the market prices of labour to its presumed value, but also to the resolution of this value of labour itself into the value of labour-power. Classical political economy's unconsciousness of this result of its own analysis and its uncritical acceptance of the categories 'value of labour', 'natural price of labour', etc. as the ultimate and adequate expression for the value-relation under consideration, led it into inextricable confusions and contradictions, as will be seen later,[41] while it offered a secure base of operations to the vulgar economists who, in their shallowness, make it a principle to worship appearances only.

Let us first see how the value (and the price) of labour-power is represented in its converted form as wages.

We know that the daily value of labour-power is calculated upon a certain length of the worker's life, and that this corresponds, in turn, to a certain length of the working day. Assume that the usual working day is 12 hours and the daily value of labour-power 3 shillings, which is the expression in money of a value embodying 6 hours of labour. If the worker receives 3 shillings, then he receives the value of his labour-power, which functions through 12 hours. If this value of a day's labour-power is now expressed as the value of a day's labour itself, we have the formula: 12

hours of labour has a value of 3 shillings. The value of labour-power thus determines the value of labour, or, expressed in money, its necessary price. If, on the other hand, the price of labour-power differs from its value, the price of labour will similarly differ from its so-called value.

As the value of labour is only an irrational expression for the value of labour-power, it follows of course that the value of labour must always be less than its value-product, for the capitalist always makes labour-power work longer than is necessary for the reproduction of its own value. In the above example, the value of the labour-power that functions through 12 hours is 3 shillings, which requires 6 hours for its reproduction. The value which the labour-power produces is however 6 shillings, because it in fact functions during 12 hours, and its value-product depends, not on its own value, but on the length of time it is in action. Thus we reach a result which is at first sight absurd: labour which creates a value of 6 shillings possesses a value of 3 shillings.[rrr]

We see, further: the value of 3 shillings, which represents the paid portion of the working day, i.e., 6 hours of labour, appears as the value or price of the whole working day of 12 hours, which thus includes 6 hours which have not been paid for. The wage-form thus extinguishes every trace of the division of the working day into necessary labour and surplus labour, into paid labour and unpaid labour. All labour appears as paid labour. Under the *corvée* system it is different. There the labour of the serf for himself, and his compulsory labour for the lord of the land, are demarcated very clearly both in space and time. In slave labour, even the part of the working day in which the slave is only replacing the value of his own means of subsistence, in which he therefore actually works for himself alone, appears as labour for his master. All his labour appears as unpaid labour.[sss] In wage-labour, on the contrary, even surplus labour, or unpaid labour, appears as paid. In the one case, the property-relation conceals the slave's labour for himself; in the other case the money-relation conceals the uncompensated labour of the wage-labourer.

We may therefore understand the decisive importance of the transformation of the value and price of labour-power into the form of wages, or into the value and price of labour itself. All the notions of justice held by both the worker and the capitalist, all the mystifications of the capitalist mode of production, all capitalism's illusions about freedom, all the apologetic

---

[rrr] Cf. *Zur Kritik der Politischen Ökonomie*, p. 40 [*A Contribution to the Critique of Political Economy*, p. 62], where I state that, in my analysis of capital, I shall solve the following problem: 'how does production on the basis of exchange-value solely determined by labour-time lead to the result that the exchange-value of labour is less than the exchange-value of its product?'

[sss] The *Morning Star*, a London free-trade organ which is so naïve as to be positively foolish, protested again and again during the American Civil War, with all the moral indignation of which man is capable, that the Negroes in the 'Confederate States' worked absolutely for nothing. It should have compared the daily cost of a Negro in the southern states with that of a free worker in the East End of London.

tricks of vulgar economics, have as their basis the form of appearance discussed above, which makes the actual relation invisible, and indeed presents to the eye the precise opposite of that relation.

World history has taken a long time to get to the bottom of the mystery of wages; but, despite this, nothing is easier to understand than the necessity, the *raison d'être*, of this form of appearance.

The exchange between capital and labour at first presents itself to our perceptions in exactly the same way as the sale and purchase of all other commodities. The buyer gives a certain sum of money, the seller an article which is something other than money. The legal mind recognizes here at most a material difference, expressed in the legally equivalent formulae: '*Do ut des, do ut facias, facio ut des, facio ut facias.*'[42]

Further. Since exchange-value and use-value are in themselves incommensurable magnitudes, the expressions 'value of labour', 'price of labour', do not seem more irrational than the expressions 'value of cotton', 'price of cotton'. Moreover, the worker is paid after he has given his labour. In its function as a means of payment, money realizes, but only subsequently, the value or price of the article supplied—i.e., in this particular case, the value or price of the labour supplied. Finally, the use-value supplied by the worker to the capitalist is not in fact his labour-power but its function, a specific form of useful labour, such as tailoring, cobbling, spinning, etc. That this same labour is, on the other hand, the universal value-creating element, and thus possesses a property by virtue of which it differs from all other commodities, is something which falls outside the frame of reference of the everyday consciousness.

Let us put ourselves in the place of the worker who receives for 12 hours of labour the value-product of, say, 6 hours of labour, namely 2 shillings. For him, in fact, his 12 hours of labour is the means of buying the 3 shillings. The value of his labour-power may vary, with the value of his usual means of subsistence, from 3 to 4 shillings, or from 3 to 2 shillings; or, if the value of labour-power remains constant, its price may rise to 4 shillings or fall to 2 shillings as a result of changes in the relation of demand and supply. He always gives 12 hours of labour. Every change in the amount of the equivalent that he receives therefore necessarily appears to him as a change in the value or price of his 12 hours of labour. This circumstance misled Adam Smith, who treated the working day as a constant quantity*ttt* into the opposite assertion that the value of labour is constant, although the value of the means of subsistence may vary, and the same working day, therefore, may represent more or less money for the worker.

Let us consider, on the other hand, the capitalist. He wishes to receive as much labour as possible for as little money as possible. In practice,

---

ttt Adam Smith only incidentally alludes to the variation of the working day, when he is dealing with piece-wages.[43]

therefore, the only thing that interests him is the difference between the price of labour-power and the value which its function creates. But he tries to buy all commodities as cheaply as possible, and his own invariable explanation of his profit is that it is a result of mere sharp practice, of buying under the value and selling over it. Hence he never comes to see that if such a thing as the value of labour really existed, and he really paid this value, no capital would exist, and his money would never be transformed into capital.

Moreover, the actual movement of wages presents phenomena which seem to prove that it is not the value of labour-power which is paid, but the value of its function, of labour itself. We may reduce these phenomena to two great classes. (1) Changes in wages owing to changes in the length of the working day. One might as well conclude that it is not the value of a machine which is paid, but that of its operation, because it costs more to hire a machine for a week than for a day. (2) Individual differences between the wages of different workers who perform the same function. These individual differences also exist in the system of slavery, but there they do not give rise to any illusions, for labour-power is in that case itself sold frankly and openly, without any embellishment. Only, in the slave system, the advantage of a labour-power above the average, and the disadvantage of a labour-power below the average, affects the slave-owner; whereas in the system of wage-labour it affects the worker himself, because his labour-power is, in the one case, sold by himself, in the other, by a third person.

For the rest, what is true of all forms of appearance and their hidden background is also true of the form of appearance 'value and price of labour', or 'wages', as contrasted with the essential relation manifested in it, namely the value and price of labour-power. The forms of appearance are reproduced directly and spontaneously, as current and usual modes of thought; the essential relation must first be discovered by science. Classical political economy stumbles approximately onto the true state of affairs, but without consciously formulating it. It is unable to do this as long as it stays within its bourgeois skin.

Part Seven
The Process of Accumulation of Capital

Chapter 25
The General Law of Capitalist Accumulation

[CAPITALIST ACCUMULATION AND SURPLUS POPULATION]

3. THE PROGRESSIVE PRODUCTION OF A RELATIVE SURPLUS POPULATION OR INDUSTRIAL RESERVE ARMY

The accumulation of capital, which originally appeared only as its quantitative extension, comes to fruition, as we have seen, through a progressive qualitative change in its composition, i.e. through a continuing increase of its constant component at the expense of its variable component.*uuu*

The specifically capitalist mode of production, the development of the productivity of labour which corresponds to it, and the change in the organic composition of capital which results from it, are things which do not merely keep pace with the progress of accumulation, or the growth of social wealth. They develop at a much quicker rate, because simple accumulation, or the absolute expansion of the total social capital, is accompanied by the centralization of its individual elements, and because the change in the technical composition of the additional capital goes hand in hand with a similar change in the technical composition of the original capital. With the progress of accumulation, therefore, the proportion of constant to variable capital changes. If it was originally say 1:1, it now becomes successively 2:1, 3:1, 4:1, 5:1, 7:1, etc., so that as the capital grows, instead of ½ its total value, only ⅓, ¼, ⅕, ⅙, ⅛, etc. is turned into labour-power, and, on the other hand, ⅔, ¾, ⅘, ⅚, ⅞, into means of production. Since the demand for labour is determined not by the extent of the total capital but by its variable constituent alone, that demand falls progressively with the growth of the total capital, instead of rising in proportion to it, as was previously assumed. It falls relatively to the magnitude of the total capital, and at an accelerated rate, as this magnitude increases. With the growth of the total capital, its variable constituent, the labour incorporated in it, does admittedly increase, but

---

uuu [Note by Engels to the third German edition:] In Marx's own copy there is here the marginal note: 'Note here for working out later: if the extension is only quantitative, then for a greater and a smaller capital in the same branch of business the profits are as the magnitudes of the capitals advanced. If the quantitative extension induces a qualitative change, then the rate of profit on the larger capital rises at the same time.'

in a constantly diminishing proportion. The intermediate pauses in which accumulation works as simple extension of production on a given technical basis are shortened. It is not merely that an accelerated accumulation of the total capital, accelerated in a constantly growing progression, is needed to absorb an additional number of workers, or even, on account of the constant metamorphosis of old capital, to keep employed those already performing their functions. This increasing accumulation and centralization also becomes in its turn a source of new changes in the composition of capital, or in other words of an accelerated diminution of the capital's variable component, as compared with its constant one. This accelerated relative diminution of the variable component, which accompanies the accelerated increase of the total capital and moves more rapidly than this increase, takes the inverse form, at the other pole, of an apparently absolute increase in the working population, an increase which always moves more rapidly than that of the variable capital or the means of employment. But in fact it is capitalist accumulation itself that constantly produces, and produces indeed in direct relation with its own energy and extent, a relatively redundant working population, i.e. a population which is superfluous to capital's average requirements for its own valorization, and is therefore a surplus population.

If we consider the total social capital, we can say that the movement of its accumulation sometimes causes periodic changes, and at other times distributes various phases simultaneously over the different spheres of production. In some spheres a change in the composition of capital occurs without any increase in its absolute magnitude, as a consequence of simple concentration[vvv]; in others the absolute growth of capital is connected with an absolute diminution in its variable component, or in other words, in the labour-power absorbed by it; in others again, capital continues to grow for a time on its existing technical basis, and attracts additional labour-power in proportion to its increase, while at other times it undergoes organic change and reduces its variable component; in all spheres, the increase of the variable part of the capital, and therefore of the number of workers employed by it, is always connected with violent fluctuations and the temporary production of a surplus population, whether this takes the more striking form of the extrusion of workers already employed, or the less evident, but not less real, form of a greater difficulty in absorbing the additional working population through its customary outlets.[www]

[vvv] The first three editions have here 'centralization' instead of 'concentration'.

[www] The census of England and Wales shows, for instance, all persons employed in agriculture (landlords, farmers, gardeners, shepherds, etc. included): 1851: 2,011,447; 1861: 1,924,110; a reduction of 87,337. Worsted manufacture, 1851: 102,714 persons; 1861: 79,242. Silk weaving, 1851: 111,940; 1861: 101,678. Calico-printing, 1851: 12,098; 1861: 12,556; a small increase, despite the enormous extension of this industry, which implies a great proportional reduction in the number of workers employed. Hat-making, 1851: 15,957; 1861: 13,814. Straw-hat and bonnet-making, 1851: 20,393; 1861: 18,176. Malting, 1851: 10,566;

Owing to the magnitude of the already functioning social capital, and the degree of its increase, owing to the extension of the scale of production, and the great mass of workers set in motion, owing to the development of the productivity of their labour, and the greater breadth and richness of the stream springing from all the sources of wealth, there is also an extension of the scale on which greater attraction of workers by capital is accompanied by their greater repulsion; an increase takes place in the rapidity of the change in the organic composition of capital and in its technical form, and an increasing number of spheres of production become involved in this change, sometimes simultaneously, and sometimes alternatively. The working population therefore produces both the accumulation of capital and the means by which it is itself made relatively superfluous; and it does this to an extent which is always increasing.[xxx] This is a law of population peculiar to the capitalist mode of production; and in fact every particular historical mode of production has its own special

---

1861: 10,677. Chandlery, 1851: 4,949; 1861: 4,686; this fall is due, among other things, to the increase in lighting by gas. Comb-making, 1851: 2,038; 1861: 1,478. Sawyers, 1851: 30,552; 1861:31,647; a small increase, owing to the spread of sawing-machines. Nail-making, 1851:26,940; 1861:26,130; a fall, owing to the competition of machinery. Tin- and copper-mining, 1851: 31,360; 1861: 32,041. As against this, however, we have cotton-spinning and weaving, 1851: 371,777; 1861: 456,646; and coal-mining, 1851: 183,389; 1861: 246,613. 'The increase of labourers is generally greatest, since 1851, in those branches of industry in which machinery has not up to the present been employed with success' (*Census of England and Wales for the Year 1861*, Vol. 3, London, 1863, p. 36).

[xxx] (The law of progressive diminution of the relative magnitude of variable capital, together with its effect on the situation of the class of wage-labourers, is suspected rather than understood by some of the prominent economists of the classical school. In this respect the greatest merit is due to John Barton, although he, like all the others, mixes up constant with fixed capital, and variable with circulating capital. He says: 'The demand for labour depends on the increase of circulating, and not of fixed capital. Were it true that the proportion between these two sorts of capital is the same at all times, and in all circumstances, then, indeed, it follows that the number of labourers employed is in proportion to the wealth of the state. But such a proposition has not the semblance of probability. As arts are cultivated, and civilization is extended, fixed capital bears a larger and larger proportion to circulating capital. The amount of fixed capital employed in the production of a piece of British muslin is at least a hundred, probably a thousand times greater than that employed in a similar piece of Indian muslin. And the proportion of circulating capital is a hundred or thousand times less . . . the whole of the annual savings, added to the fixed capital, would have no effect in increasing the demand for labour' (John Barton, *Observations of the Circumstances which Influence the Condition of the Labouring Classes of Society*, London, 1817, pp. 161–7).[44] 'The same cause which may increase the net revenue of the country may at the same time render the population redundant, and deteriorate the condition of the labourer' (Ricardo, op. cit., p. 469). With the increase of capital, 'the demand' (for labour) 'will be in a diminishing ratio' (ibid., p. 480, n.). 'The amount of capital devoted to the maintenance of labour may vary, independently of any changes in the whole amount of capital . . . Great fluctuations in the amount of employment, and great suffering may become more frequent as capital itself becomes more plentiful' (Richard Jones, *An Introductory Lecture on Political Economy*, London, 1833, p. 12). 'Demand' (for labour) 'will rise . . . not in proportion to the accumulation of the general capital. . . . Every augmentation, therefore, in the national stock destined for reproduction, comes, in the progress of society, to have less and less influence upon the condition of the labourer' (Ramsay, op. cit., pp. 90–91).

laws of population, which are historically valid within that particular sphere. An abstract law of population exists only for plants and animals, and even then only in the absence of any historical intervention by man.

But if a surplus population of workers is a necessary product of accumulation or of the development of wealth on a capitalist basis, this surplus population also becomes, conversely, the lever of capitalist accumulation, indeed it becomes a condition for the existence of the capitalist mode of production. It forms a disposable industrial reserve army, which belongs to capital just as absolutely as if the latter had bred it at its own cost. Independently of the limits of the actual increase of population, it creates a mass of human material always ready for exploitation by capital in the interests of capital's own changing valorization requirements. With accumulation, and the development of the productivity of labour that accompanies it, capital's power of sudden expansion also grows; it grows, not merely because the elasticity of the capital already functioning increases, not merely because the absolute wealth of society expands (and capital only forms an elastic part of this), not merely because credit, under every special stimulus, at once places an unusual part of this wealth at the disposal of production in the form of additional capital; it grows also because the technical conditions of the production process—machinery, means of transport, etc.—themselves now make possible a very rapid transformation of masses of surplus product into additional means of production. The mass of social wealth, overflowing with the advance of accumulation and capable of being transformed into additional capital, thrusts itself frantically into old branches of production, whose market suddenly expands, or into newly formed branches, such as railways, etc., which now become necessary as a result of the further development of the old branches. In all such cases, there must be the possibility of suddenly throwing great masses of men into the decisive areas without doing any damage to the scale of production in other spheres. The surplus population supplies these masses. The path characteristically described by modern industry, which takes the form of a decennial cycle (interrupted by smaller oscillations) of periods of average activity, production at high pressure, crisis, and stagnation, depends on the constant formation, the greater or less absorption, and the re-formation of the industrial reserve army or surplus population. In their turn, the varying phases of the industrial cycle recruit the surplus population, and become one of the most energetic agencies for its reproduction.

This peculiar cyclical path of modern industry, which occurs in no earlier period of human history, was also impossible when capitalist production was in its infancy. The composition of capital at that time underwent only very gradual changes. By and large, therefore, the proportional growth in the demand for labour has corresponded to the accumulation of capital. Even though the advance of accumulation was slow in comparison with that of the modern epoch, it came up against a natural barrier in the shape of the exploitable working population; this barrier could only be swept away by the violent means we shall discuss later. The expansion by fits and starts of the scale of production is the precondition for its equally sudden contraction; the latter again evokes the former, but the former is impossible without disposable human material, without an increase in the number of workers, which must occur independently of the absolute growth of the population. This increase is effected by the simple process that constantly 'sets free' a part of the working class; by methods which lessen the number of workers employed in proportion to the increased production. Modern industry's whole form of motion therefore depends on the constant transformation of a part of the working population into unemployed or semi-employed 'hands'. The superficiality of political economy shows itself in the fact that it views the expansion and contraction of credit as the cause of the periodic alternations in the industrial cycle, whereas it is a mere symptom of them. Just as the heavenly bodies always repeat a certain movement, once they have been flung into it, so also does social production, once it has been flung into this movement of alternate expansion and contraction. Effects become causes in their turn, and the various vicissitudes of the whole process, which always reproduces its own conditions, take on the form of periodicity. When this periodicity has once become consolidated, even political economy sees that the production of a relative surplus population—i.e., a population surplus in relation to capital's average requirements for valorization—is a necessary condition for modern industry. . . .

4. DIFFERENT FORMS OF EXISTENCE OF THE RELATIVE SURPLUS POPULATION. THE GENERAL LAW OF CAPITALIST ACCUMULATION

The relative surplus population exists in all kinds of forms. Every worker belongs to it during the time when he is only partially employed or wholly unemployed. Leaving aside the large-scale and periodically recurring forms that the changing phases of the industrial cycle impress on it, so that it sometimes appears acute, in times of crisis, and sometimes chronic, in times when business is slack, we can identify three forms which it always possesses: the floating, the latent, and the stagnant.

In the centres of modern industry—factories, workshops, ironworks, mines, etc. —the workers are sometimes repelled, sometimes attracted again in greater masses, so that the number of those employed increases on the whole, although in a constantly decreasing proportion to the scale of production. Here the surplus population exists in the floating form.

Both in the factories proper, and in the large workshops, where machinery enters as one factor, or even where no more than a division of labour of a modern type has been put into operation, large numbers of male workers are employed up to the age of maturity, but not beyond. Once they reach maturity, only a very small number continue to find employment in the same branches of industry, while the majority are regularly dismissed. This majority forms an element of the floating surplus population, which grows with the extension of those branches of industry. Some of these workers emigrate; in fact they are merely following capital, which has itself emigrated. A further consequence is that the female population grows more rapidly than the male—witness England. That the natural increase of the number of workers does not satisfy the requirements of the accumulation of capital, and yet, at the same time, exceeds those requirements, is a contradiction inherent in capital's very movement. Capital demands more youthful workers, fewer adults. This contradiction is no more glaring than the other contradiction, namely that a shortage of 'hands' is complained of, while, at the same time, many thousands are out of work, because the division of labour chains them to a particular branch of industry.*yyy*

Moreover, the consumption of labour-power by capital is so rapid that the worker has already more or less completely lived himself out when he is only half-way through his life. He falls into the ranks of the surplus population, or is thrust down from a higher to a lower step in the scale. It is precisely among the workers in large-scale industry that we meet with the shortest life-expectancy. 'Dr Lee, Medical Officer of Health for Manchester, stated that the average age at death of the Manchester . . . upper middle class was 38 years, while the average age at death of the labouring class was 17; while at Liverpool those figures were represented as 35 against 15. It thus appeared that the well-to-do classes had a lease of life which was more than double the value of that which fell to the lot of the less favoured citizens.*zzz* Under these circumstances, the absolute increase of this section of the proletariat must take a form which swells their numbers, despite the rapid wastage of their individual elements. Hence, rapid replacement of one generation of workers by another (this law does not hold for the other classes of the population). This social requirement is met by early marriages, which are a necessary consequence of the conditions in which workers in large-scale industry live, and by the premium that the exploitation of the workers' children sets on their production.

yyy During the last six months of 1866, 80–90,000 people in London were thrown out of work. This is what the Factory Report for that same half year says: 'It does not appear absolutely true to say that demand will always produce supply just at the moment when it is needed. It has not always done so with labour, for much machinery has been idle last year for want of hands' (*Reports of the Inspectors of Factories . . . 31 October 1866*, p. 81).

zzz [Added by Engels to the third German edition:] Opening address to the Sanitary Conference, Birmingham, 14 January 1875, by J. Chamberlain, at that time Mayor of Birmingham, and now (1883) President of the Board of Trade.

As soon as capitalist production takes possession of agriculture, and in proportion to the extent to which it does so, the demand for a rural working population falls absolutely, while the accumulation of the capital employed in agriculture advances, without this repulsion being compensated for by a greater attraction of workers, as is the case in non-agricultural industries. Part of the agricultural population is therefore constantly on the point of passing over into an urban or manufacturing proletariat, and on the lookout for opportunities to complete this transformation. (The term 'manufacture' is used here to cover all non-agricultural industries.)*aaaa* There is thus a constant flow from this source of the relative surplus population. But the constant movement towards the towns presupposes, in the countryside itself, a constant latent surplus population, the extent of which only becomes evident at those exceptional times when its distribution channels are wide open. The wages of the agricultural labourer are therefore reduced to a minimum, and he always stands with one foot already in the swamp of pauperism.

The third category of the relative surplus population is the stagnant population. This forms a part of the active labour army, but with extremely irregular employment. Hence it offers capital an inexhaustible reservoir of disposable labour-power. Its conditions of life sink below the average normal level of the working class, and it is precisely this which makes it a broad foundation for special branches of capitalist exploitation. It is characterized by a maximum of working time and a minimum of wages. We have already become familiar with its chief form under the rubric of 'domestic industry'. It is constantly recruited from workers in large-scale industry and agriculture who have become redundant, and especially from those decaying branches of industry where handicraft is giving way to manufacture, and manufacture to machinery. Its extent grows in proportion as, with the growth in the extent and energy of accumulation, the creation of a surplus population also advances. But it forms at the same time a self-reproducing and self-perpetuating element of the working class, taking a proportionally greater part in the general increase of that class than the other elements. In fact, not only the number of births and deaths, but the absolute size of families, stands in inverse proportion to the level of wages, and therefore to the amount of the means of subsistence at the disposal of different categories of worker. This law of capitalist society would sound absurd to savages, or even to civilized colonists. It

---

aaaa The 781 towns enumerated in the census of England and Wales for 1861 'contained 10,960,998 inhabitants, while the villages and country parishes contained 9,105,226. In 1851, 580 towns were distinguished, and the population in them and in the surrounding country was nearly equal. But while in the subsequent ten years the population in the villages and the country increased half a million, the population in the 580 towns increased by a million and a half (1,554,067). The increase of the population of the country parishes is 6.5 per cent, and of the towns 17.3 per cent. The difference in the rates of increase is due to the migration from country to town. Three-fourths of the total increase of population has taken place in the towns' (*Census, etc.*, Vol. 3, pp. 11–12).

calls to mind the boundless reproduction of animals individually weak and constantly hunted down.[bbbb]

Finally, the lowest sediment of the relative surplus population dwells in the sphere of pauperism. Apart from vagabonds, criminals, prostitutes, in short the actual lumpenproletariat, this social stratum consists of three categories. First, those able to work. One need only glance superficially at the statistics of English pauperism to find that the quantity of paupers increases with every crisis of trade, and diminishes with every revival. Second, orphans and pauper children. These are candidates for the industrial reserve army, and in times of great prosperity, such as the year 1860, for instance, they are enrolled in the army of active workers both speedily and in large numbers. Third, the demoralized, the ragged, and those unable to work, chiefly people who succumb to their incapacity for adaptation, an incapacity which results from the division of labour; people who have lived beyond the worker's average life-span; and the victims of industry, whose number increases with the growth of dangerous machinery, of mines, chemical works, etc., the mutilated, the sickly, the widows, etc. Pauperism is the hospital of the active labour-army and the dead weight of the industrial reserve army. Its production is included in that of the relative surplus population, its necessity is implied by their necessity; along with the surplus population, pauperism forms a condition of capitalist production, and of the capitalist development of wealth. It forms part of the *faux frais*[45] of capitalist production: but capital usually knows how to transfer these from its own shoulders to those of the working class and the petty bourgeoisie.

The greater the social wealth, the functioning capital, the extent and energy of its growth, and therefore also the greater the absolute mass of the proletariat and the productivity of its labour, the greater is the industrial reserve army. The same causes which develop the expansive power of capital, also develop the labour-power at its disposal. The relative mass of the industrial reserve army thus increases with the potential energy of wealth. But the greater this reserve army in proportion to the active labour-army, the greater is the mass of a consolidated surplus population, whose misery is in inverse ratio to the amount of torture it has to undergo in the form of labour. The more extensive, finally, the pauperized sections of the working class and the industrial reserve army, the greater is official pauperism. *This is the absolute general law of capitalist accumulation.* Like all other laws, it is modified in its working by many circumstances, the analysis of which does not concern us here.

[bbbb] 'Poverty seems favourable to generation' (Adam Smith, *Wealth of Nations*, Bk I, Ch. 8). Indeed, according to the gallant and witty Abbé Galiani, this is a specially wise arrangement made by God. 'God has decreed that the men who carry on the most useful crafts should be born in abundant numbers' (Galiani, op. cit., p. 78). 'Misery up to the extreme point of famine and pestilence, instead of checking, tends to increase population' (S. Laing, *National Distress*, 1844, p. 69). After Laing has illustrated this by statistics, he continues: 'If the people were all in easy circumstances, the world would soon be depopulated.'

We can now understand the foolishness of the economic wisdom which preaches to the workers that they should adapt their numbers to the valorization requirements of capital. The mechanism of capitalist production and accumulation itself constantly effects this adjustment. The first word of this adaptation is the creation of a relative surplus population, or industrial reserve army. Its last word is the misery of constantly expanding strata of the active army of labour, and the dead weight of pauperism.

On the basis of capitalism, a system in which the worker does not employ the means of production, but the means of production employ the worker, the law by which a constantly increasing quantity of means of production may be set in motion by a progressively diminishing expenditure of human power, thanks to the advance in the productivity of social labour, undergoes a complete inversion, and is expressed thus: the higher the productivity of labour, the greater is the pressure of the workers on the means of employment, the more precarious therefore becomes the condition for their existence, namely the sale of their own labour-power for the increase of alien wealth, or in other words the self-valorization of capital. The fact that the means of production and the productivity of labour increase more rapidly than the productive population expresses itself, therefore, under capitalism, in the inverse form that the working population always increases more rapidly than the valorization requirements of capital.

We saw in Part IV, when analysing the production of relative surplus-value, that within the capitalist system all methods for raising the social productivity of labour are put into effect at the cost of the individual worker; that all means for the development of production undergo a dialectical inversion so that they become means of domination and exploitation of the producers; they distort the worker into a fragment of a man, they degrade him to the level of an appendage of a machine, they destroy the actual content of his labour by turning it into a torment; they alienate [*entfremden*] from him the intellectual potentialities of the labour process in the same proportion as science is incorporated in it as an independent power; they deform the conditions under which he works, subject him during the labour process to a despotism the more hateful for its meanness; they transform his life-time into working-time, and drag his wife and child beneath the wheels of the juggernaut of capital. But all methods for the production of surplus-value are at the same time methods of accumulation, and every extension of accumulation becomes, conversely, a means for the development of those methods. It follows therefore that in proportion as capital accumulates, the situation of the worker, be his payment high or low, must grow worse. Finally, the law which always holds the relative surplus population or industrial reserve army in equilibrium with the extent and energy of accumulation rivets the worker to capital more firmly than the wedges of Hephaestus held Prometheus to the rock. It makes an accumulation of misery a necessary condition, corresponding to the accumulation of wealth. Accumulation of wealth at one pole is, therefore, at the same time accumulation of misery, the torment of labour, slavery, ignorance, brutalization and moral degradation at the opposite pole, i.e., on the side of the class that produces its own product as capital. . . .

Part Eight
The So-Called Primitive Accumulation

Chapter 32
The Historical Tendency of Capitalist Accumulation

What does the primitive accumulation of capital, i.e., its historical genesis, resolve itself into? In so far as it is not the direct transformation of slaves and serfs into wage-labourers, and therefore a mere change of form, it only means the expropriation of the immediate producers, i.e., the dissolution of private property based on the labour of its owner. Private property, as the antithesis to social, collective property, exists only where the means of labour and the external conditions of labour belong to private individuals. But according to whether these private individuals are workers or non-workers, private property has a different character. The innumerable different shades of private property which appear at first sight are only reflections of the intermediate situations which lie between the two extremes.

The private property of the worker in his means of production is the foundation of small-scale industry, and small-scale industry is a necessary condition for the development of social production and of the free individuality of the worker himself. Of course, this mode of production also exists under slavery, serfdom and other situations of dependence. But it flourishes, unleashes the whole of its energy, attains its adequate classical form, only where the worker is the free proprietor of the conditions of his labour, and sets them in motion himself: where the peasant owns the land he cultivates, or the artisan owns the tool with which he is an accomplished performer.

This mode of production presupposes the fragmentation of holdings, and the dispersal of the other means of production. As it excludes the concentration of these means of production, so it also excludes co-operation, division of labour within each separate process of production, the social control and regulation of the forces of nature, and the free development of the productive forces of society. It is compatible only with a system of production and a society moving within narrow limits which are of natural origin. To perpetuate it would be, as Pecqueur rightly says, 'to decree universal mediocrity'.[46] At a certain stage of development, it brings into the world the material means of its own destruction. From that moment, new forces and new passions spring up in the bosom of society, forces and passions which feel themselves to be fettered by that society. It has to be annihilated; it is annihilated. Its annihilation, the transformation of the individualized and scattered means of production into socially concentrated means of production, the transformation, therefore, of the dwarf-like property of the many into the giant property of the few, and the expropriation of the great mass of the people from the soil, from the means of subsistence and from the instruments of labour, this terrible and arduously accomplished expropriation of the mass of the people forms the pre-history of capital. It comprises a whole series of forcible methods, and we have only passed in review those that have been epoch-making as methods of the primitive accumulation of capital. The expropriation of the direct producers was accomplished by means of the most merciless barbarism, and under the stimulus of the most infamous, the most sordid, the most petty and the most odious of passions. Private property which is personally earned, i.e., which is based, as it were, on the fusing together of the isolated, independent working individual with the conditions of his labour, is supplanted by capitalist private property, which rests on the exploitation of alien, but formally free labour.[cccc]

As soon as this metamorphosis has sufficiently decomposed the old society throughout its depth and breadth, as soon as the workers have been turned into proletarians, and their means of labour into capital, as soon as the capitalist mode of production stands on its own feet, the further socialization of labour and the further transformation of the soil and other means of production into socially exploited and therefore communal means of production takes on a new form. What is now to be expropriated is not the self-employed worker, but the capitalist who exploits a large number of workers.

This expropriation is accomplished through the action of the immanent laws of capitalist production itself, through the centralization of capitals. One capitalist always strikes down many others. Hand in hand with this centralization, or this expropriation of many capitalists by a few, other developments take place on an ever-increasing scale, such as the growth of the co-operative form of the labour process, the conscious technical application of science, the planned exploitation of the soil, the transformation of the means of labour into forms in which they can only be used in common, the economizing of all means of production by their use as the means of production of combined, socialized labour, the entanglement of

[cccc] 'We are in a situation which is entirely new for society . . . we are striving to separate every kind of property from every kind of labour' (Sismondi, *Nouveaux Principes d'économie politique*, Vol. 2, p. 434).

all peoples in the net of the world market, and, with this, the growth of the international character of the capitalist regime. Along with the constant decrease in the number of capitalist magnates, who usurp and monopolize all the advantages of this process of transformation, the mass of misery, oppression, slavery, degradation and exploitation grows; but with this there also grows the revolt of the working class, a class constantly increasing in numbers, and trained, united and organized by the very mechanism of the capitalist process of production. The monopoly of capital becomes a fetter upon the mode of production which has flourished alongside and under it. The centralization of the means of production and the socialization of labour reach a point at which they become incompatible with their capitalist integument. This integument is burst asunder. The knell of capitalist private property sounds. The expropriators are expropriated.

The capitalist mode of appropriation, which springs from the capitalist mode of production, produces capitalist private property. This is the first negation of individual private property, as founded on the labour of its proprietor. But capitalist production begets, with the inexorability of a natural process, its own negation. This is the negation of the negation. It does not re-establish private property, but it does indeed establish individual property on the basis of the achievements of the capitalist era: namely co-operation and the possession in common of the land and the means of production produced by labour itself.

The transformation of scattered private property resting on the personal labour of the individuals themselves into capitalist private property is naturally an incomparably more protracted, violent and difficult process than the transformation of capitalist private property, which in fact already rests on the carrying on of production by society, into social property. In the former case, it was a matter of the expropriation of the mass of the people by a few usurpers; but in this case, we have the expropriation of a few usurpers by the mass of the people.[dddd]

[dddd] 'The advance of industry, whose involuntary but willing promoter is the bourgeoisie, replaces the isolation of the workers, due to competition, with their revolutionary combination, due to association. The development of large-scale industry, therefore, cuts from under its feet the very foundation on which the bourgeoisie produces and appropriates products for itself. What the bourgeoisie, therefore, produces, above all, are its own grave-diggers. Its fall and the victory of the proletariat are equally inevitable . . . Of all the classes which confront the bourgeoisie today, the proletariat alone is a really revolutionary class. The other classes decay and disappear in the face of large-scale industry, the proletariat is its most characteristic product. The lower middle classes, the small manufacturers, the shopkeepers, the artisans, the peasants, all these fight against the bourgeoisie in order to save from extinction their existence as parts of the middle class . . . they are reactionary, for they try to roll back the wheel of history' (Karl Marx and F. Engels, *Manifest der Kommunistischen Partei*, London, 1848, pp. 11, 9). Above, pp. 150, 151.

NOTES TO "CAPITAL"

1. Ferdinand Lassalle (1825–1864), German working class organizer. It was mainly against the influence of his views on the program of the German Socialist Worker's Party in 1875 that Marx wrote *Critique of the Gotha Program*; Franz Hermann Schulze-Delitsch, German economist and politician, a leader of the German Progressist Party in the 1860s.
2. "Of you the tale is told" (Horace, *Satires* I, 1).
3. amongst us, i.e., us Germans.
4. "The dead (man) clutches onto the living!"
5. None of the parts of *Capital* mentioned in this paragraph were published during Marx's lifetime. Book II was published by Engels in 1885 as Volume 2 of *Capital*; Book III was published by Engels in 1894 as Volume 3. What is here described as "the third and last volume" was eventually published by Karl Kautsky under the title *Theories of Surplus Value*, by which it is still known today. It is in three volumes.
6. "Follow your own course, and let people talk". Dante's actual words (*Divine Comedy*, Purgatorio 5: 13) were: *Vien retro a me, e lascia dir le genti* ("Come after me, and let people talk").
7. Nicholas Barbon (1640–1698), British political economist.
8. Samuel Butler (1612–1680), *Hudibras* 2: 1: 465–466: "For what is worth in any thing, but so much money as 'twill bring?"
9. An anonymous treatise on political economy of the mid-eighteenth century.
10. William Jacob (1762–1851), *An Historical Inquiry into the Production and Consumption of Precious Metals*. London, 1831. Volume 2, p. 101.
11. As Marx indicates in the *Grundrisse* (English translation, p. 833), his source here is A. M. Merivale (1806–1874) *Lectures on Colonization and Colonies*. London, 1841.
12. The passage in parentheses occurs only in the first edition.
13. Note by Engels to the fourth German edition: "I have inserted the passage in parentheses because, through its omission, the misconception has very frequently arisen that Marx regarded every product consumed by someone other than the producer as a commodity".
14. William Petty (1623–1687), early British political economist. The reference is to Petty's anonymous work *A Treatise of Taxes and Contributions*. London, 1667, p. 47.
15. Hegel, *The Philosophy of Right* § 190R: "In civil society in general [our object is] the *citizen (Bürger)* as *bourgeois*—but here at the standpoint of needs, it is the concretum for conception which we call a *human being (Mensch)*. Thus it is here for the first time, and here really the only time, that we speak of a human being in this sense."
16. Adam Smith (1723–1790), great Scottish moral philosopher and classical political economist. Marx is quoting Smith in German translation, which is the reason for the slight divergence between this quotation and Smith's original: "Equal quantities of labor, at all times and places, may be said to be of equal value to the laborer. In his ordinary state of health, strength and spirits; in the ordinary degree of his skill and dexterity, he must always lay down the same portion of his ease, his liberty, and his happiness" (Adam Smith, *An Inquiry into the Nature and Causes of the Wealth of Nations*. New York: Random House, 1937, p. 33).
17. "To encourage the others". The rest of the world was standing still after the revolutions of 1848. But in 1850 there was a revolt in China; about the same

time spiritualist "table turning" came to be fashionable in German society.
18. Fernado Galiani (1728–1787), eighteenth century Italian political economist.
19. *post festum,* "after the feast."
20. Robert Owen (1771–1858), British communist and organizer of utopian colonies; in *A New View of Society* (1813), Owen suggested parallelograms as the most appropriate layout for a workers' settlement. David Ricardo (1772–1823), British classical political economist, criticized the suggestion in *On Protection of Agriculture.* London, 1822, p. 21.
21. Marx's German says "Herr M. Wirth"—Marx's generic name for a vulgar political economist, from *Wirt* = host, inkeeper, *Wirtschaft* = economics. "Sedley Taylor" was a fictional Cambridge don against whom Engels polemicized in his Preface to the fourth German edition of *Capital,* and this name was substituted for "Herr M. Wirth" in the first English translation of Volume 1.
22. Epicurus (c. 341–c. 270 B.C.), Greek philosopher, taught that the gods existed only in the spaces between different worlds (*intermundia*) and had no influence on human affairs. The source for the attribution of this view to him is Cicero's dialogue *De natura deorum* (On the Nature of the Gods) 1: 18.
23. Marx is referring to *Capital,* Volume 3, and *Theories of Surplus Value.* See note 5, above.
24. Comte Antoine Louis Claude Destutt de Tracy (1754–1836), French philosopher and economist, founder of the "ideologues". The quotation is from Destutt de Tracy's *Elements of Ideology.* Paris, 1826, pp. 35–36.
25. "I am sorry to be obliged to add that M. de Tracy supports, by his authority, the definitions which M. Say has given of the words 'value', 'riches', and 'utility'" (Ricardo, *Principles of Political Economy,* 3rd edition. London, 1821, p. 334).
26. Quoted from the Preface. See above p. 135.
27. Shakespeare, *Much Ado About Nothing,* Act 3 Scene 3.
28. Theodor Mommsen (1817–1903), German classical historian, author of *History of Rome* (1854–1856).
29. In April, 1864, Prince Alexander Cuza, Hospodar of the Danubian Principalities (Rumania), proposed a land reform, abolishing feudal dues and tithes and legally enfranchising the serfs. The law was rejected by the Assembly, which was dominated by landed interests. In May, 1864, Cuza dissolved the Assembly and issued a Constitutional Statute endorsed by a popular plebiscite, and in this way imposed his reform on the country.
30. The great German composer Richard Wagner (1813–1883) promoted his compositions as "music of the future".
31. H. Storch, *Cours d'economie politique* (St. Petersburg, 1815), Volume 1, p. 228; H. Cherbuliez, *Richesse ou pauvrete* (Paris, 1841), p. 14.
32. Lucius Quinctius Cincinnatus, though a patrician, was reputed to have cultivated his own small farm himself. In 458 B. C. he was called out of his field to be dictator of Rome, a position which he held until 439.
33. "The thing desired for itself".
34. This unexpected judgment (unexpected from Marx, at any rate) is repeated elsewhere in Marx's writings (e.g., see above, p. 187). The conception of the justice of transactions which lies behind it is stated by Marx in Volume 3 of *Capital,* in the course of replying to the British economist James William Gilbart's (1794–1863) assertion that interest on borrowed capital is due to the borrower "by natural justice":

> It is nonsense for Gilbart to speak of natural justice in this connection. The justice of transactions between agents of production consists in the fact that these transactions arise from the relations of production as their

natural consequence. The legal forms in which these economic transactions appear as voluntary actions of the participants, as the expressions of their common will and as contracts that can be enforced on the parties concerned by the power of the state, are mere forms that cannot themselves determine this content. They simply express it. The content is just so long as it corresponds to the mode of production and is adequate to it. It is unjust as soon as it contradicts it. Slavery, on the basis of the capitalist mode of production, is unjust; so is cheating on the quality of commodities. [*Capital*, Volume 3, translated by David Fernbach. New York: Random House, 1981, pp. 460–461].

Compare also the following passages from Marx's critical notes of 1880 on Adolph Wagner's (1835–1917) *Textbook of Political Economy*:

Mr. Obscurantist foists on me the view that "surplus value," which is produced by the workers alone, remains with the capitalist entrepreneurs in a *wrongful (ungebührlicher)* manner. But I say the direct opposite: namely, that at a certain point, the production of commodities necessarily becomes "capitalistic" production of commodities, and that according to the *law of value* which rules that production, "surplus value" is due (*gebührt*) to the capitalist and not to the workers. . . .

In my presentation, the earnings of capital are not in fact "only a deduction or robbery of the worker" [as Wagner says]. On the contrary, I present the capitalist as a necessary functionary of capitalist production, and how at length that he does not only "deduct" or "rob" but forces the production of surplus value, and thus helps create what is to be deducted; further I show in detail that even if in commodity exchange *only equivalents* are exchanged, the capitalist—as soon as he pays the worker the actual value of his labor power—earns *surplus value* with full right, i.e., the right corresponding to this mode of production [*Marx Engels Werke* 19: 382, 359].

35. An allusion to Leibniz's *Theodicy*, which was of course subjected to biting satire in Voltaire's *Candide*.

36. An allusion to Goethe's *Faust*, Part I, line 2141.

37. The slave was the "speaking implement"; the animal, the "semi-mute implement"; and the plough the "mute implement". See Varro, *Rerum Rusticarum Libri Tres* 1: 17.

38. F. L. Olmsted, *A Journey in the Seaboard Slave States*. New York, 1856, pp. 46–47.

39. Jean Charles Leonard Simonde de Sismondi (1773–1842), Swiss political economist.

40. Jean-Baptiste Say (1767–1832), French political economist and popularizer of Adam Smith on the continent. The quotations are from Say's *Treatise on Political Economy*, 4th edition. Paris, 1819, Volume 2, pp. 486, 507. According to some, the views criticized in this note entitle Say to be considered a forerunner of neoclassical economics.

41. In the *Theories of Surplus Value*.

42. "I give that you may give, I give that you may do, I do that you may give, I do that you may do."

43. See Adam Smith, *The Wealth of Nations*, Book I, Chapter 8.

44. The passage in parentheses added by Engels to the fourth German edition on the basis of the French edition of 1872.

45. *faux frais*, "incidental expenses," (literally, "false costs").

46. Constantin Pecqueur (1801–1887), French political economist; the quotation is from Pecqueur's *New Theory of Social and Political Economy*. Paris, 1842, p. 435.

Bibliography

I. WRITINGS OF MARX

Original Editions

Marx Engels Werke. Berlin: Dietz Verlag, 1961–1966.
Marx Engels Gesamtausgabe. Berlin: Dietz Verlag, 1972–.
Grundrisse zur Kritik der politischen Ökonomie: Vienna: Europa Verlag. Photocopy of Soviet Edition: Moscow, 1939.
L. Krader (ed.). *The Ethnological Notebooks of Karl Marx.* Assen: Van Gorcum, 1974.
W. Endemann (ed.). *Marx: Mathematische Manuskripte.* Kronberg: Scriptor, 1974.

English Translations

Marx Engels Collected Works. New York: International Publishers, 1975–.
Marx Engels Selected Works in Three Volumes. Moscow: Progress Publishers, 1969.
Early Writings, ed. Lucio Colletti. Pelican Marx Library. New York: Random House, 1975.
The First International and After, ed. David Fernbach. Pelican Marx Library. New York: Random House, 1974.
Grundrisse, tr. Martin Nicolaus. Pelican Marx Library. New York: Random House, 1973.
The Revolutions of 1848, ed. David Fernbach. Pelican Marx Library. New York: Random House, 1973.
Surveys from Exile, ed. David Fernbach. Pelican Marx Library. New York: Random House, 1974.
Capital, Volume 1, tr. Ben Fowkes. Pelican Marx Library. New York: Random House, 1977.
Capital, Volume 2, tr. David Fernbach. Pelican Marx Library. New York: Random House, 1981.
Capital, Volume 3, tr. David Fernbach. Pelican Marx Library. New York: Random House, 1981.
Theories of Surplus Value. London: Lawrence & Wishart, 1969–72. 3 volumes.
The Letters of Karl Marx, ed. S. Padover. Englewood Cliffs, NJ: Prentice-Hall, 1979.
"The Secret Diplomatic History of the Eighteenth Century," in R. Payne (ed.), *The Unknown Karl Marx.* London: University of London Press, 1972.
"Comments on Adolph Wagner's *Lehrbuch der politischen Oekonomie.*" in Terrell Carver (ed.) *Karl Marx On Method.* Oxford: Blackwell, 1975.

II. SECONDARY LITERATURE

The following is a selected bibliography, limited to works in English, German, and French, and to literature published since 1967. For a full bibliography of Marx literature before 1967, see John Lachs, *Marxist Philosophy, A Bibliographical Guide* (Chapel Hill: University of North Carolina Press, 1967).

Books

Acton, H. B. *What Marx Really Said*. New York: Shocken, 1967.

Althusser, Louis. *For Marx*. London: Verso, 1977.

——————— and Etienne Balibar. *Reading Capital*. London: New Left Books, 1970.

Angehrn, Emil and Lohmann, Georg (eds.). *Ethik und Marx*. Koenigstein: Athenaeum Verlag, 1986.

Assoun, Paul-Laurent. *Marx et la Repetition Historique*. Paris: Presses Universitaires de France, 1978.

Avineri, Shlomo. *The Social and Political Thought of Karl Marx*. Cambridge: Cambridge University Press, 1968.

——————— (ed.). *Marxist Socialism*. New York: Lieber-Atherton, 1973.

Axelos, Kostas. *Alienation, Praxis and Techne in the Thought of Karl Marx*. Austin: University of Texas Press, 1976.

Ball, T., and Farr, J. (eds.). *After Marx*. Cambridge: Cambridge University Press, 1984.

Barth, Hans. *Truth and Ideology*. Berkeley: University of California Press, 1976.

Berlin, Sir Isaiah. *Karl Marx: His Life and Environment*. 4th edition. Oxford: Oxford University Press, 1978.

Bien, Joseph. *History, Revolution and Human Nature: Marx's Philosophical Anthropology*. Amsterdam: Gruner, 1984.

Blaug, Marc. *A Methodological Appraisal of Marxian Economics*. Amsterdam: North Holland Press, 1980.

Bloch, Ernst. *On Karl Marx*. New York: Herder and Herder, 1971.

Blumenberg, Werner. *A Portrait of Karl Marx*. New York: Herder and Herder, 1972.

Boehm-Bawerk, Eugen. *Karl Marx and the Close of His System*. with Appendices by Hilferding and von Bortkiewicz. Clifton, NJ: Kelley, 1975.

Bologh, Roslyn W. *Dialectical Phenomenology: Marx's Method*. Boston: Routledge & Kegan Paul, 1979.

Bradley, I. and Howard, M. (eds.). *Classical and Marxian Political Economy*. London: Macmillan, 1982.

Brewer, Anthony. *A Guide to Marx's* Capital. Cambridge: Cambridge University Press, 1984.

Brenkert, George G. *Marx's Ethics of Freedom*. London: Routledge and Kegan Paul, 1983.

Buchanan, Allen. *Marx and Justice*. Totowa: Rowman and Littlefield, 1982.

Callinicos, Alex. *Marxism and Philosophy*. Oxford: Oxford University Press, 1983.

Carver, Terrell. *Marx's Social Theory*. Oxford: Oxford University Press, 1982.

Castoriadis, C. *L'institution imaginaire de la Societe*. Paris: Gallimard, 1975.

Chavance, Bernard (ed.). *Marx en perspective*. Paris: Editions de l'Ecole des Hautes Etudes en Sciences Sociales, 1985.

Cohen, G. A. *Karl Marx's Theory of History: A Defence*. Princeton: Princeton University Press, 1978.

Cohen, M., Nagel, T. and Scanlon, T. (eds.). *Marx, Justice and History*. Princeton: Princeton University Press, 1981.

Colletti, Lucio. *From Rousseau to Lenin*. New York: Monthly Review Press, 1972.

Cornforth, Maurice. *Dialectical Materialism*. New York: International Publishers, 1971.

_____. *Communism and Philosophy*. London: Lawrence and Wishart, 1980.

Curtis, Michael. *Marxism*. New York: Atherton Press, 1970.

Dahrendorf, Ralf. *Die Idee des Gerechten im Denken von Karl Marx*. Hanover: Verlag fuer Literature und Zeitgeschehen, 1971.

Dostaler, Gilles. *Marx, la valeur et l'economie politique*. Paris: Anthropos, 1978.

Draper, Hal. *Karl Marx's Theory of Revolution*. 2 volumes. New York: Monthly Review Press, 1977–1978.

Duncan, Graeme. *Marx and Mill*. Cambridge: Cambridge University Press, 1973.

Dupre, Louis. *Marx's Social Critique of Culture*. New Haven: Yale University Press, 1983.

Elster, Jon. *Making Sense of Marx* Cambridge: Cambridge University Press, 1985.

Evans, Michael. *Karl Marx*. Bloomington, IN: Indiana University Press, 1975.

Fetscher, Iring. *Marx and Marxism*. New York: Herder and Herder, 1971.

Fleischer, Helmut. *Marx und Engels: Die philosophische Grundlagen ihres Denkens*. 2nd ed. Munchen: Karl Alber, 1974.

Fine, Ben. *Marx's Capital*. 2nd edition. London: Macmillan, 1984.

Foley, Duncan K. *Understanding Capital: Marx's Economic Theory*. Cambridge, MA: Harvard University Press, 1986.

Fox, John. *Understanding "Capital"*. Toronto: Progress Books, 1978.

Frantzki, Ekkehard. *Der missverstandene Marx*. Pfullingen: Neske, 1978.

Garaudy, Roger. *Karl Marx*. Westport, CT: Greenwood Press, 1976.

Geras, Norman. *Marx and Human Nature*. London: New Left Books, 1983.

Gilbert, Alan. *Marx's Politics*. New Brunswick, NJ: Rutgers University Press, 1981.

Godelier, Maurice. *Rationality and Irrationality in Economics*. New York: Monthly Review Press, 1978.

Gould, Carol. *Marx's Social Ontology*. Cambridge, MA: MIT Press, 1978.

Habermas, Juergen. *Knowledge and Human Interests*. Boston: Beacon Press, 1971.

_____. *Theory and Practice*. Boston: Beacon Press, 1973.

_____. *Zur Rekonstruktion des historischen Materialismus*. Frankfurt: Suhrkamp Verlag, 1976.

Haennimen, S. and Paldan, L. (eds.). *Rethinking Marx*. Berlin: Argument-Verlag, 1984.

Hartmann, Klaus. *Die Marxsche Theorie*. Berlin: W. de Gruyter, 1970.

Heller, Agnes. *The Theory of Need in Marx*. London: Allison and Busby, 1976.

Henry, Michel. *Marx: A Philosophy of Human Reality*. Bloomington, IN: Indiana University Press, 1983.

Hobsbawm, Eric (ed.). *The History of Marxism*. Brighton: Harvester Press, 1982.

Hoffman, John. *Marxism and the Theory of Praxis*. London: Lawrence and Wishart, 1975.

Horowitz, David (ed.). *Marx and Modern Economics.* New York: Modern Reader Paperbacks, 1968.

Howard, Dick. *Development of the Marxian Dialectic.* Carbondale, IL: Southern Illinois University Press, 1972.

Howard, M. C. and King, J. E. *The Political Economy of Marx.* New York: Longman, 1976.

——————— (eds.). *The Economics of Marx.* New York: Penguin, 1976.

Hunt, E. K. and Schwartz, Jesse G. (eds.). *A Critique of Economic Theory.* Harmondsworth: Penguin Books, 1972.

Hyppolite, Jean. *Studies on Marx and Hegel.* New York: Harper & Row, 1969.

Kamenka, Eugene. *The Ethical Foundations of Marxism.* 2nd edition. London: Routledge & Kegan Paul, 1972.

———————. *Marxism and Ethics.* London: St. Martin's Press, 1969.

Kolakowski, Leszek. *Towards a Marxist Humanism.* London: Pall Mall, 1968.

———————. *Main Currents of Marxism.* 3 volumes. Oxford: Oxford University Press, 1978.

Korsch, Karl. *Marxism and Philosophy.* New York: Monthly Review Press, 1970.

Lange, Ernst-Michael. *Das Prinzip Arbeit.* Frankfurt: Ullstein, 1980.

Lefebvre, Henri. *The Sociology of Marx.* New York: Vintage, 1968.

Little, Daniel. *The Scientific Marx.* Minneapolis: University of Minnesota Press, 1986.

Livergood, N. *Activity in Marx's Philosophy.* The Hague: Martinus Nijhoff, 1967.

Lobkovicz, Nicholas. *Theory and Practice from Aristotle to Marx.* Notre Dame: Notre Dame University Press, 1967.

Lukes, Steven. *Marxism and Morality.* Oxford: Clarendon Press, 1984.

Maarek, G. *An Introduction to Marx's 'Das Kapital'.* New York: Oxford University Press, 1979.

MacIntyre, Alasdair. *Marxism and Christianity.* New York: Shocken, 1968.

Magnis, Franz. *Normative Voraussetzungen im Denken des jungen Marx.* Munchen: Karl Alber, 1975.

Maguire, John M.. *Marx's Theory of Politics.* Cambridge: Cambridge University Press, 1978.

Mandel, Ernest. *Marxist Economic Theory.* New York: Monthly Review Press, 1968.

———————. *The Formation of the Economic Thought of Karl Marx.* New York: Monthly Review Press, 1971.

Markovic, Mihailo. *The Contemporary Marx.* Nottingham: Spokesman Books, 1974.

Markus, George. *Marxism and Anthropology.* Assen: Van Gorcum, 1985.

Matejko, Alexander (ed.). *Marx and Marxism.* New York: Praeger, 1984.

McBride, William. *The Philosophy of Marx.* New York: St. Martins, 1967.

McLellan, David. *The Young Hegelians and Karl Marx.* London, Methuen, 1969.

———————. *Marx Before Marxism.* London: Macmillan, 1970.

———————. *Karl Marx.* London: Penguin, 1975.

———————. *The Thought of Karl Marx.* 2nd edition. London: Macmillan, 1980.

McMurtry, John. *The Structure of Marx's World View.* Princeton: Princeton University Press, 1978.

Meek, Ronald L. *Studies in the Labor Theory of Value.* 2nd ed. New York: Monthly Review Press, 1973.

Meikle, Scott. *Essentialism in the Thought of Karl Marx.* London: Duckworth, 1985.

Mepham, John, and Ruben, David-Hillel (eds). *Issues in Marxist Philosophy.* 4 volumes. Brighton: Harvester, 1979–1981.

Meszaros, Istvan. *Marx's Theory of Alienation.* New York: Harper and Row, 1972.

Miliband, Ralph. *Marxism and Politics.* Oxford: Oxford University Press, 1977.

Miller, Richard. *Analyzing Marx: Morality, Power and History.* Princeton: Princeton University Press, 1984.

Moore, Stanley. *Marx on the Choice Between Socialism and Communism.* Cambridge, MA: Harvard University Press, 1980.

Molnar, M. *Marx, Engels, et la Politique Internationale.* Paris: Gallimard, 1975.

Morishima, Michio. *Marx's Economics.* Cambridge: Cambridge University Press, 1973.

Nielsen, Kai and Patten, Steven (eds.). *Marx and Morality.* Guelph: Canadian Association for Publishing in Philosophy, 1981.

Oakley, Allen. *Marx's Critique of Political Economy.* London: Routledge and Kegan Paul, 1984.

Ollman, Bertell. *Alienation.* 2nd edition. Cambridge: Cambridge University Press, 1976.

Panichas, George (ed.). *Marx Analyzed.* Lanham, MD: University Press of America, 1984.

Parkinson, G. H. R. (ed.). *Marx and Marxisms.* Cambridge: Cambridge University Press, 1982.

Parsons, Howard L. and Somerville, John (eds.). *Dialogues on the Philosophy of Marxism.* Westport, CT: Greenwood Press, 1974.

Pennock, J. Roland, and Chapman, J. W. (eds.). *Marxism, Nomos* 26 (1983).

Plamenatz, John. *Karl Marx's Philosophy of Man.* Oxford: Oxford University Press, 1975.

Post, Werner. *Kritik der Religion bei Marx.* Munchen: Kosel, 1969.

Raes, Koen (ed.). *A Marxian Approach to the Problem of Justice, Philosophica* 33 (1984).

Robinson, Joan. *An Essay on Marxian Economics.* New York: Macmillan, 1971.

Roemer, John. *Analytical Foundations of Marxian Economic Theory.* Cambridge: Cambridge University Press, 1981.

——————. *A General Theory of Exploitation and Class.* Cambridge, MA: Harvard University Press, 1982.

—————— (ed.). *Analytical Marxism.* Cambridge: Cambridge University Press, 1986.

Rosdolsky, Roman. *The Making of Marx's "Capital".* London: Pluto Press, 1977.

Rosen, Zvi. *Bruno Bauer and Karl Marx.* The Hague: Martinus Nijhoff, 1977.

Ruben, D. H. *Marxism and Materialism.* 2nd. edition. Brighton: Harvester Press, 1979.

Rubin, I.I. *Essays on Marx's Theory of Value.* Detroit: Wayne State University Press, 1972.

Sayer, Derek. *Marx's Method.* Atlantic Highlands, NJ: Humanities Press, 1979.

Schmidt, Alfred. *The Concept of Nature in Marx.* London: New Left Books, 1971.

Schmitt, Richard. *Introduction to Marx and Engels: A Critical Reconstruction.* Boulder, CO: Westview Press, 1987.

Shaw, William H. *Marx's Theory of History.* Stanford: Stanford University Press, 1978.

Sher, Gerson S. (ed.). *Marxist Humanism and Praxis*. Buffalo: Kensington Books, 1978.

Sowell, Thomas. *Marxism and Economics*. New York: Morrow, 1985.

Steedman, Ian. *Marx After Sraffa*. London: New Left Books, 1979.

Suchting, W. A. *Marx*. New York: New York University Press, 1983.

Taylor, Michael (ed.). *Rationality and Revolution*. New York: Cambridge University Press, 1987.

Thompson, E. P. *The Making of the English Working Class*. Harmondsworth: Penguin Books, 1968.

Tucker, Robert C. *The Marxian Revolutionary Idea*. New York: W. W. Norton, 1969.

—————. *Philosophy and Myth in Karl Marx*. 2nd edition. Cambridge: Cambridge University Press, 1972.

Walker, Angus. *Marx*. London: Longman, 1978.

Walton, Paul, and Gamble, Andrew. *From Alienation to Surplus Value*. 2nd edition. London: Sheed and Ward, 1976.

Wolff, Robert Paul. *Understanding Marx*. Princeton: Princeton University Press, 1984.

Wood, Allen W. *Karl Marx*. London: Routledge and Kegan Paul, 1981.

Zeleny, Jindrich. *The Logic of Marx*. Totowa: Rowman and Littlefield, 1980.

Articles

Some of the articles listed below are included in books mentioned in the previous section. Such articles will be cited by editor and title of the book.

Allen, Derek, "The Utilitarianism of Marx and Engels," 'American Philosophical Quarterly 10 (1973).

—————, "Is Marxism a Philosophy?" *Journal of Philosophy* 71 (1974).

—————, "Does Marx Have an Ethic of Self-Realization?" *Canadian Journal of Philosophy* 10 (1980).

—————, "Marx and Engels on the Distributive Justice of Capitalism," Nielsen and Patten (eds.), *Marx and Morality*.

Arneson, Richard, "What's Wrong with Exploitation?" *Ethics* 91 (1981).

—————, "Marxism and Secular Faith," *American Political Science Review*. 79 (1985).

Arthur, C. J. "Labor: Marx's Concrete Universal," *Inquiry* 21 (1978).

Atkinson, R. F. "Historical Materialism," in G. H. R. Parkinson (ed.), *Marx and Marxism*.

Bowles, S., and Gintis, H., "The Marxian Theory of Value and Heterogeneous Labor," *Cambridge Journal of Economics* 1 (1977).

Brenkert, George, "Freedom and Private Property in Marx," *Philosophy and Public Affairs* 3 (1974).

—————, "Marx and Utilitarianism," *Canadian Journal of Philosophy* 5 (1975).

Bronfenbrenner, Martin, "A Harder Look at Alienation," *Ethics* 83 (1972–73).

Buchanan, Allen, "Exploitation, Alienation and Justice," *Canadian Journal of Philosophy* 9 (1979).

—————, "Revolutionary Motivation and Rationality," *Philosophy and Public Affairs* 9 (1979–1980).

Cohen, G. A., "Bourgeois and Proletarians," Avineri, *Marxian Socialism*.
_____, "Marx's Dialectic of Labor," *Philosophy and Public Affairs* 3 (1974).
_____, "Robert Nozick and Wilt Chamberlain," in J. Arthur and W. Shaw (eds.), *Justice and Economic Distribution*. Englewood Cliffs, NJ: Prentice Hall, 1976.
_____, "Capitalism, Freedom and the Proletariat," A. Ryan (ed.), *The Idea of Freedom*. Oxford: Oxford University Press, 1979.
_____, "Freedom, Justice and Capitalism," *New Left Review* 126 (1981).
_____, "Illusions about Private Property and Freedom," Mepham and Ruben (eds.), *Issues in Marxist Philosophy*, Volume 4.
_____, "Functional Explanation, Consequence Explanation and Marxism," *Inquiry* 25 (1982).
_____, "Reply to Four Critics," *Analyse und Kritik* 5 (1983).
_____, "Reconsidering Historical Materialism," *Nomos* 26 (1983).
_____, "Restricted and Inclusive Historical Materialism," Chavance (ed.), *Marx en perspective*.
_____, "The Structure of Proletarian Unfreedom," *Philosophy and Public Affairs* 12 (1983).
Cohen, Joshua. Review of G. A. Cohen, *Karl Marx's Theory of History*, *The Journal of Philosophy* 79 (1982).
Crocker, L., "Marx's Concept of Exploitation," *Social Theory and Practice* 2 (1972).
Drucker, H. M., "Marx's Concept of Ideology," *Philosophy* 47 (1972).
Easton, Loyd D. 'Alienation and Empiricism in Marx's Thought," *Social Research* 37 (1970).
_____. "Marx and Individual Freedom," *Philosophical Forum* 12–13 (1981–1982).
Elster, Jon, "Marxism, Functionalism and Game Theory," *Theory and Society* 11 (1982).
_____, "Exploitation, Freedom and Justice," *Nomos* 26 (1983).
_____, "Further Thoughts on Marxism, Functionalism and Game Theory," Chavance (ed.), *Marx en perspective*.
_____, "Self-realization in Work and Politics: The Marxist Conception of the Good Life," *Social Philosophy and Policy* 3 (1986).
Farr, James. "Marx No Empiricist," *Philosophy and the Social Sciences* 13 (1983).
Geras, Norman, "Essence and Appearance: Aspects of Fetishism in Marx's *Capital*," *New Left Review* 65 (1971).
_____, "The Controversy About Marx and Justice," *New Left Review* 105 (1985).
Gilbert, Alan, "Marx on Internationalism and War," *Philosophy and Public Affairs* 7 (1978).
_____, "Social Theory and Revolutionary Activity in Marx," *American Political Science Review* 73 (1979).
_____, "Historical Theory and the Structure of Moral Argument in Marx," *Political Theory* 9 (1981).
Green, M., "Marx, Utility and Right," *Political Theory* 11 (1983).
Hancock, Roger, "Marx's Theory of Justice," *Social Theory and Practice* 1 (1971).
Heller, Agnes, "Die Stellung der Ethik im Marxismus," *Praxis* 3 (1967).
Hobsbawm, Eric. "Marx's Contribution to Historiography," in Robin Blackburn (ed.), *Ideology in Social Science*. New York: Vintage, 1973.

Holmstrom, Nancy, "Exploitation," *Canadian Journal of Philosophy* 7 (1977).

Hudelson, Richard, "Marx's Empricism," *Philosophy of the Social Sciences* 12 (1982).

Husami, Ziyad, "Marx on Distributive Justice," *Philosophy and Public Affairs* 8 (1978).

Itoh, Makoto, "Marx's Theory of Value," *Science and Society* 40 (1976).

LeoGrande, William M. "An Investigation into the 'Young Marx' Controversy," *Science and Society* 41 (1977).

Lukes, Steven, "Marxism, Morality and Justice," Parkinson (ed.), *Marx and Marxisms*.

—————, "Can the Base Be Distinguished From the Superstructure?" D. Miller and L. Siedentrop (eds.), *The Nature of Political Theory* (Oxford: Oxford University Press, 1983).

McBride, William, "The Concept of Justice in Marx, Engels, and Others," *Ethics* 85 (1975).

Mepham, John, "The Theory of Ideology in *Capital*," *Radical Philosophy* 2 (1972).

Miller, Richard, "The Consistency of Historical Materialism," *Philosophy and Public Affairs* 4 (1975).

—————, "Methodological Individualism and Social Explanation," *Philosophy of Science* 45 (1975).

—————, "Productive Forces and the Forces of Change," *Philosophical Review* 90 (1981).

—————, "Marx in Modern Philosophy," *Social Science Quarterly* 64 (1983).

—————, "Producing Change," in T. Ball and J. Farr (eds.), *After Marx*.

—————, "Marx and Morality" in *Nomos*, Volume XXVI: *Marxism Today* (1983).

Moore, Stanley, "Marx and the Origin of Dialectical Materialism," *Inquiry* 14 (1971).

—————, "Marx and Lenin as Historical Materialists," *Philosophy and Public Affairs* 4 (1971).

Morishima, Michio, "Marx in the Light of Modern Economic Theory," *Econometrica* 42 (1974).

Nell, Edward, "Economics—the Revival of Political Economy," in Robin Blackburn (ed.), *Ideology in Social Science*. New York: Vintage, 1973.

Nielsen, Kai, "Alienation and Self-Realization," *Philosophy* 48 (1973).

—————, "Marxism, Ideology and Moral Philosophy," *Social Theory and Practice* 6 (1980).

Parijs, Philippe van, "Marxism's Central Puzzle," Ball and Farr (eds.), *After Marx*.

Roemer, John "Property Relations vs. Surplus Value in Marxian Exploitation," *Philosophy and Public Affairs* 11 (1982).

—————, "Should Marxists Be Interested in Exploitation?" *Philosophy and Public Affairs* 14 (1985).

Ryan, Cheney, "Socialist Justice and the Right to the Labor Product," *Political Theory* 8 (1980).

Samuelson, Paul, "The Normative and Positivistic Inferiority of Marx's *Values* Paradigm," *Southern Economic Journal* 49 (1982).

Sichel, Betty A., "Karl Marx and the Rights of Man," *Philosophy and Phenomenological Research* 32 (1976–77).

Skillen, Anthony, "Marxism and Morality," *Radical Philosophy* 8 (1974).

—————, "Workers' Interest and the Proletarian Ethic: Conflicting Strains in Marxian Anti-Moralism," Nielsen and Patten (eds.), *Marx and Morality*.

Smolinski, L., "Karl Marx and Mathematical Economics," *Journal of Political Economy* 81 (1973).

Steedman, Ian, "Heterogeneous Labor, Money Wages and Marx's Theory," Chavance (ed.), *Marx en perspective*.

Van der Linden, H., "Marx and Morality: An Impossible Synthesis?" *Theory and Society* 13 (1984).

Van der Veen, Robert, "Property, Exploitation and Justice," *Acta Politica* 13 (1978).

Vandeveer, Donald, "Marx's View of Justice," *Philosophy and Phenomenological Research* 33 (1972–1973).

Wood, Allen W., "The Marxian Critique of Justice," *Philosophy and Public Affairs* 1 (1972).

——————, "Marx's Critical Anthropology," *Review of Metaphysics* 26 (1972).

——————, "Marx on Right and Justice: A Reply to Husami," *Philosophy and Public Affairs* 8 (1979).

——————, "Marx and Equality," Roemer (ed.), *Analytical Marxism*.

——————, "Marx and Morality," A. Caplan and B. Jennings, *Darwin, Marx and Freud*. New York: Plenum Press, 1984.

——————, "Justice and Class Interests," *Philosophica* 33 (1984).

——————, "Marx' Immoralismus," Angehrn and Lohmann (eds.), *Ethik und Marx*.

——————, "Marx's Immoralism," Chavance (ed.), *Marx en perspective*.

——————, "Marx, Karl," in Robert A. Gorman, (ed.), *Biographical Dictionary of Marxism*. Westport, CT: Greenwood Press, 1986.

——————, "Historical Materialism and Functional Explanation," *Inquiry* 29 (1986).

——————, "Ideology, False Consciousness and Social Illusion," in A. Rorty and B. MacLaughlin (eds.), *Perspectives on Self-Deception*. Berkeley, CA: University of California Press, 1987.

Young, Gary, "The Fundamental Contradiction of Capitalist Production," *Philosophy and Public Affairs* 5 (1976).

——————, "Justice and Capitalist Production: Marx and Bourgeois Ideology," *Canadian Journal of Philosophy* 8 (1978).

——————, "Doing Marx Justice," Nielsen and Patten (eds.), *Marx and Morality*.

Zimmerman, David, "Coercive Wage Offers," *Philosophy and Public Affairs* 10 (1981).